LINGUISTIC THEORY
IN AMERICA .

The First Quarter-Century of
Transformational Generative Grammar

LINGUISTIC THEORY IN AMERICA

The First Quarter-Century of Transformational Generative Grammar

Frederick J. Newmeyer

DEPARTMENT OF LINGUISTICS
UNIVERSITY OF WASHINGTON
SEATTLE, WASHINGTON

ACADEMIC PRESS

A Subsidiary of Harcourt Brace Jovanovich, Publishers

New York   London   Toronto   Sydney   San Francisco

ACADEMIC PRESS, INC.
111 Fifth Avenue, New York, New York 10003

United Kingdom Edition published by
ACADEMIC PRESS, INC. (LONDON) LTD.
24/28 Oval Road, London NW1 7DX

Library of Congress Cataloging in Publication Data

Newmeyer, Frederick J
    Linguistic theory in America.

    Bibliography: p.
    Includes indexes.
    1. Generative grammar--History. 2. Linguistics--
United States--History. I. Title.
P158.N4   415   79-27195
ISBN 0-12-517150-1

For Sol Saporta

Contents

Chapter 3

From *Syntactic Structures* to *Aspects of the Theory of Syntax*   61

Chapter 4

The Late 1960s   93

Chapter 5
The Linguistic Wars

Chapter 6
Syntax in the 1970s:
Constraining the Syntactic Rules

Chapter 7

On the Boundary of Formal Grammar   209

Chapter 8

Recent Developments in Syntax and Semantics   227

Preface

In this book I attempt to document the origins, birth, and development of the theory of transformational generative grammar. Despite the fact that it is now 25 years since Noam Chomsky completed his *Logical Structure of Linguistic Theory*, what I have written is, to my knowledge, the only work that combines a comprehensive account of the forging of modern linguistic theory with a detailed elaboration and explanation of its development. I have not intended the book to be an introduction to linguistics, and it cannot substitute for one. A minimal understanding of modern linguistic theory is presupposed throughout. Fortunately, there is no dearth of texts in print whose purpose is to acquaint the reader with fundamentals of theory. To my mind, the best is Neil Smith and Deirdre Wilson's lucid *Modern Linguistics: The Results of Chomsky's Revolution*, which I can recommend without reservation to the beginning student and advanced scholar alike.

To keep this book to a manageable size, I have had to slight developments in generative phonology. In fact, there is no discussion of developments in phonology since the early 1960s. My omission is compensated for in part by the existence of Alan Sommerstein's *Modern Phonology*, which covers the recent history of phonology in some detail.

The reader may be puzzled by the "in America" in the title. Why should the discussion of a scientific theory be constrained by a national boundary? In part this is a reflection of the immaturity of our science: It is a sad commentary on the state of the field that we can still talk realistically of "American linguistics," "French linguistics," and "Soviet linguistics." But more positively, my choice of title was dictated by the fact that transformational grammar HAS begun to internationalize; "in America" was necessary lest I appear to be slighting recent work of theoretical importance in Japanese, Finnish, Arabic, and other languages unknown to me.

Since there is no such thing as totally unbiased historiography, it would be utopian to imagine that an author could be free from background assumptions or beliefs that might color his or her perception of events. As a PARTICIPANT (however noncentral) in the history I describe, I might be particularly open to charges of bias. However, I feel that my participation has given me a real advantage: It has permitted me an inside view of the field that would be denied to the more displaced historian. I hope that the reader will find this to be to the book's advantage.

For those who may be interested in my background, I have been in linguistics since 1965, the year I received a B.A. in geology from the University of Rochester. Fortunately, a senior year course taught by the late William A. Coates, called "The Languages of the World," so intrigued me that I gave up any dreams I may have harbored of a career in petroleum engineering (or worse). I received a Master's in linguistics from Rochester the following year and would have stayed there longer had I not attended Chomsky's lectures at the LSA Institute at UCLA in the summer of 1966. They convinced me to transfer as soon as possible to a transformational grammar-oriented department. In 1967 I was admitted to the Ph.D. program at the University of Illinois, where I studied syntax with Robert B. Lees, Arnold Zwicky, and Michael Geis, and phonology with Theodore Lightner. My last year of graduate work was spent as a guest at MIT. After receiving a Ph.D. from Illinois in 1969, I was hired by the University of Washington, where I have been teaching ever since, with the exception of leave time spent at the University of Edinburgh, Wayne State University, and the University of London.

My earliest theoretical commitment was to generative semantics, and I contributed several uninfluential publications in defense of a deep-structureless model of grammar (1970, 1971, 1975). By 1972 or 1973, I began to have serious reservations about the direction generative semantics was taking. Since then, I have identified myself loosely as an interpretivist, without committing myself to any one particular model in that framework.

Some who know me as a Marxist may be surprised and, perhaps, disappointed that there is no obvious "Marxist analysis" given to the events I describe. For this I make no apology. There is simply no evidence that language structure (outside of limited aspects of the lexicon) is, in the Marxist sense, a superstructural phenomenon. Even if it were, however, it seems inconceivable that events taking place in such a short period of time and involving so few, so sociologically homogeneous, participants could lend themselves to such an analysis. Those interested in my views on the relationship between Marxist theory and linguistic theory may find useful my review of Rossi-Landi's *Linguistics and Economics,* published in *Language* in 1977.

A final word on chronology. Throughout the text, I cite books and articles by the year of their first publication, not by the year that they were written. Since publishing delays are uneven, this has resulted in some cases in replies appearing to be older than the publications to which they are addressed and in other possibly confusing aspects of dating. When delays are extreme or when the time lag is significant in some respect, the year of writing (in parentheses) appears after the year of publication in the reference list.

ACKNOWLEDGMENTS

My greatest debt is to those who provided me with detailed criticism of the entire pre-final manuscript: Joseph Emonds, Geoffrey Pullum, Barbara Partee, Stephen Anderson, and Jane Grimshaw. Geoffrey Pullum, in addition to his valuable written suggestions, spent many hours discussing this material with me personally, for which I am particularly grateful. The book has also benefited from comments on portions of the text by a number of other linguists, including Barbara Abbott, Michael Brame, Laurence Horn, Pauline Jacobson, Ellen Kaisse, James McCawley, Keith Percival, Jerrold Sadock, Sol Saporta, and Neil Smith. It goes without saying that none of these individuals is responsible for any of the book's faults. No doubt I shall soon regret not heeding more of their advice.

So many persons provided me with information, advice, special encouragement, etc. that I am not sure that I can remember them all. The following stand out in my mind as being particularly worthy of acknowledgment: Ann Banfield, C. E. Bazell, Woodford Beach, Christine Chiarello, Noam Chomsky, Heles Contreras, John Corcoran, Benjamin Creisler, Willa Dawson, Wolfgang Dressler, Bonny Gildin, Kenneth Hale, Morris Halle, Kirsten Johnson, Jay Keyser, Robert B. Lees, Howard Maclay, Jeffry Pelletier, Paul Peranteau, Carol Rosen, Athena Theodore, Wayne Williams, Deirdre Wilson, and Arnold Zwicky.

Finally, I am indebted to Professor A. C. Gimson for authorizing a Visiting Professorship for me at University College London, where much of this book was completed, and to Shula Chiat, Richard Hudson, Ruth Kempson, Geoffrey Pullum, Joan Pullum, Neil Smith, and Deirdre Wilson for making my stay there worthwhile.

Chapter 1

The State of American Linguistics in the Mid 1950s

1.1. A PERIOD OF OPTIMISM

If American linguistics was in a state of crisis in the mid 1950s, few of its practitioners seemed aware of it.[1] Einar Haugen (1951) in his overview of the field, wrote that "American linguistics is today in a more flourishing state than at any time since the founding of the Republic [p. 211]." Commentators boasted of the "great progress [Hall 1951:101]," "far reaching advances [Allen 1958:v]," and "definitive results [Gleason 1955:11]" achieved by structural linguistics, which was "compared in method with field physics, quantum mechanics, discrete mathematics, and Gestalt psychology [Whitehall 1951:v]." Even Kenneth Pike (1958), often critical of many of the assumptions of mainstream American linguistics, felt moved to write that "theirs [Harris's and Bloch's] is an attempt to reduce language to a formal analysis of great simplicity, elegance, and mathematical rigor, and they have come astonishingly close to succeeding [p. 204]."

More than SELF-congratulation was going on. The psychologist John B. Carroll (1953) wrote that linguistics was the most advanced of all the social sciences, with a close resemblance to physics and chemistry. And Claude

---

[1] The use of the term "American linguistics" in this chapter accurately reflects the chauvinistic attitudes of structuralists in the United States, many of whom were exceedingly insular and viewed any linguistic research carried on outside the 48 states with suspicion. The atmosphere was such that George L. Trager (1950) could write about "the usual kind of European philosophizing on the basis of insufficient evidence [p. 100]" without incurring censure. Along the same lines, Robert Hall's fascinating personal memoir, *Stormy Petrel in Linguistics* (1975), is in large part a defense of the hostile attitude toward foreign scholars prevalent at that time.

Lévi-Strauss, probably the world's foremost anthropologist, compared the discovery that language consists of phonemes and morphemes to the Newtonian revolution in physics (Lévi-Strauss 1953:350–351).

There was a widespread feeling among linguists in the 1950s that the fundamental problems of linguistic analysis had been solved and that all that was left was to fill in the details. The basic theoretical–methodological statements of Bloch's "A Set of Postulates for Phonemic Analysis" (1948) and Harris's *Methods in Structural Linguistics* (1951) seemed to render any more basic theoretical work unnecessary. In fact, many linguists felt that the procedures had been so well worked out that computers could take over the drudgery of linguistic analysis. All one would have to do (in principle) would be to punch the data into the computer and out would come the grammar![2]

There was also a feeling that computers could solve another traditional linguistic problem—translation. The idea of machine translation had been first suggested (in a memorandum by Warren Weaver) only in 1949. By 1955, such translation work was going on in three countries at half a dozen institutions. These six years were enough to convert the skeptics, as William N. Locke put it in an enthusiastic review article written in that year (Locke 1955:109).

Other postwar scientific developments seemed to be especially promising for linguistics. A new field called "information theory" proposed methods of measuring the efficiency of communication channels in terms of information and redundancy. Shannon and Weaver (1949) in their pioneering study of information theory pointed out the possible linguistic implications of the theory:

> The concept of the information to be associated with a source leads directly, as we have seen, to a study of the statistical structure of language; and this study reveals about the English language, as an example, information which seems surely significant to students of every phase of language and communication [p. 117].

Shannon and Weaver's ideas were enthusiastically received by a large number of linguists; prominent among these was Charles Hockett (1953, 1955), who set out to apply the results of information theory in the construction of a Markov-process model of human language.

Progress in acoustic phonetics also contributed to the general optimism. The spectrograph, first made public in 1945, had replaced the inconvenient

---

[2] This attitude survived among nonlinguists into the 1970s: "Settling the phonemes of a language is . . . a fairly straightforward empirical enterprise, and we suppose it already completed when the grammarian moves in [Quine 1970:16]"; " . . . the speech patterns of all languages are known to operate on a few basic principles which linguists have worked out . . . 'natural languages' all can be broken down first into phones, then into phonemes, then morphemes, then lexemes, and so on up to the higher levels of grammaticality [Fox 1970:35]."

oscilloscope as the most important tool for linguists in the physical recording of speech sounds. There was a general feeling (never expressed too clearly) that spectrograms would help decide between competing phonemicizations of a given language—a perennial problem in structural linguistics.

Finally, the synthesis of linguistics and psychology now called "psycholinguistics" was adding a new dimension to the study of language. I will return to this in Section 1.2.3.

Structural linguistics seemed so successful that it was being consciously imitated by the social sciences.[3] The anthropologist A. L. Kroeber (1952) asked "What is the cultural equivalent of the phoneme? [p. 124]," and Kenneth Pike had an answer: the "behavioreme." Pike (1954) was in the process of constructing a comprehensive theory in which "verbal and nonverbal activity is a unified whole, and theory and methodology should be organized to treat it as such [p. 2]." Not only was it a cliché "that what mathematics already is for the physical sciences, linguistics can be for the social sciences [LaBarre 1960:74]" (see also Le Page 1964:1), but many even held the view that "as no science can go beyond mathematics, no criticism can go beyond its linguistics [Whitehall 1951:v]." In this period we found the "linguistic method" being applied to the study of kinesics, folkloric texts, the analysis of the political content of agitational leaflets, and much more.

1.2. STRUCTURAL LINGUISTICS

1.2.1. The Philosophical Underpinnings

The dominant intellectual force in the United States from the 1930s to the 1960s was empiricism. The fundamental tenet of empiricism is that all nonanalytic knowledge is derived from experience alone. Clearly such a philosophical view has profound implications for every intellectual endeavor. Among other things, it entails that all learning take place through inductive generalizations mediated by sense experience. Another way of putting it is that children are born "blank slates," with no interesting predispositions structuring the acquisition of knowledge. Likewise, it goes along with an extremely strong view of theory construction in science—that for any statement, theoretical term, etc. to be meaningful, it has to be related to observation in some fairly direct way.

The intellectual origins of empiricism go back to the work of the eighteenth century British philosophers John Locke and David Hume. The famous closing paragraph of Hume's *An Enquiry Concerning Human Under-*

---

[3] This point is argued at length in Greenberg (1973).

standing captures the spirit of what came to be known as empiricism:

> When we run over libraries, persuaded of these [empiricist] principles, what havoc must
> we make? If we take in hand any volume—of divinity or school metaphysics, for instance,
> — let us ask, Does it contain any abstract reasoning concerning quantity or number?
> No. Does it contain any experimental reasoning concerning matters of fact and existence?
> No. Commit it then to the flames, for it can contain nothing but sophistry and illusion
> [Hume 1961:165].

While empiricism (or "positivism" as it was also called) was somewhat in retreat throughout the nineteenth century, it enjoyed a rebirth in the early twentieth as a result of work on the foundations of logic. Many philosophers believed that mathematical logic would give them the apparatus they lacked to formalize the distinction between mathematical truth, synthetic statements, and metaphysical nonsense. Furthermore, logic also promised to provide a formalism to make explicit the relation between a statement and the observations and procedures which could lead to its verification. Hence, twentieth-century empiricism is often called "LOGICAL empiricism" (or "logical positivism").

The wide appeal empiricist philosophy enjoyed in the intellectual community at this time is undoubtedly related to the fact that there was no period in American history in which there was greater respect for the methods and results of science. Social scientists and philosophers, envious of the dramatic achievements in nineteenth- and early twentieth-century natural science and innocent of the ethical issues which would be raised later by the atomic bomb, counterinsurgency technology, and genetic experimentation, asked: "How can we be scientific too? How can we rid ourselves of the fuzzy speculation which has characterized our field?" Logical empiricism appeared to provide an answer.

Empiricism struck an especially responsive chord in linguistics. To hard-headed fieldworkers busy with the initial descriptions of hundreds of "exotic" languages, Humboldtian speculations about "inner form" and Schleicherian pronouncements of language evolution seemed as unscientific as Greek mythology.

The American pioneer in incorporating empiricist assumptions into linguistic practice was Leonard Bloomfield. His book *Language* (1933) made explicit in a number of passages the requirement that the relationship between the corpus of data and the theoretical description had to be a direct one. The following remark is typical: "The only useful generalizations about language are inductive generalizations. Features which we think ought to be universal may be absent from the very next language that becomes accessible [p. 20]."

Bloomfield was in touch with the logical empiricist philosophers of the Vienna Circle and contributed a monograph on linguistics to their *International Encyclopedia of Unified Science*. This monograph, *Linguistic Aspects of Science* (1939a), is the clearest statement in print on the intimate relationship of empiricist philosophy, behaviorist psychology, and structural linguistics. Bloomfield (1939a) united all three in the following famous passage:

> If language is taken into account, then we can distinguish science from other phases of human activity by agreeing that science shall deal only with events that are accessible in their time and place to any and all observers (strict BEHAVIORISM) or only with events that are placed in coordinates of time and space (MECHANISM), or that science shall employ only such initial statements and predictions as lead to definite handling operations (OPERATIONALISM), or only such terms as are derivable by rigid definition from a set of everyday terms concerning physical happenings (PHYSICALISM) [p. 13].

These stringent conditions were maintained particularly by structuralists in the United States through the 1950s (see Hockett 1948a for another clear statement).[4] They were widely regarded as ruling out in principle from linguistics any statements about universals, such as the Prague School phonologists made about distinctive features, or in fact any theoretical terms at all which were not directly related to observable phenomena. Explanations were not only referred to contemptuously, but were even made to seem "un-American":

> Trubetzkoy phonology tried to explain everything from articulatory acoustics and a minimum set of phonological laws taken as essentially valid for all languages alike, flatly contradicting the American (Boas) tradition that languages could differ from each other without limit and in unpredictable ways, and offering too much of a phonological EXPLA-NATION where a sober TAXONOMY would serve as well. Children want explanations, and there is a child in each of us; descriptivism makes a virtue of not pampering that child [Joos 1958:96].

These conditions resulted in a linguistic description that was nothing more than a catalogue of observables and statements in principle extractable directly from observables by a set of mechanical procedures: "The over-all purpose of work in descriptive linguistics is to obtain a compact one–one representation of the stock of utterances in the corpus [Harris 1951:366]." Naturally, informants' judgments would have to be ruled irrelevant, as well as any description in terms of "processes," such as deletion, metathesis, and insertion. The work of earlier structuralists (such as Bloomfield himself) often WAS stated in a process framework, complete with rule ordering statements. But in later work, the discrepancies between theory and practice were pointed out, and process statements (which, like those in Bloomfield

---

[4] What follows is a synthesis of the views of the leading American structuralists of the early 1950s—in particular a synthesis of the views of Bernard Bloch, Zellig Harris, and Charles Hockett. I am well aware that if we examine the work of all self-described American "structural linguists" from the 1930s to the present, we will find an enormous diversity of assumptions and methodologies. However, I categorically reject the assertions of Hymes and Fought (1975) and many others that the ideas outlined in this and the following sections were not overwhelmingly the most favored by those American linguists in the early 1950s who took theory seriously. For more discussion on this point, see Newmeyer (in preparation).

1939b, were often highly insightful) disappeared from the literature. Hockett (1954) wrote that he could not even conceive of any meaning to "ordering" but an historical one.

The goal of structural linguistics was to "discover" a grammar by performing a set of operations on a corpus of data. Each successive operation was one step farther removed from the corpus. Since the physical record of the flow of speech itself was the only type of data considered objective enough to serve as a starting point, it followed that the levels of a grammatical description had to be arrived at in the following order:

    I. Phonemics
    II. Morphemics
    III. Syntax
    IV. Discourse

Since morphemes could be discovered only after the phonemes of which they were composed were extracted from the flow of speech, it followed that morphemic (or syntactic) information could not enter a phonemic description: "There must be no circularity; phonological analysis is assumed for grammatical analysis and so must not assume any part of the latter. The line of demarcation between the two must be sharp [Hockett 1942: 107]." This became known as the prohibition against "mixing levels" in a grammatical description.

1.2.2. Structuralist Methodology

"Structural linguistics" was a cover term for all approaches to language which shared Saussure's goal of the classification of elements as the essential one for linguistics. Whether practiced in the United States by Bloomfield and his followers, or in Prague, Paris, or Copenhagen, structuralists from the 1930s through the 1950s either tacitly or explicitly viewed language as follows:[5]

> It would be interesting from a practical viewpoint to begin with units, to determine what they are and to account for their diversity by classifying them . . . . Next we would have to classify the subunits, then the larger units, etc. By determining in this way the elements that it manipulates, synchronic linguistics would completely fulfill its task, for it would relate all synchronic phenomena to their fundamental principle [Saussure 1959: 111].

American structuralism was renowned for the rigor with which it attempted to meet these goals. It was believed quite literally that starting with

---

[5] While Lane (1970) is undoubtedly correct when he writes that "modern proponents of structuralism all acknowledge allegiance to Ferdinand de Saussure as the founding father of the method [p. 27]," Keith Percival (1977) has argued convincingly that Saussure was "resurrected" for this purpose many years after his death and had little contemporary influence.

One structuralist tendency—the Prague School—is of particular importance to the development of transformational generative grammar. I will discuss it further in Section 2.5.1.

a corpus of utterances, a grammar could be constructed through successive segmentations and classifications.

The first step in this process would be to divide the speech flow itself into a series of phones—the basic units of sound. Phones were eligible to be members of the same phoneme if they did not contrast, that is, if they were in complementary distribution or free variation in an environment. In earlier work, MEANING contrast was used as a criterion for establishing the separate phonemic status of two phones. (For example, [ɪ] and [æ] result in meaning differences in the context /b . . . d/. Hence they were to be assigned to two separate phonemes.) However, since the notion of "meaning" was too vague to satisfy empiricist strictures, more operational tests, such as the "pair test" (Harris 1951) were developed to put the notion of "contrast" on a more solid footing.

After the phonemes were discovered, the next step would be to group them into "morphs," the minimal recurrent sequences of phonemes. Since the clues for the existence of morph boundaries had to exist in an already discovered level, this was no easy task. One method was proposed by Harris (1955), who suggested that morph boundaries might be arrived at by a procedure whose first step was the calculation of the number of phonemes which might conceivably follow a sequence of phonemes in a string. Harris used by way of illustration the English sentence *he's clever*, phonemicized as /hiyzklevər/. He estimated that 9 phonemes can follow utterance-initial /h/, 14 utterance-initial /hi/, 29 /hiy/, 29 /hiyz/, 11 /hiyzk/, 7 /hiyzkl/, 8 /hiyzkle/, 1 /hiyzklev/, 1 /hiyzklevə/, and 28 /hiyzklevər/. Harris theorized that morph boundaries followed peaks—that is, that they were to be posited after /y/, /z/, and /r/.

The procedure for classifying morphs into morphemes was similar to that for classifying phones into phonemes. Two morphs were eligible to be members of the same morpheme if (in the simplest case) they were in complementary distribution and were phonemically similar. Hence, a morphemic description consisted of statements like "The morpheme {ed} has members /əd/ (in a particular environment) and /t/ (in a particular environment)." Irregularity, particularly if it was reflected by vowel alternations, was a troublesome point in structuralist morphemics. There were several different morphemic analyses of /tuk/, for example, all of which attempted to be consistent with the classificatory principle of linguistic analysis and to avoid a process description like "/ey/ goes to /u/ in the past tense of /teyk/."

The principle of complementary distribution led to a different set of procedures in syntax, since one wanted to say that two morphemes were of the same syntactic type if they were NOT in complementary distribution. One set of procedures for assigning elements to syntactic categories was Harris's (1946) "bottom-up" morpheme-to-utterance approach; another was Wells's (1947) "top-down" immediate constituent analysis. Harris classified individual morphemes into syntactic categories on the basis of their distributions. For example, any morpheme that occurred before the plural {-s} morpheme (itself arrived at via bottom-up distributional analysis) would be classified as a "noun." Lower level syntactic categories were grouped into higher ones by analogous procedures. Wells, on the other hand, started from the sentence as a whole, and by substitution procedures, divided it into smaller and smaller constituents. Since in the sentence *the King of England opened Parliament,* the sequences of morphemes, *the King of England* and *opened Parliament,* had greater substitutive possibilities than any other sequences in the sentence, the major immediate constituent break was drawn between *England* and *opened.* This procedure would be followed down to the level of the individual morphemes.

In the 1950s, Harris began to work out procedures for stating syntactic relations BETWEEN sentences. Harris's work developed out of his attempt to analyze the structure of extended discourse. The problem was that sentences could exist in many different surface forms, and the usual substitution procedures did not seem to be of much help in stating the obvious systematic relatedness which existed between various types of sentences. Hence he worked out procedures (1957, 1965) for "normalizing" complex sentence types to simpler "kernel" ones. He noted, for example, that corresponding to sentences of the form

$$N_1 V N_2$$

there often existed sentences of the form

$$N_2 \text{ is V-ed by } N_1$$

or

$$\text{it is } N_2 \text{ that } N_1 V$$

Provided that the co-occurrence relations between N_1, V, and N_2 in the three sentence types were the same, Harris set up TRANSFORMATIONS relating them. They might be stated as follows:

$N_1 V N_2 \leftrightarrow N_2$ is V-ed by N_1 (Passive Transformation)
$N_1 V N_2 \leftrightarrow$ it is N_2 that $N_1 V$ (Cleft Transformation)

It is important to remember that these transformations were stated entirely on the surface syntactic output of the prior procedures: They did not interact to form a "grammar," in the modern sense. Hence, each one stood and fell independently: "A transformation once established is not normally falsifiable by further research [Harris 1965:383]."

Despite the work of Harris and a few others, there was relatively little syntax done by structuralists. Robert Hall (1951) explained why: "Descriptive syntactic studies have also been rather rare; but, since they normally come at the end of one's analysis, the tendency is perhaps to hold them for incorporation into a more complete description [p. 120]." In fact, the little syntactic work which WAS done was, in a sense, the result of "cheating"— a complete morphemic analysis had never been worked out even for English.

Since "meaning" was not a notion which could be made operational, it in principle was not to play a role in these procedures. Bloomfield (1933) cautioned linguists about what would be involved in treating meaning scientifically:

> The situations which prompt people to utter speech, include every object and happening in their universe. In order to give a scientifically accurate definition of meaning for every form of language, we should have to have a scientifically accurate knowledge of everything in the speaker's world [p. 139].

Since this goal was, of course, unattainable, recourse to meaning was to be avoided. Nevertheless, Bloomfield was inconsistent in this regard. As argued at length in Fries (1963), Bloomfield constantly brought meaning criteria into his procedures for phonemic and morphemic analysis. Later structuralists, especially Bloch (1948) and Harris (1951), attempted to circumvent this apparent defect in Bloomfield's work by proposing meaning-independent procedures of analysis.

Bloch (1948), Householder (1952), and others were still amenable to using meaning as a "short cut" in analysis, provided the resultant analysis "could" have been achieved without meaning. Actually, the structuralist procedures were bypassed in many ways. It was therefore necessary to have some checks which could be applied to any description to ensure that it could have been arrived at operationally. The most comprehensive was that there be a BIUNIQUE relationship between elements of one level and those of the next higher level (Hockett 1951; Harris 1951). Let us take the relationship between phones and phonemes as an illustration. Biuniqueness entails that any sequence of phones in a description has to be associated with a unique sequence of phonemes and that any sequence of phonemes has to be associated with a unique sequence of phones, down to free variation. Hence, descriptions involving neutralization at either the phonetic level (Figure 1.1) or the phonemic level (Figure 1.2) were automatically ruled out.

It is easy to see how both situations are incompatible with an empiricist-based requirement that phonemes be literally extractable from the sequence of phones by mechanical procedures.

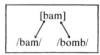

Figure 1.1

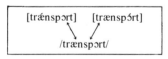

Figure 1.2

Figure 1.3

Operational considerations also demanded that a condition later termed "linearity" be placed on adjacent levels in a linguistic description. Linearity requires that the linear order of elements at one level match the linear order of the corresponding elements at the next level. Analyses representable by Figure 1.3 were therefore ruled out, assuming that phone [b] belongs to the phoneme /B/ and phone [c] belongs to the phoneme /C/.

Another necessary check was that an INVARIANT relation hold between phones and phonemes: that a phonetic segment in a given environment be invariantly assignable to a given phoneme. The weak form of invariance allowed partial intersection (overlapping) of two phonemes. Biuniqueness was not violated if, say, the [D] of [θDow] *throw* (in the dialect described in Bloch 1941) was assigned to the phoneme /r/ and the [D] of [bɛDiy] *Betty* assigned to /t/, since the environment for the identical phonetic manifestation of the two phonemes could (in principle) be recoverable from the acoustic signal. However, some structuralists (Hockett 1942; Wells 1945) disallowed even PARTIAL overlapping, resulting in the two occurrences of [D] being assigned to the same phoneme. This requirement of "once a phoneme, always a phoneme" seems to have resulted from the desire to raise the principle of complementary distribution to an inviolable strategy.

While empiricist assumptions necessitate a biunique relationship between levels within one description, it does not follow that there was necessarily a biunique relationship between the corpus of data and a description of it. The reason is that there were an indefinite number of procedures of segmentation and classification applicable to a given body of data, each consistent with empiricist methodology. This "nonuniqueness" of phonemic analyses (see Chao 1934) was a constant source of dismay to structuralists. For example, at least three different phonemicizations of the vowel nucleus in the word *bay* were proposed: /béj/ (Trager and Bloch 1941), /bée/ (Swadesh 1947), and /béi/ (Pike 1947a). The criterion of "pattern congruity" was often applied when a choice was made between alternatives. That is, the phonemicization was chosen which led to the greatest overall symmetry in the language's phonemic system. The Trager–Bloch analysis was selected as preferable by means of this criterion.[6]

---

[6] There is an interesting discussion of the criterion of pattern congruity and structural linguistics in general in Davis (1973).

1.2.3. Language and Psychology in the 1950s

The empiricist assumptions of the period under discussion had profound implications for psychology as well as for linguistics. Since all knowledge was considered to be based on experience alone, it followed that the child learned its grammar by applying elementary inductive principles to the raw speech data around it. Given that the operationalist constraint applied equally to grammarian and language learner alike, their tasks were completely analogous. Hockett (1948b) made this point clearly:[7]

> The analytical process [of the linguist] thus parallels what goes on in the nervous system of a language learner, particularly, perhaps, that of a child learning his first language. . . . The essential difference between the process in the child and the process of the linguist is this: the linguist has to make his analysis overtly, in communicable form, in the shape of a set of statements which can be understood by any properly trained person. . . [pp. 269–270].

Likewise, these assumptions entail a theory of speech perception as well. It follows that on the basis of cues in the acoustic signal alone, a hearer should be able to extract the grammatical components, just as the linguist needs (in principle) no more than an accurate record of this signal.

Despite these obvious connections between structural linguistics and its psychological counterpart, there was very little work done in what could be called "psycholinguistics" until the late 1940s. The explanation for this is not hard to find. Psychology in the 1940s was under the grip of a form of empiricism so extreme that it had no place even for the unobservable phonemes and morphemes of structural linguistics. Radical behaviorism under the leadership of B. F. Skinner would not even tolerate theoretical terms derivable by a set of mechanical operations, such as those of the structural linguist. Only the measurable responses themselves were admissible in descriptive statements. Hence, behaviorist psychology was largely ignored by practicing linguists in this period.

The marriage of structural linguistics and psychology took place after a less radical form of behaviorism was developed by the psychologist Clark Hull (see Hull 1943). Hullian psychology departed from Skinnerean in ways which made it conducive to the development of psycholinguistics. First, it was not committed to the idea that all learning takes place by reinforcement alone. In Hull's view, paired stimuli, even without direct reinforcement, could lead to learning, given that the pairing took place enough times within hearing range of the language learner. Second, it developed a notion known as the "mediating response." The mediating response was essentially a nonobservable element in the response chain, linked to observable responses on either side.

---

[7] Although many structuralists (e.g., Twaddell 1935) were unwilling to take such a "realist" position.

Now, psychologists had the theoretical apparatus they needed to capture the hierarchical nature of language as seen by structural linguists. The theoretical terms of structuralism, such as "phoneme," "morpheme," or "verb," could be thought of as mediating responses, with unique transition probabilities calculable between them. The hierarchical organization of language could be captured by the notion "associative set." An associative set for a linguistic element was considered to be all and only the responses associated with that element. For example, the mediating response *verb* would be in the associative set for the stimuli *run, hit, dance,* etc.; /t/ would be in the associative set for [t^h], [t], etc. It was further assumed that information theory would be able to provide the mathematical tools for calculating the transition probabilities from response to response. Floyd Lounsbury stated the aims of the endeavor succinctly:

> Study of the sequential or transitional structure of language behavior provides a meeting ground for linguists, information theorists, and learning theorists. The linguist, applying his own methods of analysis, discovers hierarchies of more and more inclusive units; the information theorist, usually starting with lower-level units such as letters or words, finds evidence for rather regular sequences, the points of highest uncertainty often corresponding to unit boundaries as linguistically determined, and the learning theorist, working with notions like the habit-family hierarchy, finds it possible to make predictions about sequential psycholinguistic phenomena that can be tested with information theory techniques [Osgood and Sebeok 1954:93].

By the early 1950s, an interdisciplinary field of psycholinguistics had emerged, with important seminars being held at Cornell in 1951 and Indiana in 1953. The progress reports from the latter seminar were published in the first volume of papers dealing with language and psychology, Osgood and Sebeok (1954)—a work hailed by one reviewer as "a scientific event of great importance [Olmsted 1955:59]." Among many other topics, the book dealt with issues such as the psychological verification of the phoneme and the psychological criteria which would help decide between competing linguistic analyses. The book itself inspired work conferences on many related subjects which themselves resulted in influential publications on content analysis (Pool 1959); stylistics (Sebeok 1960); aphasia (Osgood and Miron 1963); and language universals (Greenberg 1963).

Finally, for the first time a serious experimental approach to meaning was being undertaken. Charles Osgood, the leading Hullian psycholinguist, was developing his "semantic differential"—an approach to concretizing meaning through measurement of responses to word associations (see Osgood, Tannenbaum, and Suci 1957). While the linguistic community felt that Osgood's approach was rather naive, there was nevertheless hope that the most elusive notion of all—meaning—might be given an objective foundation.

1.3. CLOUDS ON THE HORIZON

So far, the picture I have painted of the self-perceived state of structural linguistics in the mid 1950s has been a uniformly rosy one. Yet hardly 10 years later its defenders were hard pressed to find an audience. And 20 years later, those linguistics students who studied it at all, learned the theory and method of structuralism the way students in the 1950s learned about Franz Bopp or August Schleicher. How did it fall so far so fast? In this section, I will answer part of this question by pointing to some of the weaknesses of the theory as perceived (if only dimly) by the structuralists themselves.

1.3.1. Crisis in Empiricist Philosophy

The crisis in linguistics which led to the downfall of structuralism and the victory of transformational generative grammar had its roots in philosophy—particularly the philosophy of science. Little by little, the philosophic and scientific underpinnings were knocked out from under structuralism. And since more than anything else structuralists felt they had SCIENTIFIC justification for their theory, when they lost that justification they had very little to appeal to.

For years, philosophers had been grappling with the question of what it might mean to say that a statement is meaningful (scientific). The strongest empiricist position possible is known as "the principle of complete verification." According to this principle, the meaning of a statement is simply a description of the ways in which it might be verified: "Whenever we ask about a sentence 'what does it mean?' . . . we want a description of the conditions under which the sentence will form a true proposition, and of those which will make it false. . . . . The meaning of a proposition is the method of its verification [Schlick 1936:341]." Strict verificationism was abandoned very early as untenable by philosophers (though not by behavioral psychologists). Various weaker forms of verificationism were put forth in the late 1930s and in the 1940s. The criteria for significance were weakened still further to the "principle of falsifiability," a statement was to be considered meaningful if it was falsifiable in principle. But still there were problems—many meaningful statements (such as any containing an existential quantifier) simply did not meet this condition. Yet it seemed counterintuitive to call them "unscientific."

By the late 1940s it was widely believed that a sentence could be considered meaningful if its constituent terms could be given what is often known as an "operational definition." That is, all terms in a scientific statement would have to be linkable directly to observables by an operation (or series of operations) performable by the investigator. Notice that the theoretical terms in structural linguistics (such as "phoneme" and "noun") had just this quality. If anybody wanted to know why the claim had been made that /k/, for example, was a phoneme of English, that person could (in principle) be provided with a list of the operations performed on the raw data to arrive at that conclusion.

In two important papers (partly surveying earlier work, partly original in nature), the philosopher Carl Hempel (1950, 1951) laid to rest any hope for an empiricist criterion for cognitive significance.[8] After reviewing the earlier, more inadequate, theories of meaningfulness, he pointed out that even the more permissive empiricist approaches to this question failed to capture the essence of what it takes for a statement to be considered scientific. There is simply no direct connection between a scientific term or statement and the empirical confirmation of a theory containing that term or statement. For example,

> the hypothesis that the agent of tuberculosis is rod-shaped does not by itself entail the consequence that upon looking at a tubercular sputum specimen through a microscope, rod-like shapes will be observed: a large number of subsidiary hypothesis, including the theory of the microscope, have to be used as additional premises in deducing that prediction [Hempel 1950:58-59].

And moreover, many fundamental scientific notions, such as "gravitational potential," "absolute temperature," and "electric field," have no operational definitions at all.

How then might a statement be judged as meaningful or not? The problem, according to Hempel, lies in attempting to ascribe meaningfulness to statements themselves in isolation. Science is more in the business of comparing THEORIES than in evaluating STATEMENTS. A theory is simply an axiomatized system which AS A WHOLE has an empirical interpretation. We can compare competing theoretical systems in regard to such characteristics as these:

> a. the clarity and precision with which the theories are formulated, and with which the logical relationships of their elements to each other and to expressions couched in observational terms have been made explicit;
> b. the systematic, i.e., explanatory and predictive, power of the systems in regard to observable phenomena;
> c. the formal simplicity of the theoretical system with which a certain systematic power is attained;
> d. the extent to which the theories have been confirmed by experimental evidence [Hempel 1951:74].

Hempel went on to write:

> Many of the speculative philosophical approaches to cosmology, biology, or history, for example, would make a poor showing on practically all of these counts and would thus prove no matches to available rival theories, or would be recognized as so unpromising as not to warrant further study or development [p. 74].

---

[8] These two papers were later merged in Hempel (1965).

Statements like these signaled the demise of empiricism as a significant force in the philosophy of science. As its philosophical props gave way, structural linguistics found itself in a distinctly unstable posture. Not surprisingly, it was relatively simple for a new theory, defective by any empiricist standards, yet nevertheless highly valued according to Hempel's four criteria, to topple it completely.[9]

1.3.2. Unresolved Problems in Structural Linguistics

The most vocal critics of structural linguistics in the 1950s, of course, were somewhat outside the mainstream. And while those critics never drew the most extreme conclusion—the bankruptcy of the theory—they nevertheless helped to create an accelerating atmosphere of uncertainty around the entire enterprise.

The most troublesome problems for structuralists involved the analysis of the suprasegmentals: stress, pitch, and juncture. Alternative analyses abounded, and no one was able to give an even half-convincing argument that their phonemicization was latent in the acoustic signal—as, of course, it had to be. James Sledd, in his 1955 review of Trager and Smith's influential *Outline of English Structure* (1951), told the truth more openly than it had ever been told before. Sledd, who had built up quite a reputation as an iconoclast, said that he simply did not hear the neat distribution of stress, pitch, and juncture phonemes of the Trager–Smith analysis, strongly implying that the authors had done nothing less than cheat.

Hill (1958) made a frank admission which could only discredit the foundations of structuralism:

> Until a few years ago, it was an assumption almost universal among linguists that a speaker, even without special training, would infallibly and automatically hear the contrasts in his own speech and that the only things he would not hear would be sounds which are not contrastive. Consequently, it would at that time have been necessary to say that any speaker who had trouble in hearing four grades of stress would be one who had only three contrasts. We have taken the position that there are speakers who have four contrasts but who still have difficulty in hearing all the distinctions they make. Such difficulties occur not only in the system of stresses, but with other sounds as well [pp. 17–18].

While Hill did not draw this conclusion, such facts are dramatic empirical disconfirmation of the principles of structural linguistics.

Kenneth Pike, in two well-known articles (1947b, 1952), pointed out many of the same problems. But Pike went further than other critics—he said that in order to assign juncture correctly you HAD to "mix levels"—to do at least part of the grammatical analysis first. Pike's alternative did not

---

[9] Hockett (1954) made many of the same points as Hempel, though, oddly, his actual descriptive work does not seem to have been affected by his change of theoretical perspective.

really represent a break from operationalism, since he outlined (very vaguely) some mechanical procedures for identifying morphemes before doing a phonemic analysis. But it is noteworthy for its clear statement of the dilemma facing competent linguists of the period—they knew what to do to get the right grammatical analysis, but their theory would not let them do it: "There must be something wrong with present-day phonemic theory if workers agree on the practical value of a procedure (and of evidence) in the field which they then rule out in theoretical discussion and in presentation [Pike 1947b: 159]."

Along the same lines, Abercrombie (1965: 114–119) chastised structuralists for their wanton use of "pseudoprocedures"—procedures which were entailed by their methodological assumptions, but which were not or (even worse) could not be carried out in actual practice.

There are a number of examples in the literature where linguists were forced to reject analyses which they knew EXPLICITLY were correct, because their theory told them otherwise. Two involve Bernard Bloch. Bloch (1947) worked out detailed procedures for assigning morphs to morphemes. After disposing of the bulk of regular and irregular verbs in English, he noted the variant phonemic shapes of the word *have* in four pronunciations of the sentence *I have seen it*:

/ày hæv síyn it/
/ày v síyn it/
/ày həv síyn it/
/ày əv síyn it/

Since /hæv/, /v/, /həv/, and /əv/ are neither in complementary distribution nor in free variation (they differ in their "social flavor"), Bloch (1947) could not escape the conclusion that they belong to FOUR SEPARATE MORPHEMES: "Reluctant as we may be to allow the multiplication of elements, we cannot escape the conclusion that the verb forms /həv/ and /əv/ belong to none of the morphemes mentioned so far [p. 417]."

An even better example can be found in Bloch's two phonological studies of Japanese (1947, 1950). The earlier paper gave an extremely elegant (though informal) description of the sound patterning of that language. But in 1950, he revised his analysis in the direction of complexity and lack of generalization. Why? Because earlier he had "confused phonemes with morphophonemes"—the earlier insightful analysis had violated biuniqueness. Hockett (1951) comments on this: "What is deceptively simple in [Bloch's] earlier treatment turns out to be quite complicated in the later—but the more complicated treatment is also obviously more accurate [p. 341]." Bloch and Hockett could not have been undisturbed by having to reject "simple" treatments for "complicated" but "accurate" ones.

By 1955, even Hockett had to agree reluctantly that one could not do an analysis of a language "objectively"—one had to "empathize" with the informant (Hockett 1955:147). But if that were the case, then what theoretical validity could operational procedures have which were designed to guarantee the correct description of a language?

Finally, in 1957 at least one observer noted a growing decline in dogmatism and confidence among practicing structural linguists:

> In the intervening years [since the early 1940s], however, it seems to me that the attitudes and behavior-patterns of linguists have changed. Naturally the fervor of that generation has waned, but even among the younger linguists there seem to be a few [*sic*] who are either as chauvinistic, as passionate, or as confident that they have discovered the whole truth . . . . Dogmatism also appears to have declined, though, to be sure, it has not vanished (and presumably never will) [Householder 1957:156].

As events in that year were to prove, they had very little to be dogmatic or confident about.

Chapter 2

The Chomskyan Revolution

2.1. OVERVIEW

Early in 1957, Noam Chomsky's *Syntactic Structures* was released by Mouton in The Hague. But it did not share the fate of most first books by unknown authors distributed by obscure publishers. Within weeks, Robert B. Lees's review of it appeared in the journal *Language*. Lees, who enjoyed a modest reputation in the field, left no doubt that the book would change linguistics. Such praise for a new approach to the study of language and such derogation of the contemporary paradigm had never been seen before in the pages of *Language*. Lees (1957) wrote that Chomsky's book was:

> one of the first serious attempts on the part of a linguist to construct within the tradition of scientific theory-construction a comprehensive theory of language which may be understood in the same sense that a chemical, biological theory is ordinarily understood by experts in those fields [p. 377].

Actually, the tone of the review as a whole made it clear that Lees regarded it as the ONLY serious attempt, and a completely successful one at that. And C. F. Voegelin (1958), in another review, noted that even if *Syntactic Structures* managed to accomplish only part of its goals, "it will have accomplished a Copernican revolution [p. 229]." The distinguished British linguist, C. E. Bazell, upon one reading of the book, remarked to a student that "linguistics will never be the same" and immediately initiated a continuing correspondence with Chomsky.

Syntactic Structures was perceived by many structuralists around the world for exactly what it was—a threat to their intellectual hegemony over the field. In the early 1960s, counterattacks by the score were directed against this "theory spawned by a generation of vipers" (Charles Hockett, quoted in Mehta 1971:175). But the structuralist critique was not successful. In the mid and late 1960s, American universities underwent the greatest expansion in history. New linguistics departments sprung up in a dozen locations and some existing ones literally quadrupled in size. The reputation of Chomsky's theory had grown to the point where, by and large, transformationalists were sought to fill the new positions. In fact, linguistics grew at a much greater rate than almost any other field—a testament to the intellectual appeal of the theory.

By 1970, if not before, it was clear that transformational generative grammar had become the "established" linguistic theory in the United States. An obvious indicator of this fact is that by that year partisans of the theory had simply stopped replying to criticism from linguists in the structuralist tradition. They had no further need to answer the old guard. Chomsky and others turned their attention to assaults on the fundamentals of the theory by psychologists and philosophers. But the increased stature of cognitive psychology and rationalist philosophy within their respective disciplines in recent years points to the growing impact that linguistic theory has had outside of linguistics proper, and to the indifferent success of the psychological and philosophical critique. The 1970s have also seen the unprecedented internationalization of a linguistic theory; transformational generative grammar has at least as many practitioners outside the United States as inside.

In recent years there has been an undeniable fragmentation of the once monolithic theory. Many alternative models of linguistic description have been proposed, some heralded as making as much of a break from mainstream transformational grammar as this theory made from structural linguistics. But with marginal exceptions, the debate has taken place well within the general framework of theoretical assumptions first articulated in *Syntactic Structures*. A truly alternative theory with any credibility has yet to emerge.

2.2. *SYNTACTIC STRUCTURES*

2.2.1. Linguistics Made a Science

The essence of Chomsky's revolution in linguistics was his gift to the field of a truly scientific perspective. Drawing (though rarely explicitly) on the contemporary changes of attitude in the philosophy of science mentioned in Chapter 1, he characterized a grammar simply as "a theory of language," and rejected the empiricist view of one as a mechanically constructable abbreviation of corpus. In short, a grammar is to be thought of as an axiomatized system generating an infinite set of sentences with their associated structural descriptions, and is to be judged for empirical adequacy by its ability to handle the primary linguistic data—the judgments native speakers can make (or, alternatively, the "intuitions" they have) about certain aspects of their language.

Chomsky attacked the structuralist–empiricist concept of a linguistic theory for imposing conditions on theory formation which were incompatible with the provision of an insightful picture of the workings of human language. Chomsky argued that in fact NO science demands that a theory be literally extractable from the primary data. Yet this was the goal that the structuralists had set for themselves. In his view, the most linguistic theory can realistically hope to construct is an EVALUATION procedure for grammars—a mechanical way of deciding between alternative grammars within a particular theory. And, as Chomsky pointed out, even an evaluation procedure is more than most sciences would hope to accomplish: "There are few areas of science in which one would seriously consider the possibility of developing a general, practical, mechanical method for choosing among several theories, each compatible with the available data [p. 53]."

Once the structuralist aim of "discovering" a grammar was abandoned, there was no longer a need to worry about a description which "mixes levels." A grammar would not result from a cookbooklike set of directions which tells the linguist to "find the phonemes first"; rather, the rules and the inventory of phonemes, morphemes, etc. might be arrived at "by intuition, guesswork, all sorts of partial methodological hints, reliance on past experience, etc. [p. 56]." This could well lead to a description in which syntactic information, say, enters into the statement of a phonological rule. But this would be a completely acceptable conclusion, since the entire question of the interdependence of levels is one to be answered by empirical investigation rather than by methodological fiat.

2.2.2. Simplicity and the Evaluation of Grammars

To say that a theory provides an evaluation procedure for grammars obviously invites the question: By what criteria are grammars to be evaluated? Clearly, the nature of a successful linguistic description had to be made explicit. Chomsky termed these criteria "external conditions of adequacy" and in *Syntactic Structures* outlined four of them:

1. The sentences generated are acceptable to the native speaker.
2. Every case of "constructional homonymity" (the assignment of more than one structural description to a sentence) describes a real ambiguity; every case of ambiguity is represented by constructional homonymity.
3. Differential interpretations of superficially similar sentences are represented by different derivational histories. (His example involved

the sentences *the picture was painted by a new technique* and *the picture was painted by a real artist.*)

4. Sentences understood in similar ways are represented in similar ways at one level of description.

Chomsky then argued for the necessity of posing "a CONDITION OF GENERALITY on grammars; we require that the grammar of a given language be constructed in accord with a specific theory of linguistic structure in which such terms as 'phoneme' and 'phrase' are defined independently of any particular language [p. 50]." The "condition of generality" (Chomsky used this term only once) seems to correspond to what were later called "linguistic universals." It comprises those theoretical terms, notational conventions, etc. which are selected and which are posited to interact in such a way as to allow the external conditions of adequacy to be met in the most linguistically revealing way. For example, since a grammar without transformational rules presumably could not meet the external conditions, such rules would have to form part of the descriptive apparatus of the theory. But what of a case where there appeared to be TWO grammars, each meeting the external conditions? Here the evaluation measure would come into play. Chomsky hoped the condition of generality might be formulable so that given two alternative descriptions, the shorter one (as measured in terms of absolute length, number of symbols, or some such criterion) would always be the one of maximum generality as well.

However, many have found Chomsky's discussion of simplicity, evaluation, and conditions of adequacy and generality in Chapter 6 of *Syntactic Structures* to be extremely confusing, and my interpretation may be biased by over 20 years of further discussion of these issues. Since he shifted his use of the word "theory" in that chapter back and forth from instances where it refers to the theory of language itself (i.e., transformational generative grammar with its particular goals and constructs) to instances where it refers to specific proposed grammars of particular languages, it is not surprising that many critics (e.g., Householder 1965) got the idea that an evaluation metric involving "simplicity" could be invoked in choosing between totally distinct theories. And since no concrete examples were given in *Syntactic Structures* of how adequacy correlates with formal simplicity, it was easy for many commentators to draw the conclusion that the simplicity metric was little more than an aesthetic—a matter of personal taste.

2.2.3. Three Models of Linguistic Description

Chomsky had two major goals in *Syntactic Structures*. First, he had the general goal of motivating linguistic theory and its formalization by means of generative grammars subject to certain conditions of adequacy. But also, he had the more narrow goal of demonstrating that only generative grammars of one particular type can meet these conditions. This model, transformational grammar, contains two types of syntactic rules: phrase structure and transformational. The latter were inspired by, and are essentially generative reinterpretations of, the identically named rules proposed by his teacher Zellig Harris in his attempt to apply the methods of structural linguistics to the analysis of discourse.

Chomsky was in the peculiar position of having to argue against two generative grammatical models—finite state grammar and phrase structure grammar—which had very few public adherents. He had to do this because these models were the closest generative interpretations of the views of language current in the 1950s. Finite state grammars bore a close resemblance to (or were identical to, as in the case of Hockett 1955) the type of device promoted by communications theorists. The sorts of descriptions which phrase structure grammars provided were (for all practical purposes) identical to those which resulted from the structuralists' procedures. So Chomsky's demonstration of the inadequacy of these two models in Chapters 3, 4, and 5 of *Syntactic Structures* was directed to—and was most convincing to—those linguists who might have been won over to his general goal of constructing a linguistic theory, but still clung to the more conservative generative analogs of earlier views of language. Clearly, a linguist who rejected the need for generative rules, external conditions of adequacy, etc. would not have been terribly impressed by Chomsky's demonstration of the superiority of transformational grammar over phrase structure grammar.

Chomsky contrasted the three models in terms of their "weak generative capacity" and their "strong generative capacity," to use terms which appeared a few years later. The former refers to their string-generating ability, the latter to their ability to assign structural descriptions to these strings. Since a grammar unable to generate all and only the sentences of a language is of no further empirical interest, the demonstration of the defect of a model in terms of weak generative capacity makes any discussion of its strong capacity unnecessary. Chomsky proved that finite-state grammars were defective in just this way in an argument taking the following form:

First Premise: No finite-state grammar is capable of generating a language containing an infinite set of strings with nested dependencies, while simultaneously excluding the infinite set of strings which contradict these dependencies.

Second Premise: A subpart of English is a language as described in the First Premise.

Conclusion: All and only the sentences of English cannot be generated by a finite-state grammar.

Chomsky proved the first premise in his 1956 paper "Three Models for the

Description of Language." The second depends crucially on the assumption that sentences of the form *if* _____ *then* _____, *either* _____ *or*, etc. can be embedded in each other without limit. While in actual speech, it is probably the case that the degree of nesting is quite restricted, speakers (with paper and pencil) can normally interpret highly complex nested constructions, such as the following one cited in Chomsky and Miller (1963) (a dependent relation holds between like-subscripted elements):

> *Anyone$_1$ who feels that if$_2$ so-many$_3$ more$_4$ students$_5$ whom we$_6$ haven't$_6$ actually admitted are$_5$ sitting in on the course than$_4$ ones we have that$_3$ the room had to be changed, then$_2$ probably auditors will have to be excluded, is$_1$ likely to agree that the curriculum needs revision [p. 286].*

Given that there is no principled limit to the nesting possibilities, it is clear that English (and, by extension, language in general) cannot be described in finite-state terms. There was no need for Chomsky even to mention the more serious defects of finite-state grammars in terms of their strong generative capacity.

Chomsky did not question the fact that phrase structure grammars are CAPABLE of weakly generating the sentences of English.[1] He rather argued that they can do so only in a cumbersome fashion and, furthermore, do not come close to assigning the correct structural descriptions to the sentences generated:

> A weaker, but perfectly sufficient demonstration of inadequacy [of phrase structure grammar] would be to show that the theory can apply only clumsily; that is, to show that any grammar that can be constructed in terms of this theory will be extremely complex, ad hoc, and "unrevealing". . . [Chomsky 1957:34].

His examples of the defects of phrase structure grammars were illustrated simultaneously with the demonstration that grammars containing the more powerful transformational rules can handle the same phenomena in an elegant and revealing manner. By far the most persuasive is his transformational analysis of the English verbal auxiliary system. While Chomsky did not attempt to state the phrase structure rules which would be involved in generating all of the possible combinations of auxiliary verbs in English

---

[1] Chomsky later (1959a) proved that the language consisting of all and only the strings [*XX*] is not a context-free language, where *X* varies over an infinite set of strings in an alphabet of two or more symbols. Postal (1964a) then demonstrated that Mohawk, an Iroquoian language, contains, as a subpart, an infinite set of sentences with this property. While he proved with this only that Mohawk sentences could not be weakly generated by a context-FREE phrase structure grammar, he also argued that a phrase-structure grammar containing context-sensitive rules would require at least thirty-six million symbols.

Both Postal's proof and Chomsky's (as cited in the text) have since been argued to be flawed. See Reich (1969) for comments on the former and Levelt (1974) for comments on the latter.

(and excluding the impossible ones), it was generally accepted at that time that such rules would have to be enormously complex. Chomsky treated the superficially discontinuous auxiliary morphemes *have . . . en* and *be . . . ing* as unit constituents generated by the phrase structure rules, and posited a simple transformational rule to permute the affixal and verbal elements into their surface positions, thus predicting all of the basic distribution of auxiliaries in simple declarative sentences. Moreover, he was able to show that the permutation rule, "the Auxiliary Transformation" (later called "Affix Hopping" by other linguists), interacts with rules forming simple negatives and simple yes–no questions to specify neatly the exact locations where "supportive" *do* appears. The ingenuity of this analysis probably did more to win supporters for Chomsky than all of his metatheoretical statements about discovery and evaluation procedures and led (in the early 1960s) even to some structuralists' taking a generative–transformational approach to syntax while at the same time (inconsistently) rejecting the assumptions of the theory itself (see, for example, Gleason 1961:171–194 and the suspiciou.ly Chomskyan analysis in Joos 1964:53ff.).

Chomsky motivated the Passive transformation in like manner. He argued that the contextual restrictions holding between the passive morpheme, the passive *by*-phrase, and the transitive verb would be extraordinarily difficult to state by means of phrase structure rules. However, one transformational rule permuting the subject and the object and adding the morphemes *be . . . en* and *by* unique to the passive construction eliminates the need for any of these special restrictions.

It is important to understand the form of these arguments. They all involve showing that a grammar with ONLY phrase structure rules is able to generate all and only the sentences of some particular subpart of English only with great complexity. Adding a transformational rule simplifies the generation of the grammatical sentences of the construction. Moreover, this simplified analysis, motivated only to meet Condition 1 of the external conditions of adequacy mentioned at the beginning of Section 2.2.2, characteristically turns out to meet Conditions 2, 3, and 4 as well—the strongest type of empirical confirmation of the analysis possible. For example, the inability of phrase structure grammar to generate discontinuous morphemes as constituents was not Chomsky's primary motivation for a transformational analysis of the auxiliary system. This analysis was justified on the basis of considerations of formal simplicity alone—one would naturally opt for a simple phrase structure rule and a simple transformational rule over a large number of cumbersome phrase structure rules. However, the generation of these morphemes as constituents turns out to be an important BY-PRODUCT of the analysis which was motivated on purely formal grounds. Likewise, the undeniable semantic correspondences between declaratives and interrogatives, affirmatives and negatives, actives and passives, etc. were not admitted by Chomsky as direct evidence for setting up transformations relating them. Rather, their relationship is incidentally explained by the syntactically motivated analysis. Had such correspondences been used as evidence for motivating the transformations, the grammar, of course, would have succeeded only in STIPULATING these relations rather than in EXPLAINING them (for further discussion see Section 2.2.5).

The transformational model of *Syntactic Structures* contained three levels: the level of phrase structure, the level of transformational structure, and the level of morphophonemics. The rules of the phrase structure level generated a finite set of "underlying terminal strings," that is, strings with phrase structure interpretations. This set was finite because there were no recursive rules applying at the phrase structure level.[2] Most phrase structure rules were context-free, such as Rule (2.1) which expands the Auxiliary node:

(2.1)   Aux → Tense (Modal) $(have + en)$ $(be + en)$

However, it was necessary to posit context-sensitive phrase structure rules as well as to account for lexical subcategorization. The following rule (taken from Chomsky 1962: 138), which subcategorizes verbs with respect to their co-occurrences within the verb phrase, is an example:

$$(2.2) \quad V \rightarrow \begin{cases} \begin{Bmatrix} V_s \\ become \end{Bmatrix} \text{ in env. } \underline{\hspace{2cm}} \text{ Pred} \\ V_t \text{ in env. } \underline{\hspace{2cm}} \text{ NP} \\ V_i \text{ in env. } \begin{Bmatrix} \# \\ Adv \end{Bmatrix} \end{cases}$$

Phrase structure rules (ordinarily context-free) then introduced the lexical items themselves:

(2.3) $V_s \rightarrow feel,\ seem,\ \ldots$

Transformational rules then mapped these underlying terminal strings into other strings, each derived string being assigned a new constituent structure. Chomsky had no term for the output of the transformational rules more technical than "a string of words." Transformations were of two fundamentally distinct types: singulary (simple) and generalized (double-based). Singulary transformations, such as Passive, the Auxiliary Transformation, and the Negative Transformation, applied within the simple phrase-

---

[2] Strictly speaking, this is not correct. Chomsky (p. 73) envisaged handling some very marginal recursive processes, such as the unlimited successive appearances of the modifier *very*, by phrase-structure rules. Technically, then, the output of this component is an infinite set of terminal strings in the *Syntactic Structures* model.

markers generated by the branching rules. Generalized transformations embedded into each other or conjoined with each other these derived phrase-markers without limit, capturing in this way the recursive property of human language. Singulary transformations could also apply after embedding, as well as before.

Many people have wondered why Chomsky did not, from the very beginning, handle recursion by the device of recursive phrase structure rules—an approach both conceptually simpler and more constrained in that base recursion limits the class of possible grammars.[3] The reason is that the interaction of the singulary and generalized transformations was a complete mystery at the time. The more conservative approach chosen by Chomsky of positing embedding transformations left open the possibility that singulary transformations might apply in a matrix clause before another sentence was embedded into it. Certainly there was no evidence that such might not be the case. A multiclausal base structure would have made this possibility difficult, if not impossible, to state formally. I will discuss this problem in some detail in the next chapter.

Chomsky further argued that at least some transformations had to be extrinsically ordered with respect to each other in the grammar. For example, the transformation which assigned number to the Verb based on the number of the subject had to be specified to follow the rule of Passive to avoid *the boy* (singular) *sees the girls* (plural) from being mapped into *the girls (plural) *is seen by the boy* (singular).

Chomsky also drew a distinction between obligatory and optional transformations. The former had to apply whenever their structural description was met. The Auxiliary Transformation and the *Do*-Transformation (which inserted the morpheme *do* before a stranded tense affix) are examples. The class of optional transformations was quite large: negatives, *wh*- and yes–no questions, and imperatives were all formed by optional rules. Hence, the underlying terminal string *you*-Pres-*will-light-the-fire* underlay all of *you will light the fire, light the fire, you will not light the fire, will you light the fire? what will you light? who will light the fire?* etc.

Those sentences derived only by the application of obligatory transformations had a special name—KERNEL STRINGS. The kernel of the language corresponded exactly to the set of simple (i.e., uniclausal) declarative affirmatives.

To complete the derivation, "we then run through the morphophonemic rules, thereby converting this string of words into a string of phonemes [Chomsky 1957:46]." The following were cited as examples of morphophonemic rules:

---

[3] But see Bach (1977a) for a defense of the view that generalized transformations are in principle more constraining than base recursion.

(2.4)   i. *walk* → /wɔk/
            ii. *take* + past → /tuk/
           iii. *hit* + past → /hit/
            iv. / . . . D/ + past → / . . . D/ + /ɪd/ (where D = /t/or/d/)

             v. / . . . C_{unv}/+ past →/ . . . C_{unv}/+/t/ (where C_{unv} is an un-
                voiced consonant)
            vi. Past → /d/
           vii. take → /teyk/
                etc.

I find the use of the expression "string of phonemes" to describe the output
of the morphophonemic rules rather misleading, since on page 59 he implied
that the generative stress rules of Chomsky, Halle, and Lukoff (1956) (see
page 39 of this volume) were part of this component. However, the precise
character of the morphophonemic component was of little importance to
Chomsky in *Syntactic Structures*.

    Each derivation in the pre-1965 model was graphically represented by
its unique TRANSFORMATION-MARKER. Such markers consisted of the specification of the phrase-markers associated with each underlying terminal
string and those singulary and generalized transformations which applied in
the derivation, in the order in which they applied.

2.2.4. Grammaticality and Acceptability

    The idea that the set of sentences which constitutes a human language
is both infinite and well-defined was, not surprisingly, resisted from the
very beginning by structuralists. In fact their last major attack on transformational generative grammar, Charles Hockett's *The State of the Art* (1968),
attempts to refute the theory by undermining just this conception. (Also,
not surprisingly, the rejection of the notion "grammatical sentence" as a
scientific idealization would become the cornerstone of the repudiation of
the theory by Chomsky's own erstwhile followers in the 1970s—see Chapter
5.) It was necessary for Chomsky, then, to motivate the need for such an
abstraction.

    The primary motivation for the idealization was the simple fact that
fundamental insights about language were inexpressible without it—namely
those analyses which fill the pages of *Syntactic Structures*. But Chomsky
also devoted a fair amount of space to arguing that any more data-bound
conception of "grammaticality," such as the idea that the set of grammatical
sentences could be equated with any particular corpus of utterances found
by the linguist in fieldwork or could be identified in any way with the notion
"high order of statistical approximation to English," simply led to absurd-
ities. His rejection of these criteria, of course, set the stage for his more
general rejection of any attempt to literally extract a grammatical description

from the primary linguistic data. It was no accident that these points were the very first which he took up in *Syntactic Structures*. For once dissuaded of the possibility of a PHYSICAL definition of grammaticality, the rational linguist would necessarily be more than half way to accepting the necessity of an abstract linguistic theory.

By what independent criteria, then, could a sentence be determined to be grammatical? The most explicit that Chomsky got was a rather vague "acceptable to a native speaker, etc. [p. 13]." But what about the numerous cases where the native speaker simply CANNOT decide—where the judgments are too subtle for even the most sophisticated informant? Chomsky wrote: "In many intermediate cases we shall be prepared to let the grammar itself decide, when the grammar is set up in the simplest way so that it includes the clear sentences and excludes the clear non-sentences. This is a familiar feature of explication [p. 14]."

Chomsky left readers of *Syntactic Structures* confused about a rather fundamental point. The rules proposed in that book generate sentences indefinitely long. In fact, the proof of the inadequacy of finite-state grammars CRUCIALLY depends on this fact—if there were an upper limit to the amount of nesting possible, the argument would not go through. Yet native speakers have very clear intuitions about multiply nested constructions a billion words long. They are utterly unacceptable. Chomsky did not address this problem in 1957, and such facts could have been used as evidence against his theory of grammaticality at that time. A solution to this problem had to await a clear statement of the competence–performance dichotomy. What Chomsky must have had in mind in *Syntactic Structures* (and what became more explicit a few years later) is that an unacceptable sentence is necessarily considered ungrammatical UNLESS some other (performance) explanation is on hand to explain its unacceptability.

The obvious theoretical desirability of not restricting in an ad hoc fashion the rules for recursive nesting combined with the obvious processing difficulty as a performance explanation would justify the generation of the billion word sentence mentioned above, despite its unacceptability.[4]

Chomsky certainly felt uneasy about relying on introspective native speaker judgments as the primary data to be explained. In fact, at one point he went so far as to write: "It is also quite clear that THE MAJOR GOAL of grammatical theory is to replace this obscure reliance on intuition by some rigorous and objective approach [p. 94, emphasis added]." In a few footnotes he did cite some independent test properties of the ungrammatical sentences he was discussing: characteristic falling intonation, difficulty of

---

[4] By the same token, linguistic theory allows for the possibility of acceptable but ungrammatical sentences. For proposals along these lines, see Otero (1972, 1973, 1976) and Emonds (1976: Chapter II). Otero's conclusions are reinterpreted without recourse to acceptable ungrammaticality in Contreras (1973) and Knowles (1974), and those of Emonds are reinterpreted in Hooper and Thompson (1973) and Koster (1978c).

learning and recall, extra long pauses between elements, lack of vowel reduction in rapid speech, etc. But none of these were proposed as GENERAL tests for ungrammaticality—a point seriously misunderstood by Hill (1961) and others who attempted to falsify transformational grammar by pointing to the failure of one or another of these tests to confirm a particular claim of ungrammaticality. After a few years, we see no further references to methods for grounding intuition objectively. No reliable test was ever developed, so Chomsky dropped the entire question without comment. It seems odd in a way that he was never taken to task for this by his critics, but then, it is difficult to imagine a realistic alternative to using native speakers as informants. The judgments linguists deal with may be subtle at times or even unreliable, but such is the nature of the data of linguistic science, and that is a fact that grammarians have learned to live with.[5]

The handling of GRADED acceptability judgments played a larger role in Chomsky's early work than it did later on. Chomsky felt that the theoretical notion "degree of grammaticalness" could be developed to explain such judgments. While he was quite vague on this question in *Syntactic Structures*, in his *Logical Structure of Linguistic Theory* (1955), from which much of *Syntactic Structures* was excerpted, he suggested that only sentences of highest order grammaticality be generated. Less than acceptable sentences would be assigned lower degrees of grammaticality, essentially on the basis of their degree of categorial violation. Hence the greater deviance of *look at the cross-eyed from* than *look at the cross-eyed kindness* could be explained on the basis of the greater "distance" of prepositions from animate nouns than that of abstract nouns from animate nouns. This notion was developed further in Chomsky (1961a). But in *Syntactic Structures* the whole question was treated in a thoroughly confusing way. The casual reader of that book comes away convinced not only that the GRAMMATICALITY of *colorless green ideas sleep furiously* illustrates the independence of grammar from meaning, but also that speakers' "intuitions about form" do not distinguish it from fully acceptable sentences. It takes a careful reading of various footnotes to realize that Chomsky is saying that EVEN THOUGH this sentence is less than fully grammatical, it is still more grammatical than (equally meaningless) *furiously sleep ideas green colorless*, demonstrating that grammaticality (relative or absolute) cannot be predicted on semantic grounds alone. Many believe that between 1957 and 1965, Chomsky changed his ideas about the nature of the intuitions native speakers have about such sentences, for in *Aspects of the Theory of Syntax*, both sentences are ruled ungrammatical. However, in *Syntactic Structures*, while defending the impossibility of grounding the notion "grammatical sentence" semantically, he simply glossed over the question of degree of

---

[5] See Carden (1976) for more recent discussion of the problems involved in grounding native speaker judgments experimentally.

grammaticalness. In his other writings of that period however, he developed
the idea in some detail.

2.2.5. Grammar and Meaning

Superficially, the relationship between syntax and semantics seems
quite straightforward in *Syntactic Structures* and can be captured by the
following quote: "I think that we are forced to conclude that grammar is
autonomous and independent of meaning . . . [p. 17]." The independence
of grammar and meaning is stressed so many times in that book that many
commentators have assumed that he simply took over the position of Harris
and Bloch, an assumption often going hand-in-hand with the implication
that this demonstrates that he had not really broken completely from structuralism. But a careful reading of *Syntactic Structures* clearly falsifies this
conclusion. First of all, the independence of grammar in no way followed
from his METHODOLOGY, as it did for the structuralists. Chomsky was clear
that the question of relation of grammar and meaning is an empirical one.
He gave example after example to illustrate his position: Speakers have
intuitions that cannot be expressed in semantic terms; neither phonemic
distinctness nor morpheme identity is wholly semantic; notions like "subject" and "object" defy strict semantic characterization; etc. In fact, Chomsky used the apparent nonparaphrase relationship between sentences like
everyone in the room knows at least two languages and *at least two languages are known by everyone in the room* as evidence that Passive (and
transformations in general) cannot be defined strictly in terms of meaning.
In other words, he was arguing that the ASSUMPTION that syntax is semantically based is false, and any theory built on this assumption must
therefore be fundamentally deficient.

Second, an understanding of how Chomsky regarded the notion "meaning" at that time helps put many of his comments in a different light. While
his theory of meaning was fairly eclectic (in footnote 10 on page 103 he
seemed to imply that much of meaning can be reduced to reference), he
was very much under the influence then of the Oxford philosophers and
their USE theory of meaning. In fact, the words "meaning" and "use" are
used almost interchangeably throughout *Syntactic Structures*:

> There is no aspect of linguistic study more subject to confusion and more in need of
> clear and careful formulation than that which deals with the points of connection between
> syntax and semantics. The real question that should be asked is "How are the syntactic
> devices available in a given language put to work in the actual use of this language [p.
> 93]?

In other words, translated into terminology he would propose a few years
later, Chomsky was not so much arguing for the autonomy of the syntactic
rules from the semantic rules as much as for the competence–performance

dichotomy. Meaning, in this view, is part of performance. As we will see, however, he regarded certain aspects of meaning as not simply matters of usage. These aspects, he felt, had to be captured formally.

Third, he regarded as theoretically significant a whole set of systematic connections between syntax and semantics. For example, he pointed out that many of the traditional assertions about the semantic basis of syntax (which he argued to be empirically false) are very nearly true. Yet, he went on to say, there would be no possibility of providing an EXPLANATION of these facts if they had simply been ASSUMED to be true. He noted other systematic connections, as in the following passage in which deep structure interpretation was foreshadowed (note again the "performance" terminology):

> The general problem of analyzing the process of "understanding" is thus reduced, in a sense, to the problem of explaining how kernel sentences are understood, these being considered the basic "content elements" from which the usual, more complex sentences of real life are formed by transformational development [p. 92].

Likewise, later claims about the relationship of T-rules and meaning were foreshadowed in statements like "we find, however, that the transformations are, by and large, meaning-preserving . . . [1956: 123]," a fact which would have never come to light if transformations "had been investigated exclusively in terms of such notions as synonymity [p. 101]."

Finally and most importantly, Chomsky proposed that grammars be evaluated on the basis of their ability to lead to insights about the meanings of sentences:

> We can judge formal theories in terms of their ability to explain and clarify a variety of facts about the way in which sentences are used and understood. In other words, we should like the syntactic framework of the language that is isolated and exhibited by the grammar to be able to support semantic description, and we shall naturally rate more highly a theory of formal structure that leads to grammars that meet this requirement more fully [p. 102].

Recall that two of the external conditions of adequacy to be imposed on grammars were their ability to handle ambiguity and paraphrase—semantic notions par excellence. Chomsky was completely explicit about the direct syntactic capturing of ambiguity:

> If the grammar of a language is to provide insight into the way the language is understood, IT MUST BE TRUE, in particular, that if a sentence is ambiguous (understood in more than one way), then this sentence is provided with alternative analyses by the grammar. In other words, if a certain sentence S is ambiguous, WE CAN TEST THE ADEQUACY OF A GIVEN LINGUISTIC THEORY by asking whether or not the simplest grammar constructible in terms of this theory for the language in question AUTOMATICALLY PROVIDES DISTINCT WAYS OF GENERATING THE SENTENCE S [1956: 123, emphasis added].

Now while this quote of Chomsky's suggests that he demanded that semantic ambiguity be captured directly by the syntax, he never once MOTIVATED a transformation by appealing to its ability to explain semantic facts. He felt that this was unnecessary because all the evidence seemed to show that transformations motivated by purely syntactic means would turn out to explain ambiguity directly. We will see in later chapters how the discovery of the fact that many T-rules motivated in this way do NOT have this property was to lead to radically different analyses of the same phenomena.

2.3. NOAM CHOMSKY

The Chomskyan revolution in linguistics was very much a revolution from the inside. Chomsky was immersed from childhood in an environment where language and its scientific study were constant topics of discussion. He was born in Philadelphia on December 7, 1928, and through his father William, a noted Hebrew philologist, he developed an interest in language structure. At the age of 10, he was reading the proofs of his father's *David Kimhi's Hebrew Grammar*. Chomsky attributes his early interest in EX-PLAINING linguistic phenomena, as opposed to simply DESCRIBING them, to his childhood exposure to historical linguistics. In a period when leading theorists tended to look upon the desire for explanation as a sort of infantile aberration, historians of language like his father, either ignorant of or indifferent to the contemporary "scientific" wisdom in the field, clung to a nineteenth-century desire to explain why a particular distribution of forms existed at a particular point in time.

As an undergraduate at the University of Pennsylvania, Chomsky's main interest was Middle East politics. In fact, he had considered leaving his studies entirely "to live on a Kibbutz and work for Arab–Jewish cooperation [quoted in Mehta 1971: 186]." In an effort to discourage him from going to Palestine, his parents introduced him to Zellig Harris, who taught at Pennsylvania and shared Chomsky's views on Zionism—and was able to function as a productive scholar at the same time. The ploy worked. Harris immediately took the 18-year-old Chomsky under his wing and gave him the proofs of his *Methods in Structural Linguistics* to examine—before Chomsky had even taken his first linguistics class! As he later remarked, "That's how I learned linguistics, by proofreading Harris' book—which was fine for me, I really learned the field [Sklar 1968: 215]."

At Harris's suggestion, Chomsky began to work on a grammar of Hebrew. The combination of his thorough understanding of historical process, the striking unsuitability of the Hebrew language to description in structuralist terms, and the intangible factor of Chomsky's own genius made him realize almost immediately that a revealing structuralist account of that language was hopeless:

> I started right off, without even asking any questions, working within the framework of generative grammar, which seemed to be the only conceivable thing, namely, trying to find a system of rules which would enable you to characterize all of the sentence

structures in the language. I very quickly discovered that if you wanted to do this properly you had to have a long sequence of ordered rules. I also noticed right off that the logical order corresponded to some extent to the historical order which I knew of. I found that if you gave it the right kind of logical order then you could explain a lot of phenomena which otherwise seemed very inexplicable. I worked on this for a couple of years in really total isolation [quoted in Sklar 1968:214].

"Total isolation" is no exaggeration. While Chomsky's Hebrew work developed into his 1949 undergraduate thesis and his 1951 M.A. thesis, *Morphophonemics of Modern Hebrew*, there is no evidence that Harris, who "didn't pay any attention to what anybody else was doing in linguistics or in anything else [Chomsky, quoted in Mehta 1971:187]," even looked at it. With the exception of Henry Hoenigswald, few linguists were then even willing to call what he was doing "linguistics," a feeling which reinforced the lingering doubts in his own mind about the fruitfulness of his approach.

Thanks to the impression he made upon the philosopher Nelson Goodman, with whom he took philosophy courses as an M.A. student at Pennsylvania, Chomsky won a prestigious Junior Fellowship in the Society of Fellows at Harvard, where he worked from 1951 to 1955. Ironically, his project was to improve the techniques of structural linguistics—he even published one paper with this goal in mind (Chomsky 1953). But little by little, his work in generative grammar became his central focus. Two individuals—the philosopher Yehoshua Bar-Hillel and the linguist Morris Halle—stand out above all others in their encouragement of Chomsky to pursue his ideas along these lines. It was Bar-Hillel who convinced him to put aside all hesitations and postulate (as his intuitions had already told him was correct) something very much like the reconstructed historical forms at the abstract morphophonemic level. And it was Halle, who Chomsky met in the fall of 1951, who, as a result of their constant discussions, was the most decisive factor in causing him to abandon any hope of a procedural approach to linguistic analysis. Here is Chomsky's own account of his moment of truth:

By 1953, I came to the same conclusion [as Halle]: if the discovery procedures did not work, it was not because I had failed to formulate them correctly but because the entire approach was wrong. In retrospect I cannot understand why it took me so long to reach this conclusion—I remember exactly the moment when I finally felt convinced. On board ship in mid-Atlantic, aided by a bout of seasickness, on a rickety tub that was listing noticeably—it had been sunk by the Germans and was now making its first voyage after having been salvaged. It suddenly seemed that there was a good reason—the obvious reason—why several years of intense effort devoted to improving discovery procedures had come to naught, while the work I had been doing during the same period on generative grammars and explanatory theory, in almost complete isolation, seemed to be consistently yielding interesting results [1979:131].

With structural linguistics now permanently in his past, Chomsky began writing *The Logical Structure of Linguistic Theory* (LSLT), his exposition of the goals, assumptions, and methodology of transformational generative grammar (one chapter of which earned him his Ph.D. from Pennsylvania). A truly incredible work of the highest degree of creativity, LSLT completely shattered the prevailing structuralist conception of linguistic theory. This 900-page volume contains the initial proposals for the formalization and evaluation of grammars which would underlie all subsequent generative research. But the American linguistic community in 1955 was not impressed. LSLT's rejection by MIT Press (the only publisher whom Chomsky felt might take the work seriously) came practically by return mail. Likewise, in the next two years his dissertation and an article on simplicity and explanation submitted to *Word* were turned down almost as rapidly. Since the only job offer he could muster at the end of the tenure of his fellowship was to teach Hebrew at Brandeis at a salary of $3500, he decided to stay at Harvard for another year.

But fortunately for Chomsky, Halle was teaching at MIT and was able to arrange for him to be hired in the Modern Language Department, with a joint appointment in the Research Laboratory of Electronics. (His responsibilities at first included teaching scientific French and German and some undergraduate linguistics, philosophy, and logic courses.) But he was able to find time to write up the notes to his introductory linguistics course, which Halle encouraged him to submit to Mouton Publishers (Mouton had just published Jakobson and Halle's *Fundamentals of Language*). By May of 1957, *Syntactic Structures* was off the presses.

As a result of Lees's review, Chomsky began to receive invitation after invitation to present his ideas, the most important of which was to the 1958 Third Texas Conference on Problems of Linguistic Analysis of English (see Chomsky 1962 in Hill 1962). Here he scored his first important coup—he succeeded in winning over the prominent young structuralist Robert Stockwell, who soon became a vigorous campaigner for the new model. While the other papers at this conference (which were in the structuralist tradition) are completely forgettable, and the content of Chomsky's is little more than an elaboration of some points in *Syntactic Structures*, Hill (1962) is wonderful reading nevertheless. The reason is that it faithfully transcribes the discussion sessions at the end of each paper. Here we can see linguistic history documented as nowhere else—Chomsky, the *enfant terrible*, taking on some of the giants of the field and making them look like rather confused students in a beginning linguistics course.

The Chomskyan Revolution was now in full motion. I will return to chart its progress in Section 2.7.

2.4. GENERATIVE GRAMMARS

Chomsky was not the first to propose generative rules as part of a description of a natural language. Indeed, Pāṇini's grammar of Sanskrit (see

Cardona 1976) antedated Chomsky by well over 2000 years. Likewise, the spirit of Bloomfield's treatment of Menomini morphophonemics (1939b) and Jakobson's of Russian conjugation (1948) is clearly that of a generative phonology, although their rules are not stated formally. Nevertheless, Chomsky's undergraduate thesis (1949) in which he proposed an explicit set of ordered rules for the syntax and phonology of modern Hebrew is the first attempt to utilize the devices of mathematical logic for an economical description of linguistic phenomena as part of a generative grammar.

The study of recursive rules has its roots in a branch of formal logic interested in the properties of combinational systems. A main developer, Emil Post (1936, 1944), worked out a number of proofs in the mathematics of specifying infinite sets by finite numbers of statements. Chomsky drew heavily on this and later work in recursive function theory, which not only provided him with the formalism he needed, but also with much terminology which has now become everyday linguistic usage, including terms like "generate" and "derivation."

Around the same time as Post's work, the Polish logician Kasimierz Ajdukiewicz (1935) was conducting research along similar lines. He developed what he called a "categorial grammar" for the artificial languages of logic. This came to be applied to natural languages by Yehoshua Bar-Hillel (1953), in what might have been the first published attempt to formulate rules for the generation of sentences in natural language. Bar-Hillel's categorial grammar was, in effect, a kind of phrase structure grammar, and later (by Bar-Hillel, Gaifman, and Shamir 1960) was proved to have the weak generative capacity of a context-free phrase structure grammar. Bar-Hillel and Chomsky were in close touch in Cambridge in the early 1950s; the former had an important effect on the latter's intellectual development at that time.

By the early 1950s many logicians simply ASSUMED that a natural language was defined by a set of recursive rules, though they shrank from the enormity of the task of trying to state them:

> We may alternatively construct the English language by taking as the alphabet the strings of letters already classified as words . . . . Then a sentence is a string in this alphabet formed according to standard rules of sentence formation. We may then regard English sentences as "words" in this alphabet and the rules of formation of English sentences as rules of word formation (i.e., spelling) in this alphabet . . . . As in all natural languages . . . the rules of word and sentence formation in English are so complicated and full of irregularities and exceptions that it is almost impossible to get a general view of the structure of the language, and to make generally valid statements about the language [Rosenbloom 1950: 153].

Along the same lines, in an article which had a profound influence on Chomsky, Quine (1953) discussed the grammarian's goal of formally specifying "K, . . . the infinite class of all those sequences, with exclusion of the inappropriate ones as usual, which COULD be uttered without bizarreness reaction. *K* is the class which the grammarian wants to approximate in his formal reconstruction . . . [p. 53].''

It is interesting to note that Zellig Harris and Charles Hockett, two structural linguists with some training in formal logic, at times (uncharacteristically) wrote of the sentence generating properties of grammars:

> A grammar may be viewed as a set of instructions which generates the sentences of the language [Harris 1954:260].

> The description must also be prescriptive . . . in the sense that by following the statements one must be able to generate any number of utterances in the language, above and beyond those observed in advance by the analyst—new utterances most, if not all, of which will pass the test of casual acceptance by a native speaker [Hockett 1954:232].

Since such views clashed head-on with their usual methodological assumptions, it is not surprising that they did not develop them. Certainly (as pointed out in Corcoran 1972), Harris never conceived of his transformational rules as being the "instructions." Even so, once dissuaded of his teacher's overall goals, it is hardly surprising that Chomsky applied them for just this purpose.

2.5. GENERATIVE PHONOLOGY

2.5.1. The Prague School

One structuralist school of language—the Prague School—had such an important influence on generative grammar that it seems appropriate to discuss it in this chapter. Broadly, the name describes the circle of scholars active in Prague and Vienna in the 1920s and 1930s. One leading member, Prince N. S. Trubetskoi, contributed *Grundzüge der Phonologie* (1939), the basic Prague School statement of phonology—the area in which it had the greatest impact on modern linguistic theory. Prague School phonology was brought to the United States in the 1940s and further elaborated by Trubetskoi's colleague Roman Jakobson.

The Prague School phonologists shared with their American counterparts the fundamental structuralist view that a linguistic description consists of an inventory of elements meeting the condition of biuniqueness. But in crucial respects, their theoretical outlook was diametrically opposed to that of other structuralists. Most importantly, they made it perfectly clear that their overall goal was explanation rather than taxonomy. Their requirement of biuniqueness, then, which guaranteed that a description WOULD be a taxonomy, was regarded as an empirical hypothesis rather than (as it was to the Americans) an a prioristic assumption. For this reason they were not obsessed with developing the "correct" set of operational procedures by which an analysis might be obtained. Furthermore, since they had no hesitation about imputing psychological reality to their linguistic descriptions, native speaker judgments were not ruled out as admissible evidence. This enabled them to develop phonetic theory to a rather sophisticated degree. While the Bloomfieldians had always been suspicious of phonetics, given its essentially impressionistic basis, the Pragueans, not shrinking from impressionistic data, were able to make important cross-language generalizations about phonetic universals. Jakobson insightfully incorporated these results in the first major theoretical study of language acquisition, his remarkable *Kindersprache, Aphasie, und allgemeine Lautgesetze* (1941).

For the Prague School, the phoneme was not simply a notational device but, rather, a complex phonological unit consisting of a set of DISTINCTIVE FEATURES. This concept of the phoneme represented an important advance for several reasons. First, because it turned out that the phonemic systems of every language in the world were characterizable in terms of a small number of binary feature oppositions. Second, because features allowed the formulation of generalizations impossible to state in other structuralist models. For example, the assimilation of nasals to following stops in English could be described by positing an abstract (unspecified for point-of-articulation features) nasal "archiphoneme" before stops and a general rule which then filled in the redundant features. Third, features made possible the development of a mechanical EVALUATION procedure—since redundant features could be left unspecified in the basic feature matrix (which would be filled in by rules), the most highly valued analysis would be regarded as the one with the minimal number of feature specifications per phoneme.

A great amount of work took place in the 1950s to characterize precisely those features relevant for the description of all human languages. The results were reported in two important books: Jakobson, Fant, and Halle's *Preliminaries to Speech Analysis* (1952) and Jakobson and Halle's *Fundamentals of Language* (1956). The universal inventory was reduced to 12 binary distinctive features, some defined in absolute acoustic terms (e.g., vocalic versus nonvocalic) and some in relative acoustic terms (e.g., grave versus acute).

From the above discussion it should be clear to anyone with the slightest familiarity with generative phonology how great a debt is owed to the Prague School phonologists. Roman Jakobson probably exerted a greater influence on transformational generative grammar than any other linguist. However, he himself never broke completely with structuralism to embrace without fundamental reservations Chomsky's view of linguistic theory. This was left to his student, Morris Halle, who began his collaboration with Chomsky in 1953. Together they developed the theory of generative phonology within a comprehensive theory of human language.

2.5.2. Morris Halle

Even before his collaboration with Chomsky began, Halle had built a reputation for himself in linguistics. In a period in which experimental acoustics was being heralded as the most promising direction for linguistic research to take, Halle was one of America's leading acousticians. The publication of *Preliminaries to Speech Analysis* (the research for which was carried out at the Acoustics Laboratory at MIT) not only resulted in American linguists taking seriously for the first time Roman Jakobson and the Prague School, but made Halle a public figure in the field.

Halle, who was born and educated in Latvia, emigrated to the United States in 1940. He studied engineering at the City College of New York before being drafted in 1943. After the war, he received a degree in linguistics from the University of Chicago. At the urging of Giuliano Bonfante (who was then at Chicago) he went to Columbia University to study with Roman Jakobson in 1948, and followed Jakobson to Harvard a year later. His Harvard Ph.D., which he received in 1955, was awarded on the basis of his dissertation "The Russian Consonants: A Phonemic and Acoustical Study." In somewhat revised form, this later appeared as the second half of *The Sound Pattern of Russian* (1959).

Halle had worked on the MIT Research Laboratory of Electronics acoustics project while a student, and was hired by that university's Modern Language Department (to teach German and Russian) in 1951. In addition to his scholarly activities, he was instrumental in initiating the Ph.D. program in linguistics at MIT, which he supervised from 1960 until he stepped down in 1977.

Halle combines in a rare fashion the qualities of productive scholar and organizer–administrator. While transformational generative grammar would no doubt have succeeded had he lacked one of these two attributes, it does not seem too far-fetched that its history would have been very different had he lacked both.

2.5.3. Early Generative Phonology

Generative phonology, in essence, synthesized three contemporary trends in linguistics. First, it incorporated the unformalized insights about phonological processes which characterized the work of Edward Sapir and (in much of his work) Leonard Bloomfield, and those American linguists from a more "anthropological" tradition, such as Mary Haas, Morris Swadesh, C. F. Voegelin, and others. Second, it drew from the American structuralists the practice of explicit formalization of all rules. And finally, it owed to the Prague School the overall explanatory goals of phonological theory along with the notion of the distinctive feature.

Chomsky and Halle teamed with Fred Lukoff in 1956 to publish the first generative phonological analysis—"On Accent and Juncture in English." This paper, which proposed a retreatment of English suprasegmentals, hit structuralism where it was weakest. In place of the four degrees of phonemic stress which previous treatments hypothesized, they were able to predict the full range of phonetic stress possibilities with only a simple phonemic accented–unaccented distinction. They argued that this economy was possible only by assuming a set of ordered rules sensitive to underlying junctures placed at certain morpheme boundaries. Since their analysis resulted in a nonbiunique relation between phonemics and phonetics and violated the prohibition against mixing levels, it was totally incompatible with structuralist methodology. But, they argued, four important benefits resulted from abandoning these methodological constraints: The constituent organization imposed to state the stress rules most simply coincided with that which would be required for other levels of description; the binary phonemic feature of "accent" made special suprasegmental phonemes unnecessary; the simplicity and symmetry of the rules proposed contrasted markedly with the inelegant structuralist account; and the rules predicted how native speakers could assign stress patterns to new utterances in a consistent and uniform manner.

The first major work of generative phonology was Halle's *The Sound Pattern of Russian* (1959). While his specific rules for Russian would be modified many times, the book is remembered primarily for its argument against the structuralist concept of the phoneme. This argument not only was regarded as the most compelling one for generative phonology at the time, but even reappeared in its broad structural outline 10 years later to be used against the level of syntactic deep structure (see Section 5.4.1). Hence, it is worth paraphrasing:

> Consider the phonetic representations (C in Table 2.1) and the morphophonemic representations (A in Table 2.1) of four Russian phrases:

TABLE 2.1

Gloss	A	B	C
was he getting wet	{m'ok l, i}	/m'ok l, i/	[m'ok l, i]
were he getting wet	{m' ok bi}	/m'og bi/	[m'og bi̵]
should one burn	{ž'eč l, i}	/ž'eč l, i/	[ž'eč l, i]
were one to burn	{ž'eč bi}	/ž'eč bi/	[ž'eǯ bi̵]

Since there are instances where the velar stops ([k] and [g]) are in contrast, the relationship between A and C violates biuniqueness. Structuralists would therefore have to set up an intermediate phonemic level (B) to insure a biunique relation holding between all levels of description. On the other hand, [č] and [ǯ] never contrast, and in structuralist grammar would have to be identical at phonemic level B. But consider the consequences of this. A grammar with level B has no choice but to break down the generalization that obstruents are voiced before voiced obstruents into two distinct statements: once as a morphophonemic (A to B) rule applying to {k}; once as an allophonic (B to C) rule applying to /č/. Only by abandoning biuniqueness, and with it level B, can we capture this generalization by one unitary rule statement.

By Chomsky and Halle (1960), the analysis of English stress had been simplified still further. By incorporating syntactic categorial information into the stress rules, they were able to dispense with underlying phonemic accent entirely and, at the same time, eliminate the phonemic /ɨ/ required in the 1956 paper. That year also saw the publication of Stockwell (1960), the first attempt to incorporate pitch into a generative description.

The major theoretical discussion of generative phonology prior to Chomsky and Halle's *The Sound Pattern of English* (1968), was Halle's article "Phonology in Generative Grammar" (1962). Halle gave the first clear statement of the economy gained by formulating phonological rules in terms of distinctive features rather than in terms of indivisible phonemes. He pointed out that in the latter approach, Rules (2.5) and (2.6) would be equally complex:

$$(2.5) \qquad /a/ \rightarrow /æ/ \text{ in the env.} \_ \left\{ \begin{array}{c} /i/ \\ /e/ \\ /æ/ \end{array} \right\}$$

$$(2.6) \qquad /a/ \rightarrow /æ/ \text{ in the env.} \_ \left\{ \begin{array}{c} /i/ \\ /p/ \\ /z/ \end{array} \right\}$$

But under an analysis in which the rules were stated in terms of features, Rule (2.5) would be vastly simpler to state than Rule (2.6)—a clear demonstration of how feature theory can provide a definition of the intuitive notions "natural class" and "natural phonological process." He further argued (using the familiar example of Sanskrit vowel sandhi) that the OR-DERING of rule statements would, at one and the same time, lead to both a minimization of feature specifications and an analysis which intuitively was the most insightful as well. While this was by no means the first example given of phonological rule ordering, it WAS the first concrete illustration of the theoretical interrelatedness of this concept with that of distinctive features and the simplicity criterion for evaluating alternative analyses.

Halle broke ground in three other important areas in this article. First, he explained how differences between dialects could be explained by hypothesizing that they contained the same set of rules applying in different orders. Second, he gave a broad overview of how generative phonology was suited to the description of language change. He suggested that rule addition characteristically takes place at the end of the grammar (or at the end of "natural subdivisions" in it). Hence, it is no accident that the synchronic order of rules characteristically mirrors their relative chronology, a point first observed by Bloomfield (1939) in his study of Menomini. He went on to give what he claimed was an example of a case (from the history of English) where two phonemes which had merged, later reappeared, the reemerging phonemes corresponding exactly to their historical antecedents. Since such a phenomenon would be utterly inexplicable under a structuralist account, it pointed more strongly than any purely synchronic data could to the need for an abstract level of representation not simply extractable from the superficial phonetic data.

Finally, Halle gave the first theoretical explanation of the diminished language learning ability of the adult:

> I propose to explain this as being due to deterioration or loss in the adult of the ability to construct optimal (simplest) grammars on the basis of a restricted corpus of examples. The language of the adult—and hence also the grammar that he has internalized—need not, however, remain static: it can and does, in fact, change. I conjecture that changes in later life are restricted to the addition of a few rules in the grammar and that the elimination of rules and hence a wholesale restructuring of his grammar is beyond the capabilities of the average adult [p. 64].

While few of Halle's specific theoretical claims stand unaltered today, except in the most general terms, the importance of "Phonology in Generative Grammar" should not be underestimated. This article was the closest thing to a "*Syntactic Structures* of phonology"—the basic theoretical statement that would direct research in this area of linguistics for years.

2.6. LANGUAGE AND PSYCHOLOGY AFTER CHOMSKY

2.6.1. The Psychological Implications of the Theory

Chomsky did not bring up the question of the psychological implications of transformational generative grammar in *Syntactic Structures*; as he wrote later, it would have been "too audacious" for him to have done so. But Lees in his review did not shrink from this. He closed the review with a frontal attack on inductivist learning theory, arguing that there could be no alternative but to conclude that the grammar the linguist constructed was "in the head." But if that be the case, then how could these highly abstract principles possibly be learned inductively? "It would seem," he wrote, "that our notions of human learning are due for some considerable sophistication [1957:408]."

It was Chomsky's 1959 review of B. F. Skinner's *Verbal Behavior* that drove home the fact that his theory of language was more than a neat manipulation of arcane symbols—it was a psychological model of an aspect of human knowledge. Chomsky's review represents, even after the passage of 20 years, THE basic refutation of behaviorist psychology. Of all his writings it was the Skinner review which contributed the most to spreading his reputation beyond the small circle of professional linguists. So powerful were his arguments that no linguist has even attempted to answer them, and behaviorist psychology has been on the retreat since its publication.

Chomsky took in turn each basic construct of behaviorism, which he demonstrated either to lead to false predictions or to be simply devoid of content:

> a critical account of his book must show that . . . with a literal reading (where the terms of the descriptive system have something like the technical meanings given in Skinner's definitions) the book covers almost no aspect of linguistic behavior, and that with a metaphoric reading, it is no more scientific than the traditional approaches to this subject matter, and rarely as clear and careful [Chomsky 1959b: 31].

How then could verbal behavior be explained? While its complexities defied any simplistic treatment, Chomsky wrote that "the actual observed ability of a speaker to distinguish sentences from nonsentences, detect ambiguities, etc., apparently forces us to the conclusion that this grammar is of an extremely complex and abstract character, and that the young child has succeeded in carrying out what from the formal point of view, at least, seems to be a remarkable type of theory construction [p. 57]." Chomsky went on to argue that this seemed to indicate that rather than being born "blank slates," children have a genetic predisposition to structure the acquisition of linguistic knowledge in a highly specific way:

> The fact that all normal children acquire essentially comparable grammars of great complexity with remarkable rapidity suggests that human beings are somehow specially designed to do this, with data-handling or "hypothesis-formulating" ability of unknown character and complexity [p. 57].

Just as the changes of attitude of philosophers of science toward theory construction by the 1950s had helped create an atmosphere more conducive to the acceptance of linguistic theory, the fact that a significant number of psychologists had begun to have serious reservations about behaviorism made these points of Chomsky's seem less cataclysmic than they would have if they had been written a few years earlier. In an important paper, Lashley (1951) had argued that underlying many forms of complex behavior, such as language, piano playing, whip snapping, etc. there have to be extremely abstract mechanisms not analyzable in terms of simple associative principles. And Lenneberg (1964) gave considerable evidence that human language shares more fundamental properties with clearly innately predisposed activities, like walking, than with wholly learned culturally determined ones. The late 1940s and the 1950s also saw scores of papers questioning either some of the more extreme behaviorist conclusions from animal behavior studies or the degree to which these results could be applied to human behavior.

Chomsky did not and to date has not convinced a majority of practicing psychologists of the correctness of nativistic explanations of human language ability. But from the early 1960s on, a growing core has accepted the general validity of such explanations. No statement more dramatically illustrates this point than the following by the one-time behaviorist George

Miller (1962): "I now believe that mind is something more than a four-letter, Anglo-Saxon word—human minds exist and it is our job as psychologists to study them [p. 761]."[6]

2.6.2. The Psychological Reality of Linguistic Constructs

Many experiments were carried out in the early 1960s relating to the problem of native speakers' intuitions about their language. Two are worth mentioning. Maclay and Sleator (1960) tested whether naive native speakers would make the same judgments as trained linguists in regard to the grammaticality and meaningfulness of sentences. They did find a rough correlation, but concluded that the problem would require considerably more sophisticated experimental techniques before any real conclusions about the adequacy of the linguist's subjective data could be drawn. Miller and Isard (1963) found a decreasing order of memorizability and audibility over masking noise progressing from fully grammatical sentences to grammatical but semantically anomalous ones to fully ungrammatical ones. While these two experiments gave some slight support to the use of intuitive judgments, it was soon realized that the entire question of such judgments was too complex to be tested by simple experiments of this sort, and psycholinguists turned their primary attention elsewhere.

More fruitful experimental work was involved in testing the psychological reality of the constructs of the theory itself. In a famous experiment, Fodor and Bever (1965) showed that clicks inserted in various positions in sentences tended to be perceived at hypothesized clause boundaries, thereby confirming the psychological reality of linguistic structure. Along the same lines Lieberman (1965) showed that perception of stress is a function of syntactic structure. His demonstration that stress levels cannot be judged correctly in isolation even by trained linguists provided strong evidence against the structuralist–empiricist view that the acoustic signal alone provides all the necessary perceptual cues. Rather, an abstract level of syntactic representation would have to be postulated to explain even the perception of phonological features. Later experiments as well have tended to bear out claims about the psychological reality of syntactic structure, both surface and deep (see Fodor, Bever, and Garrett 1974 for discussion).

Despite an initial confirming study by Miller (1962), further experimental work has simply failed to bear out the assumption that the transformational rules themselves have any psychological reality, a problem to which I will return in Section 8.3.2.

---

[6] Maclay (1973) is an interesting discussion of the attitudes of psycholinguists before, during, and after the Chomskyan revolution.

2.7. WINNING THE REVOLUTION

2.7.1. Robert B. Lees

Any discussion of the revolutionary period of transformational generative grammar must begin with a portrait of Robert B. Lees. I have already noted the impact of his review of *Syntactic Structures*. But the debt that linguistic theory owes him far exceeds that one piece of writing. Lees's book *The Grammar of English Nominalizations* (see Section 3.2.1) was to linguistic analysis what *Syntactic Structures* was to linguistic theory. It meant that the opponents of the theory had the burden of responding to (and finding alternatives to) highly detailed analyses of many central syntactic phenomena in English. But most importantly of all, Lees was a campaigner. At every conference, at every forum, there was Lees—to tear apart the structuralist view of language and defend the transformational view in as articulate and methodical a manner as is humanly imaginable. Nobody who was around linguistics in the late 1950s and early 1960s can talk about that period without recalling Lees's colorful style and unyielding determination to win victories for the new theory, and without recalling how moved they were by his charismatic presence—whichever position in factional debate they held then or hold now.

Lees never earned his Bachelor's degree in chemical engineering—World War II (in which he was trained as a meteorologist) intervened. But the four postwar years in which he worked at the Argonne National Laboratories were influential to his future linguistic research. He was involved in a project whose goal was to develop a methodology for counting carbon isotopes—the same project which led to Willard Libby's discovery of carbon-14 dating. This naturally led him to see in Morris Swadesh's observations about lexical loss in Salish, a process which could be described by a familiar first-order rate-equation and resulted in his working out the mathematical equations involved in glottochronology (Lees 1953). While Lees, of course, soon saw the limitations of the method, the fame which he gained through his work in glottochronology was indispensible in giving him the credibility he needed as "Chomsky's Huxley" several years later.

Disenchanted with chemistry, Lees entered the University of Chicago Linguistics Department in 1947 where he received his M.A. in 1950. After editing a book on English for Turkish speakers and working at several other jobs, Lees in 1956 accepted Victor Yngve's invitation to come to MIT to work on his machine translation project. While the project held little interest for him (in fact, Yngve fired him in short order), it was there he began his collaboration with Chomsky, whose views he began to champion and develop creatively in his own right. *The Grammar of English Nominalizations* earned him his MIT Ph.D. in 1959 in the Department of Electrical Engineering (there was no Linguistics Department there at the time). After a brief stint at IBM, he accepted a position at the University of Illinois, where he built one of the leading linguistics programs in the United States. Since 1969, he has taught at Tel-Aviv University, where he has also built a successful program.

2.7.2. The Ascendancy of Transformational Generative Grammar

Lees's review meant that *Syntactic Structures* could not be ignored. But the structuralist camp in America was sharply divided on how best to curtail the growth of the new theory. The minority faction, led by Archibald A. Hill, chose the bold tactic of confronting it directly with the intent of snuffing it out before any serious damage could be done. In fact, Hill organized the Third Texas Conference alluded to in Section 2.3 primarily for the purpose of exorcising the demon of generative grammar. But, as we have seen, the plot backfired, with the theory benefiting immensely from the exposure which the conference provided it. Hill was equally unsuccessful in his published attack on transformational grammar (Hill 1961), which Chomsky's reply (1961a) more than adequately disposed of. Interestingly, most of the earliest published attacks on the theory were by non-Americans (see Reichling 1961; Uhlenbeck 1963; Dixon 1963a, 1963b, 1964; Winter 1965; and the responses in Chomsky 1966a). The boldness of the counterattackers seems to have increased in proportion to their distance from Cambridge, Massachusetts.

But most structuralists in the United States initially wrote about transformational grammar as if it were just one approach out of many possible ones by which language might be studied. The sense they seemed to wish to convey was that while Chomsky's theory might be interesting, it was nothing to make a fuss about. So we find Joos (1961) making almost wholly sympathetic remarks about generative grammar in his discussion of linguistic prospects in the United States, Gleason (1961) adding a chapter on transformations to his introductory text, and Harris (1965) describing Chomsky's approach to transformations as "virtually the same" as his own. One might surmise that by diminishing the significance of transformational generative grammar, they hoped to render it harmless.

Charles Hockett, who was to remark in later years that the transformationalists' studies "are as worthless as horoscopes" [quoted in Mehta 1971:218], far from attempting to demolish Chomsky's ideas, spoke and wrote in the early 1960s as if he had been 90% converted to the new paradigm. In his presidential address to the Linguistic Society of America in 1964 (published as Hockett 1965), he actually characterized the publication of *Syntactic Structures* as one of "only four major breakthroughs [Hockett 1965:185]" in the history of modern linguistics, on a par with Sir William Jones's address to the Asiatic Society in 1786 and the publication of Karl Verner's "Eine Ausnahme der ersten Lautverschiebung" and Ferdinand de Saussure's *Cours de Linguistique Générale*. Later in this address he confessed:

> I know how I would have reacted to [the abrasive style of the *Junggrammatiker*], because I know my reaction to the similar tone of Robert B. Lees's review, which appeared in 1957, of Chomsky's *Syntactic Structures*, and of the introductory remarks in his *Grammar of English Nominalizations*, published in 1960. We do not enjoy being told that we are fools. We can shrug off an imprecation from a religious fanatic, because it does not particularly worry us that every such nut is sure he holds the only key to salvation. But when a respected colleague holds our cherished opinions up to ridicule, there is always the sneaking suspicion that he may be right [p. 187].

Hockett's Linguistic Institute lecture series in 1964 (published in 1966 as *Language, Mathematics, and Linguistics*) is also indicative of the olive branch which he was extending to transformationalists in that period. In those lectures, he not only advocated, but even attempted to contribute to, the study of algebraic models of grammar.

One can speculate that Hockett's drastic about-face around 1966 was caused in part by the spurning (or, more accurately, ignoring) of his conciliatory gestures by the generativists. But its main cause was surely his abhorrence of the frankly rationalist underlying assumptions of Chomsky's *Aspects of the Theory of Syntax*, published in 1965. Chapter One of this book so repelled Hockett that he felt compelled to revise the preface of *Language, Mathematics, and Linguistics* for the express purpose of condemning it. Hockett (1966) wrote:

> This chapter is a *reductio ad incredible* of the mistakes we have been making in linguistics for the last thirty or forty years; my study of it, after the present essay was completed, was responsible for the radical change of view reported in this Preface [p. 8].

Hockett devoted a year to the preparation of his oddly titled *The State of the Art* (1968), which he intended to be the ultimate answer to Chomsky. Among other memorable quotes in this monograph we find "Chomskyan–Hallean 'phonology' . . . is, in my opinion, completely bankrupt [Hockett 1968:3]." But by 1968 transformational generative grammar had so thoroughly won the field that Hockett's efforts were in vain. Aside from eliciting an articulate reply from George Lakoff (1969a), the impact of *The State of the Art* has been nil.

One structuralist stands out from the rest in his attitude toward transformational generative grammar. While Bernard Bloch never publicly endorsed the new theory, he did confide to at least two colleagues, "Chomsky really seems to be on the right track. If I were younger, I'd be on his bandwagon too." Bloch's actions certainly bear out the attitude expressed in this quotation. As editor of *Language,* he unhesitatingly published the crucial Lees review of *Syntactic Structures*. And several years later, in an unprecedented action, he actually inserted an editorial comment in a published review in that journal. The review was Postal's (1966) vicious but justified attack on Dixon's *Linguistic Science and Logic*. Bloch's comment added insult to injury by bolstering Postal's case against Dixon.[7] Bloch also was responsible for placing *The Morphophonemics of Modern Hebrew* and *The Logical Structure of Linguistic Theory* in the Yale University linguistics library as early as 1958.

The debate over generative phonology continued to rage long after transformational syntax had won a significant degree of acceptance [see Chomsky (1964b); Chomsky and Halle's (1965) reply to Householder (1965); and Postal's (1968) reply to Lamb (1963)]. This is hardly surprising, since structuralists never had much to say about syntax. Sol Saporta, another early 1960s convert from structuralism, recalls that he immediately adopted the *Syntactic Structures* syntactic model, yet (inconsistently) resisted generative phonology for several years. To one degree or another, such a reaction was not atypical.

One of the earliest criticisms of the transformationalists and one which has survived to the present day (see Hagège 1976; Hall 1977) is the supposed English language orientation of the theoretical work within this model. American structuralists, whose roots are in the Boas tradition which prioritized the description of indigenous languages, and European scholars alike have united to condemn what many have implied is at best poor linguistics, at worst a reflection of American chauvinism and arrogance. Yet even the earliest work was not as English-centered as many believe. For example, of the six faculty members in the MIT Linguistics Department in the late 1960s, four were known primarily for their work in languages other than English: Kenneth Hale for Amerindian and Australian; G. Hubert Matthews for Amerindian; Paul Kiparsky for general Indo-European; and Morris Halle for Russian. In addition, it will be recalled that Chomsky wrote a partial generative grammar of Hebrew BEFORE attacking English. And of the 28 doctoral dissertations written in linguistics at MIT in the 1960s, 17 (or 61%) dealt primarily with languages other than English, including those by Stephen Anderson (West Scandinavian), George Bedell (Japanese), Thomas Bever (Menomini), James Fidelholtz (Micmac), James Foley (Spanish), James Harris (Spanish), Richard Kayne (French), Paul Kiparsky (various languages), Sige-Yuki Kuroda (Japanese), Theodore Lightner (Russian), James McCawley (Japanese), Anthony Naro (Portuguese), David Perlmutter (various languages), Sanford Schane (French), Richard Stanley (Navaho), Nancy Woo (various languages), and Arnold Zwicky (Sanskrit).

It goes without saying, of course, that the majority of published syntactic analyses have dealt with English. This is an inevitable consequence of the American origins of the theory and the value placed on native speaker judgments as data. But as more and more non-English speakers have

[7] Dixon was later to become a productive contributor to transformational theory (see, for example, Dixon 1970, 1972, 1977).

adopted transformational generative grammar, the percentage of work involving English has steadily declined, and by now transformational studies have appeared on literally hundreds of languages. It might also be pointed out that the first concerted attempt to train American Indians as professional linguists was undertaken at MIT (under the impetus of Kenneth Hale), where in recent years native Navaho and Hopi speakers have received Ph.D.s.

From the beginning, Chomsky and Halle were able to attract some of the brightest young scholars in the United States to the new way of doing linguistics. Not only Lees, but also G. Hubert Matthews, Fred Lukoff, Edward Klima, Keith Percival, and John Viertel were part of Victor Yngve's machine translation project when they came into contact with generative grammar, a fact which exacerbated the theoretical differences which already existed between Chomsky and Yngve (see Yngve 1960, 1961; Miller and Chomsky 1963). Jerrold Katz and Jerry Fodor, philosophy students at Princeton, were won over and hired by MIT around 1960, as were Paul Postal and Jay Keyser from Yale. As Searle (1972) put it, "Chomsky did not convince the established leaders of the field but he did something more important, he convinced their graduate students [p. 17]." Many of the earliest transformationalists, such as Emmon Bach, Carlota Smith, Charles Fillmore, and Kenneth Hale were students or recent Ph.D.s who adopted the new theory despite the indifference or open hostility of their teachers.

The 1960s were a decade of rebellion, and the intellectual and political ferment going on in American universities at that time provided an ideal atmosphere for the intellectual movement sweeping linguistics, which was bent on overthrowing the rigid dogmas of American structuralism. Just as students began en masse to question the "common sense" political assumptions of their upbringing which they felt were rationalizing an imperialist foreign policy and oppresssive domestic policy by the American government, they began to question the "common sense" pseudoscientific assumptions of empiricism in linguistics. The appeal of nonobvious explanatory ideas in linguistics at this time was a reflection of the openness of students to such ideas in politics as well.

Far from substituting one dogma for another, as Hagège (1976) would have it, the transformationalists encouraged—in fact, rewarded—students for questioning EVERY assumption in linguistics, including those of transformational generative grammar itself. Paul Newman (1978) has stressed:

> While there was a general consensus that "the other guys" were wrong and that the basic linguistic/philosophical tenets of generative grammar were essentially right, there was a singular absence of dogma or rigidity. Everyone was encouraged to test the theory on a new language, to explore linguistic areas not yet treated, and to experiment with different kinds of formal devices—always with the freedom to modify or reject the then-standing TG theory as necessary. Of great importance in understanding the growth and spread of generative grammar is the fact that this freedom extended to students who, in key places, were permitted to follow their own lines of research, challenge the views of

their teachers (generativist or not), take part in the continual discussion and debate, and otherwise participate actively in the creation and dissemination of this new theory. In the final analysis, generative grammar was a creative, liberating movement, which freed linguistics as a discipline and as a profession from the straitjacket of the post-Bloomfieldian period. Whatever the other factors involved, a great part of its success must be ascribed to this [pp. 928-929].

The missionary zeal with which "the other guys" were attacked may have led some linguists, along with Wallace Chafe (1970), to be "repelled by the arrogance with which [the generativists'] ideas were propounded [p. 2]," but overall the effect was positive. Seeing the leaders of the field constantly on the defensive at every professional meeting helped recruit younger linguists far more successfully and rapidly than would have been the case if the debate had been confined to the journals. Lees and Postal, in particular, became legends as a result of their uncompromising attacks on every structuralist-oriented paper at every meeting.

Postal's fame derived in large part from his book *Constituent Structure*, published in 1964. He attempted to show that each of the models of grammatical description in competition with the transformational generative model was equivalent in weak generative power to phrase structure grammar and was therefore inadequate as a model of human language. This involved reinterpreting the GOALS of the formulators of these models as being identical to those of the transformationalists, opening Postal to charges of gross distortion and rewriting history (for interesting commentary on this point, see Thorne 1965). Needless to say, Postal's approach had the effect of strengthening the resolution of practicing structuralists to resist the new model. But their students were profoundly impressed—no single publication was more instrumental in drawing students into the transformationalist camp.

The quality of the first two classes to enter MIT (in 1961 and 1962) was instrumental to the early success which the theory achieved. Not one individual who has failed to contribute to linguistic theory is found in its list, which includes Thomas Bever, James Foley, Bruce Fraser, Jeffrey Gruber, Paul Kiparsky, S.-Y. Kuroda, Terence Langendoen, Theodore Lightner, James McCawley, Barbara Hall Partee, Peter Rosenbaum, Sanford Schane, and Arnold Zwicky. None found difficulty in finding jobs upon graduation; by the end of the 1960s Illinois, California—San Diego, UCLA, Texas, and Ohio State stood beside MIT as departments in which transformational grammar predominated.

Halle and Chomsky had the policy of encouraging their students to integrate themselves into American linguistic life from the moment they entered MIT. It was not unusual in the early 1960s to see even first year graduate students from that institution presenting and commenting on papers at meetings. The combative spirit may have gotten a bit out of hand at times, as even undergraduate advocates of the theory such as Thomas Bever and James Fidelholtz got into the act, embarrassing their teachers as they ruthlessly lit into linguists old enough to be their grandparents.

There were other factors which contributed to the theory's rapid success. First, the field in the late 1950s was very small. For example, the Linguistic Society of America in 1957 had only slightly more than 1000 members in the entire world, the vast majority of whom would not have considered themselves "linguists." Simultaneous sessions at meetings were not instituted until 1968. This meant that a new idea could be disseminated rapidly to the entire profession.

Second, by sheer coincidence, the Ninth International Congress of Linguists was held in Cambridge, Massachusetts in 1962, with Halle and William Locke (who was Chairman of the Modern Languages Department at MIT) on the Local Arrangements committee. After Zellig Harris turned down his invitation to present one of the five major papers at the plenary session (the others were by Kurylowicz, Benveniste, Martinet, and Andreyev), there was no trouble in replacing him by Chomsky. Chomsky's paper, "The Logical Basis of Linguistic Theory" (1964a), thus reached an international audience, giving him the appearance of being THE spokesperson for linguistics in the United States. There was no question in the mind of anybody at MIT that transformational generative grammar would become the established paradigm for linguistics after that point.

Third, transformational grammar was blessed from the beginning with extraordinarily gifted teachers, writers, and explainers:

> a number of the early generativists were extremely good teachers. The outsider—outraged by the belligerent polemics of generative lectures and writings—could not know that, in the classroom, a Halle at MIT or a Stockwell at UCLA functioned as a sympathetic and dedicated teacher, prepared to spend long hours explaining the intricacies and nuances of the new model. Students were attracted to generative grammar because, among other reasons, their teachers made it intellectually challenging and exciting [Newman 1978:928].

Two pieces of pedagogical writing greatly advanced the theory in this period—Emmon Bach's *An Introduction to Transformational Grammars* (1964a), which made it accessible and interpretable to beginning students, and Paul Postal's "Underlying and Superficial Linguistic Structure," published in the *Harvard Educational Review* in 1964, which acquainted educators and psychologists with its basic goals.

And finally, there was enough money available in the late 1960s in America for university expansion that young transformationalists did not have to contend with Old Guard-dominated departments before or after finding employment. It did not matter that Hockett and Hall were at Cornell, Trager and Smith at Buffalo, or Harris and Hiż at Pennsylvania. New departments could always be founded which could be used by transformationalists as academic bases from the very beginning. MIT was particularly favored in this respect. Chomsky (1979) has commented:

> We were able to develop our program at MIT because, in a sense, MIT was outside the American university system. There were no large departments of humanities or the related social sciences at MIT. Consequently, we could build up a linguistics department without coming up against problems of rivalry and academic bureaucracy. Here we were really part of the Research Laboratory of Electronics. That permitted us to develop a program very different from any other and quite independent [p. 134].

The affiliation with the Research Laboratory of Electronics arose as a result of the classification of linguistics at MIT as a "communication science," thus placing it under the purview of the laboratory. This affiliation guaranteed that vast sums of money (largely military in origin) would trickle down into the department, enabling the kind of support for a linguistics program that no other university could hope to match.[8]

2.8. THE GROWTH OF THE FIELD

The period of the Chomskyan Revolution was one of unprecedented growth in the field of linguistics in the United States. Measured by every imaginable statistic, the discipline grew by enormous proportions throughout the 1960s. Tables 2.2 through 2.6 provide documentation of this fact: LSA membership grew (Table 2.2); the number of departments and programs increased (Table 2.3); more institutions offered degrees (Table 2.4); enrollments increased (Table 2.5); and more degrees were conferred (Table 2.6).[9]

Now it is of course well known that the 1960s saw the expansion of almost every area of American higher education. But the growth rate of linguistics was considerably above the average, suggesting that it was the appeal of transformational generative grammar rather than economic growth alone to which this expansion must be attributed. For example, in 1956–1957, 16 doctorates were awarded in linguistics out of a total 8752 in all fields by American universities—that is .18%. But by 1972–1973, the percentage had almost TRIPLED to .51% (177 out of 34,790).

---

[8] Newmeyer and Emonds (1971) have discussed at length the funding of linguistic research in the United States. The point is made that while, of course, the source of funding is irrelevant to the ultimate CORRECTNESS of a theory, it is by no means irrelevant to a (partial) explanation of one's ACCEPTANCE. It is tempting to speculate on the speed with which transformational grammar would have won general acceptance had Chomsky and Halle's students had to contend with today's more austere conditions, in which not just military, but ALL sources of funding have been sharply curtailed, and the number of new positions has been declining yearly.

[9] Tables 2.3–2.6 and 2.8–2.12 report United States statistics only.

TABLE 2.2
Linguistic Society of America Membership, 1950–1978

December	Active LSA membership	December	Active LSA membership
1950	829	1965	3263
1951	822	1966	3495
1952	914	1967	3814
1953	978	1968	4166
1954	1022	1969	4231
1955	1090	1970	4383
1956	1178	1971	4723
1957	1354	1972	4263
1958	1501	1973	4258
1959	1633	1974	4148
1960	1768	1975	4279
1961	1951	1976	4112
1962	2180	1977	4108
1963	2602	1978	4258
1964	2918		

Source: LSA Bulletins.

Since around 1971 growth has leveled off and LSA membership has actually declined. This has gone hand-in-hand with an employment picture aptly described by Levy *et al.* (1976: 14) as "bleak." It is my impression that reduced funding to higher education rather than disenchantment with linguistics is primarily responsible for this, and that our field has suffered

TABLE 2.3
Organization of Linguistics Departments and Programs, 1963–1972

Organizational arrangements	1963	1966	1969–1970	1971–1972
Department of linguistics	13	23	31	42
Department of linguistics and languages (or other subject)	4	8	10	12
Interdepartmental program or committee	14	25	52	78
Linguistics courses offered in other departments	43	29	30	39
Languages	(7)	(4)	(4)	(2)
English	(14)	(14)	(17)	(24)
Anthropology	(4)	(7)	(5)	(4)
Other	(18)	(4)	(4)	(9)
Interdepartmental courses only	3	1	11	2
Total	77	86	134	173

Source: Levy et al. (1976: 114).

TABLE 2.4
Number of Institutions Offering Each Linguistics Degree, 1963–1975

Degree offered	1963	1966	1969–1970	1971–1972	1974–1975
Ph. D. in linguistics	25	29	39	45	45
Ph. D.—linguistics concentration	9	16	17	13	19
Master's in linguistics	26	38	49	66	70
Master's—linguistics concentration	9	27	34	37	33
Bachelor's in linguistics	16	22	40	49	66
Bachelor's—linguistics concentration	4	16	27	35	46

Source: Levy *et al.* (1976:116) and *Guide to Programs in Linguistics: 1974–1975* (Center for Applied Linguistics and the Secretariat of The Linguistic Society of America).

less than others oriented toward basic scholarly research. By way of confirmation, it is worth pointing out that between 1970 and 1975, while the number of first-year graduate students in physics declined by 41%, in English by 35%, and in history by 31%, linguistics actually saw an INCREASE of 49%.

It is much more difficult of course to document the growth of transformational generative grammar WITHIN the field of linguistics. Many articles and presented papers reflect diverse (and sometimes contradictory) influ-

TABLE 2.5
Enrollment for Advanced Degrees in Linguistics, 1960–1975

Year	Enrollment	Increase	Percentage
1960	407		
1961	558	151	37.1
1962	739	181	32.4
1963	882	143	19.4
1964	1083	201	22.8
1965	1298	215	19.9
1966	1482	184	14.2
1967	1567	85	5.7
1968	1740	173	11.0
1969	1846	106	6.1
1970	1884	38	2.1
1971	2043	159	8.4
1972	2220	177	8.7
1973	2294	74	3.3
1974	2316	22	1.0
1975	2597	281	12.1

Source: Levy *et al.* (1976:119) and U. S. Office of Education, *Enrollment for Advanced Degrees.*

TABLE 2.6
Degrees Conferred in Linguistics, 1955–1977, by Level

Year	Bachelor's	Master's	Ph.D.
1955–1956	38	41	18
1956–1957	25	31	16
1957–1958	20	73	30
1958–1959	31	72	21
1959–1960	57	70	26
1960–1961	41	90	31
1961–1962	64	105	33
1962–1963	54	103	38
1963–1964	57	114	48
1964–1965	67	173	60
1965–1966	113	229	84
1966–1967	132	232	70
1967–1968	126	340	97
1968–1969	192	343	90
1969–1970	220	338	109
1970–1971	254	352	150
1971–1972	296	373	139
1972–1973	443	452	177
1973–1974	431	455	145
1974–1975	434	506	166
1975–1976	534	523	151
1976–1977	—	—	190

Source: *Earned Degrees Conferred.*

ences and assumptions, while individuals and departments often resist such categorizations as "transformationalist" or "stratificationalist." Table 2.7 represents my estimation of the percentage of papers at winter LSA meetings from 1961–1966 which either presuppose or defend transformational generative grammar. After about 1966 such attempts at quantification be-

TABLE 2.7
Papers at Winter LSA Meeting Presupposing or Defending
Transformational Generative Grammar, 1961–1966

Year	Number of papers	Number of transformationalist papers	Percentage of transformationalist papers
1961	31	4	13
1962	33	2	6
1963	45	8	18
1964	52	16	31
1965	37	14	38
1966	40	22	55

come quite impossible, given the questioning of certain theoretical fundamentals by many transformationalists (see Chapter 5) and the concomitant
adoption by nontransformationalists of many of the assumptions of the
dominant theory. Yet even so, William Bright, editor of *Language*, could
remark in the March 1975 *LSA Bulletin*: "It is clear that the overwhelming
majority of papers submitted [to *Language*], and of those published, take
for granted certain principles of generative grammar [p. 12]." Most indicative of transformationalist hegemony, perhaps, is the fact that almost all
journals with largely American editorial boards founded in the last decade
have had a clear transformationalist orientation. Among such journals are
Papers in Linguistics (1969), *Linguistic Inquiry* (1970), *Linguistic Analysis*
(1975), and *Linguistics and Philosophy* (1977).

It is an unfortunate fact that women and racial minorities have not
fared much better in linguistics (whether pre- or postgenerativist) than in
other disciplines. As Table 2.8 illustrates, female students in linguistics have
consistently tended to drop out of the field at a greater rate than male
students. Linguistics B.A.s have always gone to a higher percentage of

TABLE 2.8
Percentage of Degrees Conferred in Linguistics to Women, 1955–1977, by Level

Year	Linguistics			Percentage of Ph.D.s awarded to women—all fields
	Bachelor's	Master's	Ph.D.	
1955–1956	45%	39%	6%	10%
1956–1957	56	55	6	11
1957–1958	60	38	27	11
1958–1959	55	43	33	11
1959–1960	28	30	12	11
1960–1961	44	38	23	11
1961–1962	36	35	19	11
1962–1963	35	45	26	11
1963–1964	35	39	21	11
1964–1965	45	36	15	11
1965–1966	43	39	33	12
1966–1967	56	39	30	12
1967–1968	62	40	21	13
1968–1969	61	46	24	13
1969–1970	62	52	21	13
1970–1971	67	51	25	14
1971–1972	63	53	24	16
1972–1973	65	50	29	18
1973–1974	73	55	42	19
1974–1975	70	55	36	21
1975–1976	69	60	48	23
1976–1977	—	—	38	—

Source: *Earned Degrees Conferred.*

TABLE 2.9
Composition by Sex and Rank of Linguistics Faculties, 1964–1979[a]

Year	Number of departments surveyed	Below Assistant professor			Assistant professor			Associate professor			Full professor		
		Male	Female	Percentage female	Male	Female	Percentage female	Male	Female	Percentage female	Male	Female	Percentage female
1964-1965	27	36	5	12	89	6	6	59	5	8	130	4	3
1974-1975	45	28	23	45	116	43	27	103	22	18	215	18	8
1978-1979	40	7	6	46	64	49	43	106	24	18	196	16	8

Sources: 1964-1965: *University Resources in the United States for Linguistics and Teacher Training in English as a Foreign Language: 1965;* 1974-1975: *Guide to Programs in Linguistics:* 1974-1975; 1978-1979: *LSA Bulletin, No. 80.*

[a] Survey restricted to departments offering a Ph.D. in linguistics. The number of faculty at all levels appears inflated because many linguistics departments do not distinguish between their "core" faculty and those primarily associated with some other department.

TABLE 2.10
Rates of Unemployment and Underemployment (Combined) in Linguistcs, by Sex, 1973

Degree level	Men	Women
Ph.D.	5.5%	16.4%
Ph.D. candidate	8.0	31.3
Master's	30.4	21.1
Overall	7.8	19.2

Source: Levy et al. (1976:249).

women than M.A.s, and M.A.s to a higher percentage than Ph.D.s, suggesting a channeling of women out of the field. However, this situation seems to be improving faster in linguistics than elsewhere. At the Ph.D. level, women are closing the gap on men more rapidly in linguistics than in academia as a whole.

As far as academic hiring is concerned, conditions have been improving for women, but very slowly. Table 2.9 illustrates that women are far outnumbered by men in linguistics positions at American universities and are heavily concentrated in the lower (nontenured) rungs of the academic ladder. As tenure is becoming increasingly difficult to obtain, there is a real danger that the gains that women have made will be reversed in the coming years. A 1973 survey (see Table 2.10) indicated as well that unemployment and underemployment were considerably more acute among women in linguistics than among men. I suspect (but can provide no documentation) that things are worse today.

The most overt forms of discrimination are, for obvious reasons, impossible to document. Perhaps the best example of antifemale (and anti-

TABLE 2.11
Minority Group Members as Percentage of Linguistics Faculty, by Rank, 1972

Minority group	Rank					
	Instructor/ lecturer	Assistant professor	Associate professor	Full professor	Total	Total number
Black	—	2.3%	1.5%	.5%	1.4%	10
Spanish-speaking	4.6%	1.5	4.4	2.7	2.9	21
Asian	2.3	5.0	4.4	3.1	4.1	30
American Indian	—	—	.5	—	.1	1
Total	7.0	8.9	10.8	6.3	8.5	
Total number	3	23	22	14		62

Source: Levy et al. (1976:229).

TABLE 2.12
Ph.D.s in Linguistics Awarded to Minority Group Members, by Sex, 1974–1977

Year	Total number	Black Women	Black Men	Asian American Women	Asian American Men	Hispanic Women	Hispanic Men	American Indian Women	American Indian Men
1974	145	1	0	1	1	1	3	1	1
1975	166	0	4	0	0	0	0	0	1
1976	151	1	1	1	0	0	0	0	0
1977	190	2	2	4	3	2	2	0	0

Source: Summary Report, Doctorate Recipients from United States Universities, Commission on Human Resources, National Research Council.

Asian) bias among linguists, and one which seemingly disallows any alternative conclusions, is reflected in an admission in the March 1974 LSA Bulletin that "the number of females and Orientals participating in the [LSA] meetings increased significantly when the abstracts were read masked, and they have been so read ever since [p. 15]." By the same token, the first year that Chicago Linguistic Society abstracts were read anonymously, the percentage of women presenting papers rose from 25 to 34.

A 1972 survey (Table 2.11) shows an insignificant number of minority group faculty members in linguistics. While I know of no more recent tabulations of minority hiring, the percentage of minorities receiving Ph.D.s in linguistics continues to be tiny (see Table 2.12). It seems to be the case that most black linguists in the United States are involved in work which might be considered "race-related": pidgins and creoles, African languages, and Black English.

Chapter 3

From *Syntactic Structures* to *Aspects of the Theory of Syntax*

3.1. INTRODUCTION

In this chapter, I will sketch the progress made in linguistic theory between 1957 and 1965, the publication date of Chomsky's *Aspects of the Theory of Syntax*. This period, which was characterized by total agreement by transformational-generative grammarians on almost all major issues, was capped by three complementary works, which collectively would define a research strategy for the next decade: Katz and Fodor (1963), which took the initial steps to incorporate semantics into linguistic theory; Katz and Postal (1964), with its hypothesis that underlying structures alone serve as input to the semantic component; and Chomsky (1965), which, by eliminating generalized transformations in favor of phrase structure recursion, allowed, for the first time, a level of "deep structure" to be defined.

3.2. REVISIONS IN THE SYNTACTIC COMPONENT: 1957–1965

3.2.1. *The Grammar of English Nominalizations*

Syntactic Structures sketched but a small handful of transformational rules—the presentation of a grammar fragment was not Chomsky's main purpose in that book. While Chomsky (1962) expanded on his initial account somewhat in what had originally been a 1958 conference paper, the first book-length study of syntax giving extensive rule motivations and derivations was Robert B. Lees's *Grammar of English Nominalizations* (1960).

Since virtually all of Lees's specific analyses have long since been revised, it is hard to appreciate the importance the book had at the time. By working out in fine detail the embedding transformations involved in the derivation of the various complement and relatival structures in English, Lees succeeded in demonstrating that the theory of transformational generative grammar could be applied insightfully to the analysis of a huge body of material. To a skeptical audience of linguists, this was an achievement of the highest order. Today, many remember *Grammar of English Nominalizations* primarily for its comprehensive analysis of English compound nouns, which would not undergo substantial revision for almost twenty years.[1]

No important book-length studies of syntax appeared between Lees (1960) and Katz and Postal (1964). Those five years, however, saw a number of important groundbreaking studies of the following topics: comparatives (Lees 1961); indirect object constructions (Fillmore 1962); German word order (Bach 1962); cleft sentences (Lees 1963); pronouns (Lees and Klima 1963); passives and imperatives (Lees 1964); negatives (Klima 1964); and determiners, adjectives, and relative clauses (Smith 1964).

3.2.2. The "Traffic Rule" Problem

While Chomsky, in *Syntactic Structures,* gave several examples to illustrate that singulary transformations had to be ordered with respect to each other, he left open many important questions about rule ordering. For example, are the generalized transformations also ordered with respect to each other? Can singulary transformations apply in a matrix ("higher") sentence before a generalized transformation embeds a constituent ("lower") sentence into it? What other factors determine ordering relations among transformations? That these ordering restrictions, whatever they were, had to be rather complex was realized after the discovery was made that transformations can reapply to structures created in part by their first application. For example, Lees pointed out that a passive sentence can be

---

[1] *The Grammar of English Nominalizations* contains the first published use of the asterisk to designate ungrammatical sentences. Fred Householder (1973) takes credit for the notation:

> I suppose that I may be somehow responsible myself for the spread of this notation; in the summer of 1958 I taught a course in "morphology–syntax" at the Michigan Linguistic Institute, in which I complained that the problems we had to solve . . . never included specification of ungrammatical strings. For one or two special problems we did get some sample ungrammatical strings and listed them, using the asterisk to mark them. Andreas Koutsoudas and R. B. Lees were auditors in that class, and both of them adopted the asterisk (as well as the double-arrow notation for transformations, which was devised in the same class), as did Emmon Bach in his text (though I don't think he was in that 1958 class) [p. 366].

It took editors of linguistics texts several years to accommodate themselves to the presence of ill-formed sentences in their books. The first proofs of Katz and Postal's *An Integrated Theory of Linguistic Descriptions* (1964) were returned to them with all the ungrammatical sentences "corrected" to the closest grammatical equivalents!

nominalized, and then this nominalization can serve as one term in the structural description for a second application of Passive:

(3.1) a. *The invader destroyed the citadel*   (underlying constituent sentence)

b. *The citadel was destroyed by the invader*   (by Passive)

c. *The people regretted the citadel's destruction by the invader*   (by Nominalization and Embedding)

d. *The citadel's destruction by the invader was regretted by the people*   (by Passive)

Lees (1960:54–57) proposed a number of tentative answers to the first two questions, all of them too vague to merit repeating here. However, two of his specific answers to the third question are of particular historical interest. The first is the claim that all obligatory transformations are ordered to follow all optional transformations. Lees's (1960) sole motivation for this was his belief that from this ordering "we might expect to gain a deeper insight into how a grammar can be used by a speaker in the production of sentences (since only the optional rules need to be provided with external inputs), etc. [p. 3]." Lees himself recognized that this would entail a complication in the formulation of certain rules. For example, Reflexive, an obligatory rule, would be required to "look back" to an earlier stage in the derivation before various optional transformations had applied, since only at that point could the restriction of that transformation to apply within simple clauses be stated: "The only alternative is to use the full power of transformational rules to look back into the derivational history of complex strings and identify all the simplexes within them [Lees 1960; 101]." Lees dropped the segregation of optional and obligatory rules a few years later, pointing out (in the Preface to the 1964 edition) that it was based on the mistaken notion that the grammar could be conceived of directly as a processing and perception model. He also pointed out that the fact that certain rules seemed both to have to precede and follow other rules would make this restriction impossible to formulate. However, Lees, in segregating the two rule types into distinct blocks, had not only anticipated similar proposals for grammatical organization which would be advanced many years later by supporters of "trace theory" (see Chapter 8), but had also been forced to propose the first GLOBAL RULE in transformational syntax (see Chapter 5).

Lees proposed another ordering restriction that would soon be abandoned, yet reintroduced (without acknowledgment) many years later. This was that all ellipsis transformations be ordered at the very end of the grammar. At that time, such rules were allowed to delete any element freely. For example, one rule of Lees's, "Pseudo-Intransitive," optionally deleted a nominal following a verb in the class containing *breathe, eat, hammer, read, steal*, etc. Hence, *the boy steals* was derived from all of *the boy steals books, the boy steals money, the boy steals food*, etc. This meant that deletions were unrecoverable and the grammar therefore undecidable—given the output of the T-rule and the rule's formal statement, it would not be possible to recover the input uniquely. Lees proposed that by segregating ellipsis rules in this way, at least THE REST of the grammar would be decidable. While his proposal was soon abandoned in favor of a general prohibition against nonrecoverable deletion (see Section 3.2.6), recent interpretivist work has revived the segregation of ellipsis rules (see Section 8.2.1).

Fillmore (1963) proposed a general solution to the traffic rule problem, one which in its essentials is still accepted today. He noted first that no cases were known of ordering among the generalized transformations, although the theory allowed such ordering. Second, he pointed out that there was no solid evidence that a singulary transformation ever had to apply to a matrix sentence before another sentence was embedded into it by a generalized transformation. Third, there were many examples of cases where singulary transformations had to apply to a constituent sentence before embedding and then again to the entire matrix–constituent complex after embedding. These facts suggested to Fillmore the following organization of the transformational component. First, the singulary transformations apply within that sentence which, by virtue of its not containing special markers to that effect, does not allow another sentence to be embedded into it. Then this sentence can be embedded by a generalized transformation into a matrix sentence, whose embedding symbol marks the site of the embedding. Singulary transformations then apply to the phrase-marker resulting from this embedding. Depending on the number of constituent sentences, this "recycling" of embedding and singulary transformations continues to apply until all embedding has taken place. Figure 3.1 schematically illustrates the order of operations in the derivation of a sentence from three source sentences.

This predictability of ordering between embedding and singulary transformations and the nonordering of embedding transformations with respect to each other was a major motivation for Chomsky's (1965) proposal to eliminate them entirely (see Section 3.5.2).

3.2.3. The Derived Constituent Structure Problem

Since it was generally the case that a string created by the application of a transformational rule itself would serve as input to another transformation, it was necessary that constituent structure be mechanically assigned to the derived string. For simple permutations, deletions, substitutions, and adjunctions this was no great problem—Postal (1962:26–31) gave a somewhat improved version of the original Chomsky (1955) proposal for breaking down each transformation into the elementary transformational operations

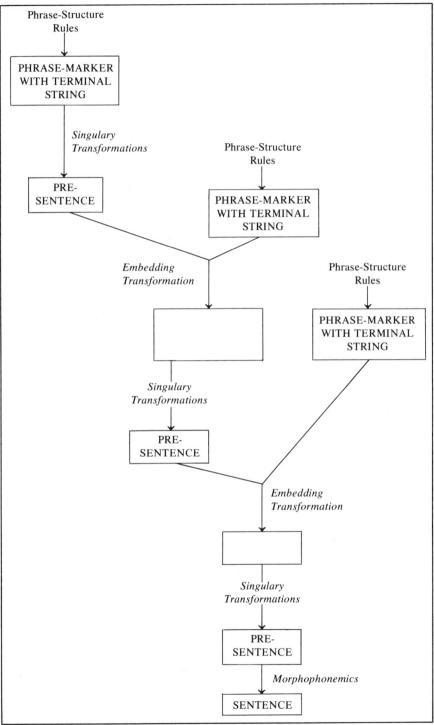

Figure 3.1

it performed, each of which was associated with a simple algorithm for derived constituent structure imposition.

But special problems remained. The first had to do with the assignment of constituent structure to elements actually CREATED by the application of a transformation: the *be + en* and *by* of passive, the *for* of *for John to go,* the expletive *it* of *it's good to be here,* and the *of* of *John is the signer of the check* are examples. To deal with this problem, Chomsky (1957:73–74) had proposed to assign automatically the *by*-phrase created by Passive to the category "Prepositional Phrase" by virtue of its formal resemblance to *by*-phrases generated by the phrase-structure rules. By implication, the constituent structure of the other examples would be handled in a like manner. Yet this was not considered a satisfactory solution—in fact, Chomsky himself (1965:104) later described it as "ad hoc." For the sole purpose of avoiding this ad hoc principle, Lees (1964) proposed that the *be + en* and *by* be generated by the phrase-structure rules; we also find independent evidence presented for this solution in Katz and Postal (1964) and Chomsky (1965) (see Section 3.2.4).

A much more serious problem had to do with the assignment of derived constituent structure to sentences formed by generalized transformations. In the earliest work, as much as possible of what would later be considered "the future transformational history" was taken care of along with the embedding. For example, in the derivation of *we persuaded him to play the flute* the generalized transformation not only embedded *he play the flute* into *we persuaded* COMP *him,* but also deleted the embedded subect *he.* The reason for this was that since so little was known about ordering relations among the various types of transformations, it was felt to be extremely undesirable to have a transformation which would apply after embedding with both matrix and constituent sentences as its domain to delete the embedded subject. Hence, the embedding transformation had to perform two operations at once. But this led to great complications in the precise specification of its structural output.

Once the traffic rule problem had been solved by Fillmore, this resolved itself almost instantaneously. We find proposals in Chomsky and Miller (1963) and Katz and Postal (1964) that all embedding take place at unexpanded modes in the matrix sentence, and that the constituent sentence keep the node label "S" after embedding. Given that, there was no difficulty in formulating a transformational rule such as Equi-Noun Phrase-Deletion, which, though singulary (nonembedding), has to apply across clause boundaries.

It should be clear that if a constituent sentence is to keep its internal structure intact after embedding, the embedding transformation has a very restricted syntactic role to play. This provided one more argument for their elimination (see Section 3.5.2).

3.2.4. Underlying Trigger Morphemes

As I have just mentioned, Lees (1964) proposed that the (*be* + *en*) and *by*-phrase of the passive construction be generated by optional phrase-structure rules, whose presence would trigger obligatory passivization. Katz and Postal (1964) and Chomsky (1965) suggested that the *by*-phrase be generated as an optional expansion of the manner adverbial. The syntactic motivation for this was that it would explain the apparent fact (see G. Lakoff 1970: 156–157 for a number of counterexamples) that passives are limited to verbs which take manner adverbials freely and that it would allow the rule to generalize to generate "pseudo-passives" such as *the proposal was argued against vehemently*, since the simple category "Verb" rather than "Verb-Transitive" could then appear in the rule.

More importantly, arguments were put forward for introducing the negative (Neg), imperative (I), and question (Q) morphemes by optional phrase-structure rules and for deriving negatives, imperatives, and questions by obligatory transformations dependent on the presence of the appropriate morpheme.

Lees (1960) was the first to suggest generating Neg in the base. He argued that it would be difficult to state restrictions preventing double negatives (e.g., *not never) if *not* were inserted by an optional transformation. Klima (1964), in his extensive analysis of English negation, gave considerably more evidence to support this. His arguments rested on the many similar syntactic properties of the word *not* and words in the class of negative preverbal adverbs, such as *never, scarcely, hardly, rarely, seldom,* and *barely*. By way of example, consider the following sentences:

(3.2)   a. *Max won't come, not even if you beg him*
        b. **Max will come, not even if you beg him*

Apparently, *not even* requires negation in the preceding clause. But this negation can be a property of a negative adverb, as well as the word *not*:

(3.3)   *Max will never come, not even if you beg him*

Klima explained these and other facts by positing an abstract negative morpheme to be present in the underlying structures of sentences containing *not* and the negative adverbials. This morpheme made possible a single statement of the identical co-occurrence restrictions shared by these elements.

Lees (1964) also proposed an underlying imperative morpheme. His argument rested on the special co-occurrence restrictions of imperative sentences. For example, while *be* in declaratives does not allow *do*-support:

(3.4)   **He doesn't be silly*

We do find *do* with negative imperatives with *be*:

(3.5)   *Don't be silly*

Furthermore, imperatives have a number of restrictions not found in declaratives: They do not allow *have* + *en*, modals, tensed verbs, etc. Lees proposed capturing these facts by imposing restrictions on the underlying occurrence of the imperative morpheme, which would be positioned in the auxiliary to trigger *do*-support in appropriate contexts.

Katz and Postal's arguments in *An Integrated Theory of Linguistic Descriptions* for the imperative and question morphemes were also based primarily on co-occurrence restrictions holding between particular items. In previous analyses, *you will drive the car, drive the car,* and *will you drive the car?* had been derived from the same underlying structure. But note:

(3.6) $\left\{ \begin{array}{l} Maybe \\ Yes \\ Perhaps \\ Certainly \end{array} \right\}$ *you will drive the car*

(3.7) $\left\{ \begin{array}{l} *Maybe \\ *Yes \\ *Perhaps \\ *Certainly \end{array} \right\}$ *drive the car*

(3.8) $\left\{ \begin{array}{l} *Maybe \\ *Yes \\ *Perhaps \\ *Certainly \end{array} \right\}$ *will you drive the car?*

How could the prohibition against imperatives and questions co-occurring with sentence adverbials be captured in the grammar? Only, they reasoned, by assuming that the morphemes I and Q occur in underlying structure and by stating the appropriate restriction between the co-occurrence of these markers and the class of sentence adverbials. They further argued for a *wh*-marker, to be present in underlying structure associated with the element to be questioned. Their analysis of *wh*- questions (which space limitations do not allow me to repeat) is unquestionably the most convincing section of *An Integrated Theory*, and laid the basis for all subsequent work on the syntax of questions. The arguments in this section also stand out as being the only ones in the book for underlying markers not based largely on primarily semantic co-occurrence restrictions (see Chapter 4).

3.2.5. The Abandonment of the Notion "Kernel Sentence"

In the *Syntactic Structures* model, the notion "kernel sentence" had a certain intuitive appeal, since the class of sentences formed by the application of only obligatory transformations corresponded exactly to the class of uniclausal declarative affirmatives. But as we have seen, more and more transformations were made obligatory in the early 1960s, subject to the presence of underlying markers. That took away a clear formal character-izability of such sentences—a huge variety of non-uniclausal declaratives would become "kernels" if the definition did not change, and no obvious definition presented itself to replace the old one.

Furthermore, Lees suggested (in the Preface to the 1964 edition of *The Grammar of English Nominalizations*) that in German it was probably the case that one rule out of a set of rules has to be chosen in the derivation of EVERY sentence. (He unfortunately did not give any data in support of this.) But since there is a free choice as to WHICH rule is chosen, German has, strictly speaking, no kernel sentences at all.

For these reasons, the notion "kernel sentence" was simply dropped from the technical vocabulary of linguistic theory by the mid 1960s.[2]

3.2.6. Recoverability of Deletion

Chomsky (1964b:39–40) observed that interrogative pronouns which replace (i.e., delete) an entire noun phrase can be derived only from those noun phrases which are singular and indefinite. Thus (3.9a) and (3.9b) are well-formed, while (3.10) (derived from a definite) and (3.11) (derived from a plural) are rather odd:

(3.9)   a. *Who do I know with a scar?*
          b. *Who do I know who was expelled?*

(3.10)   **Who do I know with the scar?*

(3.11)   **Who do I know who were expelled?*

Relative clauses and nondeleting interrogatives, however, are not subject to this restriction:

(3.12)   a. *You know the boy with the scar*
          b. *You know the boys who were expelled*

(3.13)   a. *Which boy has the scar?*
          b. *Which boys were expelled?*

Chomsky further noted that the distribution of deleting interrogatives cor-responds exactly to the distribution of the indefinite pronouns *some (one, thing)* in English. Seemingly, the transformation forming this type of inter-rogative has to be limited to strings containing indefinite pronouns. But why should this be the case and why should nondeleting interrogatives and

---

[2] There was also a persistent tendency on the part of many to confuse kernel sentences with underlying terminal strings. This confusion is found even in Lees (1960:2), if I read him correctly.

relatives behave differently? Chomsky suggested that this could be explained if it were assumed, first, that each category has associated with it a "designated element" as a member. This designated element might actually be realized (e.g., *it* for abstract nouns), or might be an abstract "dummy element." Furthermore, he hypothesized that:

> It is this designated representative of the category that must appear in the underlying strings for those transformations that do not preserve, in the transform, a specification of the actual terminal representative of the category in question. In other words, a transformation can delete an element only if this element is the designated representative of a category, or if the structual condition that defines this transformation states that the deleted element is structurally identical to another element of the transformed string.[3] A deleted element is, therefore, always recoverable [1964b:41].

This condition, then, automatically EXPLAINS why interrogatives formed by deletion of a noun phrase are more restricted in their distribution than relative pronouns (which occur in structures with recoverability-guaranteeing head nouns) and nondeleting interrogatives.

Matthews (1961) had proposed the same condition for totally different reasons. He noted that with free deletion, the set of sentences generated by the syntactic component is not decidable. But he reasoned that it is inconceivable that a grammar could ever be learned or an utterance processed if the language were NOT decidable. (Recall that it was his intention to avoid this consequence that prompted Lees [see Section 3.2.2] to suggest that free deletions occur in a block at the end of the grammar.) Chomsky's purely syntactic arguments gave Matthews's formally motivated proposal the empirical support it needed.

There were other reasons for adopting the condition on recoverability of deletion. Early syntactic analyses tended to bear out the idea that there is direct correlation between the number of underlying sources a sentence has and its degree of ambiguity. On independent syntactic grounds, two underlying structures had been motivated, for example, for *flying planes can be dangerous* and *John doesn't know how good meat tastes*, each structure corresponding to one of the interpretations. But nonrecoverable deletion of the object noun phrase in the derivation of *John is eating* results in an INFINITE number of underlying structures for this sentence. As Chomsky pointed out, however, speakers do not interpret this sentence as being infinitely ambiguous—they interpret it as being simply vague, with the understood object of *eating* paraphrasable by the indefinite pronoun *something*. Since this indefinite pronoun is what was motivated independently as the designated element for the category "Noun Phrase," the condition

---

[3] Katz and Postal (1964:81) later extended this to allow deletion of terminal symbols mentioned in the structural description of the rule, as, for example, the deletion of *you* and *will* in a popular formulation of the Imperative transformation.

on recoverability of deletion seemed to have semantic as well as syntactic motivation.

3.2.7. Subcategorization

In the earliest work in transformational generative grammar, phrase-structure rules both introduced lexical categories and subcategorized them. It was pointed out as early as 1957 (by G. H. Matthews, in class lectures) that branching rules are not the appropriate device to capture lexical sub-categorization, because the subcategories are typically cross-classified with respect to each other. For example, nouns in English can be either common or proper, human or nonhuman, with the classes intersecting to create four subclasses, all actually occurring (see Figure 3.2):

	HUMAN	NONHUMAN
COMMON	boy	book
PROPER	Charlie	Egypt

Figure 3.2

Two sets of phrase-structure rules of equal complexity can generate these elements:

(3.14)   i. $N \to \left\{ \begin{array}{l} N \text{ human} \\ N \text{ nonhuman} \end{array} \right\}$

      ii. $N \text{ human} \to \left\{ \begin{array}{l} N \text{ human and common} \\ N \text{ human and proper} \end{array} \right\}$

      iii. $N \text{ nonhuman} \to \left\{ \begin{array}{l} N \text{ nonhuman and common} \\ N \text{ nonhuman and proper} \end{array} \right\}$

      iv. N human and common $\to$ *boy*, . . .

      v. N human and proper $\to$ *Charlie*, . . .

      vi. N nonhuman and common $\to$ *book*, . . .

      vii. N nonhuman and proper $\to$ *Egypt*, . . .

(3.15)   i. $N \to \left\{ \begin{array}{l} N \text{ common} \\ N \text{ proper} \end{array} \right\}$

      ii. $N \text{ common} \to \left\{ \begin{array}{l} N \text{ common and human} \\ N \text{ common and nonhuman} \end{array} \right\}$

      iii. $N \text{ proper} \to \left\{ \begin{array}{l} N \text{ proper and human} \\ N \text{ proper and nonhuman} \end{array} \right\}$

      iv. N common and human $\to$ *boy*, . . .

      v. N common and nonhuman $\to$ *book*, . . .

      vi. N proper and human $\to$ *Charlie*, . . .

      vii. N proper and nonhuman $\to$ *Egypt*, . . .

It was argued that subcategorizing lexical categories by branching rules leads to fundamental generalizations about English not being capturable. Examples (3.14), and (3.15), while containing the same number of symbols, differ in their empirical claims. Example (3.14) makes the claim that common nouns and proper nouns form natural classes in English, since they can be referred to by one symbol, but not the classes of human nouns and nonhuman nouns. Example (3.15) makes the opposite claim. It allows the classes of human nouns and nonhuman nouns to be referred to by one symbol, but not the classes of common nouns and proper nouns. Yet, clearly, both binary classes are "natural" ones and should not have to be characterized by a conjunction of symbols. For example, the class of human nouns must be referred to by the rule that accounts for the distribution of the relative and interrogative pronouns *who, whom,* and *whose.* The common-proper distinction is relevant to the statement of the occurrence of the determiner. When one considers that these distinctions also cross-classify with a large number of others (e.g., count–mass; agent–nonagent; concrete–abstract) it becomes clear that literally thousands of separate phrase-structure rules and sublexical categories would be needed, the degree of loss of generality increasing for each additional distinction covered by the set of rules.

Various suggestions were made to deal with this problem in the early 1960s (Schachter 1962; Stockwell and Schachter 1962; Bach 1964b), but since these had little impact, even in the short run, I will discuss the solution offered in Chomsky (1965). Chomsky noted that a similar problem occurs in phonology, where subcategorization typically involves cross-classification rather than hierarchy. For example, some rules must refer to the class of all obstruents, others to the (overlapping) class of all alveolars. The solution in phonology is to consider each segment to be composed of a set of binary distinctive features. In this way, both classes can be referred to by the small number of features which characterize them without loss of generality. Chomsky suggested that an analogous solution could be applied to syntactic subcategorization—each syntactic category has associated with it a set of syntactic features, introduced not by branching rules, but by feature-introducing rules, such as (3.16), which replaces (3.14) or (3.15):

(3.16)   N → [±N, ±Human, ±Common]

In addition to the formal simplicity of (3.16) compared to (3.14) or (3.15), (3.16) allows both the classes of human nouns and common nouns to be referred to by a single symbol.

With this step, it became possible to separate the lexicon from the expansion rules of the base. Lexical items under the new approach were insertable into the modified phrase-marker (now terminating in "complex symbols" of feature matrices) if their syntactic features matched those features generated by the subcategorization rules. The separation of the lexicon had the desirable consequence that the various idiosyncratic grammatical, semantic, and phonological properties of lexical items did not have to be specified by the rewriting rules at all—they could be listed as part of the lexical entry of each item.

I will return to Chomsky's proposals concerning the structure of the lexicon (and the more difficult question of context-sensitive subcategorization) in Section 3.5.1.

3.3. THE INCORPORATION OF SEMANTICS INTO THE MODEL

Hardly a mention was made of semantics during the first five years after the publication of *Syntactic Structures*. Yet it was never forgotten that linguistic theory would be tested for adequacy partly by the degree to which the structures generated by the syntactic rules formed a suitable basis for semantic interpretation. In fact, the syntactically motivated underlying structures in this period almost without exception captured in significant ways various aspects of the meaning of the sentences under investigation. Chomsky took note of this fact in 1962: "In general, as syntactic description becomes deeper, what appear to be semantic questions fall increasingly within its scope . . . [Chomsky 1964a:936]." For the first time, Chomsky went on to raise the possibility of an independent semantic theory:

> it is not entirely obvious whether or where one can draw a natural bound between grammar and "logical grammar" in the sense of Wittgenstein and the Oxford philosophers. Nevertheless, it seems clear that explanatory adequacy for descriptive semantics requires, beyond this, the development of an independent semantic theory (analogous, perhaps, to the general theory of grammar as described above) that deals with questions of a kind that can scarcely be formulated today, in particular, with the question: what are the substantive and formal constraints on systems of concepts that are constructed by humans on the basis of presented data [Chomsky 1964a:936]?

The task of developing this theory was undertaken not by Chomsky, but by two young Princeton philosophers, Jerrold Katz and Jerry Fodor, who had come to MIT specifically to work with Chomsky.

3.3.1. Katz and Fodor (1963)

The number of fundamental questions which Katz and Fodor had to answer in their attempt to construct a semantic theory was simply overwhelming. First, they had to address the question of the goals of the theory itself. What is its lower bound? Its upper bound? Second, they not only had to posit a set of primitives for the theory, but they also had at least to attempt to answer the question of their epistemological character. Are all semantic constructs universal and, by implication, innate? And if not all, then which? Finally, there was still the unresolved problem of the relationship between semantic theory and grammatical theory. This not only involved the question of how transformational rules affect meaning, but also the question of which traditionally semantic problems have purely "syntactic" solutions and which require special "semantic" rules of a still unknown character.

In their view, a line can—and has to—be drawn between a speaker's ability to interpret a sentence by virtue of linguistic knowledge and the ability to assign a SPECIFIC interpretation to that sentence by virtue of that speaker's beliefs about the world. Put another way, the setting (context) of an utterance might limit the number of interpretations actually assigned to it by participants in the discourse, but the full range of interpretations is part of the speaker's linguistic competence and has to be accounted for by the semantic theory. To give a concrete example, the sentences *Our store sells horse shoes* and *Our store sells alligator shoes* are not normally interpreted as ambiguous—the former is typically interpreted as ' . . . shoes for horses,' the latter as ' . . . shoes from alligator skin.' Now, surely, Katz and Fodor argued, it is not the job of a semantic theory to incorporate the purely cultural, possibly temporary, fact that shoes are made for horses, but not for alligators, and that shoes are made out of alligator skin, but not out of horse hide. Both sentences, then, must be regarded as ambiguous— the upward bound of the semantic theory is set to exclude the role that nonlinguistic facts play in the interpretation of sentences. To do otherwise, they argued, would require that a semantic theory be nothing less than a theory of all human behavior.

As for the lower bound of the theory, they asserted that its goals are to describe and explain speakers' ability to (a) determine the number and content of the readings of a sentence; (b) detect semantic anomalies; (c) decide on paraphrase relations between sentences; and (d) mark "every other semantic property that plays a role in this ability [Katz and Fodor 1963 : 176]."

There are two interrelated components which Katz and Fodor posited to explain this ability. The first they called the "dictionary," which contained, for each lexical item, a characterization of the role it plays in the interpretation of the sentence. The second component was made up of a set of rules called "projection rules." These rules determined how the structured combinations of lexical items assigned a meaning to the sentence as a whole.

The dictionary entry for each item consisted of a grammatical portion (grammatical markers) and a semantic portion containing semantic markers, distinguishers, and selectional restrictions. The grammatical markers were simply the lexical (and sublexical—this paper was written before the introduction of syntactic features) categories to which the lexical item belonged. The marker–distinguisher distinction is more difficult to describe. In their own words:

> Semantic markers are the elements in terms of which semantic relations are expressed in a theory . . . . The semantic markers assigned to a lexical item in a dictionary entry are intended to reflect whatever systematic semantic relations hold between that item and the rest of the vocabulary of the language. On the other hand, the distinguishers assigned to a lexical item are intended to reflect what is idiosyncratic about its meaning. Generally speaking, a change in the system of semantic markers has extensive consequences throughout the semantic theory . . . . But a change in a distinguisher merely alters the relation between one item and its synonyms [Katz and Fodor 1963 : 187].

Markers, then, but not distinguishers, were to enter into the statement of selectional restrictions. Which aspects of the meaning were to be represented by markers and which by distinguishers was determined in part by evidence about disambiguations speakers can make. For example, their dictionary entry for *bachelor* was represented (initially) as in Figure 3.3, with markers in parentheses and distinguishers in square brackets.

Since there is no marker (Young) in the path of the ''knight'' or the ''fur seal'' reading, this entry predicts that speakers interpret *The old bachelor finally died* as ambiguous. If they do not, then (Young) would have to be taken to be a marker in the paths of those readings and [knight serving under the standard of another knight] and [fur seal without a mate during the breeding time] as their respective distinguishers.

Katz and Fodor made it clear that the EVALUATION of a semantic theory involves markers only—hence their goal was to posit as few markers as possible in each dictionary entry. By implication, markers are theoretical primitives, defined independently of any language, and consequently, part of every human being's language learning facility. We can see, then, why it was so important for Fodor and Katz for the marker–distinguisher distinction to go through. While it might not seem implausible to maintain that

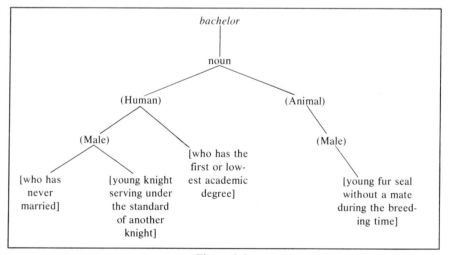

Figure 3.3

notions like "human," "animal," "male," etc. are (to some extent) un-learned, surely no one could reasonably attribute innateness to such concepts as "knight serving under the standard of another knight" or "fur seal without a mate at breeding time."

However, Bolinger (1965) cast considerable doubt on the tenability of the marker–distinguisher distinction. He gave as evidence sentences such as the following:

(3.17) a. *He became a bachelor*
        b. *The seven-year-old bachelor sat on the rock*
        c. *Lancelot became the unhappiest of all the bachelors after his wife died*
        d. *That peasant is a happy bachelor*
        e. *The bachelor wiggled his flippers*

Since (3.17a–c) rule out the "never married" sense of *bachelor*, selectional restrictions, to capture this, would seemingly have to make reference to markers such as (Nonbecoming), (Adult), and (Unmated), eliminating entirely the distinguisher on the leftmost path of Figure 3.3. By the same token, (3.17d) is incompatible with the "young knight" reading, apparently necessitating the marker (Noble); (3.17e) is incompatible with all but the "fur seal" reading, hence a marker such as (Phocine) would be necessary! In this way, Bolinger succeeded in replacing all four distinguishers by a series of markers.[4] Whatever the epistemological character of semantic constructs, then, it seems clear that Katz and Fodor did not succeed in motivating a neat twofold division corresponding directly to the universal–language-specific or innate–learned distinctions.

In the Katz–Fodor framework, the first step in the interpretation of an entire sentence was the plugging in of the lexical items from the dictionary into the syntactically generated phrase-marker, given the existence of a compatibility relation between the grammatical markers in the lexical entry and the categories in the phrase-marker. After insertion, projection rules then applied upward from the bottom of the tree, amalgamating the readings

---

[4] Though it should be stressed that Bolinger did not consider the possibility that the sentences of (3.17) might be only PRAGMATICALLY unambiguous—a possibility congenial to the marker–distinguisher distinction.

J. D. Fodor (1977: 146) has pointed out that the existence of synonymous lexical items in a language whose meaning must be represented in the distinguisher is incompatible with the Katz–Fodor claim that distinguishers can appear only once in the dictionary:

Also, the existence of the English word *spinster* means that the distinguisher [*who has never married*] in the Katz and Fodor dictionary entry for *bachelor* would have to be converted to a semantic marker. Even the highly idiosyncratic and unsystematic concept of being without a mate during the breeding season would have to be represented by a semantic marker if there were also a word in English meaning, for instance, a young male rabbit without a mate during the breeding season [p. 146].

of adjacent nodes to specify the reading of the node which immediately dominated them. As an example, consider the phrase-marker represented by (3.18) (we are assuming that the dictionary entries have already been inserted into the phrase-marker):

(3.18)

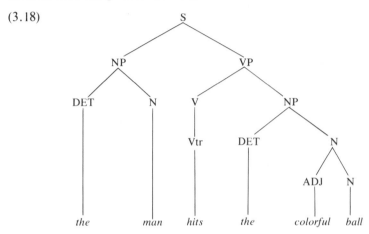

First, the projection rule operating on heads and modifiers combined the readings of *colorful* and *ball* to give the reading of the noun *colorful ball*. The projection rule for articles and nouns then applied twice, amalgamating the readings of *the* and *man,* and *the* and *colorful ball*. Third, the Main Verb–Object Projection Rule resulted in a reading of the verb phrase *hits the colorful ball*. Finally the reading of the entire sentence was attained by the application of the Subject–Verb Phrase Projection Rule.

Since any lexical item might have more than one reading, if the projection rules applied in an unconstrained fashion the number of readings of a node would simply be the product of the number of readings of those nodes which it dominated. However, selectional restrictions forming part of the dictionary entry of each lexical item served to limit the amalgamatory possibilities. For example, the verb *hit* contains a selectional restriction limiting its occurrence to objects with the marker (Physical Object). The sentence *the man hits the colorful ball* would thus be interpreted as meaning ' . . . strikes the brightly-colored round object,' but not as having the anomalous reading ' . . . strikes the gala dance,' since *dance* does not contain the marker (Physical Object).

While Katz and Fodor's proposals regarding the general goals of a semantic theory were immediately accepted by theoretical linguists and were to underlie most of the work done in semantics for years afterward, their specific claims about the structure of the semantic component were largely ignored due to their extreme inadequacy. We have already seen the defects in the marker–distinguisher distinction. Many saw even more serious problems with their conception of projection rules. Put simply, the rules as proposed in their paper are utterly trivial. They hypothesized four distinct projection rules, but, in reality, all had the identical function of combining readings of adjacent nodes without regard to their category or the internal syntactic or semantic structure of the nodes being combined. Since structural information was lost as the projection rules applied, the reading of an entire sentence actually contained LESS semantic information than the phrase-marker (with lexical entries inserted) before the first application of a projection rule! Given the final "semantically interpreted" sentence, there was no way to tell where the reading of one subpart of the sentence stopped and another started.[5]

In the years following the appearance of Katz and Fodor's work, attention turned from the question of character of the semantic rules to that of the syntactic level most relevant to their application.

3.3.2. Levels of Syntactic Structure, Transformations, and Meaning

The first paper to make a specific claim about the relationship between transformations and meaning was Fodor (1961). Fodor was aware that, as the syntactic rules were formulated at that time, the relationship was a fairly indirect one. For example, while many transformational rules preserved meaning, not all did—*John swept the floor* and *John did not sweep the floor* were related by an optional transformation. Likewise, while sentences whose derivations included the same set of phrase-structure rules were often paraphrases, there were a number of cases where they were not, as the examples just given also illustrate. Fodor therefore put forward a rather weak claim about the relation of transformations and meaning, though it was the strongest which seemed feasible at the time: If two sentences are paraphrases and the same transformation is applied to each, then the resultant transforms are also paraphrases. In a reply to Fodor, Katz (1962) showed that even this exceedingly weak claim was deficient:

> For instance, the matrix sentence "The man hit the man" can, by the same transformation rule, now have the sentence fragment "old" embedded in it in front of either occurrence of "man." Thus, assuming the matrix and fragment each to be a paraphrase of itself . . . , a P-related [i.e., "paraphrase-related"] pair is transformed by the same rule into sentences that are not P-related: "The old man hit the man" and "The man hit the old man [p. 41]."

Katz and Fodor devoted very little space to this problem in their ensuing paper on the structure of a semantic theory. They recognized that there was no single level at which their projection rules seemed suited to

---

[5] Katz refined the projection rules considerably in later publications (1967, 1972). They still retained their essentially amalgamatory character, however. A useful discussion of Katz's later work is found in J. D. Fodor (1977).

apply with maximum generality. On the one hand, they did not want the rules to apply SIMPLY to the output of the transformations, since they would not be able to predict the ambiguity inherent in a sentence derived from more than one underlying source. On the other hand, it would not do for the projection rules to apply to the output of the phrase-structure rules, since transformations not only changed meaning, but actually introduced elements with semantic content. They therefore arrived at the compromise of positing TWO types of projection rules. The first type, P1 rules, interpreted sentences produced without the aid of optional transformations (i.e., kernel sentences). The second type, P2 rules, introduced to the final interpretation the contribution of the optional transformational rules. Katz and Fodor never made the P2 rules precise.

An answer to the question of how transformations affect meaning and at which syntactic level the projection rules apply followed with the publication of Katz and Postal's *An Integrated Theory of Linguistic Descriptions* (1964). Katz and Postal concluded that ALL information necessary for the application of the projection rules is present in the underlying syntactic structure, or, alternatively stated, that transformational rules do not affect meaning. This conclusion quickly became known to all linguists simply as the "Katz–Postal Hypothesis."

Katz and Postal first attempted to motivate the meaning-preserving nature of the singulary transformations. (This was necessary, of course, only for the optional transformations—what could it mean to claim that the input to and output of an obligatory rule had different interpretations?) Logically, they pointed out, there are three ways they might behave with respect to meaning:

(3.19)   a. No singulary transformations affect semantic interpretation.
          b. All singulary transformations affect semantic interpretation.
          c. Some singulary transformations affect semantic interpretation and some do not.

Katz and Postal argued that simply on a priori methodological grounds, (3.19a) was preferable to (3.19b), just as both were preferable to (3.19c). And it was (3.19a), which on empirical grounds as well, seemed to have the most support. This alternative entails that it is the UNDERLYING P-marker in the derivation of a sentence which is most suited to semantic interpretation. For a number of reasons, this appeared to be correct. First, rules such as Passive distort the underlying grammatical relations which the projection rules are clearly sensitive to. Hence, it seemed logical to do interpretation before Passive, not after. Second, it was typically the case that discontinuities were created by T-rules (*look . . . up, have . . . en*, etc.) and never the case that a discontinuous underlying construction BECAME continuous by the application of a transformation. Naturally, then, it made sense to interpret such constructions at an underlying level where their semantic unity is reflected by syntactic continuity. Finally, while there were many motivated examples of transformations which DELETED elements contributing to the meaning of the sentence (the transformations forming imperatives and comparatives, for example), there were very few which had been proposed which INSERTED such elements. The rule which Chomsky (1957) had proposed to insert meaningless supportive *do* was typical in this respect.

There were apparent counterexamples to the Katz–Postal hypothesis, of course. Consider Passive first. Recall from Section 2.2.5 that Chomsky had actually used the apparent meaning-changing property of this rule as evidence that transformations could not be defined in terms of synonymy. Katz and Postal reconsidered the data and reported that THEIR intuitions told them that BOTH *every one in the room knows at least two languages* and *at least two languages are known by everyone in the room* are ambiguous, allowing Passive to behave in accord with the meaning-preserving hypothesis. Oddly, they ignored other well-known examples which could not be explained away so easily. For example, Wang (1964) had pointed out that *everybody loves somebody* and *somebody is loved by everybody* are quite resistant to ambiguous interpretation, at least for many speakers.

Four other examples of meaning-changing rules in *Syntactic Structures* were those which formed negatives, imperatives, yes–no questions, and *wh*-questions. I have already (in Section 3.2.4) described how in the following years special underlying morphemes Neg, I, Q, and *wh* were posited, which functioned to trigger the obligatory application of these once optional rules. With such morphemes in the underlying structure to serve as input to the relevant projection rule, there appeared to be no further counterexamples among the singulary transformations (but see Section 4.4.2!).

Turning to generalized transformations, Katz and Postal gave the first account of how the various constituent sentences involved contributed to the meaning of the entire sentence. The simple amalgamatory aspect of combining the reading of the constituent with the reading of the matrix was to be handled by a special P2 projection rule for that purpose. But that more than simple amalgamation was involved was indicated by the fact that syntactically and semantically distinct sentences could be formed from the same simplex sentences combined by exactly the same embedding transformations. For example; consider (3.20a–b):

(3.20)   a. *I know that the boy who John likes hates Mary*
          b. *The boy who I know that John likes hates Mary*

In (3.20a) Relativization applied before Complementation, in (3.20b) Complementation before Relativization. The semantic interpretation of complex sentences, then, had to involve reference to the transformation-marker, which kept track of the order of embeddings. There still remained cases such as (3.21a–b), which differ syntactically only by virtue of the embedding taking place at a different position within the same matrix sentence:

(3.21)   a. *The man who is happy likes the man who is sad*
         b. *The man who is sad likes the man who is happy*

Katz and Postal solved the problem of their interpretation simply by arbitrarily specifying that the leftmost embedding take place first. In that way, the transformation-markers of the two sentences (and hence the readings assigned to them) would differ in the appropriate ways.

Finally, they argued that those generalized transformations which, in the past, had been hypothesized to change meaning, in reality did not do so. Most of their attention was centered on the derivation of nominalizations. Both the factive and the manner readings of sentences such as *I don't approve of his drinking* had been derived from the same underlying phrase-markers, roughly *I don't approve of it* and *he drinks*. Different generalized transformations then carried these identical underlying structures through different derivational paths to the surface. Katz and Postal argued at length for deriving each nominalization from a structure containing a head noun representing its abstract semantic quality, such as "act," "fact," "manner." Given such an analysis, each of the two readings of *I don't approve of John's drinking* would be derived from a different underlying structure, so the generalized transformations involved would not violate their hypotheses.

Their arguments for an abstract underlying structure for nominalizations are too detailed to go into here. But these, and many of the other arguments in their book, utilized a novel heuristic for motivating rules and structures which they outlined as follows:

> Given a sentence for which a syntactic derivation is needed; look for simple paraphrases of the sentence which are not paraphrases by virtue of synonymous expressions; on finding them, construct grammatical rules that relate the original sentence and its paraphrases in such a way that each of these sentences has the same sequence of underlying P-markers. Of course, having constructed such rules, it is still necessary to find INDEPENDENT SYNTACTIC JUSTIFICATION for them [Katz and Postal (1964: 157), emphasis in original].

The Katz–Postal hypothesis and the accompanying heuristic seemed so intuitively appealing that they soon came to be adopted without hesitation by a large majority of practicing syntacticians. The consequences of this will be discussed in depth in the following two chapters.

3.4. SOME ASSUMPTIONS MADE EXPLICIT

Several notions were implicit in the very earliest work in transformational generative grammar: the competence–performance dichotomy and the concepts "linguistic universal" and "level of adequacy." However, since they were not made precise until the early 1960s (or at least not given their familiar labels until then), I have saved discussion of them for this section.

3.4.1. Competence and Performance

Chomsky (1964a: 915), in coining the terms "competence" and "performance" to refer to language knowledge and language use, respectively, was (as he explicitly acknowledged) giving a modern reinterpretation to the Saussurean notions of *langue* and *parole*. But it is just as well that Chomsky avoided Saussure's terms, given the very fundamental differences in how the two linguists viewed the respective constructs. For Saussure, *langue* was an inventory of elements, not a system of generative rules. Moreover, to Saussure syntax was part of *parole*, while the social function of language came under *langue*! Better examples of pre-Chomskyan understanding of the concepts of competence and performance can be found in the work of Edward Sapir (1921) and Stanley Newman (1941), both of whom gave explicit examples demonstrating how linguistic knowledge contributed to, but had to be kept distinct from, the actual use of language.

While Chomsky always stated clearly that the boundaries of linguistic competence could not be set by methodological fiat, but themselves were the subject of empirical investigation, many linguists have taken his definition of competence ("what one knows about one's language") in the broadest sense possible. Along these lines we find discussions of "communicative competence" (Hymes 1971) and attempts to incorporate every conceivable linguistic phenomenon (and many nonlinguistic ones), from strategies for successful communication to belief systems, into the grammatical model on the grounds that they involve things speakers "know" about their language. I will return to these proposals in Chapters 5 and 7.

Chomsky, for his part, has tended to ascribe to performance many phenomena which seem, in relevant respects, strictly grammatical. For example, after making a few brief remarks about so-called "free word order" phenomena in languages like German and Russian, he commented: "In general, the rules of stylistic reordering are very different from the grammatical transformations, which are much more deeply embedded in the grammatical system. It might, in fact, be argued the former are not so much rules of grammar as rules of performance [Chomsky 1965:127]." Many have wondered, along with G. Lakoff (1973), how these rules, whose inputs and outputs seemingly have to be stated in structural terms, could be anything other than rules of grammar (i.e., rules of competence).[6]

---

[6] For characterization and discussion of the notion "stylistic transformation," see Banfield (1973a) and Emonds (1976:187–188).

3.4.2. Linguistic Universals

As I have already mentioned, Chomsky in *Syntactic Structures* referred to the "condition of generality" which must be posed by the theory: "We require that the grammar of a given language be constructed in accord with a specific theory of linguistic structure in which such terms as 'phoneme' and 'phrase' are defined independently of any particular language [p. 50]." While he left no room for doubt in this and other passages that the general form of linguistic rules and the vocabulary of the theory itself were universal, he was not actually to use the term "universal" until around 1962. One can only speculate that the atmosphere of the 1950s, hostile to any but "inductive" generalizations, made him discreet enough to avoid that emotionally charged term.

Katz and Postal (1964: 160–161) and Chomsky (1965: 27–30) classified universals into two types—SUBSTANTIVE and FORMAL. The substantive universals are those concepts out of which particular statements in a linguistic description are constructed, as, for example, the syntactic categories, phonological distinctive features, and semantic markers. Traditional grammar, in so far as it claimed (or assumed) that all the languages in the world could be described by the same set of phonetic features or syntactic categories embodied a theory of substantive universals.

Formal universals are more abstract. They specify the formal conditions that every grammatical description must meet, including the character of the rules that appear in grammars and the ways in which they can be interconnected:

> For example, consider the proposal that the syntactic component of a grammar must contain transformational rules (these being operations of a highly special kind) mapping semantically interpreted deep structures into phonologically interpreted surface structures, or the proposal that the phonological component of a grammar consists of a sequence of rules, a subset of which may apply cyclically to successively more dominant constituents of the surface structure (a transformational cycle, in the sense of much recent work on phonology). Such proposals [are examples of formal universals] [Chomsky 1965: 29].

3.4.3. Levels of Adequacy

Chomsky (1964a) outlined two levels of success that might be attained by a grammatical description. The lower, the level of OBSERVATIONAL ADEQUACY, is attained "if the grammar presents the primary data correctly [p. 924]." The higher, the level of DESCRIPTIVE ADEQUACY, is achieved "when the grammar gives a correct account of the linguistic intuition of the native speaker, and specifies the observed data (in particular) in terms of significant generalizations that express underlying regularities in the language [p. 924]." The theory itself would achieve the level of EXPLANATORY

ADEQUACY by providing "a general basis for selecting a grammar that achieves the second level of success over other grammars consistent with the relevant observed data that do not achieve this level of success. In this case, we can see that the linguistic theory in question suggests an explanation for the linguistic intuition of the native speaker [p. 924]."

Chomsky illustrated the various levels of adequacy by giving several examples from syntax and phonology. One of them involved the alternate phonetic shapes of the lexical item *telegraph*, which appears as (3.22), (3.23), and (3.24) in the contexts #____#, *-ic, -y*, respectively:

(3.22)   téligrǽf

(3.23)   tèligrǽf

(3.24)   tilégrif

Observational adequacy is achieved by a grammar which simply states the above facts. To achieve the level of descriptive adequacy, the grammar would have to treat these variant shapes as special cases of general rules applying to many other items. Explanatory adequacy would be attained by

> the linguistic theory associated with it provid[ing] a framework for phonological rules and an evaluation measure meeting the following condition: the most highly valued set of rules of the appropriate form selected to generate a set of items from which the variants of "telegraph" are excluded would be the set of rules that in fact predict this contextual variation for "telegraph" [Chomsky 1964a:926].

This example and the others offered by Chomsky indicate that there might well be several descriptively adequate treatments of the stress and vowel reduction alternations exhibited by the variants of *telegraph* and related items in English. An explanatorily adequate linguistic theory would be able to select one of them as preferred, on principled grounds.

In the generativist view, the ultimate explanation of a linguistic phenomenon involves the demonstration that it follows from some independently motivated aspect of universal grammar—that is, that it has its roots in the innate human linguistic facility: "The problem of . . . explanatory adequacy . . . is essentially the problem of constructing a theory of language acquisition, an account of the specific innate abilities that make this achievement possible [Chomsky 1965:27]." Chomsky has repeatedly stressed that the intrinsic INTEREST of language as an object of investigation is the fact that its structural properties are to a large extent innate and therefore underivable from such notions as "communicative function," and "speaker intent." A clear defense of this view can be found in Chapter 2 of his *Reflections on Language* (1975), where he devotes a number of pages to the demonstration that the structure-dependent property of transformational rules admits no "external" explanation of any sort, and concludes:

[Structure-dependence] seems to be a general property of an interesting class of linguistic rules, innate to the mind. Following what I take to be Searle's [(1969)] suggestion, let us try to account for it in terms of communication. I see no way of doing so. Surely this principle enters into the function of language; we might well study the ways in which it does. But a language could function for communication (or otherwise) just as well with structure-independent rules, so it would seem. For a mind differently constituted, structure-independent rules would be far superior, in that they require no abstract analysis of a sentence beyond words. I think that the example is typical. Where it can be shown that structures serve a particular function, that is a valuable discovery. To account for or somehow explain the structure of UG [= universal grammar], or of particular grammars, on the basis of functional considerations is a pretty hopeless prospect, I would think . . . [Chomsky 1975b: 57–58].

3.5. THE *ASPECTS* MODEL

I have already made reference to the two major theoretical innovations in Chomsky's *Aspects of the Theory of Syntax* (1965): base (phrase structural) recursion and the elimination of branching rules for lexical subcategorization in favor of rules introducing complex symbols (complexes of syntactic features). Figure 3.4 illustrates the organization of the *Aspects* model:

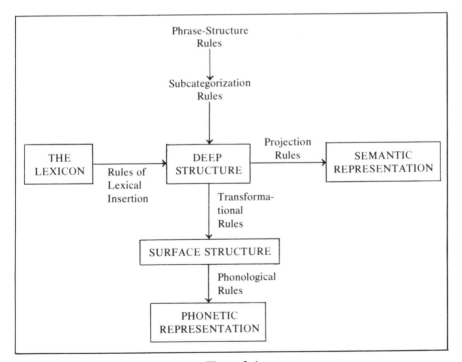

Figure 3.4

Since all recursion in this model is handled by the phrase-structure rules, it follows that each derivation contains a single formal object consisting of a lexically specified P-marker, serving as input to the transformational rules. This formal object Chomsky named the "deep structure" of the sentence. The term "deep structure," like so much of the technical vocabulary of transformational generative grammar, has its historical antecedents. For example, the nineteenth century linguist, Wilhelm von Humboldt, had used the term *innere Form* in a very similar way. Charles Hockett (1958), in one of the many passages in which he reached inspired theoretical conclusions, never to be developed or to manifest themselves in an actual analysis, referred to the "deep grammar" of a sentence:[7]

> It is as though the whole network of structural relationships between forms . . . constituted a complex intertwining of various kinds of valences, only one layer of which is immediately apparent to the analyst. This most apparent layer constitutes, we shall say, SURFACE GRAMMAR. Beneath it lie various layers of DEEP GRAMMAR, which have much to do with how we speak and understand but which are still largely unexplored, in any systematic way, by grammarians [p. 249].

Chomsky may simply have appropriated and modified slightly Hockett's terminology. At any rate, given the adoption of "deep structure" for the level of structure serving as input to the transformations, "surface structure" naturally suggested itself as the term to be applied to the structure defined by the output of these rules.

The term "deep structure" has had the unfortunate effect of inviting a metaphorical interpretation by the linguistically unsophisticated. As Chomsky later (1975b) complained, "[the term] has led a number of people to suppose that it is the deep structures and their properties that are truly 'deep,' in the nontechnical sense of the word, while the rest is superficial, unimportant, variable across languages, and so on. This was never intended. [p. 82]." Even practicing linguists have confused the notion "deep structure," which is simply a level of grammatical description, with the innate linguistic mechanisms common to all humans: "Besides being explicit, generative grammars propose to include an underlying or deep structure which reflects innate patterns controlled by the brain [Lehmann 1978:50]." Such profound misunderstandings have been only too common.

---

[7] Even Robert Hall the most virulent antimentalist of them all, could write in a book published as late as 1966:

> The surface characteristics of the various pidgins and creoles may often be quite far from those of English, French, or the other Indo-European languages; but, on a deeper level of grammar, all varieties of Pidgin English and creoles that have grown out of them have an underlying identity of structure with English, and similarly with the French-based, Spanish-based, and Portuguese-based pidgins and creoles [p. 58].

One can speculate that Chapter 1 of *Aspects* drove home to Hall, as it did to Hockett (see Section 2.7.2) the mentalist implications of such a position. Certainly, we find nothing comparable in Hall's work after 1966.

3.5.1. The Level of Deep Structure

The level of deep structure in *Aspects* is defined by the application of three sets of rules: phrase-structure rules, subcategorization rules, and rules of lexical insertion. Chomsky referred to the first two collectively as the "base rules."

The provision of categorial and functional (or "relational") information is the task of the phrase-structure rules, which generate a phrase-marker, each node of which is labeled with a particular category symbol. Functional information, or "grammatical relations," are then defined as wholly derivative relations between categories. For example, the notions "Subject-of," "Predicate-of," "Direct-Object-of," and "Main-Verb-of" are defined at one point (Chomsky 1965:71) in the following way:

(3.25)   a. Subject-of [NP immediately dominated by S]
          b. Predicate-of [VP immediately dominated by S]
          c. Direct-Object-of [NP immediately dominated by VP]
          d. Main-Verb-of [V immediately dominated by VP]

Chomsky suggested that while these definitions correctly characterize deep structure grammatical relations, sentences with topicalized noun phrases such as *this book I really enjoy*, in which two NP's appear to be immediately dominated by the S node, point to the fact that other definitions for surface relations are needed. He mentioned, but did not expand on, a proposal by Paul Kiparsky that the relations "Topic-of" and "Comment-of" might be the appropriate ones for surface structure.

Chomsky (1965) attributed universality to the definitions of (3.25): "These definitions must be thought of as belonging to general linguistic theory; in other words, they form part of the general procedure for assigning a full structural description to a sentence, given a grammar . . . [pp. 71–72]."

Dozens of pages of *Aspects* are devoted to the interrelated questions of subcategorization, selection, and lexical insertion. The subcategorization rules include the context-free variety described in Section 3.2.7 and two types of context-sensitive rules: strict subcategorization rules and selectional rules. The former subcategorize lexical categories in terms of the syntactic frames in which they appear. For example, Chomsky suggested (3.26) as the phrase-structure rule expanding the node VP:

$$(3.26) \qquad VP \rightarrow \left\{ \begin{array}{l} \text{copula Predicate} \\ V \left\{ \begin{array}{l} \text{(NP) (Prep-Phrase) (Prep-Phrase) (Manner)} \\ S \\ \text{Predicate} \end{array} \right\} \end{array} \right\}$$

In that case, since verbs are generated before NP, before NP Prep-Phrase, before S, before Predicate, etc., the subcategorization rules make available to the verb the features +[___NP], + [___NP Prep-Phrase], + [___S], + [___Predicate], etc., the actual feature assigned dependent upon the actual context of the verb in the phrase-marker.

Selectional rules subcategorize verbs on the basis of the syntactic features of the subject and object. For example, an intransitive verb generated following a human subject is automatically assigned the feature + [+ Human___]. Chomsky devoted quite a bit of space to motivating the assignment of inherent features to nouns and subcategorizing verbs by the selectional rule, rather than vice versa. Since the opposite position, which leads to enormous complication, had never (nor has ever since) been advocated, it is not necessary to repeat his arguments.[8]

Finally, lexical items in *Aspects* are substitutable into the base phrase-marker if their syntactic features are nondistinct from those generated by the base rules. For example, a verb such as *discuss*, lexically provided with the feature + [[+ Human] ____[+ N]] is unsubstitutable in the base phrase-marker (3.27), blocking the derivation of the deviant sentence *the chair discussed the problem* at the level of deep structure:

(3.27)

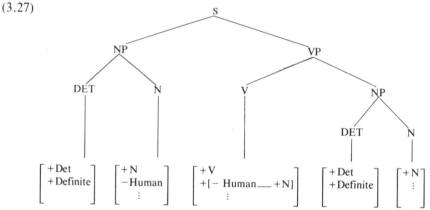

Chomsky considered an alternative analysis which removes subcategorization from the base rules entirely and has each lexical category single-branch to a fixed "dummy symbol," designated Δ. The rules of lexical insertion must in this analysis all be context-sensitive, since they play the role of the subcategorization rules of the first proposal, allowing insertion of a lexical item (replacing Δ), given compatibility of features of the item inserted with its neighbors.

Chomsky seemed to prefer the first, "matching format," to the second,

---

[8] Although Bach (1968) later pointed out several problems with Chomsky's formulation. Chomsky chose to make subject and object selection mutually dependent for each verb, rather than providing each verb with distinct subject and object selection features, a position later defended in Bresnan (1972a). The latter alternative, favored by G. Lakoff (1970a), now seems more popular, although no one has ever claimed that the issue has great empirical significance.

"substitution format," stating that while there was not a great deal of empirical evidence to support one or the other, the former was more restrictive and hence a priori more desirable—a claim which he did not attempt to motivate in any detail. In subsequent work, the question has received very little attention, with some linguists (e.g., G. Lakoff 1970) adopting the matching format, but most (e.g., McCawley 1968b; Emonds 1976; and Chomsky himself 1970, 1971) adopting the substitution format.

Note that both of these approaches involve selectional restrictions being stated as SYNTACTIC restrictions between LEXICAL ITEMS (i.e., that selectional deviance be accounted for before the application of both the semantic projection rules and the syntactic transformations). This claim would lead to a major controversy (see Section 4.4.1).

3.5.2. The Transformational Component

As we have seen, the following claims led to Chomsky's decision to eliminate generalized transformations in favor of base recursion:

(3.28)   a. There is no order between embedding transformations. A singulary transformation never applies in a matrix sentence before a constituent sentence is embedded into it. (See Section 3.2.2.)
          b. Constituent sentences keep their internal structure intact after embedding. (See Section 3.2.3.)
          c. Generalized transformations themselves contribute nothing to the interpretation of the sentence. (See Section 3.3.2.)

Chomsky incorporated Fillmore's proposal that the set of singulary transformations "recycle" after each embedding in the most direct way possible—he proposed that the transformational rules apply cyclically (preserving their linear order) from the most deeply embedded S to the highest S. Hence, any transformation might have as many applications as there were levels of deep structure embedding.

Now in no way does the principle of cyclic application FOLLOW from base recursion, although base recursion does have the virtue of eliminating in principle many ordering possibilities. George Lakoff's (1968c) argument that a noncyclic grammar would have to be nonfinite is of special historical importance, then. I will return to this and to further discussion of the cyclic principle in Section 6.6.2.

Note that the principle of base recursion also obviates the need for transformation-markers—another point which was cited in its favor.

Aspects imputed to transformational rules a filtering function by which they would prevent certain well-formed base structures from being realized as grammatical sentences. Chomsky cited the following two (somewhat simplified) base-generated strings to illustrate this point:

(3.29)   a. Δ *fired the man (# the man persuaded John to be examined
              by a specialist #)* by Passive
          b. Δ *fired the man (# the boy persuaded John to be examined by
              a specialist #)* by Passive

The problem is to block (3.29b), which clearly underlies no well-formed
surface structure. Chomsky's solution consisted of an argument of the
following form:

(3.30)   a. The Relative Clause Transformation deletes the boundary-
              symbol "#" as it deletes (i.e., pronominalizes) the noun
              phrase in the relative clause.
          b. This transformation will delete *the man* in (3.29a), but not *the
              boy* in (3.29b), since the latter deletion is nonrecoverable.
          c. # will therefore appear in the surface structure in (3.29b), but
              not in (3.29a).
          d. Any surface structure containing an internal # is ungrammat-
              ical.
          e. Example (3.29b) is therefore ungrammatical.

It is interesting that Chomsky chose this method to filter the ungrammatical sentence derived from (3.29b), since he had at least two others open
to him. He could have, by an extension of the mechanism for capturing
selectional restrictions, blocked (3.29b) at the level of deep structure by
requiring that head nouns in relative clause structures select identical nouns
in the relative clause. Or he could have left the task of explaining the
deviance to the semantic rules. Since (3.29b) receives no interpretation,
seemingly the semantic rules would have to block it anyway.

Perlmutter (1971:1-3) pointed out that Chomsky chose the transformational over the deep structural filtering solution because, first, conditions
on identity had been proposed repeatedly for transformations, but had never
been claimed to be operative in the base and, second, there were no other
clear examples of selectional restrictions holding between items in separate
clauses. Chomsky's not even considering the semantic alternative simply
illustrates his reluctance at that time to attribute any nontrivial role to that
component.

Before *Aspects*, syntactic relatedness between sentences was expres-
sible only in transformational terms. But the adoption of a separate lexicon
and syntactic features made an alternative—lexical—treatment possible:

> There may be some point to allowing a lexical item to appear in several categorial
> positions . . . —for example, in the case of words such as "proof," "desire," "belief."
> Suppose that these are specified as taking Sentential Complements of various forms, but
> are permitted to enter either the Noun or Verb position. Then the lexical insertion rule
> will place them in either the frame " . . . N that S . . . " or the frame " . . . V that

S . . . ," in the positions of the Noun and Verb, respectively. Hence it will not be necessary to derive the former by transformation from the latter, as is necessary, for example, in the case of " . . . proving that S . . . [Chomsky 1965:219]."

By what criteria, then, would it be determined whether a process was lexical or transformational? In *Aspects*, Chomsky had only one—productivity. In keeping with the idea that "all properties of a formative that are essentially idiosyncratic will be specified in the lexicon [p. 87]," Chomsky proposed to handle lexically those "quasi-productive" processes which would necessarily have been considered transformational at an earlier time. The rules involved in the formation of forms such as *horror, horrid, horrify; terror, (*terrid), terrify;* and *candor, candid, (*candify)* were cited as examples [p. 186].

In retrospect, it is interesting to recall that in *Aspects* Chomsky considered PRODUCTIVE the processes involved in the formation of *destruction, refusal,* etc., and hence felt that "clearly" [p. 184] they were to be derived transformationally. Soon, however, his criteria for "productivity" were to become more stringent, and he would opt for a lexical treatment of all derived nominals (see Chapters 4 and 6).

3.5.3. Syntax and Semantics

Chomsky's views in *Aspects* on the relationship between grammar and meaning are decidedly peculiar—perhaps even contradictory. On the one hand, in a passage he restated his earlier position on the independence of the two notions:

> For the moment, I see no reason to modify the view, expressed in Chomsky (1957) and elsewhere, that although, obviously, semantic considerations are relevant to the construction of a general linguistic theory (that is, obviously the theory of syntax should be designed so that the syntactic structures exhibited for particular languages will support semantic interpretation), there is, at present, no way to show that semantic considerations play a role in the choice of the syntactic or phonological component of a grammar or that semantic features (in any significant sense of this term) play a role in the functioning of the syntactic or phonological rules [Chomsky 1965:226].

But on the other hand, he uncritically adopted the Katz–Postal hypothesis with its assumption that everything necessary for semantic interpretation is present in the deep structure. Assuming Katz–Postal, semantic considerations CLEARLY "play a role in the choice of the syntactic component"—a syntactic analysis which results in an ambiguous sentence having only one deep structure must be rejected.

Furthermore, he simply refused to take a position on the question of whether semantic features play a role in the functioning of the syntactic rules: "We call a feature 'semantic' if it is not mentioned in any syntactic rule, thus begging the question of whether semantics is involved in syntax [Chomsky 1965:142]." If, as Chomsky seemed to imply, any semantic

feature which appears in a syntactic rule is to be considered syntactic BY
DEFINITION, then it seems fair to conclude that in 1965 he could not have
regarded the independence of grammar as a very strong empirical hypothesis.

The overall impression that one gets about Chomsky's position on this
question is one of extreme agnosticism. For example, he was quite open to
the possibility that selection might be handled by the semantic rules, rather
than at the level of deep structure. Going to the other extreme, he even
considered plausible an alternative which later would be called "generative
semantics"—the first published proposal along these lines: "Alternatively,
one might raise the question whether the functions of the semantic component as described earlier should not be taken over, *in toto* by the
generative syntactic rules [Chomsky 1965: 158]." While Chomsky did not
advocate this position, he certainly considered it reasonable.

Aspects of the Theory of Syntax, as the most ambitious general exposition of syntactic theory since *Syntactic Structures*, has deservedly played
the role of the "Bible" of our field. An old saying about the other Bible
(the holy one) is that even the Devil could use it for his own purposes. As
we will see in the following chapters, EVERY post-*Aspects* tendency,
whether on the side of the angels or on the side of the Devil, found Chomsky's remarks about the relationship of syntax and semantics in that book
vague enough to suit its own purposes.

Chapter 4

The Late 1960s

4.1. TOWARD ABSTRACT SYNTAX

Until around 1965, generative theoreticians were united on virtually every important issue. In one sense, this is hardly surprising—*Aspects* was written by Chomsky with constant feedback from the faculty and students at MIT, who made up at least 90% of the transformational grammarians in the world at that time. But there was more to it than that. By 1965 numerous studies had appeared which demonstrated conclusively that the theory could be applied insightfully to the analysis of the most complex linguistic phenomena. The most noteworthy was Peter Rosenbaum's 1965 MIT dissertation *The Grammar of English Predicate Complement Constructions* (Rosenbaum 1967). Rosenbaum did for *Aspects* what Lees had done for *Syntactic Structures*, showing that base recursion and the principle of cyclic application provided a satisfactory framework for the analysis of the fundamental syntactic processes in English.

Yet, even by late 1965, the first public signs of division had appeared. In the fall of that year, Paul Postal argued at a colloquium at MIT that adjectives were members of the category ''verb''—a conclusion quite uncongenial to Chomsky's view of English syntax. The following spring, John Robert Ross, a graduate student and instructor at MIT, and George Lakoff, a part-time instructor at Harvard and associate in its computation laboratory, organized a series of Friday afternoon seminars in Harvard's William James Building, devoted to challenging analyses then favored by Chomsky. In the fall of 1966, with Chomsky on leave in Berkeley, Ross and Lakoff brought their opposition into the open in the classes which they were

93

teaching that semester. Ross's class in universal grammar at MIT drew dozens of students; Lakoff's in syntactic theory at Harvard well over 100. The real fight began upon Chomsky's return early in 1967. For several years, however, the sides were very uneven. Aside from Chomsky and his current students at MIT (most of whom speedily reconverted from their infatuation with the Ross–Lakoff approach), a large majority of theoretical linguists held positions very much at odds with those of the field's founder and driving force. And throughout the late 1960s the rift grew, as measured both by the intensity of the feeling of the participants and in the number of theoretical issues at stake.

The primary point of contention at that time centered around the AB-STRACTNESS of underlying syntactic structure. While of course all grammatical structures are "abstract," the notion "degree of abstractness" came to be identified with "degree of distance of deep structure from surface structure," or as contemporary eyes saw the issue, with "degree of closeness of deep structure to semantic representation." By this definition, the deep structures posited by many linguists were becoming very abstract indeed. To give one typical (and much discussed) example, Ross and Lakoff argued that the deep structure of (4.1) was not (4.2.)—as an analysis along the lines sketched in *Aspects* would suggest—but rather the highly abstract (4.3):

(4.1)   *Floyd broke the glass.*

(4.2)

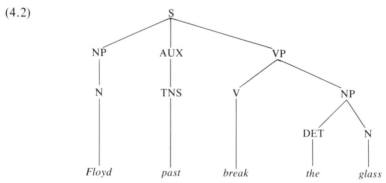

Going hand-in-hand with abstract deep structures was a drastic reduction in the inventory of grammatical categories. For example, abstract syntacticians argued that adjectives, prepositions, auxiliaries, and negative elements were all members of the category "Verb" in deep structure. Numerous arguments were adduced for "lexical decomposition" as well—the representation of the component elements of a lexical item structurally in the underlying phrase-marker. Example (4.3) illustrates this: The verb *break* is derived from (roughly) 'cause + come about + be + broken'. The

(4.3)

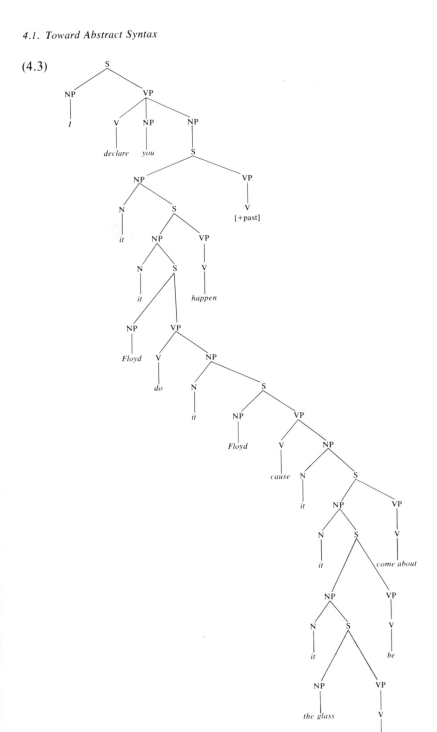

arguments for abstract deep structures typically resulted in sentences with radically different surface structures, for example, (4.4a) and (4.4b), being considered identical at the deepest level of syntactic representation:

(4.4)   a. *Seymour sliced the salami with a knife*
        b. *Seymour used a knife to slice the salami*

By the end of the decade, abstract syntacticians had simply abandoned the notion "deep structure" entirely—this level had been driven back so far that it made no theoretical sense to distinguish it from semantic representation.

As we will see, these radical conclusions were arrived at almost entirely by conventional modes of argumentation, based on the assumptions of Katz and Postal and *Aspects*. This, of course, is a major factor in the explanation of their widespread acceptance. The counterattack, initiated by Chomsky's lectures in the spring of 1967 (which were published as Chomsky [1970]), required an abandonment of certain of these assumptions, and for that reason, if for no other, Chomsky was faced with an uphill struggle. It was not until the mid 1970s, in fact, that the nonabstract alternative was to reassert itself as the dominant model of syntactic description.

In the remainder of this section I will outline in some detail the reasoning which led to the conclusion that deep structures were highly abstract. I have chosen the expository device of presenting these arguments by paraphrasing the authors' own words, without providing immediate critical commentary on their adequacy. The reader should NOT conclude from this that I either endorse the assumptions underlying the arguments, or feel that the arguments go through even GRANTING the assumptions. In fact, I do neither. For the sake of historical continuity, however, it seems best to delay their evaluation until Section 4.4.

4.1.1. Arguments Based on the Katz–Postal Hypothesis

By far, the main impetus for the adoption of highly abstract deep structures came from the Katz-Postal hypothesis. This might seem surprising: There is nothing in the notion that all interpretation takes place at deep structure which, per se, leads to abstractness. One could easily imagine a model consistent with Katz–Postal in which deep structures were quite "shallow," and were mapped onto their respective interpretations by a rich set of interpretive rules. In fact, the possibility that the projection rules might themselves CONTRIBUTE to the meaning is not ruled out under the Katz-Postal hypothesis. But recall the utterly trivial nature of the projection rules of the mid 1960s. Their triviality led to their simply being ignored, and invited a search for a syntactic solution to every semantic problem. Whatever Chomsky's actual views may have been in 1965, many interpreted his comment that "the syntactic component of a grammar must specify, for

each sentence, a DEEP STRUCTURE that determines its semantic intepreta-
tion. . . [Chomsky 1965:16]" as an endorsement of just that position.
Hence syntacticians saw themselves faced with the task of "finding" deep
structures which represented every aspect of the meaning of the sentence
under investigation—a task which led to evermore abstract deep structures.

   It follows automatically from the Katz–Postal hypothesis and the Katz–
Fodor conception of the projection rules that every ambiguity must be
represented by a deep structure difference. Here are a few examples of
abstract deep structures motivated on that basis:

> Sentences like (4.5a), containing a reason adverbial and a negative, are
> ambiguous between one reading in which the adverbial has wider scope
> and another in which the negative has wider scope. A natural way of
> representing this ambiguity in deep structure is by phrase-markers (4.5b)
> and (4.5c), respectively:

(4.5)   a. *I don't steal from John because I like him*
          b.

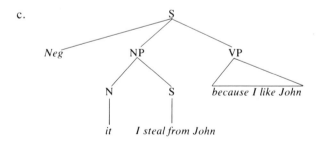

          c.

[PARAPHRASING G. LAKOFF 1970a]

> Sentences like (4.6) are ambiguous between one reading in which *John* and
> *Mary* left jointly and another in which they left separately. Therefore deep
> structures must allow for both phrasal conjunction (4.7a) and sentence
> conjunction (4.7b):

(4.6)   *John and Mary left*

(4.7)   a.

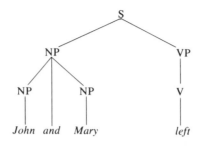

b.

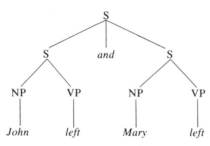

[PARAPHRASING LAKOFF AND PETERS 1969]

It also followed that since projection rules did not supply aspects of meaning, anything UNDERSTOOD as part of the meaning had to be in the deep structure. Some examples of arguments constructed on that basis:

(4.8) has an understood verbal sense ('writing', 'reading', etc.). This must be represented in the deep structure. (4.9) is a plausible candidate:

(4.8)   *John began the book*

(4.9)

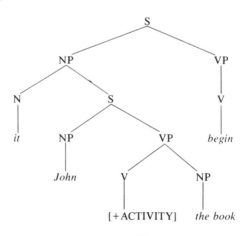

[PARAPHRASING NEWMEYER 1975]

Nouns as well as verbs have tense. (4.10) can be understood to mean either the girl who WAS beautiful (when I saw her) or who IS beautiful (now). Therefore nouns are derived from full sentences in which the understood tense can be represented.

(4.10)   *I was watching the beautiful girl*

[PARAPHRASING BACH 1968]

Consider (4.11):

(4.11)   *John agreed that Harry was an idiot*

One cannot simply "agree"; one must agree with SOMEONE. Hence, the deep structure of (4.11) is roughly (4.12):

(4.12)

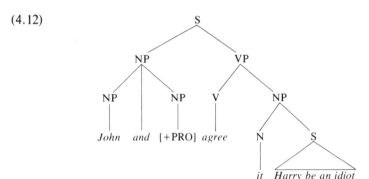

[PARAPHRASING LAKOFF and PETERS 1969]

Occasionally, arguments were adduced for abstract deep structures on the grounds that such structures would provide a more optimal input to the semantic projection rules than nonabstract ones:

Consider the synonymous (4.13a) and (4.13b):

(4.13)   a. *I regret that*
           b. *I am sorry about that*

The only way to avoid two separate projection rules doing the same work (one for V NP, one for ADJ NP) is to consider *sorry (about)* to be a verb in deep structure.

[PARAPHRASING G. LAKOFF 1970a]

Consider the following two noun phrases:

(4.14)   a. *John's beliefs*
           b. *John's tenets*

There is ample evidence for deriving (4.14a) from a deep structure like (4.15):

(4.15)

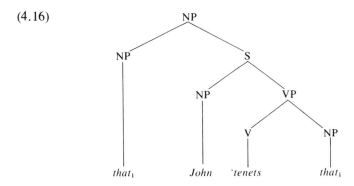

Even though there is no verb which stands in the same relation to *tenet* as *believe* to *belief*, *tenet* must be derived from a verb, as shown in (4.16). Otherwise we would need two totally distinct projection rules, one for (4.14a) and one for (4.14b):

(4.16)

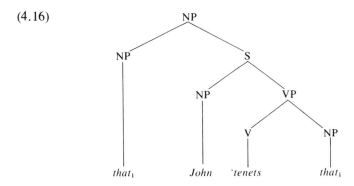

[PARAPHRASING G. LAKOFF 1970a]

Normally the "uppermost verb phrase" is the one negated and questioned. The projection rule for questions and negatives will therefore pick out *like ice cream* in (4.17a) and (4.17b) as the constituent questioned and negated, respectively:

(4.17)   a. *Does John* [_VP_ *like ice cream*]
          b. *John does not* [_VP_ *like ice cream*]

Now consider (4.18a–c):

(4.18)   a. *John shot Bill near the house*
          b. *Did John shoot Bill near the house?*
          c. *John did not shoot Bill near the house*

Notice that the element questioned and negated in (4.18b) and (4.18c), respectively, is *near the house*. Therefore this phrase must be a verb phrase, and the deep structure of (4.18a) must be (4.19):

(4.19)

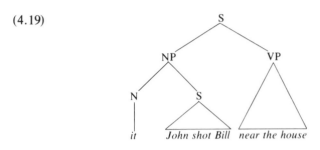

[PARAPHRASING G. LAKOFF 1970a]

4.1.2. Arguments Based on *Aspects* Hypotheses about Deep Structure

While in *Aspects*, Chomsky only hesitantly put forward a particular formalism for capturing strict subcategorization and selectional restrictions and even more hesitantly suggested that the latter should be stated at deep structure at all, the majority of syntacticians from 1965 to 1967 (during which period abstract syntax saw its fastest development) accepted his proposals without question. Many arguments were constructed for abstract deep structures based on the idea that such structures would enable an economical statement of strict subcategorization and selectional restrictions. A common argument was that the grammar could be simplified by reducing the number of possible deep structure configurations and hence the number of strict subcategorization features needed. Two examples:

Rosenbaum (1967) derives the verbs *try, expect,* and *insist (on)* from configurations (4.20a–c), respectively, necessitating three subcategorization features, something like [+___S], [___N^S], and [___P^N^S]:

(4.20)   a.   b.

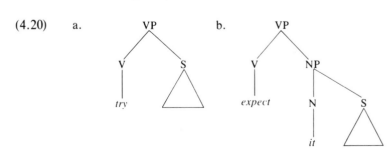

c.

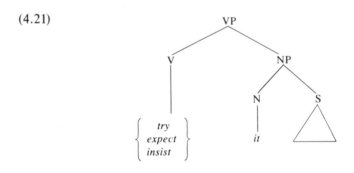

However, we can derive all three from (4.21), necessitating only one feature [+___N^S]:

(4.21)

This allows us to simplify the phrase-structure rules and eliminate unneeded features. The different properties of the three verbs which the different subcategorizations predict automatically (such as lack of *it* with *try* and the preposition following *insist*) will be handled by rule features triggering obligatory transformations. This entails no complication, since we need rule features anyway.

[PARAPHRASING R. LAKOFF 1968]

Note the following pairs:

(4.22)   a. *The oil and water mixed*
           b. *The chemist tried to mix oil and water*

(4.23)   a. *John and Mary married*
           b. *The priest married John and Mary*

It would appear that the verbs *mix* and *marry* have to be subcategorized both for phrasally conjoined subjects and phrasally conjoined objects. However, if we derive (4.22b) from a complex causative deep structure like

(4.24) and (4.23b) in like manner, we can eliminate phrasal object conjunction entirely:

(4.24)

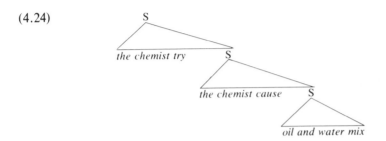

[PARAPHRASING LAKOFF and PETERS 1969]

Probably the most commonly used of all arguments for the purpose of motivating abstract deep structures was the shared selectional restriction argument. Typically, it took the following form:

The selectional restrictions holding between A and B in sentence S and between C and D in sentence S' are essentially the same. We can capture this within the Aspects framework by positing substructures within S and S' where A and C, and B and D, have the same representation. The restriction now need be stated only once.

Here are a few examples:

Consider sentences (4.25a) and (4.25b). An analysis in the spirit of those in Chomsky (1965) would derive them from deep structures (4.26a) and (4.26b), respectively:

(4.25)   a. *Seymour sliced the salami with a knife*
          b. *Seymour used a knife to slice the salami*

(4.26)   a.

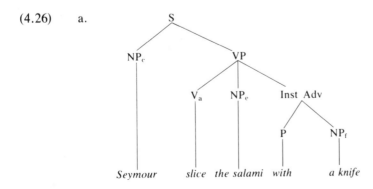

b.

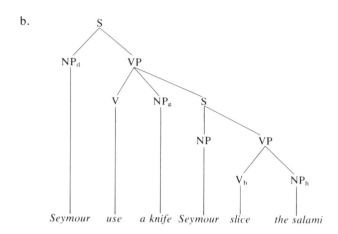

Seymour   use   a knife Seymour slice   the salami

But notice the selectional correspondences holding between the two sentences. The class V_a occurring before instrumental adverbs = the class V_b of complements to the verb *use*. Only animate nouns can be NP_c in (4.26a); likewise only animates can be NP_d in (4.26b). The same co-referentiality restrictions blocking $NP_e = NP_f$ and $NP_c = NP_f$ in (4.26a) seem to block $NP_g = NP_h$ and $NP_d = NP_g$ in (4.26b). And so on. Clearly, it is undesirable to have to state these restrictions twice. Yet this is what would be necessary if the sentences were derived from two different deep structures. Therefore BOTH (4.25a) and (4.25b) are derived from (4.26b), and the selectional restrictions need to be stated but once.

[PARAPHRASING G. LAKOFF 1968a]

Observe the parallels between (4.27a), (4.27b), and (4.27c):

(4.27)   a. *America attacked Cuba*
          b. *The American attack on Cuba (was outrageous)*
          c. *America's attack on Cuba (was outrageous)*

Clearly, the noun phrases which can be the subject of the verb *attack* in (4.27a) and the pseudo-adjective and the possessive which can occur before the noun *attack* in (4.27b) and (4.27c) are, in an intuitive sense, the same. In other words, we have a case of shared selectional restrictions. But the restriction in (4.27a) is superficially one between a noun phrase and a verb, in (4.27b) between an adjective and a noun, and in (4.27c) between a noun phrase and a noun. That means three SEPARATE selectional restrictions, UNLESS we derive them all from the same deep structure. We can do that by deriving the noun *attack* in (4.27b) and (4.27c) from the verb *attack* and the pseudo-adjective *American* from the noun *America*. In that way we need state the selectional restriction only once—as one between subject and verb.

[PARAPHRASING POSTAL 1969]

Action nominalizations are subject to the same selectional restrictions as the noun *act*. Note:

(4.28) a. *The act (of destroying the building) disturbed us*
        b. *The destroying of the building disturbed us*

(4.29) a. **The act (of destroying the building) was delicious*
        b. **The destroying of the building was delicious*

This can be explained if action nominalizations are derived from a structure like the following:

(4.30)

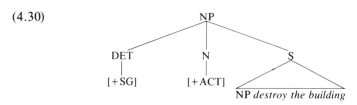

[PARAPHRASING FRASER 1970]

The possible subjects of sentences (4.31a) and (4.32a) correspond to the possible prepositional objects of the sentences (4.31b) and (4.32b).

(4.31) a. $\left\{ \begin{array}{l} Martha \\ *My\ toenail \end{array} \right\}$ *is amazed at your brilliance*

        b. *Your brilliance is amazing to* $\left\{ \begin{array}{l} Martha \\ *my\ toenail \end{array} \right\}$

(4.32) a. $\left\{ \begin{array}{l} Harold \\ *Rice \end{array} \right\}$ *is pleased with your success*

        b. *Your success is pleasing to* $\left\{ \begin{array}{l} Harold \\ *rice \end{array} \right\}$

These identical selectional restrictions can be captured by positing that the (a) and (b) sentences have the same underlying subject–verb–object order in deep structure.

[PARAPHRASING POSTAL 1971]

4.1.3. Conventional Syntactic Arguments for Abstract Deep Structures

Abstract syntacticians found to their delight that many "classic" forms of syntactic argumentation also led to the positing of deep structures far removed from surface structure. For example, it had always been considered uncontroversial that rule statements utilizing the curly-bracket notation for expressing disjunctions are undesirable—one would naturally seek a deeper generalization which rendered the use of this convention unnecessary. Even the highly nonabstract Emonds (1976), for example, argues that particles and prepositions must be members of the same category. If they were not, several rules would have to refer to two categories disjunctively.

As George Lakoff (1971a) put it: "Transformational grammar has . . . a formal device for expressing the claim that a generalization does not exist. That formal device is the curly-bracket notation [p. 291]."

Many arguments were designed in the late 1960s to show that unless two categories were collapsed into one (with the resultant "abstract" consequences), curly-brackets would be necessary. Some examples:

> Adjectives must belong to the "Verb" category because both are moved by the rule of Adjective Shift, which transforms (4.33a) and (4.34a) into (4.33b) and (4.34b), respectively:

(4.33)   a. *the man old* (FROM *the man who is old*)
          b. *the old man*

(4.34)   a. *the man sleeping* (FROM *the man who is sleeping*)
          b. *the sleeping man*

[PARAPHRASING G. LAKOFF 1970a]

> Adjectives are dominated by NP at some point in their derivation, as in (4.35), which underlies *Henry is hungry*. If they were not, Pronominalization would have to be stated with curly-brackets to allow the definite pronoun *it* to replace adjectives as well as NP's—note sentence (4.36):

(4.35)

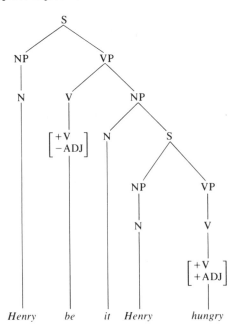

(4.36)   *John is happy, but he doesn't look it*

[PARAPHRASING ROSS 1969a]

> Prepositional phrases are noun phrases, as is evidenced by their both being movable by the rules of *Wh*-Movement and Heavy-NP-Shift:

(4.37)   *you gave the book* [_{PP}*to*[_{NP}*whom*]]→
           [_{NP}*who*] *did you give the book to*/[_{PP}*to whom*] *did you give the book*

(4.38)   a. *I gave* [_{NP}*the book which Mary brought me*] *to Sue* →
               I gave to Sue [_{NP}*the book which Mary brought me*]
           b. *I insisted* [_{PP}*on the fact that I was neutral*] *throughout the dis-*
               cussion →
               I insisted throughout the discussion [_{PP} *on the fact that I was*
               neutral]

                                                        [PARAPHRASING POSTAL 1971]

  A variety of arguments were constructed to show that the capturing of
a linguistically significant generalization demanded a deep structure quite
far removed from surface structure:

  Consider the pairs of sentences in (4.39a–c):

(4.39)   a. *I know someone who is working on English adverbs* ~ *I know*
               someone working on English adverbs
           b. *I saw something that was horrible* ~ *I saw something horrible*
           c. *I never speak to anyone who is a behaviorist* ~ *I never speak to*
               a behaviorist

Uncontroversially, the second sentence in (4.39a) and (4.39b) is derived
from the first. But clearly the same relationship holds between the sentences of (4.39c), and must be captured by the same rule. Therefore, all surface
nouns are derived from relative clauses.

                                                        [PARAPHRASING BACH 1968]

  The verb *seem* must take an object complement in deep structure. That is,
the deep structure of (4.40a) is (4.40b). If *seem* were deeply intransitive,
the rule of *Neg*-Raising would have to be greatly complicated to allow it to
apply out of subject complements as well as object complements.

(4.40)   a. *John seems to me to be a fool*
           b.

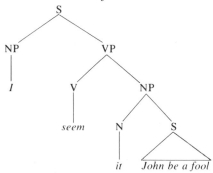

                                                  [PARAPHRASING R. LAKOFF 1968]

The widely held assumption that transformational rules may refer only to constituents motivated many abstract analyses. This assumption was at least implicit in Chomsky's (1965:194) argument that the bracketing of *the man saw the boy* is [*the man*] [*saw the boy*], not [*the man saw*] [*the boy*]:

> Sentence (4.41a) must contain substructure (4.41b), since the pronoun *it* can refer to *the metal hardened*, which therefore must be a constituent:

(4.41)   a. *The scientist hardened the metal, but it took him a year to bring it about*

　　　　　　b.

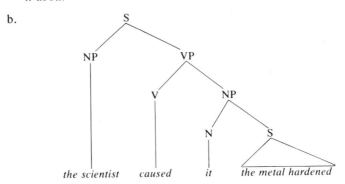

[PARAPHRASING G. LAKOFF 1968b]

In (4.42a), the pronoun *it* can refer to *John marry Mary*. Hence, the latter is a constituent, and negation must be a predicate outside of the sentence it negates, as in (4.42b):

(4.42)   a. *John didn't marry Mary, although the fortune teller had predicted it*

　　　　　　b.

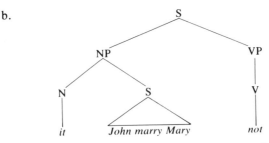

[PARAPHRASING G. LAKOFF 1970b]

A variety of other arguments for abstract structures appeared in the late 1960s which (in form, at least) were quite traditional:

> Sentences like (4.43a) and (4.43b) are derived from their full sentence paraphrases, roughly (4.44a–b). Passive applies in the derivation of (4.43a),

Reflexive in the derivation of (4.43b). Given this, we can explain the nonexistence of *self- . . . -able* forms like (4.43c), based on the well-known fact that Passive and Reflexive are mutually exclusive:

(4.43) a. *The book is readable*
        b. *John is self-motivating*
        c. **John is self-shaveable*

(4.44) a. *One is able to read the book*
        b. *John motivates himself*
        c. **John is able to be shaved by himself*

                                                   [PARAPHRASING CHAPIN 1967]

Notice that the rules of Subject Raising and *Neg*-Raising apply to nonfactive verbs like *believe* but not to factive verbs like *regret*:

(4.45) a. *I believe that John left*
        b. *I believe John to have left*

(4.46) a. *I believe that John didn't leave*
        b. *I don't believe that John left*

(4.47) a. *I regret that John left*
        b. **I regret John to have left*

(4.48) a. *I regret that John didn't leave*
        b. **I don't regret that John left*   (≠ 4.48a)

We can explain this if we assume that every factive verb takes a complement headed by the noun *fact*, as in (4.49):

(4.49)

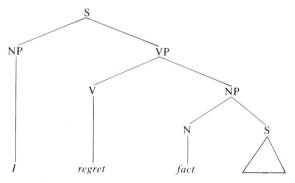

The nonextractability of subjects and negatives now follows automatically from the constraint proposed in Ross (1968) prohibiting movement out of a clause with a lexical head noun.

                              [PARAPHRASING KIPARSKY and KIPARSKY 1970]

4.1.4. Novel or Unusual Argument Types for Abstract Deep Structures

In the following pages I will mention a few types of arguments which seem to have appeared for the first time in the late 1960s (and, in general, seem to have disappeared soon afterward). What they have in common is that, without exception, they reinforced the other arguments for very abstract deep structures.

One very commonly used argument in this period was based on the idea that if two putative syntactic categories share some syntactic feature, they are in reality members of the SAME category. I will give two well-known examples:

Adjectives and verbs are both subcategorized with respect to the features [±STATIVE] and [± ____S]. Note:

(4.50)   a.   *Look at the picture*   [+VERB, −STATIVE]
         b.   **Know that Bill went there*   [+VERB, +STATIVE]

(4.51)   a.   *Don't be noisy*   [+ADJECTIVE, −STATIVE]
         b.   **Don't be tall*   [+ADJECTIVE, +STATIVE]

(4.52)   a.   *John hoped that Bill would leave*   [+VERB, +____S]
         b.   **John elapsed that Bill would leave* [+VERB, −____S]

(4.53)   a.   *John was sure that Bill would leave*   [+ADJECTIVE,
              +____S]
         b.   **John was fat that Bill would leave*   [+ADJECTIVE,
              −____S]

Therefore, adjectives and verbs are members of the same category "Verb."
                                          [PARAPHRASING G. LAKOFF 1970a]

The verb *force* requires that the verb in the next lower sentence be [−STATIVE]:

(4.54)   a.   *I forced John to eat his dinner*
         b.   **I forced John to know the answer*

But note:

(4.55)   **I forced John to have eaten his dinner*

Clearly, the auxiliary *have* must be marked [+STATIVE]. But if so, it shares a feature with a true verb and is therefore a verb itself.
                                          [PARAPHRASING ROSS 1969b]

Many arguments were given citing analyses from other languages to bolster some particular analysis for English. In general, these were only supporting arguments—I do not believe that it was ever regarded as a sufficient condition to establish an abstract structure for English that such a structure could be motivated easily in some foreign language. Nevertheless, these arguments were regarded as very persuasive and were cited frequently:

The complementizer *for* and its following NP are dominated by NP as in (4.56):

(4.56)

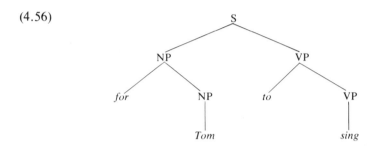

"This accords with the fact that in many languages the complementizer corresponding to *for* appears as a case attached to all nouns that are part of this NP [R. Lakoff 1968:27]."

[PARAPHRASING R. LAKOFF 1968]

Support for (4.57b) as the deep structure of (4.57a) comes from the fact that in "various African, Asian, and Indian languages, it appears that the only way to say, for example, *I shot John in the yard* is to say something equivalent to *My shooting John was located in the yard* [R. Lakoff 1968:67]."

(4.57)   a. *I shot John in the yard*

b.   *it S was in the yard*

[PARAPHRASING R. LAKOFF 1968]

The fact that in many American Indian languages, such as Mohawk and Hidatsa, and in African languages, such as Gã, a language of Ghana, adjectives are transparently verbal supports the analysis of G. Lakoff (1970a), in which adjectives are claimed to be verbs in deep structure.

[PARAPHRASING ROSS 1969a]

The analysis of prepositions as underlying verbs receives support from Indonesian, where (4.58a) is (4.58b), translated literally as (4.58c):

(4.58)   a. *He ran to the river*
         b. *Dia berlari sampai sungai*
         c. 'He ran arrived river'

[PARAPHRASING BECKER and ARMS 1969]

Finally, at least once, an abstract analysis was motivated by appealing to a native speaker's supposed INTUITIONS ABOUT UNDERLYING STRUC- TURES. G. Lakoff (1970a) cited sentence pairs like the following:

(4.59)   a. *I enjoy movies*
         b. *Movies are enjoyable to me*

He argued that these sentences were transformationally related, and that the rule relating them "has applied to the sentence containing the adjective. We know this from our intuitions about what the underlying subjects and objects are . . . [G. Lakoff 1970a:126]."

4.2. THE BIRTH OF GENERATIVE SEMANTICS

Up to 1967, a battery of arguments by many leading transformational grammarians led consistently in one direction—to deep structures extremely distant from surface structure and at the same time exhibiting semantic relations far more straightforwardly than the more shallow deep structures suggested in Chomsky (1965) and argued for in depth in Rosenbaum (1967). Yet in no way had the fundamental ASSUMPTIONS of Katz and Postal (1964) and Chomsky (1965) been challenged. Quite the contrary, in fact—as we have seen, the abstract analyses arrived at crucially depended on their essential correctness.

But this resulted in a paradoxical situation. The more abstract deep structures became, the more ANOTHER aspect of Chomskyan deep structure seemed incompatible with these results. This was the hypothesis that at deep structure, all lexical items be inserted into the phrase-marker. G. Lakoff (1970a) had argued that in the same fashion that one could motivate abstract deep structures based on selectional restrictions holding BETWEEN lexical items, one could motivate—in fact was forced to motivate—abstract structures based on restrictions holding WITHIN lexical items. Given that it was correct to derive *John thickened the sauce* from (roughly) *John caused*

– *the sauce thicken*, it was absolutely necessary to derive *John killed Bill* from (roughly) *John caused – Bill die*. Otherwise, two separate (and unrelated) projection rules would be necessary to interpret causative sentences. Since he did not question the *Aspects* assumption that lexical items were inserted at deep structure, Lakoff had no choice but to posit the following deep structure for this sentence:

(4.60)

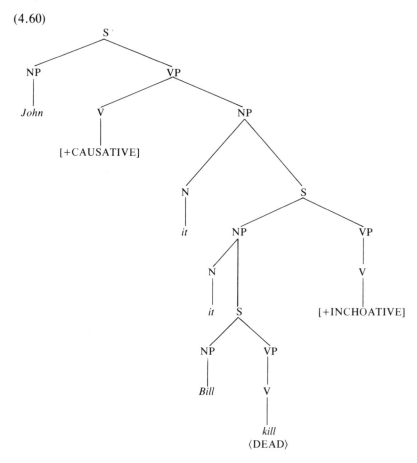

That is, *kill* had to be inserted in the deep structure with the meaning 'dead' (in angle brackets), marked not only to undergo the transformations merging its features with the higher abstract verbs of causation and inchoation but marked TO MEET OBLIGATORILY THEIR STRUCTURAL DESCRIPTION AS WELL.

Clearly, having *kill* in the deep structure prior to the application of the collapsing rules led to loss of generalization. It not only demanded structural description features, but forced the unnatural lexical representation of *kill* as ⟨DEAD⟩.

The step to take was obvious—allow deep structures to represent meanings only, and insert the lexical item *kill* only AFTER the collapsing transformation (soon to be christened "Predicate Raising") applied. The fact that, by 1967, deep structures all but represented the meaning of the sentence anyway (at least given the abstract syntacticians' view of meaning at the time), made this step a completely natural one to take.

The idea of getting rid of deep structure as an independent level was first suggested in a widely circulated letter which George Lakoff and John R. Ross wrote to Arnold Zwicky in March 1967 (now published as Lakoff and Ross 1976).[1] They characterized the defining criteria for the level of deep structure as Chomsky conceived it in *Aspects* by the following four properties:

1. The base of the simplest syntactic component.
2. The place where co-occurrence and selectional restrictions are defined.
3. The place where basic grammatical relations are defined.
4. The place where lexical items are inserted from the lexicon.

But, they argued, all the evidence pointed to Properties 1, 2, and 3 being none other than semantic representation—no "intermediate" level of deep structure had these properties. And as far as Property 4 is concerned, they pointed to examples like those discussed above to illustrate that some transformations have to apply before lexical items enter the derivation.[2]

The new deep structureless theory, now dubbed "generative semantics," won virtually all of the abstract syntacticians to its banner. I will describe its fate in considerable detail in the next chapter.

4.3. CHOMSKY'S RESPONSE TO ABSTRACT SYNTAX

Chomsky launched his counteroffensive to abstract syntax upon his return from Berkeley at the beginning of 1967—at about the same time that its practitioners were transforming themselves into generative semanticists. The principle document of this counteroffensive, his paper "Remarks on Nominalization" (Chomsky 1970), argued that fundamental syntactic generalizations can be captured only if the syntactic deep structure level exists, and is moreover much LESS abstract than was commonly held at the time— less abstract even than the pre-abstract syntax analyses sketched in *Aspects*.

[1] George Lakoff had actually proposed as early as 1963 that the rules of the base generate semantic structures. However, the not very widely circulated mimeographed paper in which he proposed this (now published as G. Lakoff 1976a) was largely forgotten during the later years of the decade.

[2] Lakoff and Ross's specific example of post-transformational lexical insertion involved idioms, not causatives.

Concentrating on nominalizations, a central area of syntax, he argued that, contrary to previous analyses (including his own), those which are clearly nouns in surface structure are not derived transformationally from verbs. Rather, they are entered as nouns in the lexicon. Borrowing a term from Chapin (1967), he characterized this view as the "lexicalist hypothesis" and strongly implied that this hypothesis should be extended to rule out ALL category-changing transformational rules.

Given that "Remarks" was destined to underlie most of the work in syntax done in the 1970s, it is hard to appreciate today how unsuccessful it was when it appeared in 1967. The fact is that it convinced very few at that time who were not Chomsky's own students (a group whose members, presumably, were predisposed to be convinced). I will try to explain why as I develop Chomsky's ideas.

4.3.1. The Arguments for the Lexicalist Hypothesis

Chomsky devoted the bulk of the "Remarks" paper to arguing that "derived nominals,"[3] illustrated by the boldface italic words in (4.61), should be entered in the lexicon directly as nouns, rather than be derived by a transformational rule from their related verbs (or adjectives):

(4.61)   a. *John's **refusal** of the offer*
        b. *Mary's great **skill** at tennis*
        c. *the **payment** of one hundred dollars to the fund*
        d. *Helen's **marriage** to Terry*
        e. *an itinerant **laborer***

In the remainder of this section I will paraphrase Chomsky's three principal arguments for this position:

> **Argument I:** Derived nominals (DN's) occur in sentences correspond- ing to base structures, but never to transformationally derived structures. This is explained automatically if DN's are deep structure nouns—the structural description of Raising-to-Object, Particle Movement, Dative Movement, etc. blocks nouns from undergoing those rules, automatically predicting the ungrammaticality of the (d) phrases of Examples (4.62)– (4.64):

(4.62)   a.   *John believed that Bill was a fool* $\longrightarrow$ RAISING-TO-OBJECT
        b.   *John believed Bill to be a fool*
        c.   *John's belief that Bill was a fool* $\longrightarrow\!\!\!\times\!\!\!\longrightarrow$
        d.   **John's belief of Bill to be a fool*

---

[3] The term "derived nominal" created no end of confusion, since these were just those nominalizations which Chomsky claimed were NOT derived transformationally. Presumably they were so labeled because they exhibit derivational morphology.

(4.63)   a.   *John looked up the answer* ⟶ PARTICLE MOVEMENT
          b.   *John looked the answer up*
          c.   *John's looking up of the answer* ⟶⥇⟶
          d.   **John's looking of the answer up*

(4.64)   a.   *John gave the book to Bill* ⟶ DATIVE MOVEMENT
          b.   *John gave Bill the book*
          c.   *John's gift of the book to Bill* ⟶⥇⟶
          d.   **John's gift of Bill of the book*

    Argument II: A transformational rule should capture a regular productive relationship. But the relationship between DN's and their corresponding verbs is highly IRREGULAR. Not only does every verb not have a corresponding DN, but every DN does not have a corresponding verb. Furthermore, the meaning relation between verbs and DN's is highly idiosyncratic. Consider, for example, the relation between *do* and *deed, marry* and *marriage, ignore* and *ignorance*. Where no verb corresponding to a DN exists, a transformational account must invent a totally abstract verb marked to meet obligatorily the structural description of the nominalization transformation. The lengths the transformational account has to go to make the underlying forms "mean the same" as the derived forms reduces to vacuity the hypothesis that transformational rules do not change meaning. On the other hand, a lexical treatment of DN's is the natural way to capture their irregular behavior—the lexicon, after all, is the repository of what is idiosyncratic in language. We can capture lexically the shared features of the verb *refuse* and the noun *refusal*, for example, by considering *refuse* to be lexically neutral between N and V, and allowing the entry to contain a "N" branch and a "V" branch. The properties common to *refuse* and *refusal* need to be represented only once in the neutral entry, while their distinct properties can be represented on the appropriate branch.

    That still leaves the problem of the similarity of co-occurrence restrictions holding within sentences and those holding within noun phrases. For example, consider (4.65a) and (4.65b):

(4.65)   a.   [$_{NP}$*John*] [$_V$*proved*] [$_{NP}$*the theorem*]
          b.   *Several of* [$_{NP}$*John*]'*s* [$_N$*proofs*] *of* [$_{NP}$*the theorem*]

We still have to capture the fact that the noun phrase subject of *prove* corresponds to the noun phrase in the determiner of *proof*, and the noun phrase object of *prove* corresponds to the noun phrase in the prepositional phrase following *proof*. The transformationalist account does this automatically by deriving phrases like (4.65b) from full sentences.

    A lexicalist account can handle these facts as well, if a formalism is devised that exploits the internal similarities of the major categories. Assume rules (4.66a–c) as the basic phrase-structure rules of English (oversimplified, of course):

(4.66)   a. $S \rightarrow \bar{\bar{N}} \ \bar{\bar{V}}$
          b. $\bar{\bar{X}} \rightarrow [\text{Spec}, \bar{X}]\bar{X}$ (Spec = specifier)
          c. $\bar{X} \rightarrow X . . .$ (where X can be N, A, or V)

Now the deep structures of (4.65a–b) will be (4.67a–b), respectively:

(4.67)   a.

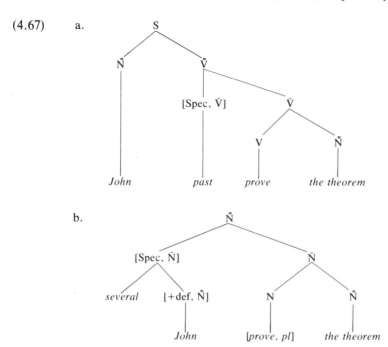

Now note that

> the internal structure of the nominal [(4.67b)] mirrors that of the sentence [(4.67a)]. The strict subcategorization features of the lexical item *prove* take account of the phrases V̄ and N̄ dominating the category to which it is assigned in [(4.67a), (4.67b)], respectively. Its selectional features refer to the heads of the associated phrases, which are the same in both cases [Chomsky 1970:211].

Put simply, this "X-bar convention" allows the co-occurrence restrictions holding within sentences to be generalized to hold within noun phrases as well, thereby eliminating what is perhaps the major motivation for a transformational treatment of DN's.[4]

Argument III: The structures that DN's occur in resemble noun phrases in every way. They can contain determiners, prenominal adjectives, and prepositional phrase complements, but disallow adverbs, nega-

---

[4] The X-bar convention was seen to provide a solution to the long-standing problem of characterizing the notion "head of a phrase." Lyons (1968) had pointed out a serious problem with the current transformationalist view of base rules—it was unable to capture the generalization that noun phrases have nouns as heads, verb phrases have verbs as heads, etc. (that is, that such constructions are endocentric). The rules of (4.66), by formally capturing this relationship, were seen as a plus for the lexicalist approach. For interesting early discussions of the problem of endocentricity, see Postal (1964b) and the reply in Robinson (1970).

tion, aspect, and tense. This follows automatically if DN's are lexical nouns—we would expect them to have the same distribution as ordinary nouns. A transformational analysis is forced to posit ad hoc conditions on the T-rule to ensure that the underlying sentences end up looking like surface noun phrases.

4.3.2. The Initial Failure of Lexicalism

Why was Chomsky so extremely unsuccessful in his initial attempt to win support for the lexicalist alternative to abstract syntax? There are several reasons. First, there was the half-hearted nature of his counterattack. Whereas the abstract syntacticians proselytized for their model with the zeal of born-again Christians (in the fall of 1966 Ross lectured for 18 hours in 3 days at the University of Illinois), Chomsky confined his rebuttal to lectures at MIT and the "Remarks" paper. This is hardly surprising—in the late 1960s he had far weightier issues on his mind than the abstractness of underlying syntactic structure. As the American war against Vietnam escalated, Chomsky found more and more of his time devoted to political rather than linguistic activism.

Second, there were Chomsky's own tactical blunders. Since the conclusions of "Remarks" went contrary to all of the work that had been done in syntax in the previous several years, Chomsky carried a heavy burden— he had to win over the majority. But he chose the wrong strategy to win his fight. With few exceptions, he did not challenge the ARGUMENTS of the abstract syntacticians which, as we shall see, were exceedingly vulnerable. Rather, he challenged their CONCLUSIONS. That is, he developed his own arguments for lexicalism. That meant that any flaws (real or apparent) in his own presentation counted against him, while he himself, because of his strategy, missed scoring many corresponding "points" against the majority. And there were enough perceived flaws in his reasoning (as we shall see) to deter most syntacticians from budging an inch.

Another tactical blunder of Chomsky's was his adoption of the terms "lexicalism" and "lexicalist hypothesis" to describe his position. Since they contrasted with "transformationalism" and "transformationalist hypothesis," they had obvious built-in negative emotional overtones. To the unsophisticated, it seemed that Chomsky was leading an astonishing rearguard attack on transformational grammar itself. It was easy to conclude that Chomsky was actually advocating unilluminating solutions to problems over motivated ones, since in the minds of many, phrase-structural and lexical solutions were devoid of interest, and the transformational component was the EXPLANATORY component of the grammar. While such a confused reaction may have been inevitable WHATEVER terminology Chomsky may have chosen, the negative consequences would have been lessened in intensity had he taken greater care in this regard.

Finally, numerous objections were raised to Chomsky's three principal arguments for his hypothesis.[5] Many counterexamples were found to the claim that transformationally derived structures are nonnominalizable. Chomsky discussed one himself: *John's rejection by the committee,* where Passive (apparently) preceded the application of a transformation forming the DN (for discussion of other rules which seem to feed nominalization, see especially Ross 1973a, Postal 1974, and Pullum 1978). Moreover, Newmeyer (1971, 1976) pointed out that even if Chomsky's observations are correct, a precyclic Nominalization makes identical predictions to the lexicalist hypothesis, as far as the productivity argument is concerned.

Chomsky attempted to explain away the Passive case by allowing the rule of Passive to apply WITHIN NOUN PHRASES. Thus, *rejection* could be a noun in the lexicon and *John's rejection by the committee* could be derived without a Nominalization transformation. But this was perceived as a totally ad hoc maneuver by many linguists (see McCawley 1975). If Passive "applies within noun phrases," then why don't the other cyclic transformations apply as well? What principle determines that the domain of Dative Movement, say, is only S, but that of Passive is both S and NP?

Chomsky's arguments based on the irregularity of the verb–DN relation did not convince many of his opponents for several reasons. First, the generative semantic hypothesis that lexical items are inserted AFTER transformations such as Nominalization apply obviated the need for abstract verbs with structural description features, which Chomsky saw as the major defect of the transformational account. Second, since Chomsky made no specific proposal for accounting for the paraphrase relationship between, say, *John's refusal was unexpected* and *the fact that John refused was unexpected,* few abstract syntacticians saw any reason to give up their Nominalization transformation, which, though no doubt messy, would account for the relation automatically.

Note in addition that the X-bar notation, at least in the preliminary "Remarks" version, was met with nothing but bewilderment. While, formally, it claimed parallel internal structures between adjective, noun, and predicate phrases, in order for the co-occurrence arguments to go through, Chomsky needed a formalism which imputed parallel internal structures to NOUN PHRASES and SENTENCES. Yet rules (4.66 a–c) do not predict such a parallel at all. But they do predict apparently nonexistent parallels between adjective phrase, noun phrase, and verb phrase "specifiers," i.e., between *more, very,* etc. ([Spec, $\bar{A}$]), determiners ([Spec, $\bar{N}$]), and auxiliaries ([Spec, $\bar{V}$]). Finally, the X-bar notation entailed that not only lexical categories, but major categories as well, be subcategorized with respect to syntactic features. Chomsky himself (1965: 188) had earlier rejected this possibility be-

---

[5] It may appear that I am guilty of anachronism in this section, since many of the specific points raised were not written, much less published, until the 1970s. However, most if not all of the arguments below were well known and frequently discussed in the late 1960s.

cause of its lack of empirical motivation and its concomitant weakening of linguistic theory.

The argument based on the identical internal structures of phrases containing DN's and "ordinary" nouns was regarded at that time as by far the most convincing one for the lexicalist hypothesis. Indeed, every attempt to actually characterize the properties of the Nominalization transformation (see Fraser 1970, for example) led to numerous ad hoc conditions being placed on it just to make the output look like a noun phrase. Yet even here, the facts seemed to be less clear-cut than Chomsky would have them. Ross (1973a) and Bedell (1974) pointed out that, rather than there being two poles, with noun phrases (containing DN's) at one pole and sentences (containing gerunds) at the other, there is an entire CONTINUUM of construction types, from very "sentence like" at one pole (4.68a) to very "unsentence like" at the other (4.68f):

(4.68)   a. *that John proved theorems*
         b. *for John to prove theorems*
         c. *John's proving theorems*
         d. *John's proof of theorems*
         e. *John's proofs of theorems*
         f. *John's book of theorems*

Whatever the INTERPRETATION of this observation may have been (and there have been several), it tended to diminish the force of Chomsky's final argument.

Finally, a major barrier to the acceptance of "Remarks" was its extreme inexplicitness on almost every point. No rules other than (4.66a–c) were formalized, yet, as Botha (1976) has pointed out, "Remarks" contains no fewer than 20 vaguely adumbrated grammatical processes, most quite unfamiliar. Furthermore, Chomsky, introduced 3 novel TYPES of processes—rules of analogy, nonamalgamatory projection rules, and lexical redundancy rules—practically without comment. It is hardly surprising, then, that his paper had little impact outside MIT. In 1967, generative semantics appeared to be the wave of the future, and lexicalism nothing but a dead end.

4.4. A CLOSER LOOK AT THE ARGUMENTS FOR ABSTRACT SYNTAX

In Section 4.1 I presented the arguments for highly abstract deep structures just as the abstract syntacticians themselves developed them—that is, without questioning their validity. But even before the 1960s ended, two important props had been knocked out from under the entire abstract syntactic enterprise. First, it became generally acknowledged that selectional restrictions were NOT defined at an intermediate level of structure, such as the deep structure of *Aspects*. Second, counterexample after counterexample was constructed to the Katz–Postal hypothesis, upon which so many arguments for abstract deep structures were based. And many of the more "syntactic" arguments for abstract syntax began to be questioned with increased vigor as well. While few hard-core generative semanticists were moved by any of these points, the fact that counterarguments to their conclusions were in the air in the 1960s helped contribute to the formation of a pool of "undecideds," which would facilitate the victory of nonabstract syntax in the 1970s.

4.4.1. The Question of Selectional Restrictions

Jackendoff (1972) and McCawley (1968a, b) independently put forward arguments that selectional restrictions are defined, not at the level of deep structure, but at the level of semantic representation.

Jackendoff's most convincing examples involved sentences like the following:

(4.69)   a.   *I ate something that was the result of what Bill acknowledged to be a new baking process*
         b.   **I ate something that was the result of what Bill acknowledged to be a syntactic transformation*

Intuitively, (4.69b) is ill-formed because *a syntactic transformation* is abstract and one cannot eat an abstraction. Yet this noun phrase is not the direct object of *eat* in the deep structure of (4.69b), but is deeply embedded inside its direct object. To capture the **eat–a syntactic transformation* restriction at the level of deep structure, Jackendoff argued, would involve the selectional machinery duplicating all the work of the semantic component. However, if selection is handled semantically, the restriction of *eat* to nonabstract objects can be stated simply AFTER the projection rules have amalgamated the readings of the material in the object in *eat*, characterizing the object in (4.69a) as "nonabstract" and that in (4.69b) as "abstract."

McCawley's arguments are even better known. First, as can be easily concluded by observing the sentences of (4.70), deep structure selection would require an unacceptably large number of "syntactic features" at that level to block their generation. Seemingly, their deviance should be attributed to semantic or pragmatic factors, rather than syntactic:

(4.70)   a.   **That verb is in the indicative tense*
         b.   **Bernstein's theorem is nondenumerable*
         c.   **John diagonalized that differentiable manifold*
         d.   **That election is green*
         e.   **I ate three phonemes for breakfast*

f. *He pronounces diffuseness too loud
g. *My hair is bleeding
h. *That unicorn's left horn is black

Second, and more important, paraphrases have the same selectional restrictions. Any verb in English that can take *bachelor* for its subject can take *unmarried man* as well. By the same token, (4.71b) is deviant for the same reason as (4.71a):

(4.71) a. *My sister is the father of two
        b. *My buxom neighbor is the father of two

It is not clear how the *Aspects* approach, which considers selectional restrictions as restrictions holding between lexical items, could account for these facts. Yet they lend themselves quite naturally to a restriction stated at the level of semantic representation.

Finally, whenever grammatical features and semantic features are in conflict, selection is based on the latter, not the former. There are many verbs in German, for example, that occur with only semantically female subjects, but none that take only grammatically feminine subjects. Likewise, despite (4.72), it is not the case that the verb *count* requires a grammatically plural object:

(4.72) a. *I counted the boy
        b. I counted the boys

Count in fact CAN take a grammatically singular object as long as that object is semantically plural:

(4.73) I counted the crowd.

One would think that the discovery that selection is semantic would have been perceived to WEAKEN the case for abstract syntax. After all, if selectional restrictions are not defined syntactically, then it is clearly illegitimate to use them to "find" a syntactic level. If selectional restrictions are semantic, any arguments for a deep structure for a particular sentence based on them are going to end up motivating something close to the semantic representation as the deep structure. Put simply, arguments for deep structure based on selectional restrictions are going to lead INEVITABLY to generative semantics.

This point seemed to be totally lost on abstract syntacticians, who regarded selection being semantic as INDEPENDENT EVIDENCE for generative semantics (see Lakoff and Ross 1976). Their reasoning seemed to be that one less thing statable at deep structure is one more argument for scrapping that level entirely. But at the same time, they failed to reevaluate their many arguments for abstract deep structures based on the assumption that selectional restrictions defined an independent syntactic level.[6]

Abstract syntacticians simply assumed without argument that strict subcategorization restrictions were semantic as well (see R. Lakoff 1968: 17; McCawley 1968a: 136; Lakoff and Ross 1976: 160). Naturally, analogous reasoning led them to see this as one more argument for abandoning deep structure. But here, the case for a semantic treatment is much less persuasive than with selectional restrictions. Oehrle (1975) and Wasow (1976) cite numerous examples of strict subcategorization not predictable from meaning:

> Or consider the difference between *dine, devour* and *eat* with respect to transitivity: *dine* is intransitive, *devour* requires an object, and *eat* takes an optional object. Although the meanings of these words are subtly different, nothing in those differences predicts the difference with respect to transitivity (i.e., all seem to designate two-place predicates involving both some sort of food and a consumer of food) [Wasow 1976: 282].

4.4.2. Problems with the Katz–Postal Hypothesis

So intuitively appealing was the Katz–Postal hypothesis that no abstract syntactician even questioned it. And as we have seen, incredibly abstract deep structures resulted from using it as a heuristic. It was the assumption of Katz–Postal which would lead most of all to deep structures resembling the formulas of symbolic logic translated into phrase-structure notation (see Section 5.4.4). Every difference of logical scope led to another level of embedding in the deep structure and another "verb" corresponding to a logical operator.

Yet there were lingering doubts throughout the mid 1960s that deep structures were semantically complete and unique, and that under no circumstances did a T-rule change meaning. Chomsky expressed these doubts in a footnote to *Aspects* (1965: 224), where he reiterated his feeling that *everyone in the room knows at least two languages* and *at least two languages are known by everyone in the room* differed in meaning. Yet he conceded that both interpretations might be "latent" in each sentence. A couple of years later he gave his doubts even stronger voice, though he neither gave specific examples nor made specific proposals: "In fact, I think that a reasonable explication of the term 'semantic interpretation' would lead to the conclusion that surface structure also contributes in a restricted but important way to semantic interpretation, but I will say no more about this matter here [Chomsky 1967: 407]."

---

[6] Chomsky has continued to maintain (in class lectures) that at least SOME selection is syntactic, citing as evidence sentences like **the boy who was turned by magic into a swarm of bees dispersed.* For a critical evaluation of the arguments against syntactic selection, see Seegmiller (1974).

In the last few years of the 1960s there was a great outpouring of examples from Chomsky and his students of superficial levels of syntactic structure playing an important role in determining semantic interpretation. Taken as a whole, they seemed to indicate that any strong form of the Katz-Postal hypothesis had to be false—everything needed for semantic interpretation was NOT present in the deep structure. And, while one could still legalistically maintain that transformations did not CHANGE meaning, one would have to concede that all of meaning was not DETERMINED before the application of the transformational rules. Some examples:

> The following sentences clearly differ in meaning, suggesting that Passive is a meaning-changing transformation:

(4.74)   a. *Many arrows did not hit the target*
           b. *The target was not hit by many arrows*

> Klima's (1964) rule placing negatives also changes meaning:

(4.75)   a. *Not much shrapnel hit the soldier*
           b. *Much shrapnel did not hit the soldier*

> Note that in (4.74) and (4.75) it is the SURFACE ORDER of quantifier and negative that determines the interpretation. The element on the left in surface structure is interpreted as having "wider scope."
>   [PARAPHRASING JACKENDOFF 1969]

> The *some–any* transformation of Klima (1964) also changes meaning, as is evidenced by the nonsynonymy of (4.76a–b):

(4.76)   a. *I couldn't answer some of the questions*
           b. *I couldn't answer any of the questions*
>   [PARAPHRASING PARTEE 1971]

> The scope of elements like *only* and *even* is determined by their surface structure position:

(4.77)   a. *Only John reads books on politics*
           b. *John only reads books on politics*
           c. *John reads only books on politics*
>   [PARAPHRASING KURODA 1969]

> Consider questions (4.78a–c) and their "natural responses" (4.79a–c), respectively:

(4.78) a. *Was John told to look out for an ex-convict with a red **shirt**?*
   b. *Was John told to look out for a red-shirted **ex-convict**?*
   c. *Was John told to look out for an ex-convict with a shirt that is **red**?*

(4.79) a. *No, John was told to look out for an ex-convict with a red **tie***
   b. *No, John was told to look out for a red-shirted **car salesman***
   c. *No, John was told to look out for an ex-convict with a shirt that is **green***

Loosely put, the focused (questioned) element seems to be part of the phrase which contains the intonation center, and the presupposition expressed by the sentence is, equally loosely put, the remainder of the sentence. Notice that a variety of phrases containing the intonation center can act as focus. The following are also natural responses to (4.78a):

(4.80) a. *No, he was told to look out for an ex-convict with a **carnation***
   b. *No, he was told to look out for an **automobile salesman***

The crucial point is that focusable phrases are SURFACE STRUCTURE phrases. Note question (4.81) and its natural responses (4.82a–c):

(4.81) *Is John certain to **win**?*

(4.82) a. *No, he is certain to **lose**.*
   b. *No, he's likely not to be **nominated**.*
   c. *No, the election won't ever **happen***

Therefore, the interpretation of focus and presupposition must take place at surface structure.

[PARAPHRASING CHOMSKY 1971]

The meanings of certain modal auxiliaries depend on their surface structure position. Note:

(4.83) a. *I shall go downtown*
   b. *Shall I go downtown?*

In (4.83a), *shall* is essentially a tense-marker. In (4.83b), it means 'should.' This suggests that the interpretation of the meaning of *shall* takes place after the transformation forming questions.

[PARAPHRASING CHOMSKY 1971, who cites JOSEPH EMONDS]

Consider:

(4.84) *John hit Bill and then George hit him*

If *him* is unstressed, it refers to *Bill*. If *him* is stressed, it refers to *John*. This suggests that the interpretation of anaphoric expressions must follow stress placement and clearly not take place at deep structure.
[PARAPHRASING CHOMSKY 1971, who cites ADRIAN AKMAJIAN and RAY DOUGHERTY]

Consider the following:

(4.85)   a. *Einstein has visited Princeton*
          b. *Princeton has been visited by Einstein*

In (4.85a), there is the presupposition that Einstein is still alive. No such presupposition holds in (4.85b). This suggests that the presupposition does not hold under passivization or, alternatively, that presupposition is determined at the level of surface structure.
[PARAPHRASING CHOMSKY 1971]

If we assume that (4.86b) is a passivized form of (4.86a), as seems natural, then the scope of (certain) adverbs must be interpreted at surface structure. In (4.86a) *cleverly* modifies *the doctor;* in (4.86b) it modifies *John*:

(4.86)   a. *The doctor cleverly has examined John*
          b. *John cleverly has been examined by the doctor*

[PARAPHRASING FILLMORE 1966 and JACKENDOFF 1972]

Consider the meaning difference between (4.87a) and (4.87b):

(4.87)   a. *It is certain that nobody will pass the test*
          b. *Nobody is certain to pass the test*

We must conclude that either Subject Raising is a meaning-changing transformation or (more naturally) that the relative scope of *certain* and *nobody* is determined after the application of this rule.
[PARAPHRASING PARTEE 1971]

Taken at face value, these examples struck right at the heart of the abstract syntactic analyses. They strongly suggested that criteria based on meaning are all but worthless for motivating deep structures. But, by and large, generative semanticists were not impressed—by this point they had raised the Katz–Postal hypothesis to axiomatic status. To deal with the above facts they developed a theoretical construct—the global rule—which allowed them to keep their abstract syntactic analyses intact and comply with the letter, if not the spirit, of the Katz-Postal hypothesis. I will return to this in the next chapter.

On the other hand, the discovery that surface structure was relevant to semantic interpretation was seen as strong independent if indirect support for Chomsky's faltering lexicalist hypothesis. While surface interpretation and lexicalism are logically independent, the realization that superficial syntatic properties play an essential role in the grammar was naturally a shot in the arm for lexicalism, which began to gain credibility as a result. I will outline the further development of this model in Section 5.2 and in Chapter 6.

4.4.3. The Syntactic Arguments for Abstract Syntax

The arguments for abstract deep structures NOT based on selectional restrictions or the Katz-Postal hypothesis have not fared much better than the others over the years. This is most of all true of the category reduction arguments—those arguments which purported to show that C's are really D's, where C and D are both hypothesized syntactic categories. McCawley himself (1977a) pointed out that abstract syntacticians tended to recognize SUFFICIENT conditions for membership in the same category, but never NECESSARY ones. For example, contrast (4.36) (repeated here for convenience) with (4.88a-c):

[4.36]   *John is happy, but he doesn't look it*

(4.88)   a. **John is happy, but I can't imagine why he is it*
          b. **John isn't happy, but he hopes to become it*
          c. **John is happy, and I'm it too*

For Ross, (4.36) provided sufficient justification for adjectives being NP's. He never felt obligated to discuss the prima facie counterexamples (4.88a-c).

Along the same lines, abstract syntacticians provided arguments that prepositional phrases were noun phrases [based on sentences like (4.37)-(4.38)] and were also verb phrases [based on sentences like (4.18)], but made no attempt to explain this apparent contradiction. Even if one of these two alternatives were correct, it certainly raised questions which no abstract syntactician attempted to answer. For example, if PP's are NP's, then why can't (4.89a) be passivized to (4.89b)? If PP's are VP's, then why should VP-Deletion treat *lives near the school* as a constituent, as (4.90a-b) show that it does:

(4.89)   a.   *John ate at the table*
          b.   **At the table was eaten by John*

(4.90)   a.   *John lives near the school and Bill lives near the school too*
         b.   *John lives near the school and Bill does too*

Other counterarguments to abstract analyses of this type are found in Schachter (1973) and Baker (1975).

Chomsky (1971) gave some examples which cast considerable doubt on the assumption that *it* replaces only constituents—a test which [as we have seen from (4.41)] often led to highly abstract structures. Note:

(4.91)   *Ten errors were committed by the Red Sox and the Yankees, but it would never have happened with any two other teams*

Consistency would lead to the conclusion that the derived subject and following passivized verb be considered a noun phrase constituent of the sentence, clearly a reductio of the entire test.

One argument for joint category membership was immediately attacked by lexicalists (Chomsky 1970) and has been subject to many critiques since then, the most exhaustive by Culicover (1977). This is the argument that two categories must be conflated if they share features. Chomsky pointed out that not only adjectives and verbs share the feature "stative," but nouns as well. This would lead logically to nouns, adjectives, and verbs all being in the same category. Note:

(4.92)   a.   *Be a hero.*   [−STATIVE]
         b.   **Be a person.*   [+STATIVE]

While such a conclusion was not repellent to abstract syntacticians—Bach (1968), in fact, had proposed it on independent grounds—the same type of test could have been used to conflate ALL categories into one. Very few grammarians would have found such a conclusion acceptable.

4.5. CASE GRAMMAR

In the late 1960s, the relatively shallow deep structures of *Aspects* were attacked from another quarter. In a number of interesting papers, Charles Fillmore (1966, 1968, 1969a, 1971a,b) developed an alternative model of grammar whose distinguishing feature is that at the deepest syntactic level, a sentence consists of a verb and an unordered series of semantic CASES, drawn from a universal vocabulary.

Fillmore was worried in particular about the seeming inability of the *Aspects* model to represent both categorial and functional information pertaining to prepositional phrases. His starting point was the observation that *Aspects* could not adequately capture the fact that expressions such as *in the room, toward the moon, on the next day, in a careless way, with a sharp knife,* and *by my brother* are simultaneously prepositional phrases and adverbials of location, direction, time, manner, instrument, and agent, respectively. His solution was that prepositional phrases in underlying syntactic structure be reanalyzed as noun phrases with an associated prepositional "case-marker," both NP and case-marker being dominated by a case symbol capturing that NP's semantic function in the sentence. Generality, he claimed, then demanded that EVERY NP (even those which, as surface subjects, have no associated preposition) be so represented in underlying structure.

Notice how similar Fillmore's methodology was to that of the other abstract syntacticians. Both were driven by the desire to represent at deep structure as much semantic information as possible, with the consequence of that level being pushed closer to semantic representation.

While the specific set of case relationships (and their definitions) has varied from paper to paper, the following list (from Fillmore 1971a) is typical (LOCATIVE has been added from Fillmore 1968):

(4.93)   a. AGENT (A), the instigator of the event
         b. COUNTERAGENT (C), the force or resistance against which the action is carried out
         c. OBJECT (O), the entity that moves or changes or whose position or existence is in consideration
         d. RESULT (R), the entity that comes into existence as a result of the action
         e. INSTRUMENT (I), the stimulus or immediate cause of an event
         f. SOURCE (S), the place from which something moves
         g. GOAL (G), the place to which something moves
         h. EXPERIENCER (E), the entity which receives or accepts or experiences or undergoes the effect of an action (earlier called "Dative")
         i. LOCATIVE (L), the case which identifies the location or spacial orientation of the state or action identified by the verb

I will give a few brief examples (one semantic, one syntactic, one lexical) of the benefits Fillmore felt would accrue by taking "case" to be a primitive notion, in each case paraphrasing Fillmore himself:

I. Semantic benefits. The theory of *Aspects* claims that deep structure is an adequate base for semantic interpretation. This is clearly false. In each of the sentences of (4.94), the noun phrase *the door* bears the same semantic relation to the verb, yet would be considered a deep structure subject in (4.94a) and a deep structure object in (4.94b–d). Conversely, *the door* in (4.94a), *John* in (4.94b), and (4.94d), and *the wind* in (4.94c) all manifest different semantic relations with respect to the verb. Yet in the *Aspects* model, all would be considered deep structure subjects:

(4.94) a. *The door opened*
  b. *John opened the door*
  c. *The wind opened the door*
  d. *John opened the door with a chisel*

Case grammar can capture these relationships straightforwardly. *Open* is a verb which takes an obligatory OBJECT, with an optional AGENT and/ or INSTRUMENT. Hence, at the level of case structure the relevant semantic information is represented directly.

II. Syntactic benefits. Case information can be used to predict which noun phrase will become the subject if more than one noun phrase occurs in a sentence. The following case hierarchy holds for English (Fillmore 1971:42):

(4.95) a. AGENT
  b. EXPERIENCER
  c. INSTRUMENT
  d. OBJECT
  e. SOURCE
  f. GOAL
  g. LOCATION
  h. TIME

If two noun phrases are present in the sentence, the one higher on the hierarchy becomes subject. For example, since AGENT is higher than OBJECT, we predict the grammaticality of (4.94b) rather than (4.96a); since INSTRUMENT is higher than OBJECT, we predict (4.94c) rather than (4.96b):

(4.96) a. **The door opened by John*
  b. **The door opened with/by the wind*

Rules which lead to violations of the hierarchy, like Passive, "register" their violation by means of special morphological elements—*be* + *en* in the case of Passive. There are lexical exceptions to the hierarchy, as well, however. For example, the verb *please* is lexically marked to violate the subject choice rule: hence the grammaticality of (4.97), in which an OB-JECT has been chosen subject in place of the higher ranked EXPERIEN-CER:

(4.97) *The play pleased me*

III. Lexical benefits. By entering verbs in the lexicon associated with their case frames, considerable simplification in that component can be attained. *Like* and *please*, for example, can be regarded as being synony-mous, each with the case frame +[___O + E]; they differ only in their subject selection features. We can give the verb *show* the same semantic representation as *see*, their entries differing only in that the frame feature for *show* contains an A, while that for *see* does not:

(4.98)   a. see; +[____O + E]
         b. show; +[____O + E + A]

Case grammar, at least superficially, seemed a much greater departure from the *Aspects* model than the previously described abstract syntactic model which developed alongside it. Abstract syntax explicitly BASED its conclusions on *Aspects*; case grammar explicitly based its conclusions on the INADEQUACY of *Aspects*. This led Fillmore to break with that theory even before abstract syntax had become generative semantics:

> [Deep structure] is an artificial intermediate level between the empirically discoverable "semantic deep structure" and the observationally accessible surface structure, a level the properties of which have more to do with the methodological commitments of grammarians than with the nature of human languages [Fillmore 1968:88].

One would think, then, that Fillmore would have been in the vanguard of the generative semantic "movement." Nothing could be further from the truth, however. Despite Fillmore's rhetorical abandonment of deep structure, the case structures he posited were far too shallow to please abstract syntax, much less generative semantics. Fillmore (1968) considered the basic structure of a sentence to consist of

> the "proposition," a tenseless set of relationships involving verbs and nouns (and embedded sentences, if there are any), separated from what might be called the "modality" constituent. This latter will include such modalities on the sentence-as-a-whole as negation, tense, mood, and aspect [p. 23].

But contemporaneously with the publication of this paper, generative semanticists were constructing arguments that not only were the "modalities" depropositional, but the cases, "semantic primitives" in Fillmore's view, were themselves decomposable into more basic units. A dramatic testimony to the relative shallowness of the level of case structure is the fact that Stockwell, Schachter, and Partee (1973), an ambitious attempt to construct a complete grammar of English, is based on the compatibility of case grammar and the lexicalist hypothesis!

Fillmore, to be sure, drew case grammar somewhat closer to generative semantics by analyzing the former BENEFACTIVE case preposition *for* as a higher predicate (1971b). But this hardly satisfied generative semanticists, who pointed out (correctly) that the same argumentation should lead to an analogous treatment for ALL cases—that is, to an abandonment of case grammar in favor of generative semantics.

While generative semanticists have attacked case grammar for not being semantically revealing, lexicalists have concentrated on its syntactic shortcomings (see expecially Dougherty 1970a, Chomsky 1972a, and Mellema 1974). Above all else, they have pointed out flaws in the subject selection hierarchy. At best, lexicalists have argued, the subject selection rules would simply supplement the familiar movement transformations, not resulting in any particular support for case grammar. But at worst, they would complicate them considerably, which alternative being correct depending on the correct interpretation of case grammar's rather vague claims about how and where the subject selection rules function in the grammar.

While work in case grammar has always been somewhat outside of "mainstream" transformational work in syntax and semantics, the theory has nevertheless attracted quite a number of adherents over the years, and its possibilities continue to be explored. Two adaptations which deserve mention are the "lexicase" approach of Starosta (1971, 1973) and the "localist" hypothesis of J. Anderson (1971, 1977). Fillmore himself now (1977) appears to have developed a more "functionalist" approach to subject selection in particular and case grammar in general. In fact, the theory has been taken in well over a dozen different directions, with its proponents differing among themselves over such fundamental questions as the number of cases (from three to over a dozen have been proposed) and the means of their identification. While many would agree that there is something right about the notion of "semantic case," the foundational crisis from which case grammar has never emerged has made generative grammarians extremely hesitant to regard it as anything more than a convenient, if somewhat arbitrary, way of classifying the roles that noun phrases play in sentences.

4.6. ABSTRACT SYNTAX: A SUMMARY

While it lasted, abstract syntax wore the mantle of orthodoxy, and that more than anything else explains its phenomenal success. The conclusions of Katz and Postal (1964) about underlying structure fully determining meaning and Chomsky (1965) about selectional restrictions being determined at the deepest level of syntactic structure were too intuitively pleasing to be questioned. When the abstract syntacticians themselves realized that selectional restrictions were semantic, that only spurred them on to greater abstractness. Chomsky was right after all, they seemed to be saying—the deepest level of syntactic structure just happens to be semantic representation.

Chomsky was unable to put together a viable alternative to abstract syntax before it took the inevitable step to generative semantics. Partly as a result of his vacillation in taking the arguments of the abstract syntacticians head on, and partly as a result of the weakness of his initial counterproposals, linguistics entered the 1970s very much under generative semantic hegemony.

It took several years of the most acrimonious battles linguistics had seen in over a decade before the nonabstract current was again dominant in syntax. Those battles will be the subject of Chapter 5.

Chapter 5

The Linguistic Wars

5.1. INTRODUCTION

This chapter gets its title from Paul Postal's apt term for the state of hostility which existed between the two rival camps of theoreticians in the late 1960s and early 1970s. But it could just as easily have been called "The Fall of Generative Semantics." In 1968, there was hardly a theoretician who was not committed to, or attracted to, this new model. Around 1970 and 1971 many commentators—and not just its practitioners—saw generative semantics as being as important and dramatic a break from classical transformational grammar as the latter was from structural linguistics. George Lakoff traveled around the world speaking on "Why Transformational Grammar Died" and wrote with confidence about the "crumbling foundations" of the field (1972a).

But Lakoff's state of euphoria must have been short-lived. Even by 1972, to judge from the quantity and tone of papers written relevant to factional debate, generative semantics was on the defensive. Most significantly, its own adherents began to abandon ship. A dramatic indicator of this fact is the remarkable paper by generative semanticist Jerry Morgan (1973a), which demolished step by step many of the fundamental hypotheses of the model—hypotheses which Morgan himself had played a key role in fashioning. Today many of these hypotheses have no public adherents at all, and the term "generative semantics" itself evokes nostalgia rather than partisan fervor.

The successful war against generative semantics, then, is the subject matter of this chapter. But I must warn the reader at the outset that I am giving an overly one-sided picture of the confrontation. For expository reasons, it seems best simply to sketch very roughly the counterposed interpretive model (in Section 5.2), which will be developed in more detail in Chapter 6. The rest of this chapter will be devoted to explaining the claims and documenting the collapse of generative semantics. Hence, this chapter will focus far more on the weaknesses of the latter than the former. This seems the correct expository strategy since the former continued to develop after the latter had all but disappeared. It would make far too fragmentary and repetitive a presentation to describe the specific claims along with the strengths and weaknesses of the interpretive model before, say, 1973 in this chapter and after that year in the next. Also, since generative semantics, at least in its later stages, rejected the traditional GOALS of a linguistic theory, while the interpretive model did not, it seems best to treat its development and that of its rival more or less separately.

5.2. THE 1970 INTERPRETIVE MODEL

Chomsky and his students in the late 1960s set to work to develop a model of grammar consistent with the evidence supporting the lexicalist hypothesis and refuting the Katz–Postal hypothesis. Since Chomsky had for several years been referring to the *Aspects* model, correctly if immodestly, as the "Standard Theory," it was logical for him to dub this revised model the "Extended Standard Theory" (EST). While "The EST" is how this model was commonly known during these years, for reasons which I will clarify in Section 5.3, I will refer to it as "the interpretive model" and to its supporters as "interpretivists."

While there were some rather strong disagreements among interpretivists even in 1970, all seem to have shared a number of basic assumptions. It is worth outlining them here before tracing their development in Chapter 6, since quite a few generative semantic claims were made in reaction to these interpretivist views.

First of all, all interpretivists in this period agreed that the lexicalist hypothesis of Chomsky (1970) (see Section 4.3.1) was correct. This resulted in rather "shallow" deep structures, of course. It was agreed that rules operating in the lexicon ("lexical redundancy rules") would handle nonproductive relationships, such as those between verbs and derived nominals, though such rules were rarely formulated (see Jackendoff 1972 for the most explicit examples).

By 1970, all interpretivists agreed that anaphoric definite pronouns were present in the deep structure. Earlier, it had been generally assumed that pronouns replaced full noun phrases under identity with another noun phrase by means of a transformational rule (Lees and Klima 1963; Ross

1967; Langacker 1969). In that way, for example, (5.1a) would be mapped into (5.1b):

(5.1)   a. *Harry$_i$ thinks that Harry$_i$ should win the prize*
        b. *Harry$_i$ thinks that he$_i$ should win the prize*

However, by the end of the 1960s, it came to be accepted that such an approach faced insuperable difficulties. The most serious problem for the strict transformational treatment involved the analysis of sentences discovered by Emmon Bach and Stanley Peters involving crossing co-reference. An example from Bach (1970) is:

(5.2)   *The man who shows he$_i$ deserves it$_j$ will get the prize$_j$ he$_i$ desires*

Given the assumption that pronominalization is a transformation operating on full NP's, sentence (5.2) would require a deep structure with an infinite number of embeddings, since each pronoun lies within the antecedent of the other:

(5.3)

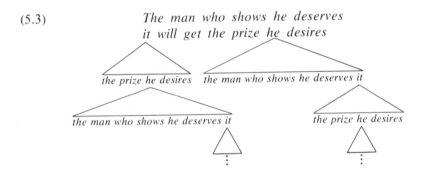

It was argued that this paradox entailed (at least) that pronouns had to be present in deep structures, which then further entailed that there must be an interpretive rule which assigned co-referentiality between pronouns and noun phrases already present in the sentence.

Below are paraphrased three other arguments which were cited as evidence for an interpretive over a transformational approach to pronominalization:

Consider the phrases *the bastard* in (5.4a) and *the bum* in (5.4b). They are interpreted as co-referential to *Charlie* and *Harry*, respectively. Such "anaphoric epithets" obey many of the same conditions on co-reference as ordinary pronouns (see G. Lakoff 1976b):

(5.4)   a. *I wanted Charlie to help me, but the bastard wouldn't do it*
        b. *Although the bum tried to hit me, I can't really get too mad at Harry*

How could epithets replace full NP's? What principle would decide which epithet an NP would be turned into?

[PARAPHRASING JACKENDOFF 1972]

It would be next to impossible to find full noun phrases to serve as syntactic antecedents for the pronouns in boldface italics:

(5.5)   a. *Lips that touch liquor shall never touch **mine***
         b. *You can have an ice cream, a soda, or **both***
         c. *Each of Mary's sons hated **his** brothers*

[PARAPHRASING DOUGHERTY 1969]

If pronouns replace full NP's, what would block *There*-Insertion from applying before Pronominalization, resulting in (5.6c)?:

(5.6)   a. *some students$_i$ believe that some students$_i$ are running the show*
             → THERE- INSERTION
         b. *some students$_i$ believe that there are some students$_i$ running the show* → PRONOMINALIZATION
         c. **Some students believe that there are they running the show*

[PARAPHRASING BRESNAN 1970a]

Some interpretivists (Jackendoff 1972, Wasow 1972) took the position that NO deletion or pronominalization rules be allowed in the grammar, other than the deletion of constants. The question of pronominalization and deletion will be returned to in Sections 5.4.4 and 6.2.3.

Another point of agreement followed from the rejection of the Katz–Postal hypothesis; namely, that there are levels more shallow than deep structure relevant to semantic interpretation. However, there was widespread disagreement over the specification of those levels (see Section 6.6.3).

Finally, all interpretivists in 1970 advocated the Structure Preserving Constraint (see Section 6.2.2) and some version of the X-bar convention (see Sections 4.3.1 and 6.4).

5.3. SOME PROBLEMS OF TERMINOLOGY

Picking the correct terminology to refer to each of the rival models is no easy task. On the one side, we find "lexicalism," "interpretive semantics" (or simply "interpretivism"), and "The Extended Standard Theory"; on the other, "generative semantics." Yet the several terms for the former are definitely distinct in their referents.[1] "Lexicalism" in its narrow sense refers to a particular position on the derivation of derived nominals; in its broad sense, to the position that NO transformation changes category labels. Interpretive semantics in its broad sense refers to the position that interpretive semantic rules apply to syntactic structures. Now lexicalism (in either sense) DOES entail interpretivism in its broad sense—if transformations do not do all the work, then they clearly must be supplemented by interpretive semantic rules. But unfortunately "interpretivism" has come to be used in a narrow sense as well—as the position that interpretive rules apply to superficial syntactic structures as well as to deep structures. Lexicalism certainly does NOT entail this position; Katz (1972), for example, combines lexicalism with deep structure interpretation only. For a while, "The Extended Standard Theory" served well as the name of the predominant interpretivist model—the model with the lexicalist hypothesis in its broad sense and interpretive semantics in its narrow sense. But since the mid 1970s, a variety of interpretivist models have been proposed, and the term "Extended Standard Theory" has fallen into disuse. When no confusion will result, I will use the terms "interpretivism," "interpretive semantics," and "the interpretive model" interchangeably to refer to the 1970 model AND its later modifications, and to its advocates as "interpretivists."

While the term "generative semantics" has no competitors (except for Pieter Seuren's (1972) "semantic syntax," which is better chosen, but never caught on), it is nevertheless a misnomer. This is because:

> (i) any theory of semantics must be generative in the sense that it must provide a formal means of generating the infinite class of semantic representations and (ii) what is crucial about Generative Semantics is its claim about the HOMOGENEITY of semantic and syntactic representations and the homogeneity of the mapping between them [Postal 1970a: 98].

The term caught on, despite its inaccuracy, perhaps partly because it seemed like such a natural counterposition to "interpretive semantics," but also because the central figures like Lakoff and Ross used it from the outset. (The first line of Lakoff and Ross's (1976) "Is Deep Structure Necessary?" was "We believe semantics may be generative. . . [p. 160].")

Another complicating question, partly terminological and partly substantive, is that of DIRECTIONALITY. Superficially, at least, a major difference between generative and interpretive semantics is that of directionality of derivation. The former posits a "smooth" derivation, "progressing" directly from semantic representation to surface structure; the latter posits a far more complex interrelation of components. G. Lakoff (1971a) and Postal (1972) on one side and Chomsky (1972a) on the other have stressed

---

[1] For further remarks on the logical independence of the referents of these various terms and an interesting discussion of the mixed positions which were adopted in the 1960s, see Partee (1971).

that these apparent differences in directionality have no empirical consequences. Yet as Zwicky (1972) has argued at length, this point is correct
only if the two theories are compared only at the highest level of abstraction—their ability to generate sets of quadruples (P, s, d, S), where P is a
phonetic representation, s a surface structure, d a deep structure, and S a
semantic representation: "if the only empirical test of a device is its ability
to generate a particular set, then clearly no two devices which generate the
same set can be empirically distinct [Zwicky 1972: 104]."

Zwicky went on to point out that once the rival theories are provided
with more explicit content than the simple ability to generate the quadruples
(P, s, d, S), directionality indeed becomes an empirical issue.[2] However,
he concluded: "there is at the moment no credible framework available in
which questions of directionality can be profitably raised. I look forward to
theories embodying very strong substantive universals, theories in which
these questions CAN be treated [p. 108]."

5.4. EARLY GENERATIVE SEMANTICS

As we have seen, the crucial step from abstract syntax to generative
semantics involved the rejection of the idea that lexical insertion must
precede the transformational rules. By taking this step, abstract syntacticians had abandoned the level of syntactic deep structure altogether. And
by rejecting this level, generative semantics had rejected an assumption that
had gone unchallenged since the inception of transformational generative
grammar—that syntactic and semantic processes are fundamentally distinct.
Figure 5.1 depicts the initial generative semantic model of 1967–1968:

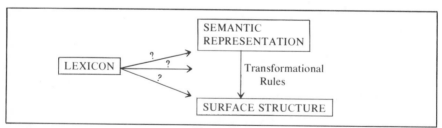

Figure 5.1

Note that this model suggests that semantic representations and syntactic
representations must be of the same formal nature—otherwise there would

[2] It is interesting to recall that Chomsky (1957) had attributed empirical significance to
directionality in this sense: "Each transformation that I have investigated can be shown to be
irreversible in the sense that it is much easier to carry out the transformation in one direction
than in the other, just as in the case of the passive transformation discussed above [p. 80]."

(at some point) be a cut off point between syntactic and semantic rules and hence a ''deep structure.'' This consequence was happily endorsed by generative semanticists, who saw no aspect of meaning that could not be represented in phrase-marker form. In fact, as we have seen (in Section 4.2), it was the apparent fact that by doing syntax, one was inevitably led to semantic representation as the natural input to the syntactic rules which made the generative semantic conclusion such an obvious one to take. In Ross's (1972) words: ''Where syntactic evidence supports the postulation of elements in underlying structure which are not phonetically manifested, such elements tend to be relevant semantically [p. 106].''

Still to be worked out was the question of exactly how and where lexical items entered the derivation. McCawley (1968c) solved the problem in part by proposing that lexical items themselves be structured composites of semantic predicates and/or arguments. For example, the entry for *kill* would be:[3]

(5.7)

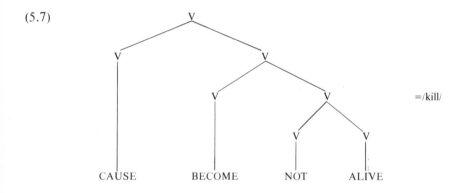

After various applications of transformational rules had created a substructure in the derivation corresponding to a P-marker in the lexicon, that substructure would be eligible for replacement by the phonological matrix associated with the lexical P-marker. While McCawley in 1968 hesitantly suggested that lexical insertion transformations might apply in a block at the level of shallow structure (the point between the cyclic and post-cyclic rules) and later (1974) proposed cyclic insertion, generative semanticists never did agree on the locus of lexical insertion, nor even whether it occurred at some independently definable level at all.

The remainder of this section will further develop the case that was made for generative semantics and chart its progress during the five or so years in which it flourished. Section 5.5 will treat its later development.

---

[3] The idea that lexical items have their own internal syntax which mirrors sentence-level syntax was first put forward in Weinreich (1966).

5.4.1. Against the Level of Deep Structure

Generative semanticists realized that their rejection of the level of deep structure would be little more than word-playing if the transformational mapping from semantic representation to surface structure was characterized by a major break before the application of the familiar cyclic rules—particularly if the natural location for the insertion of lexical items was precisely at this break. They therefore constructed a number of arguments—some quite ingenious—to show that no such break existed. The most compelling were modeled after Halle's argument (see Section 2.5.3) that the positing of an independent phonemic level between underlying phonological representation and phonetic representation resulted in one general process having to be stated twice in the phonology. Some examples:

In the *Aspects* model, the deep structures of (5.8a) and (5.8b) are (5.9a) and (5.9b), respectively:

(5.8)   a. *John likes pork*
           b. *John likes meat from pigs*

(5.9)   a.

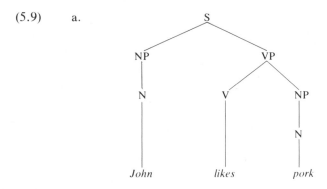

           b.

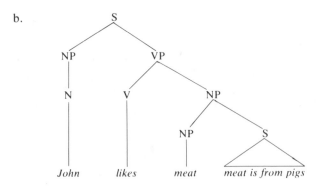

The syntactic rules of Relative Clause Formation/Reduction apply to (5.9b) to derive (5.8b). However, given that (5.9a) underlies (5.8a), the same two rules will have to apply IN REVERSE IN THE SEMANTICS to map (5.9a) into its semantic representation, something like [MEAT WHICH COMES FROM PIGS]. The only way to avoid these double rule statements is to take this semantic representation as the initial representation in the derivation and form (5.8a) by optionally replacing the semantic material by the word *pork*. If this optional lexical transformation does not apply, (5.8b) results.

[PARAPHRASING POSTAL 1970a]

If deep structure exists, the transformation forming *respective(ly)* constructions will have to apply once in the syntax and once in the semantics.

[PARAPHRASING MCCAWLEY 1968a]

If the deep structure of a sentence like *John began the book* were NP⌢*begin*⌢NP, as the lexicalist hypothesis demands, the rule of Subject Raising would have to apply once in the syntax and once in the semantics.

[PARAPHRASING NEWMEYER 1970]

The rule of Adverb Preposing has to be stated twice in the *Aspects* model; once relating deep structures to semantic representations, once relating deep structures to surface structures.

[PARAPHRASING G. LAKOFF 1972b]

Many arguments were constructed to show that cyclic rules have to precede lexical insertion, thereby depriving deep structure of what Chomsky (1971) saw as its crucial defining feature—the locus of lexical insertion. For example, Postal (1970a) argued at great length that (5.10b) was the underlying syntactic structure of (5.10a) (which he considered to be essentially identical to its semantic representation:[4]

(5.10)   a. *Max reminded me of Pete*
          b.

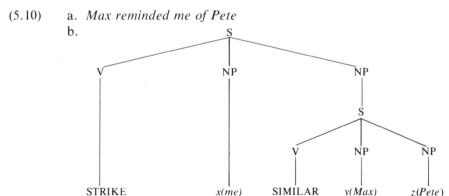

<hr>

[4] While the question is logically independent of other assumptions, most generative semanticists assumed underlying *VSO* order for English (see McCawley 1970c). The refutation of this in Berman (1974) is generally accepted as valid (but see the critique of Berman's reply to McCawley in S. Anderson and Chung 1977).

He argued that the only way that *Max* could end up as the surface structure subject was by having it raised by the cyclic rule of Subject Raising, which must have applied prior to the lexical insertion of *remind*.

Analogously, G. Lakoff (1971a) argued that the lexical item *dissuade* could be inserted only after the application of Passive, and McCawley (1970a) suggested that the meanings of *suicide* ('killing oneself'), *malinger* ('pretend to be sick'), and *under surveillance* ('being watched') pointed to the application of Reflexive, Equi, and Passive, respectively, prior to their insertion.

Several other types of arguments were constructed in support of uniform deep structureless derivations:

> Word-internal structures can be modified externally. Note that (5.11) is ambiguous between (5.12a) and (5.12b):
>
> (5.11)   *I almost killed John*
>
> (5.12)   a. *I almost caused John to die*
>   b. *I caused John almost to die*
>
> This is strong evidence for syntactic lexical decomposition and, therefore, against the level of deep structure.
>
> [PARAPHRASING MORGAN 1969a]

> Prelexical transformations are subject to the same movement constraints as postlexical ones. Just as the constraint proposed in Ross (1968) prevents (5.13a) from being transformed into (5.13b), it predicts that there can be no verb *sneep* with a meaning such that (5.14b) is a paraphrase of (5.14a):
>
> (5.13)   a. *John saw Mary laying a wreath at the grave of the unknown what?*
>   b. **What did John see Mary laying a wreath at the grave of the unknown?*
>
> (5.14)   a. *John saw Mary laying a wreath at the grave of the unknown hippie*
>   b. **John sneeped Mary laying a wreath at the grave of the unknown*
>
> [PARAPHRASING MORGAN 1969a]

> Syntactic lexical decomposition combined with the restriction that lexical items replace only constituents allows us to characterize the notion "possible lexical item." No lexical item could correspond to the circled material in (5.15), since it does not form a constituent.

(5.15)

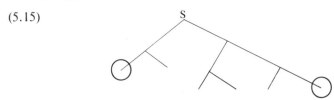

In contrast, the nonexistence of a lexical item meaning 'cause to become not obnoxious' is simply an accidental gap—the rule of Predicate Raising creates a structure which could be replaced by a lexical item with this meaning.

[PARAPHRASING McCAWLEY 1968c]

5.4.2. Rule Government

Early transformational grammar, from Lees's (1960) subcategorization of verbs into dozens of sublexical categories, each category appearing in the structural description of some transformation, to G. Lakoff's (1970a) subcategorization of every verb in the language with respect to every transformational rule, claimed that rule government was essentially arbitrary and unpredictable. Yet it was always known that this was not really the case. Among other things, the semantics of the lexical items involved seemed relevant. Lees's categories, for example, each have, by and large, their own defining semantic characteristics. Zwicky (1968) took note of the possible semantic nature of rule government and called for a motivated treatment in which "some natural syntactic classes might be referable to semantic classes in the same way that some phonological classes might be referable to phonetic classes [p. 101]." Even Jackendoff (1972) agreed in principle with the desirability of this undertaking: "If the difference in grammatical behavior has something to do with the meanings of the items in question, then that is the best possible case, since the rule has only to refer to the properties already present—if the meaning of the item is learned, its behavior is known automatically [p. 24]." [5]

Part of the great promise of generative semantics, then, was its being able to provide a natural means to express the apparent generalization about semantic rule government. Since in this model the governed rules apply to nonlexicalized bundles of semantic predicates, generative semantics PRE-DICTS that rule government be semantic, whereas the interpretive model is no more than compatible with such a possibility. (Generative semantics still had to deal with lexical exceptions, of course. For example, *probable* would somehow have to be prevented from being inserted if Subject Raising had applied, given the ungrammaticality of **John is probable to leave*.)

Given that confirmation of the hypothesis that rule government was semantic would have been the strongest possible empirical support for generative semantics, it seems astonishing in retrospect that so little work was done to test it. In fact, the only work of significance along these lines is Green (1974), whose results are highly inconclusive, to say the least (see Section 5.6.3).

[5] One of the more bizarre exchanges in the generative–interpretive debate involved Jackendoff (1968b), the interpretivist, claiming that *Neg*-Raising applies to a semantic class of verbs, and G. Lakoff (1970b), the generative semanticist, claiming in reply that it does not, and is THEREFORE a syntactic rule.

5.4.3. Global Rules

   Generative semanticists were still faced with the problem of handling all of the apparent counterexamples to the Katz–Postal hypothesis—those which had led interpretivists to posit rules of semantic interpretation operating off of derived structures.

   Consider (5.16a–b):

(5.16)   a. *Many men read few books*
         b. *Few books were read by many men*

The difference in meaning between (5.16a) and (15.6b)[6] seemed to suggest, as we have seen, either that Passive is a meaning-changing transformation or, alternatively, that it is the surface ordering of quantifiers which determines meaning. Neither option was open to generative semanticists. Since, for them, the deep structure and the meaning were identical, they could not speak of a transformation "changing" meaning or countenance meaning being interpreted at some derived level of structure.

   It was no problem for generative semanticists to find initial structures for (5.16a) and (5.16b) to represent their meaning. All of the usual arguments for abstract structures led them to posit something like (5.17a) and (5.17b), respectively, as their semantic representations, although there was disagreement on the details:

(5.17)   a.

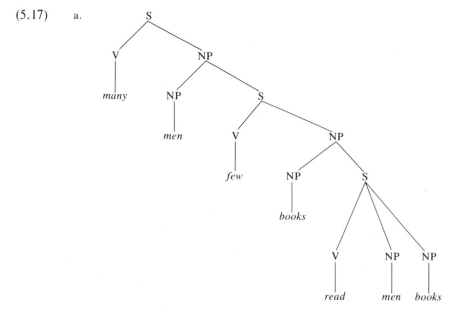

   [6] In the late 1960s and early 1970s most parties seem to have reverted to Chomsky's original intuition (see Sections 2.2.5 and 3.3.2) that sentences containing more than one quantifier are both unambiguous and nonvague as regards scope.

b.

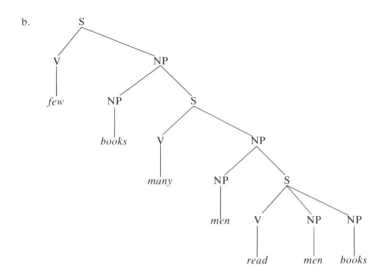

The problem, as Partee (1970) succinctly pointed out, was in insuring that (5.17a) would not be mapped into (5.16b) by undesired passivization and that (5.17b) WOULD undergo this rule to guarantee that it not underlie (5.16a). The solution arrived at by G. Lakoff (1971a) was to let the rules of Passive and Quantifier Lowering apply freely to (5.17a) and (5.17b). By the end of the transformational derivation, then, both have been mapped into both (5.16a) and (5.16b). However, the strict transformational derivation was to be supplemented by another type of rule—a GLOBAL RULE (or GLOBAL DERIVATIONAL CONSTRAINT). This was stated roughly as follows: if one logical predicate "asymmetrically commands" (roughly, `is in a higher sentence than') another in semantic representation, it precedes it·in derived structure. In this way (5.16a) and (5.16b) are filtered out as sentences derivable from (5.17b) and (5.17a), respectively.

Note that this global rule technically allows both the Katz–Postal hypothesis and the hypothesis that the deepest syntactic level is semantic representation to be maintained. Needless to say, any evidence that derived structure is relevant to semantic interpretation could be—and was—reinterpreted as a global rule in just this fashion.

Soon many examples of other types of processes were found which could not be stated in strict transformational terms but seemed to involve conditions holding between derivationally nonadjacent phrase-markers (i.e., were global). Many of these involved PRESUPPOSITION. Morgan (1969b), using standard abstract syntactic argumentation, postulated that the presuppositions of a sentence are, in semantic representation, represented as complements of an abstract performative verb of presupposing conjoined to the left of the sentence. The semantic representation of (5.18a), then, would be approximately (5.18b):

(5.18)   a. *John doesn't realize that his fly is open*

b.

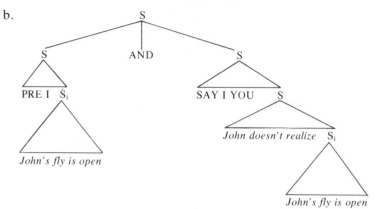

G. Lakoff (1971a) gave several examples of grammatical processes which seemed to refer, globally, to the presuppositions of the sentence. For example, he argued that the well-formedness of (5.19b) beside ill-formed (5.20b) indicates that the rule of *Will*-Deletion can only apply "if it is presupposed that the speaker is sure that the event will happen [G. Lakoff 1971b:260].":

(5.19)   a. *The Red Sox will play the Yankees tomorrow*
           b. *The Red Sox play the Yankees tomorrow*

(5.20)   a. *The Red Sox will beat the Yankees tomorrow*
           b. **The Red Sox beat the Yankees tomorrow*

Also, he argued, lexical insertion transformations have to refer globally to presuppositions. Drawing on work by Fillmore (1969b, 1971a), he suggested that the meanings of lexical items contain both assertions and presuppositions. In this view, *assassinate* asserts 'kill' and presupposes that its object is an important public figure. Hence, Lakoff argued, the insertion transformation for *assassinate* differs from that for *kill* only in that in the former case this rule is conditioned globally by the above presupposition.

The first global rules proposed all referred to a level of syntactic structure and a level of semantic structure. This left their proponents open to the charge that global rules were no more than rules of semantic interpretation "in reverse." In response to this accusation, George Lakoff wrote his famous "Global Rules" paper (1970c), in which he attempted to establish that global rules have purely SYNTACTIC motivation. Below are briefly (and inadequately!) paraphrased two much-discussed global rules of this type:

In Classical Greek, adjectives and participles agree in case with their subjects. But this cannot be stated by a simple transformational rule of Case Agreement. The reason is that these elements agree with the DERIVED case of what WAS their cycle-final subject. Hence, Case Agreement must be stated as a global rule that applies late in the derivation, but has the power to "look back" to see what grammatical relations existed at an earlier stage of the derivation.

[PARAPHRASING G. LAKOFF 1970c, ANDREWS 1971]

Be in English contracts regularly under reduced stress:

(5.21) a. *There is this much wine in the bottle*
        b. *There's this much wine in the bottle*

(5.22) a. *The concert is here at two o'clock*
        b. *The concert's here at two o'clock*

But note:

(5.23) a. *I wonder how much wine there is in the bottle*
        b. **I wonder how much wine there's in the bottle*

(5.24) a. *Tell Harry where the concert is at two o'clock*
        b. **Tell Harry where the concert's at two o'clock*

(5.23b) and (5.24b) are ungrammatical because stress lowering (and subsequent contraction) have occurred immediately preceding a place where movement or deletion took place. Stress lowering, which is in the phonology, must be stated with a global condition blocking it from applying before a deletion site.

[PARAPHRASING KING 1970, G. LAKOFF 1970c]

It is important to understand that Lakoff's definition of "global rule" was broad enough to encompass almost any conceivable grammatical process which was not a transformation:[7]

> Those of us who have tried to make transformational grammar work have attempted to patch up the classical theory with one ad hoc device after another: my theory of exceptions (G. Lakoff 1970a), Ross' constraints on movement transformations (1968), the Ross (1968)–Perlmutter (1971) output conditions, Postal's crossover principle (1971) and anaphoric island constraints (1969), Jackendoff's surface interpretation rules (1972), Chomsky's lexical redundancy rules and his analogy component (1970), and so on. In a recent paper (G. Lakoff 1971a), I suggested that most, if not all, of these ad hoc patching attempts were special cases of a single general phenomenon: global derivational constraints . . . constraints [stating] well-formedness conditions on configurations of corresponding nodes in nonadjacent trees in a derivation [G. Lakoff 1970c:627–628].

The only attempt to constrain the power of global rules involved limiting the points in a derivation to which they might make reference:

> It is assumed that derivational constraints will be restricted to hold either at particular levels in a derivation (semantic representation, surface structure, shallow structure and

---

[7] I have updated the references in the quotation. Lakoff (1971a) also described extrinsic rule ordering statements as global constraints.

deep structure, if such exists), or to range over entire derivations or parts of derivations holding between levels [G. Lakoff 1971a:234].

At first it was suggested that any particular global rule could refer to at most two nodes (G. Lakoff 1971a:234). This was later increased to ''hopefully no more than three or four [G. Lakoff 1972c:87].''

5.4.4. Logic and Semantic Representation

In the late 1960s, McCawley, Bach, and G. Lakoff independently made an interesting discovery. As the inventory of syntactic categories became more and more reduced, those remaining bore a very close correspondence to the categories of symbolic logic. The three categories whose existence generative semanticists were certain of in this period—sentence, noun phrase, and verb—seemed to correspond directly to the proposition, argument, and predicate of logic (logical connectives were incorporated into the class of predicates, as were quantifiers). This was an exhilarating discovery for generative semanticists and indicated to them more than anything else that they were on the right track. For, now, the deepest level of representation had a ''natural'' language-independent basis, rooted in what Boole had called ''The Laws of Thought.'' And this level was arrived at, it seemed to them, strictly by traditional syntactic language-independent argumentation. What is more, they were confident that analogous argumentation would lead to the same base rules with the same categories for EVERY language in the world (the ''universal base hypothesis''). As Bach (1968) observed:

> The base component suggested here looks in some ways very much like the logical systems familiar from the work of modern logicians like Rudolf Carnap, Hans Reichenbach, and others. In particular, such systems do not have any subdivision of ''lexical items'' into nouns, verbs, and adjectives. Much more basic is the distinction between variables, names, and general ''predicates'' which can be n-placed with respect to the number of terms that can cooccur as their arguments. It should not be surprising that a system of universal base rules should turn out to be very close to such systems, which are after all the result of analyzing the most basic conceptual relationships that exist in natural languages [p. 121].

The universal base hypothesis, not surprisingly, was seen as one of the most attractive features of generative semantics.

The suitability of classical symbolic logic for expressing semantic representations in natural language was explored more by James McCawley than by anyone else. McCawley (1970b) found existing versions of symbolic logic insufficient in one essential way: ''It is necessary for the semantic representation to separate a clause into a 'proposition' and a set of noun phrases, which provide the material used in identifying the indices of the 'proposition' . . . [p. 173].'' Hence, his semantic representation of (5.25a) was (5.25b):[8]

---

[8] McCawley later (1970a:230ff.) listed many other respects in which his proposals for semantic representation differ from the more usual variants of symbolic logic.

(5.25) a. *The man killed the woman*
        b.

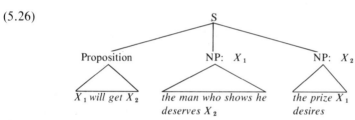

In other words, the argument places in the "Proposition" are filled by variables (called "indices" by McCawley), which are bound by the NP operators external to it. A transformational rule substitutes these external NP's for the indices, those indices remaining after the substitution rule applies being realized as pronouns.

McCawley presented two major arguments for deriving noun phrases from bound variables. First, he claimed, it provided a solution to the Bach–Peters paradox not involving interpretive rules (i.e., a solution compatible with generative semantics). The semantic representation of (5.2) would be (5.26):

(5.26)

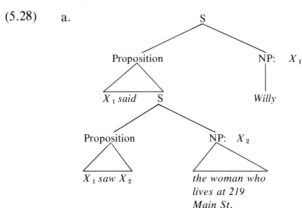

Second, he claimed, it allowed a natural syntactic treatment of *de dicto–de re* ambiguities. The *de dicto* interpretation of (5.27) (in which Willy identifies the woman as living at that address) is represented by (5.28a); the *de re* interpretation (in which the speaker makes the identification) is represented by (5.28b):

(5.27) *Willy said that he had seen the woman who lives at 219 Main St.*

(5.28) a.

b.

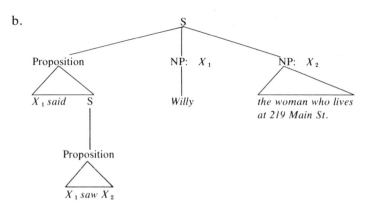

By around 1970, generative semanticists, particularly George Lakoff, were using the term "natural logic" freely—in fact, they had raised it to the level of a slogan for the generative semantic "movement." However, the meaning of the term was never fully clarified. In some cases it seemed to refer to a field of inquiry (as in the following quotation), in others to a set of conditions on a successful linguistic description (G. Lakoff 1972b:589), and in still others to a new logical system to replace the inadequate arbitrary ones of the logicians (McCawley 1971:285-286):[9] "Natural logic is the study of REASONING in natural language [G. Lakoff 1974:162]."

Generally, examples cited to illustrate the need for natural logic involved subtle interactions of grammatical and logical phenomena. The following is typical:

> The expression *would rather* is a positive polarity item:

(5.29)   a.   *I would rather go*
           b.   **I wouldn't rather go*

> But note the acceptability of (5.30):

(5.30)   *I didn't meet anyone who wouldn't rather go*

> One might think, then, that an even number of negatives renders the sentence acceptable. But this is not so, since (5.31) is ungrammatical:

(5.31)   **I didn't meet the man who wouldn't rather go*

> Double negatives are permissible only when they result in a sentence that is LOGICALLY EQUIVALENT to a positive. This shows the inseparability of grammar and logic and the hopelessness of the *Aspects* model and its interpretivist successor, which attempt to maintain a strict separation of the two.
>
> [PARAPHRASING G. LAKOFF (1971b), based
> on work by BAKER (1970)]

---

[9] These three uses of the term are not necessarily incompatible, although they may be. Stalker (1973) describes at length the difficulty in interpreting what exactly "natural logic" is.

5.4.5. The Appeal of Generative Semantics

I have already hinted at the essential reason for the rapid initial adoption of generative semantics by such a large portion of the linguistic community. Its characterization of the relation between syntax and semantics was both familiar, in that it was based on pre-*Aspects* assumptions, and conceptually simple. Traditionally, grammarians have set their goal as explicating the relation between form and content—generative semantics set out to capture this relation in as direct (and therefore in as an intuitively plausible, or common-sensical) way as possible. As Kuroda (1972) pointed out: "One seems to witness here [in generative semantics] a more faithful reemergence of the time-honored view of language that it is a correlation of the inner content of meaning and the outer form of sound representation [p. 3]." [10]

In an influential essay, Paul Postal (1972) elevated to principle the desirability of the generative semantic view of uniform (or "homogeneous") derivations:

> What I wish to suggest briefly is that because of its a priori logical and conceptual properties, this theory of grammar [with semantic representations and surface structures which are formally homogeneous] is the basic one which generative linguists should operate from as an investigatory framework, and that it should be abandoned, if at all, only under the strongest pressures of empirical disconfirmation. In short, I suggest that the Homogeneous I framework has a rather special logical position vis-à-vis its possible competitors within the generative framework, a position which makes the choice of this theory obligatory in the absence of direct empirical disconfirmation [p. 135].

In short, Postal's view that generative semantics is A PRIORI preferable to interpretive semantics (and hence the burden of proof is to be placed on partisans of the latter) was widely accepted at the time.

There were sociological reasons as well for the early successes of generative semantics. Many of the earliest transformational grammarians, at home with the Katz–Postal hypothesis, naturally adopted generative semantics in the late 1960s. But by then, they had radiated into teaching positions all over the United States, while almost all interpretivists were at MIT. This not only gave generative semantics the aura of a national "movement," but it meant that 10 times as many students were being taught generative semantics as were being taught interpretive semantics. The "clubby" ingroup atmosphere which then characterized (and still, to a certain extent, characterizes) the MIT Linguistics Department contrasted sharply with the missionary zeal of the generative semanticists, and further

---

[10] Interestingly, Chomsky (personal communication) has offered the opinion that the history of transformational grammar would have been more "rational" if generative semantics had been the original position, with interpretivism a subsequent development, given the fact that the former more directly captures the grammarian's classic goal. Along the same lines, he suggests that the only valid criticism of his research into the Port-Royal grammar (see Chomsky 1966b) comes from commentators like H. E. Brekle (1969), who have implied that this seventeenth century linguistic model is more directly an antecedent of generative semantics than of the *Aspects* theory.

helped to guarantee a slow, arduous reassertion of MIT hegemony within transformational grammar.

The allusion to generative semantics as a "movement" or a "crusade" is not simply a figure of speech. The public lectures given by Lakoff, Ross, McCawley, Postal, and others resembled political rallies as much as academic seminars. The 1968 Linguistic Institute at the University of Illinois, at which Lakoff, Ross, and McCawley preached the new gospel to hundreds, stands out not only as the high-water mark in the ascendant tide of generative semantics, but also as the epitome of the mixing of reasoned argument with pure showmanship and pure salesmanship.

The epicenter of generative semantics was the Department of Linguistics at the University of Chicago, where James McCawley (and later Jerrold Sadock and Noriko McCawley) taught. McCawley's charisma was certainly an important factor in spreading the model. Many of the "second generation" of generative semanticists—including Jerry Morgan, Georgia Green, Robert Binnick, and Alice Davison—were McCawley's students. Also instrumental in this regard was the Chicago Linguistic Society, whose published proceedings (particularly in the 1968–1972 period) provided a vehicle for the rapid dissemination of the latest generative semantic hypotheses. The CLS, which holds yearly meetings organized by Chicago students, further helped to give generative semantics a national (and later international) presence which interpretivists had nothing comparable to match.

5.4.6. The Chicago and Berkeley Linguistic Societies

The excitement that pervaded the Chicago meetings in this period is impossible to characterize adequately in print. Linguists traveled from across the United States just to HEAR ABOUT the latest developments in generative semantics. CLS papers, like the following, were to define a research strategy for the majority of the theoretical linguists in America:

CLS volume	Author and date	Title of paper
4	James McCawley (1968c)	"Lexical Insertion in a Transformational Grammar without Deep Structure"
5	Laurence Horn (1969)	"A Presuppositional Analysis of *Only* and *Even*"
5	George Lakoff (1969b)	"On Derivational Constraints"
5	Jerry Morgan (1969b)	"On the Treatment of Presupposition in Transformational Grammar"
5	Paul Postal (1969)	"Anaphoric Islands"
5	John R. Ross (1969c)	"Guess Who?"
7	David Gordon and George Lakoff (1971)	"Conversational Postulates"

The CLS itself was not officially committed to generative semantics any more than it was officially committed to generative grammar. In fact, each volume contained one or two interpretivist papers, and even an occasional paper from completely outside the generative tradition was presented at the meetings. But the combination of the commitment of the CLS officers to generative semantics and the insularity of the interpretivists guaranteed that the views of generative semanticists would dominate the meetings.

The CLS was originally founded on 19 January 1951 by ``a group of interested people from the Chicago area,'' as they classified themselves at the time. In the words of the Society's principal founder, Eric Hamp, its purposes were

> to foster linguistic studies; to encourage free exchange of ideas with related disciplines; to disseminate the fruits of linguistics to other potential consumers, professional and non-professional; to develop intellectually honest and socially affable and fruitful relationships with non-linguists [Peranteau 1973:np].

For the first 13 years of its existence, the CLS did little more than hold monthly meetings at various colleges in the Chicago area, featuring both local and outside speakers. In November 1964, Doris Bartholomew, who was then a graduate student at the University of Chicago, sent a letter to various linguistics departments in the Midwest proposing that the CLS sponsor an all-day regional conference for the following April. As a result, in April 1965, the First Regional Meeting of the Chicago Linguistic Society was held.

By the time that the decision had been made to publish the proceedings of each conference (1968), control of the Society had (in effect) passed into the hands of graduate students at the University of Chicago. This led to continuing friction between the Department of Linguistics at the University of Chicago and others in the Chicago area during the late 1960s and early 1970s:

> This total identification of the Chicago Linguistic Society with the University of Chicago, certainly a foreign idea to the founders and earlier members of the society, has been a subject of some acrimonious debate. Opponents maintain that there was a species of coup and that they were neither consulted about plans and programs, nor asked for help. Students running the organization countered these claims by pointing out how poor response was from other schools. Theoretical arguments about what is proper linguistics have added to the dissension.
>
> It is a fact that since 1968, efforts have been made each year to include other schools in the society. A letter was usually written in September, but there was little, if any, response. This year, 1973, even the letter has been dropped. Effectively, the Chicago Linguistic Society is now an organization of University of Chicago students.
>
> . . . The takeover by the University of Chicago students now loomed as very important since these students were primarily interested in transformational generative studies of linguistics. With the success of the Fifth [Regional Meeting], the issue of just what should be the linguistic emphasis at the meetings became moot. The controlling

faction in the society and the eagerness of TG linguists to have a central yearly conference combined to direct the CLS into assuming a new role. The regional meetings became the best national source for new papers in transformational grammar.

If the apparent "coup" by University of Chicago students had raised hackles, the generativization of CLS brought sharp recriminations. Former members of the society, believers in other theories, criticized the new emphasis and ended their association with the society, in some cases starting their own speaker programs. At this time, from the point of view of satisfying the largest audience, this drift of CLS toward one theory has been highly successful. A change of fashion, however, might cause problems for the society [Peranteau 1973:7-9].

By 1973, the FIRST printing of each CLS volume had risen from 1000 copies a few years before to 2500. While, unfortunately, exact total sales figures are not available, given the fact that all of the early volumes were reprinted, one can estimate with assurance that tens of thousands of CLS volumes have been sold. Attendance at regional meetings peaked in 1974 and 1975 at around 400. Since then, attendance has declined somewhat, and the initial press run has been decreased to 2000. The primary reason for this is undoubtedly economic—less travel money is available, and more, more expensive, books are competing for linguists' paychecks. Also, the publication of papers from the Berkeley and North Eastern (see Section 6.7.1) Linguistic Societies has cut into the Chicago Society's sales, attendance, and relative importance. And finally, the decline of generative semantics has diminished the relative prestige of the Linguistics Department at Chicago, with a corresponding decline in the prestige of the meetings it sponsors. While, of course, the composition of the papers at each CLS meeting has changed with the times, this (somewhat intangible) factor cannot be overlooked.

Interestingly, the Berkeley Linguistics Society was formed in 1974 at the SUGGESTION of the CLS, which went so far as to provide an organizational loan. At the time, the CLS was forced to reject 80% or more of all abstracts, due to the huge number of submissions. The officers of that society hoped that a "fraternal" organization on the West Coast would ease its burden somewhat. As an organization run by graduate students at the University of California–Berkeley, the BLS has, not surprisingly, sponsored meetings whose papers reflect the orientation of the department at that university. While papers from many different perspectives have been presented, the BLS is best known for informal pragmatic and descriptivist studies. Tables 5.1 and 5.2 give a statistical summary of the BLS.

TABLE 5.1.
Berkeley Linguistics Society—
Attendance at Yearly Conferences

BLS 1	(1975)	150
BLS 2	(1976)	118
BLS 3	(1977)	209
BLS 4	(1978)	197

Source: Berkeley Linguistics Society.

TABLE 5.2. .
Berkeley Linguistics Society, Proceedings of Annual Meetings—
Number of Volumes Sold

	1975	1976	1977	1978	Total by volume
BLS 1	401	188	197	131	917
BLS 2	—	312	309	124	745
BLS 3	—	—	446	211	657
BLS 4	—	—	—	272	272
Total by year	401	500	952	738	

Source: Berkeley Linguistics Society.

5.5. LATE GENERATIVE SEMANTICS

While holding the positions described in Section 5.4 was sufficient for considering oneself a "generative semanticist," a number of linguists working in this model, in particular George Lakoff, continued to elaborate and enrich its theoretical devices. This elaboration is the subject of the following section. While it must be stressed that not all generative semanticists followed Lakoff, it is definitely the case that, because of his stature, the claims outlined in this section came to be seen by many linguists as intrinsic to generative semantics. By 1972, Lakoff's model appeared as in Figure 5.2 (an oversimplified diagram based on the discussion in G. Lakoff 1974a):

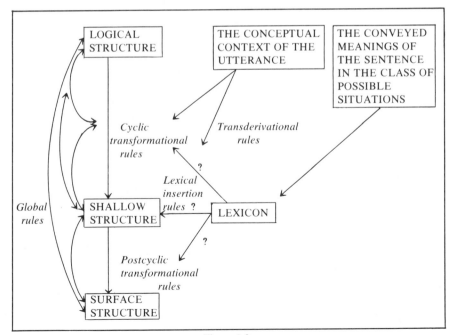

Figure 5.2

5.5.1. Beyond Global Rules[11]

In the 1970s, generative semanticists began proposing grammatical mechanisms which far exceeded the power of global rules. This was necessitated by the steady expansion of the type of data that was considered relevant to the construction of a theory of grammar. As the list of phenomena that generative semanticists felt required a "grammatical" treatment expanded, so did the number of formal devices and their power. Arguments motivating such devices invariably took the following form:

(5.32)   a. *Phenomenon P has in the past been considered to be simply "pragmatic," that is, part of performance and hence outside the bounds of a formal grammatical treatment.*

   b. *But P is reflected both in morpheme distribution and in the "grammaticality" judgments that speakers are able to provide.*

   c. *If anything is the task of the grammarian, it is the explanation of native-speaker judgments and the distribution of morphemes in a language. Therefore, P must be handled in the grammar.*

   d. *But the grammatical devices now available are insufficient for this task. Therefore, new devices of greater power must be added.*

Jerrold Sadock was the first person to defend in depth the idea that, what in the past had been considered "pragmatic" phenomena, were amenable to grammatical treatment. For example, Sadock (1969) argued that the German sentence (5.33) is "clearly ungrammatical [p. 297]" due to its mixing of polite and familiar forms. He therefore concluded that underlying structures would have to encode the relative status of speaker and hearer:

(5.33)   *Machen Sie deinen Koffer zu!*

Sadock also argued (1970, 1975) that even indirectly conveyed illocutionary forces have to be represented in the deepest level of syntactic structure—again on the basis of morpheme distribution. For example, since the word *please* occurs only with requests, its occurrence in *Could you close the door, please* suggested to Sadock that this sentence must contain a performative verb of requesting in its underlying representation.

Sadock never took step (5.32d)—he felt that the existing syntactic mechanisms sufficed to handle the phenomena in question. But the work of

---

[11] Much of the material in this section will be treated in greater detail in Section 7.2.

George Lakoff in the early 1970s was largely devoted to motivating this step. His arguments were typically based on "grammaticality" judgments such as those of (5.34a–b):

(5.34) a. *John told Mary that she was ugly and then shé insúlted hím*
         b. **John told Mary that she was beautiful and then shé insúlted hím*

He noted that the "grammaticality" of (5.34a) and the "ungrammaticality" of (5.34b) are relative to our culture, which praises beauty and condemns ugliness—"those with other beliefs may disagree [G. Lakoff 1971c:333]." Since, "one's judgment of the well-formedness of sentences seems to vary with one's beliefs or assumptions [p. 332]," he concluded that rules of stress placement had to make reference to such beliefs or assumptions—an ability clearly beyond the bounds of the grammar as they were conceived in 1970. He also argued that in order to provide a full account of the possible antecedents of anaphoric expressions, even deductive reasoning must enter into a grammatical description (1971b). Note that the antecedent of *too* in (5.35), "the mayor is honest," is not present in the logical structure of the sentence, but must be deduced from it and its associated presupposition "Republicans are honest":

(5.35) *The mayor is a Republican and the used-car dealer is honest too*

The attempt to handle all aspects of conveyed meaning grammatically led Lakoff to develop a mechanism of great expressive power—the TRANS-DERIVATIONAL CONSTRAINT. A transderivational constraint is a constraint on one derivation subject to properties of another. They were first suggested (in unpublished work) around 1970 by David Perlmutter and Paul Postal, who were puzzled by the fact that the rule of Extraposition-from-NP seems to apply to (5.36a) to derive (5.36b), but not to (5.37a) to derive (5.37b):

(5.36) a. *A woman that was pregnant took the job*
         b. *A woman took the job that was pregnant*

(5.37) a. *A woman that was attractive took the job*
         b. *A woman took the job that was attractive*

Perlmutter and Postal suggested that the incorrect reading of (5.37b) was blocked by a transderivational constraint sensitive to the fact that this sentence, but not (5.36b) is ambiguous.[12]

---

[12] The Perlmutter–Postal conception of transderivational constraints has been developed in several papers by Judith Aissen and Jorge Hankamer (see Aissen and Hankamer 1972; Hankamer 1972, 1973; Aissen 1973.)

Lakoff further developed transderivational constraints (1971a, 1972b) to handle presuppositions, suggesting that they need not be part of the logical structure of a sentence if rules dependent on presuppositional information have transderivational power. Such power became clearly necessary with the assumption that rules could be sensitive to conveyed meanings in the class of possible contexts in which such meanings were appropriate— there was no way that a "situation" could be considered part of the logical structure of the sentence. Gordon and Lakoff (1971) proposed a set of transderivational constraints called CONVERSATIONAL POSTULATES to handle conversationally conveyed aspects of meaning such as indirect illocutionary force and conversational implicature, treating them essentially as context-dependent entailments.

5.5.2. Fuzzy Grammar

The chain of reasoning in (5.32a–d) led, as we have seen, to any judgment a speaker can make being considered a "grammaticality" judgment. But, as is well known, such judgments are not generally an either–or matter. Some sentences are more acceptable than others. G. Lakoff (1973) illustrated this point by citing sentences (5.38a–f), which according to his judgments grow gradually less acceptable from (a) to (f):

(5.38)   a. *John is the kinda fella that accidents naturally happen to him*
          b. *John is the kinda fella that it's likely that accidents'll happen to him*
          c. *John is the kinda fella that people think accidents naturally happen to him*
          d. *John is the kinda fella that I know that accidents happen to him*
          e. *John is the kinda fella that I realize that accidents happen to him*
          f. *John is the kinda fella that you find out that accidents happen to him*

Lakoff concluded that such graded judgments falsify the notion that sentences should be either generated (i.e., be "grammatical") or not generated (i.e., be "ungrammatical"). Rather, some mechanism has to allow for their being assigned grammaticality TO A CERTAIN DEGREE. On the basis of his own "subjective judgment," he assigned them the following well-formedness ratings:

(5.39)   (5.38a) = (.8); (5.38b) = (.7); (5.38c) = (.6); (5.38d) = (.5);
          (5.38e) = (.4); (5.38f) = (.3)

Lakoff called a grammar that is capable of generating sentences with a particular degree of assigned grammaticality a "fuzzy grammar," and explicitly viewed such a grammar as entailing only a slight extension of the mechanisms already available to generative semantics.

Between 1972 and 1974, a number of generative semanticists, most notably John R. Ross, argued in many papers that ALL of the constructs of linguistic theory, not just the notion of "grammaticality," are nondiscrete (or "squishy"). For example, Ross (1973a) argued that the boundary between sentences and nouns is fuzzy rather than discrete. Constructions at the left end of the "nouniness squish (5.40)" are more sentencelike; those at the right end are more nounlike. This squish is further elaborated in (5.41):

(5.40)   *that* > *for–to* > Q > *Acc Ing* > *Poss Ing* >
Action Nominal > Derived Nominal > Noun

(5.41)   a. *that* = *that*-clause (*that Max gave the letters to Frieda*)

b. *for–to* = *for* NP *to* VX (*for Max to have given the letters to Frieda*)

c. Q = embedded questions (*how willingly Max gave the letters to Frieda*)

d. *Acc Ing* = [$^{NP}_{+Acc}$] V + *ing* X (*Max giving the letters to Frieda*)

e. *Poss Ing* = NP's V + *ing* X (*Max's giving the letters to Frieda*)

f. Action Nominal $\left(\left\{ \begin{array}{l} Max's \\ the \end{array} \right\} giving\ of\ the\ letters\ to\ Frieda \right)$

g. Derived Nominal $\left(\left\{ \begin{array}{l} Max's \\ the \end{array} \right\} gift\ of\ the\ letters\ to\ Frieda \right)$

h. Noun (*spatula*)

To show that these complement types are hierarchically grouped, Ross gave many examples of phenomena which apply, say, to (5.41a–d), but not (e–h); (c–f), but not (a–b) or (g–h); (d–h), but not (a–c); etc. For example, the rule of Preposition Deletion, which deletes the *at* which is lexically associated with the word *surprised*, must apply before *that* and *for–to*, may apply before Q, and may not apply before complements of greater nouniness (an asterisk inside parentheses indicates that the enclosed material must not occur; an asterisk outside parentheses that it must occur):

(5.42)   a. *I was surprised (*at) that you had hives*
           b. *I was surprised (at) how far you could throw the ball*
           c. *I was surprised *(at) Jim's victory*

Ross (1973a) proposed to capture these generalizations formally by allowing elements to be members of a category to a degree:

> Thus in particular, I propose that the previously used node S, sentence, be replaced by a feature [αS], where α ranges over the real numbers in [0,1]. Each of the complement types in (1-2) [=my (Example 5.40)—F.N.] would be given a basic value of α, and rules, filters, and other types of semantactic [*sic*] processes, would be given upper and lower threshold values of α between which they operate [p. 188].

In addition to grammaticality and category distinctions, it was also argued that the notions of "rule applicability" (Ross 1974), "island strength" (Rodman 1975), "clause-mate" (Ross 1975), "grammatical relation" (Lawler 1977), and the basic constructs of semantics (G. Lakoff 1972e, 1973) are all also fuzzy.[13]

5.5.3. The End of Grammatical Theory

Not surprisingly, as the terms "grammatical" and "acceptable" began to be used interchangeably, the competence–performance dichotomy began to lose more and more of its original force. As early as 1972, McCawley used the term "competence" with a meaning that encompassed much of what had previously been considered part of performance:

> I take "linguistic competence" here as referring to a speaker's internalized system for relating meanings to possible ways of expressing them and the characteristics of linguistic and extra-linguistic contexts under which particular ways of expressing them are appropriate [McCawley 1972:np].

George Lakoff (1974a) took a further step in the annihilation of the competence–performance distinction. In response to the interviewer's question: "Modern linguistics was always operating with strong dichotomies. Is it your explicit purpose to transcend all these boundaries and distinctions?" Lakoff replied:

> Yes. In fact, that is one of the most interesting things coming out of generative semantics. We have found that one cannot just set up artificial boundaries and rule out of the study of language such things as human reasoning, context, social interaction, deixis, fuzziness, sarcasm, discourse types, fragments, variation among speakers, etc. Each time we have set up an artificial boundary, we have found some phenomenon that shows that it has to be removed. That is not to say that there are no bounds on the study of linguistics. I only suggest that at this point in history the boundaries are disappearing daily, and one should not be too surprised if the domain of the field continues to expand [p. 178].

---

[13] Lakoff and Ross acknowledged their debt for the notion of fuzzy grammar to the logician Lofti Zadeh and his work in "fuzzy set theory" (see especially Zadeh 1965, 1971).

And not much later, the next logical step was taken as linguistic theory itself was abandoned. Echoing Twaddell (1935) and other structuralists, Lakoff (and his collaborator, Henry Thompson) came to characterize theoretical constructs simply as "convenient fictions":

> From this point of view, abstract grammars do not have any separate mental reality; they are just convenient fictions for representing certain processing strategies. Likewise, abstract transformational derivations are just convenient fictions for representing aspects of linguistic structure [Lakoff and Thompson 1975:295].

5.5.4. On the Inevitability of These Developments

It is worth asking whether or not generative semantics HAD to take the course outlined in this section. The fact that not all generative semanticists followed Lakoff down this path suggests that the answer is "no." Yet there is a sense in which these developments were inevitable. The cornerstone of generative semantic argumentation was the Katz–Postal hypothesis, which led to the strategy of motivating underlying structures by appealing to the meaning of the sentence. But no construct in linguistics is fuzzier than "meaning of a sentence." In particular, the boundary between semantic and pragmatic facts was not understood in the least in the early 1970s and is barely understood today. Given this, it is hardly surprising that, more and more, the domain of "meaning" was expanded to include virtually any construct relevant to understanding, from quantifier scope to strategies for indicating sarcasm. As the data base of grammatical theory expanded (and with it the amount of information needed to be encoded into underlying structure), the content of the theory declined correspondingly. The Lakoff and Thompson quotation just cited simply represents the Katz–Postal hypothesis carried to its logical conclusion.

5.6. THE EARLY DEBATE

5.6.1. A Period of Acrimony

It is hard today to appreciate the vehemence with which the debate between generative semanticists and interpretive semanticists was carried out in the late 1960s and early 1970s. At times, the heat of the debate grew so intense that even in print the rhetoric exceeded the bounds of normal partisan scholarship—witness Dougherty's (1974) description of a paper of McCawley's as "Machiavellian [p. 267]" and George Lakoff's (1972d) accusation that Chomsky "fights dirty when he argues. He uses every trick in the book [p. 70L]." As can easily be imagined, the discussion sessions after conference papers provided an arena for far stronger sentiments. The high point (or low point) of this was surely the one after George Lakoff's "Global Rules" paper at the 1969 Linguistic Society of America meeting, in which for several minutes he and Ray Jackendoff hurled amplified obscenities at each other before 200 embarrassed onlookers. There is hardly a need to mention the personal animosities engendered, many of which smoulder still.

As might be expected, the controversy over hiring decisions made by linguistics departments was one particularly bitter aspect of the internecine warfare. For example, the replacement of two generative semanticists at the University of Massachusetts by interpretivists served to solidify partisans of the former model in their opposition to interpretivism. On the other side of the fence, the hiring of a noninterpretivist by MIT in 1970 to fill a vacant position so outraged the students there (who almost unanimously would have preferred an interpretivist) that it has been suggested (by Joseph Emonds, personal communication) that this event represents the turning point in the struggle. From that point onward, the students there consciously set out to "reconquer the field."

In the following pages, I will attempt to identify the more substantive issues of the debate, and explain why, in general, generative semantics came away very much the loser.

5.6.2. The Globality Debate

The most emotional issue, perhaps oddly, was the question of the existence of global rules. I write "perhaps oddly" because even prior to the birth of generative semantics it had always been assumed that history of derivation had to play a role in determining applicability of transformations. Recall the original Lees proposal, which I outlined in Section 3.2.2. And as recently as 1968, Chomsky had discussed in some detail "a rather abstract condition that takes into account not only the structure to which the operation applies but also the history of derivation of this structure [p. 28]." In fact, during the debate itself NOBODY denied that transformations needed to be supplemented with rules of a different formal nature. And to argue about which was preferable, an interpretive rule determining the scope of logical elements or a global rule describing the same thing, seemed especially senseless to many—after all, the two simply seemed to be inverses of each other.

But at a more metatheoretical level, linguists did indeed perceive a difference between the two approaches. George Lakoff (whose positions, for better or worse, came to be identified with the "official" generative semantic line) repeatedly implied that to claim that something was to be handled by a global rule was to make no claim at all about it (other than the negative claim that a transformational rule could not handle it). Derived structure rules of interpretation, as hazily formulated as they were, seemed to many to be at least in principle limitable in their scope. Whatever empirical differences there may have been between global rules and derived structure rules of semantic interpretation (and there may not have been any), this perceived limitability helped give the latter the edge over the former.

The debate around the Greek case and English contraction phenomena has continued for many years. Baker and Brame (1972) and Quicoli (1972) proposed the following solution to the former: An index is assigned to an NP and its modifiers which indicates their being in the same simple S; a late rule assigns case to the modifier based on that of its coindexed NP. As stated, this makes the same empirical predictions as the Lakoff–Andrews global treatment. Lakoff (1972c) replied, however, that the indexing solution, as opposed to the global solution, involved "arbitrary markers" and "an infinite number of different grammatical elements," and hence was to be rejected. Few viewed this as a particularly persuasive criticism, since the indexing solution seemed to be little more than a formalization of the global rule. Since then, Quicoli has presented massive evidence (still uncontested) that the facts are far more complicated than suggested by Lakoff and Andrews. When they are taken into account, he argues, they require little if any alteration of the indexing solution, but enormous complication of the global account, including the modification of the rule of Equi solely to "encode" information from an earlier stage in the derivation—the very solution which Lakoff found so abhorrent.

Selkirk (1972) has offered a nonglobal solution to the contraction phenomena very much in the spirit of the Baker–Brame–Quicoli treatment of the Greek data. She proposed (essentially) that transformations that move or delete constituents do not move to delete the word boundaries associated with them, and that the presence of these word boundaries blocks stress reduction and contraction. Here, the Lakoff defense that this would involve "arbitrary coding devices" was even weaker, since word boundaries have independent motivation. Furthermore, since Selkirk's solution succeeded in relating (at least in principle) the contraction phenomena to other boundary phenomena in French, it was the global alternative which emerged looking the more ad hoc.

By the mid 1970s, partisans of global rules were clearly on the defensive. Those proposed seemed, for the most part, to be based on a faulty analysis of the data or to lend themselves to an indexing or interpretive rule solution. Despite the numerous unclarities and problems with this alternative approach, they came to be more and more favored, since they at least enabled the phenomenon under investigation to be concretized and, in many cases, pointed the way to a principled solution.

Global rules continue to be posited today by various linguists. But in general they are seen as a descriptive statement for organizing recalcitrant data, rather than as an explanatory device. Certainly few today would agree that a grammar with global rules "is as much an innovation over transformational grammar as transformational grammar is over phrase structure grammar [G. Lakoff 1970c:638],'' or at least not with the positive connotations that the quotation is intended to convey.

5.6.3. The Deep Structure Debate

Needless to say, the question of the existence of the level of deep structure was an issue that caused its share of rancor. Since the most common arguments against this level involved arguments for syntactic lexical decomposition, it was on lexical decomposition that the interpretivists most frequently trained their guns. They claimed to be able to show, and by and large were perceived as successful in doing so, that the syntactic and semantic behavior of lexical items simply does not match those of their supposed syntactic sources, and therefore the strongest argument for lexical decomposition is invalid.

For example, J.A. Fodor (1970) gave a syntactic argument against deriving *melt* from something like 'cause to melt.' Under such a derivation, Fodor argued, (5.43b) should be grammatical and a paraphrase of (5.43a):

(5.43) a. *Floyd caused the glass to melt on Sunday by heating it on Saturday*
        b. **Floyd melted the glass on Sunday by heating it on Saturday*

Bowers (1970) attacked Postal's underlying representation of *remind* [see (5.10b)] from a semantic rather than a syntactic angle, by pointing out that Postal's analysis predicts that the contradictory nature of (5.44a) should entail (5.44b) being contradictory as well. But it is not, as (5.44c) (in which modifiers have been added for clarity) clearly illustrates:

(5.44) a. *I perceive that Larry is similar to Winston Churchill, although I perceive that Larry is not similar to Winston Churchill*
        b. *Larry reminds me of Winston Churchill, although I perceive that Larry is not similar to Winston Churchill*
        c. *For some reason Larry reminds me of Winston Churchill, although I perceive that Larry is not really similar to him at all*

Many more arguments of this type were constructed against lexical decomposition. The generative semanticists' only recourse was to say that the lexical items *melt, remind*, etc. do not have exactly the same semantic representations as *cause to melt, perceive to be similar*, etc., but have meanings which are either more restricted or less restricted. While nobody denied the truth of this claim, it made this type of argument for lexical decomposition and against deep structure extremely unpersuasive.

Generative semanticists also attempted to motivate syntactic lexical decomposition by pointing to the fact that their crucial rule of Predicate Raising can be motivated uncontroversially in languages as diverse as Japanese, Eskimo, and Blackfoot (see Frantz 1974). Hence, they claimed, it stands to reason that it should be at work in English too. But this was not seen as an especially compelling argument. It seemed to be the case that whenever generative semanticists needed a prelexical transformation to collapse two clauses, they postulated Predicate Raising at work; to raise a noun phrase to a higher clause, Subject Raising; to make an object a subject, Passive. No motivation for the application of these rules was ever given, aside from the need to get from Point A (semantic representation) to Point B (a constituent which a lexical item could replace). But given enough ingenuity and enough rules for whose application no formal statement nor external motivation was required, and whose application could be assumed to be optional or obligatory at will, it was obviously always going to be easy to get from A to B.

The internal modification arguments for lexical decomposition did not fare much better. Chomsky (1972a) and Kac (1972) pointed out that lexical decomposition predicts far more ambiguities than actually occur. If the ambiguity of *John almost killed Bill* is an argument for decomposition of *kill*, then the fact that the sentence is not obviously four (or more) ways ambiguous should count as an argument against it, since the semantic representation of *kill* contains (at least) CAUSE-BECOME-NOT-ALIVE, each of which should be modifiable by *almost*.

Likewise, it did not prove impossible to come up with examples of lexical items whose "syntactic" derivation seemed to violate constraints on transformations. For example, Dowty (1972) noted that *cuckold* in *John cuckolded Bill* means 'had sexual intercourse with a woman who is the wife of', apparently violating the Complex NP Constraint, and Wasow (1976) (citing Howard Lasnik) argued that if *tincture of* or *include* were derived syntactically, then their derivations must have violated the Coordinate Structure Constraint, since they mean 'a solution of alcohol and' and 'contain something else and', respectively. While no doubt paraphrases could be found whose sources would not lead to the constraint violation, this simply indicated to many the hopelessness of the strategy of doing syntax by searching for paraphrases.

But by far the most intractable problem for the generative semanticists was the fact that they were still left with the problem of accounting for a primary function of the renounced level of deep structure—the specification of morpheme order. For example, the order of articles, adjectives, negatives, numerals, nouns, and noun complements within a noun phrase simply does not follow from anything semantic. Thus, generative semantics would require some sort of template or filter to ensure the correct order—in itself a sneaking-in of an important aspect of deep structure. But the filter could not be statable without considerable loss of generality. For example, Green (1974), in her effort to make Dative Movement semantically governed, posited 14 underlying semantic classes of Dative Movement predicates, which, after the application of various rules, end up in structures like V NP_a P NP_b or V NP_b NP_a. Now, a model with deep structure can express this surface generalization very simply—by positing a phrase-structure rule like (5.45) and a Dative Movement transformation like (5.46):

(5.45)   VP → V NP PP

(5.46)   V NP_a $\begin{Bmatrix} to \\ for \end{Bmatrix}$ NP_b → V NP_b NP_a

Green attempted to express this regularity by postulating that her 14 rules are in some sense part of a "conspiracy" that guides them to the "target structures" V NP_a *to/for* NP_b and/or V NP_b NP_a. But as Oehrle (1977) pointed out, this target structure cannot be a property of the grammar as a whole, but only of its subpart forming sentences with "dative predicates." Hence, each rule in the grammar would need to be marked with a feature of some sort to indicate whether or not it was subject to a particular conspiracy/target structure. A treatment with a level of deep structure and a phrase-structure rule like (5.45) faces no such problem.

5.6.4. Other Issues

The debate focused on many other issues as well, and on most, generative semantics emerged the loser. Nowhere is this as true as in the debate over syntactic categories. To begin with, generative semantics, even if it had been successful in reducing the UNDERLYING set of categories to three members, clearly did not succeed in reducing the TOTAL number to three. There is a difference between nouns, verbs, adjectives, adverbs, quantifiers, prepositions, etc. in surface structure, regardless of what is needed at the most underlying level. Hence, there seemed to be no substance to the generative semantic claim that it succeeded in reducing the inventory of substantive universals. How WOULD generative semantics distinguish nouns from verbs? McCawley (1970b) explained: "The difference between nouns and verbs is that nouns but not verbs are subject to a transformation which replaces a relative clause by its predicate element [pp. 169–170]." But as Bresnan (1972a:198) pointed out, such an approach is really nothing more than using a class of transformations as categories in disguise. Nothing is gained by replacing ad hoc (if such they be) categories by ad hoc transformations. Bresnan discussed the problem at length, arguing that the deep structure/category approach makes an important prediction that the generative semantic approach does not—categories predict a CLUSTERING of syntactic properties. For generative semantics, the grammar would be no more complicated if there were no correlation at all between "derived" category and syntactic behavior.

By 1972 or 1973 all of the issues discussed in this section had been fully debated at conferences, in unpublished (and some published) work, and at a personal level. Generative semantics was on the retreat.

5.7. THE LATER DEBATE: THE COLLAPSE OF GENERATIVE SEMANTICS

In this section, I will probe further the amazingly rapid decline of generative semantics. We still have not arrived at an adequate explanation for the fact that a model whose followers were ''motivated only by personal loyalty to Chomsky'' (as popular wisdom had it in 1967), would half a dozen years later be the dominant syntactic theory, with a corresponding decline of its rival.

This is not to say that ALL generative semanticists abandoned their beliefs, and certainly not to say that all became interpretivists (although some did; examples are Emmon Bach, D. Terence Langendoen, and David Lightfoot). Many adopted newer approaches to language with rather different assumptions from both, like relational grammar or Montague grammar. Many others were simply ''neutralized.'' But most significantly, students entering linguistics from around 1971 or 1972 on were not interested in becoming generative semanticists. And this is the fact which I will attempt to explain.

5.7.1. The Generative Semantic Dynamic

It is tempting to think that it was the weight of the interpretivist counterattack that led to the demise of generative semantics. While it played an important role, it was not the deciding factor. For one thing, generative semanticists saw enough defects in the interpretive model (some of which I will outline in Chapter 6) for the interpretivist critique to lose some of its force. For another, the majority of the published critiques of generative semantics, including the most comprehensive ones (Wasow 1976; Brame 1976; Oehrle 1977) did not appear until after that model had begun to crumble.

No, the fact is that generative semantics DESTROYED ITSELF. Its internal dynamic led to a state of affairs in which it could no longer be taken seriously by anyone interested in the scientific study of human language. Generative semantics simply gave up on attempting to EXPLAIN grammatical phenomena, leaving the field open to its competitors.

The dynamic that led to the abandonment of explanation for pure description flowed irrevocably from the decision to abandon scientific idealizations and therefore consider ANY speaker judgment and ANY fact about morpheme distribution as a matter for grammatical analysis. In retrospect, it is easy to see how aprioristic such a decision was—it is no more NECESSARY that, say, the distribution of the morpheme *please* in English and the distribution of clitic pronouns in Spanish be treated within the same general framework (i.e., formal grammar) than it is that any two physical phenomena be derivable from the same set of equations.

Attributing the same theoretical weight to each and every fact about language had disastrous consequences. Since the number of facts is, of course, absolutely overwhelming, simply DESCRIBING the incredible complexities of language became the all-consuming task, with formal explanation postponed to some future date. Fillmore (1972) explicitly noted the data-collecting consequences of the generative semantic view of language: The ordinary working grammarian "finds himself in the age of what we might call the New Taxonomy, an era of a new and exuberant cataloguing of the enormous range of facts that linguists need eventually to find theories to deal with [p. 16]."

This "exuberant cataloguing of . . . facts" became a hallmark of generative semantics, as every counterexample to a claim (real or apparent) was greeted as an excuse to broaden still further the domain of formal grammar. The data fetishism reached its apogee in fuzzy grammar. Many staunch generative semanticists who had followed every step of Lakoff's and Ross's up to that point, turned away from fuzzy theoretical constructs. "Of course there's a squish," they objected. "There's always a squish. It's the nature of data to be squishy. And it's the purpose of a theory to extract order from squishy data." Generative semantics, it became all too clear, was not such a theory.[14]

The substitution of "squishy" lists of sentences for rules and derivations took on a life of its own. Generative semanticists squealed with delight at the "horrors," "monstrosities," "mind snappers," and "wonders" (Postal 1976) which no theory seemed to be able to explain. Bill Darden (1974) captured the nihilistic outlook of his generative semanticist co-thinkers admirably in the following quote (which dealt specifically with natural phonology): "The multitude of views can be taken as evidence that we have reached that happy state when no one can be sure that he knows anything— except that everyone else is wrong [np]."

Now it needs to be pointed out that very few interpretivists in the early 1970s were either formalizing rules or presenting grammar fragments.[15] But

[14] Apparently Ross's mid 1970s squishes lacked significance even when evaluated on their own terms. Gazdar and Klein (1978) point out that "it is crucial to Ross' argument [for squishes] in this paper [=Ross 1975], as in his others, that the matrices exhibit statistically significant scalar properties that would not typically show up on an arbitrary matrix. He does not subject his matrices to any kind of significance test, nor does he seem to be aware that such testing is necessary [p. 666]." After applying the "appropriate statistical technique" (Guttman scaling) to Ross's major clausematiness "squishoid," they conclude from the results that "Ross' squishoid provides no backing whatever for his claim that grammars require a quantifiable predicate of clausematiness [p. 666]."

For arguments that fuzzy logic is formally unsuitable for the linguistic goals which Lakoff and Ross wish to apply it, see Morgan and Pelletier (1977).

[15] Yet interpretivists (Ray Dougherty, in particular) never had any hesitation about condemning generative semanticists for this. It is interesting to note that, aside from various Montague treatments (see Section 8.5), the most comprehensive formalized fragment of English grammar in the late 1970s is Levi (1978), a work very much in the (early) generative semantic tradition.

for generative semanticists, not doing so became a matter of PRINCIPLE: "I think that the time has come to return to the tradition of INFORMAL descriptions of exotic languages . . . [G. Lakoff 1974a:153]." To students entering linguistics in the early 1970s, increasingly trained in the sciences, mathematics, and philosophy, the generative semantics positions on theory construction and formalization were anathema. It is little wonder that they found nothing of interest in this model.[16]

Not surprisingly, commentators began to see in generative semantics the seeds of a structuralist–empiricist counterrevolution. The first to make this point explicit, Ronat (1972), compared Postal's (1970a) heavy reliance on co-occurrence facts to support his abstract analysis of the verb *remind* to the methodology of Harris and other Bloomfieldians (see also Dougherty 1974). By the time that the consummate critique of the philosophical implications of late generative semantics, Katz and Bever (1976), had been published, that model had been abandoned even by most of its erstwhile supporters. Nevertheless, the following passage from their article is worth quoting, since it was the realization of its point that led many linguists to turn their backs on generative semantics:

> The three cases just considered show how generative semantics has distorted grammar by including within its goals a complete theory of acceptability. This assimilation of the phenomenon of performance into the domain of grammaticality has come about as a consequence of an empiricist criterion for determining what counts as grammatical. In almost every paper Lakoff makes explicit his assumption that the explanatory goal of a grammar is to state all the factors that influence the distribution of morphemes in speech. On this view, any phenomenon systematically related to cooccurrence is *ipso facto* something to be explained in the grammar. Since in actual speech almost anything can influence cooccurrence relations, it is no wonder that Lakoff repeatedly discovers more and more new kinds of "grammatical phenomena." In fact, the generative semanticist program for linguistic theory represents, if anything, a more extreme approach than even Bloomfieldian structuralism, which recognized that a variety of phenomena concerning language are extragrammatical [Katz and Bever 1976:58].

5.7.2. "The Best Theory"

Probably no metatheoretical statement by a generative semanticist did more to undermine confidence in that model than Paul Postal's paper "The Best Theory," to which I alluded in Section 5.4.5. Interpreted at one level this paper is no more than a routine plea for a theory without unneeded apparatus and with as tight constraints as possible on the apparatus which

---

[16] Robin Lakoff (1974) has attempted to provide the generative semantic rejection of formalism with explicit POLITICAL motivation, arguing that "undue obeisance to formalism [xiv–23]" discourages women from the field. While she did not state whether mathematics and the sciences should also abandon formalism as a step toward sexual equality, she did, astonishingly, explicitly leave open the possibility that the "indisposition toward formalism among women" might be "inherent"!

it does have. But that is not how "The Best Theory" was generally interpreted. Postal contrasted two hypothetical models, one with just As and another with both Bs and Cs, where A, B, and C are distinct components or rule types. Surely, Postal argued, the first, more "homogeneous" theory is preferable. Generative semantics is then preferable to interpretive semantics, since it is more homogeneous—it postulates a single mapping from semantic representation to surface structure without the level of deep structure intervening, whereas the latter has (at least) two distinct rule types and an extra level.

As long as Postal was attributing no CONTENT to A, B, and C, nobody could object. But Postal did not consider what it would mean if A were simply an unconstrained "rule of grammar," while B and C were highly constrained rule types of definite form and specific function. In that case, it is the LATTER alternative which is preferable, not the former. But as things stood around 1970, it was the third possibility that best described the situation. Interpretivists, at least in principle, were committed to constraining (or at least characterizing) B and C, whereas generative semanticists steadily weakened the content of A by ever increasing the type of data that it had to cover. Postal's paper drove home better than any interpretivist critique succeeded in doing the point that generative semantics was constructing a more homogeneous theory only by ceasing to make specific claims about language.

Generative semanticists typically responded to criticism of this type by arguing that the two theories were simply incomparable by virtue of the differing conceptual status of their primitives. In generative semantics, such primitives were all "natural":

> The same considerations of naturalness obtain in syntax [as in phonology]. The theory of generative semantics claims that the linguistic elements used in grammar have an independent natural basis in the human conceptual system . . . . In generative semantics, possible grammars are limited by the requirement [sic] that the nonphonological elements used have a natural semantic basis, independent of the rules of the grammar of any particular natural language [G. Lakoff 1972c:77–78].

But such argumentation did not get very far. Many saw through its transparently aprioristic character. Emonds (1973) wrote:

> Lakoff refuses to consider the merits of their [interpretivist] analysis, which employs categories which are well-motivated internal to language (syntactically). This refusal seems to me like requiring that philosophy define a priori the notions of science, in which case we never would have gotten to gravity, relativity, etc. [p. 56].

But even more importantly, the naturalness "requirement" was seen as little more than a terminological trick. Taken literally, it embodied the claim that all syntactic behavior could be expressed in "natural" semantic terms. But stated this way, NOBODY ever held such a position—how could one possibly explain the radically different syntactic behavior of the adjective *possible* and the modal *may* in strictly semantic terms, for example? In other words, all of the "natural" categories of generative semantics would have to be supplemented by a set of "unnatural" (derived) categories, rules, or whatever to explain all of the regularities (and irregularities) of language which could not be formulated in strictly semantic terms.

All the appeal to "naturalness" did, in effect, was to bequeath to the interpretivists the task of searching for syntactic regularity.

5.7.3. Generative Semantic Style[17]

One last characteristic trait of generative semantics which clearly speeded its downfall was the whimsical style of presentation which pervaded so much written in that framework. This is not to say that all generative semanticists were prone to such practice, nor that partisans of that model alone were, but such practice certainly became a hallmark of generative semantics. This manifested itself in titles of papers and books (5.47), names of rules and constraints (5.48), example sentences (5.49), and in the prose itself (5.50):

(5.47)   a. *You Take the High Node and I'll Take the Low Node* (Corum *et al.* 1973)
b. "If You Hiss or Anything, I'll Do It Back" (Cantrall 1970)
c. "Tracking the Generic Toad" (Lawler 1973)

(5.48)   a. "Richard" (Rogers 1974)
b. "Q-Magic" (Carden 1968)
c. "Stuffing" (Ross 1972b)

(5.49)   a. *Norbert the narc only reports potheads* (Lawler 1973)
b. *Tums's taste is wall-to-wall Yucksville* (Ross 1973c)
c. *Symbolic logic—and, by the way, who invented it?—isn't my cup of Postum.* (Sadock 1974)

(5.50)   a. "The winner gets to say 'Nyaah, nyaah!' to the loser." (G. Lakoff 1973:286)
b. "In summing up this awesome display of cosmic mysteries with scarcely a hint here and there of a denouement, we are reminded of the immortal words of Harry Reasoner." (L. Horn 1970:326)
c. "It is no longer necessary to assume that instrumental verb formation occurs in one swell foop." (Green 1972:84)

Such stylistic traits only served to give extra credibility to the charge of lack of seriousness, which the generative semanticists were more than open to as a result of their abandonment of the task of constructing a

---

[17] I am indebted to Ann Banfield and Joseph Emonds for first making me aware of the issue discussed in this section. For remarks in a similar vein, see Percival (1971), Sampson (1976), and Hagège (1976).

formalized theory of language. Indeed, it is tempting to speculate that generative semantic style is but a classic example of content both shaping form and dominating it. Certainly not all generative semanticists would agree with one ex-partisan that ''we went out of our way to be funny in our papers so that once our ideas were refuted we could get ourselves off the hook by saying, 'Oh, did you take us seriously? Couldn't you see that we were just fooling around?' [personal communication].'' But most, I suspect, would acknowledge a kernel of truth in it.

In addition to the way this stylistic practice reflected on generative semantics itself, linguists outside of American culture were totally offended by it. Even highly fluent nonnative speakers of English found many generative semantic papers impossible to read, by virtue of the culture-bound slang and topical examples that permeated them. Even NATIVE speakers were baffled at times. Stephen Isard, an American linguist resident in Britain, recalls that he had to serve as interpreter for a colleague to help him through Ross's example sentence *It is said that the tacos Judge Bean won't go for* (Ross 1973b: 164). *Tacos, Judge Bean,* and *go for* were all unfamiliar to him. Of course, the sentence *It is said that the oranges John won't ask for* would have served just as well to make the relevant theoretical point.

5.7.4. The Generative Semanticists' Organizational Problems

Generative semanticists were never able to take full advantage of the numerical and geographical head start which they had over the interpretivists. Of the leading members of that tendency, only James McCawley was able to build a stable base and following. Paul Postal, working for IBM, had no students at all, while John R. Ross was always very much under Chomsky's shadow at MIT, a fact which for obvious reasons deterred students at that university from becoming generative semanticists. And George Lakoff, by associating himself with four different institutions (Harvard, Michigan, The Center for Advanced Studies in the Behavioral Sciences, and The University of California, Berkeley) during the crucial years of 1969–1972, relinquished any possibility of building the kind of program that Halle and Chomsky had succeeded in building at MIT.

Once at Berkeley, Lakoff did attempt this. But by 1972 it was already too late. Neither the linguistics department there nor the Berkeley Linguistics Society (over which he exerted considerable influence at first) ever became the vehicles for the dissemination of his ideas that he hoped they would. And by coming out almost yearly with a newly named theory, from ''fuzzy grammar'' (1973) to ''global transderivational well-formedness grammar'' (1974b) to ''cognitive grammar'' (Lakoff and Thompson 1975) to ''dual–hierarchy grammar'' (1975a) to ''linguistic gestalt theory'' and ''experiental linguistics'' (1977), Lakoff has not presented himself to the linguistic world as a consistent theoretician.

5.8. THE LEGACY OF GENERATIVE SEMANTICS

While generative semantics now appears to few, if any, linguists to be a viable model of grammar, there are innumerable ways in which it has left its mark on its successors. Most importantly, its view that sentences must at one level have a representation in a formalism isomorphic to that of symbolic logic is now widely accepted by interpretivists, and in particular by Chomsky. It was generative semanticists who first undertook an intensive investigation of syntactic phenomena which defied formalization by means of transformational rules as they were then understood, and led to the plethora of mechanisms such as indexing devices, traces, and filters, which are now part of the interpretivists' theoretical store. Even the idea of lexical decomposition, for which generative semanticists have been much scorned, has turned up in the semantic theories of several interpretivists, as Wasow (1976:296) has pointed out. Furthermore, many proposals originally mooted by generative semanticists, such as the nonexistence of extrinsic rule ordering, post-cyclic lexical insertion, and treating anaphoric pronouns as bound variables, have since turned up in the interpretivist literature, virtually always without acknowledgment.

While late generative semantics may have proven itself THEORETICALLY bankrupt, the important initial studies which it inspired on the logical and sub-logical properties of lexical items, on speech acts, both direct and indirect, and on the more general pragmatic aspects of language are becoming more and more appreciated as linguistic theory is finally developing means to incorporate them. In Chapter 7, I will describe these studies, and the various attempts to deal with the semantic–pragmatic aspects of language, within both the theoretical framework of generative semantics and in later models.

Finally, one might say that generative semantics has won a Pyrrhic victory of sorts. The interpretive model has its own internal dynamic—a dynamic which has led its practitioners to strike rule after rule from the transformational roster, until, for some interpretivists, the transformational component has been entirely eliminated. As a result, there are now various interpretivist models whose interpretive components mirror in crucial ways the distinguishing features of the transformational component of the early generative semanticists. It is not clear that in these models (whose development I will outline in Chapter 8), a boundary between syntactic processes and semantic processes can be defined any more than it could in early generative semantics.

Chapter 6

Syntax in the 1970s:
Constraining the Syntactic Rules

6.1. THE CRUCIAL NEED FOR SYNTACTIC CONSTRAINTS

There had never been any doubt that the expressive power of transformational rules was far too great. Chomsky noted even in his 1955 work *The Logical Structure of Linguistic Theory* that such rules were so powerful that, as a consequence, transformational generative grammar made rather weak claims about what could or could not be a possible human language. Several specific proposals from the mid 1960s such as the condition on recoverability on deletion (Section 3.2.6), the base recursion hypothesis (Section 3.5.2), and the A-over-A Principle (Section 6.2.1) were explicitly seen as helping to reduce the expressive power of transformational rules.

But around 1970, the task of power reduction took on a new urgency. Studies by Stanley Peters and Robert Ritchie (1969, 1971, 1973) demonstrated that the situation was far worse than imagined. Put simply, Peters and Ritchie proved that the weak generative capacity of a transformational grammar was that of an unrestricted rewriting system (Turing machine). What this meant was that transformational rules were so unconstrained that transformational grammar as formulated then made no claim at all about any human language except that its sentences could be generated by some set of rules.[1] They showed further that the situation was not alleviated by either the recoverability condition or the principle of cyclic application. One last consequence was that the universal base hypothesis (Section 5.4.4) was unfalsifiable and hence devoid of content. They proved that ANY system of base rules could serve as a "universal" base of a descriptively adequate

---

[1] The Peters–Ritchie results are summarized in very readable form in Bach (1974:201–202).

grammar. Peters and Ritchie concluded that transformational grammar had to be constrained far more tightly than it was in the currently available version.

The Peters–Ritchie findings served as silent witness to almost all of the significant work in syntax in the 1970s. There was hardly a paper written that did not appeal to the increased restrictiveness of the theory that followed as a consequence of the adoption of the proposals in its pages. Constraint after constraint was put forward to limit the power of the grammar.

It is worth mentioning that the Peters–Ritchie findings drove one more nail into the generative semantic coffin. They showed that the main problem to be addressed was not the proliferation of category and rule types; it was the lack of constraints on the rules themselves. Thus the generative semanticists, who saw the former as the greater problem, found themselves in an extremely vulnerable position as the implications of the Peters–Ritchie results became more widely appreciated.

This chapter will be devoted, then, to discussing the many proposals for restricting the power of the syntactic rules which were made in the early and mid 1970s. Since this task, rather than the task of producing actual grammar fragments, was what consumed the attention of syntacticians in that period, the following pages serve to document the significant syntactic work carried on at that time.

Most of the work described in this chapter is in the interpretivist framework. So much so, that it can be considered a sequel to Section 5.2, in which the early interpretivist model was outlined. Yet, as always, complicating factors, partly terminological and partly substantive, cloud the issue. For purely sociological reasons, many linguists whose work was objectively interpretivist would have left the field rather than agree to have that label applied to them. Moreover, the relationship BETWEEN the various constraints is quite complex. Some are clearly compatible, some compatible only granted certain questionable assumptions, and some quite incompatible. Furthermore, compatibility between two proposed constraints was certainly no guarantee that a linguist who advocated one would advocate the other—any number of factors ranging from purely linguistic to purely sociological led to the wide range of "mixed" positions. I will delay my brief discussion of "who believed which and why" until Section 6.7 except in cases in which the delay would lead to confusion.

6.2. CONSTRAINTS ON TRANSFORMATIONS

The following three sections describe three important classes of constraints proposed to restrict the applicability of transformational rules: constraints on extraction (Section 6.2.1), the Structure Preserving Constraint (Section 6.2.2), and constraints on the application of deletion rules (Section

6.2.3). I will, however, devote an entire major section (Section 6.3) to a set of constraints originally proposed in Chomsky (1973), since they are intimately interwoven with an important modification of syntactic theory—the trace theory of movement rules.

6.2.1. Constraints on Extraction

Chomsky (1964a) noted the ambiguity of (6.1):

(6.1)   *Mary saw the boy walking to the railroad station*

In one reading, bracketed as (6.2a), *walking to the railroad station* is understood as a reduced relative clause. In the other, bracketed as (6.2b), it can be paraphrased *walk to the railroad station*:

(6.2)   a. [$_{NP}$[$_{NP}$*the boy*] [*walking to the railroad station*]]
         b. [$_{NP}$*the boy*] [*walking to the railroad station*]

He pointed out that the question formed from (6.1), (6.3), has only the second reading:

(6.3)   *Who did Mary see walking to the railroad station?*

He offered the following explanation. If a rule is stated so that it can apply ambiguously to one node and to another node of the same category which dominates it, the rule may in fact apply only to the dominating node. In (6.2a), since *the boy* is itself dominated by an NP, no NP (such as *who*) may be extracted from that position by a transformational rule. However *the boy* in (6.2b) and any *wh*-phrase in that position CAN be extracted—there is no dominating NP.

Apparent counterexamples like (6.4a–b) forced Chomsky to give up this "A-over-A Principle" very rapidly (Chomsky 1964b):

(6.4)   a. [$_{NP}$*who*] *would you approve of* [$_{NP}$*my seeing* ____]
         b. [$_{NP}$*what*] *are you uncertain about* [$_{NP}$*my giving* ____ *to John*]

However, the question of how extraction transformations might be constrained was returned to and treated in great detail in J. R. Ross's classic 1967 MIT dissertation "Constraints on Variables in Syntax." Ross too found the A-over-A Principle inadequate, and proposed a number of constraints on transformations designed to do its work without generating (6.4a–b). The four most important are

A. The Complex Noun Phrase Constraint
B. The Coordinate Structure Constraint
C. The Left Branch Condition
D. The Sentential Subject Constraint

They are informally stated below, along with a diagram schematically illustrating their effect and a sentence whose ungrammaticality the constraint
predicts:

   A. Complex Noun Phrase Constraint. *No element may be extracted
from a sentence dominated by a noun phrase with a lexical head noun.*

(6.5)

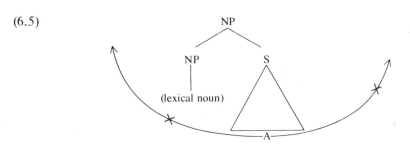

(6.6)   * [ₙₚwho] do you believe [ₙₚthe claim [ₛthat Bill saw   ____]]

   B. Coordinate Structure Constraint. *No conjunct in a coordinate structure may be moved, nor may any element in a conjunct be moved.*

(6.7)

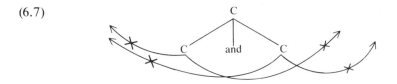

(6.8)   * [ₙₚwhat] was John eating [ₙₚ[beans] and ____]

   C. Left Branch Condition. *No noun phrase on the left branch of another
noun phrase may be extracted from that noun phrase.*

(6.9)

(6.10)   * [ₙₚwhose] did you like [ₙₚ____ [ₙbook]]

   D. Sentential Subject Constraint. *No element may be extracted from
the sentential subject of a sentence.*

(6.11)

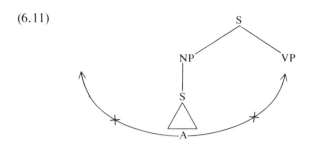

(6.12)   * [NP*what*] [NP[S*that John will eat* _____]] is likely?

The importance of Ross's thesis cannot be overestimated—the fact that it is second only to *Aspects of the Theory of Syntax* in number of citations in publications dealing with questions of syntax bears witness to its significance. Chapter 4, in which the bulk of the constraints are motivated, has served as a model in many a classroom for syntactic argumentation. And since the rules most relevant to the constraints (*Wh*-Question and Relative Movement, and Topicalization) operate at fairly shallow levels of syntactic structure, Ross's own abstract syntactic/generative semantic biases at the time of writing did not serve to discredit his results even after generative semantics fell by the wayside.

As might be expected, there have been innumerable minor and several major revisions of Ross's work since 1967. The eight most important major counterproposals are mentioned very briefly below:

A. (Chomsky 1973). See Section 6.3.
B. (Grosu 1972). The Complex NP Constraint, the Coordinate Structure Constraint, and a constraint on extraction from adverbial subordinate clauses can be replaced by a single constraint making use of the notions "nucleus" and "satellite."
C. (Kuno 1973). The Sentential Subject Constraint can be generalized to exclude any extraction process which results in "incomplete" subjects.
D. (G. Horn 1977). Almost all of Ross's constraints can be replaced by a single one—no constituent can be extracted from a noun phrase.
E. (Cattell 1976). Most of Ross's constraints can be replaced by "The NP Ecology Constraint"—the number and identity of argument NP's within a syntactic configuration must remain constant under the operation of movement rules.
F. (Culicover 1976). The "Binary Principle" involving the structural notion "master of" can replace most of Ross's constraints.

G. (Shir 1977). Most of Ross's constraints have a semantic explanation—extraction can take place only out of clauses which are semantically dominant (not presupposed and without contextual reference).

H. (Bresnan 1976b). Ross's constraints can be reinterpreted essentially
as a constraint involving unbounded movements or deletions and
the COMP node.

It seems safe to say that not one of these revisions has not been found
to be any less fraught with problems than those put forward in *Constraints
on Variables in Syntax* itself. The widespread use of the term "Ross-Con-
straint" to refer to extraction constraints in general is suggestive of the
importance—and resilience—of Ross's original proposals.

6.2.2. The Structure-Preserving Constraint

In 1967, John Kimball, then a student at MIT, made an interesting
observation. He noted that, by and large, cyclic transformations yield outputs which correspond to structures generable by the phrase-structure rules
(see Kimball 1972b). At the same time, his fellow students Stephen Anderson and Joseph Emonds made proposals that seemed to have the potential
of providing a means for capturing this insight. Anderson, in an effort to
extend McCawley's (1968b) concept of the base component, suggested that
(in effect) phrase-structure rules "check" the output of each transformational rule (see S. Anderson 1976). And Emonds, noting the increasing
length of derivations in this period of abstract syntax, put forward the idea
that the phrase-structure rules apply AFTER the transformations, lest important generalizations about surface order go uncaptured.

Emonds's 1970 dissertation *Root and Structure Preserving Transformations*, which fuses his and Anderson's proposals in a nonabstract framework, advances a formal explanation of WHY a class of transformations has
this structure preserving property. Emonds devoted the next several years
to a thoroughgoing revision of this work, the culmination of which is *A
Transformational Approach to English Syntax* (1976), widely agreed to be
the most impressive detailed analysis of English structure within the framework of transformational generative grammar.

The core of Emonds's analysis is the Structure-Preserving Constraint.
Put simply, this constraint states that a transformational rule can move an
element of category C only into a position in a phrase-marker held by a
node of category C. This is captured formally by allowing deep structure
nodes to go unfilled, "holding a place" for a structure preserving rule to
move an element under its domination. Any empty nodes (symbolized by
"Δ") remaining in surface structure result in ungrammaticality. To illustrate, consider Emonds's derivation (6.14a–b) of sentence (6.13):

(6.13)   *Germany was defeated by Russia*

(6.14)   a.

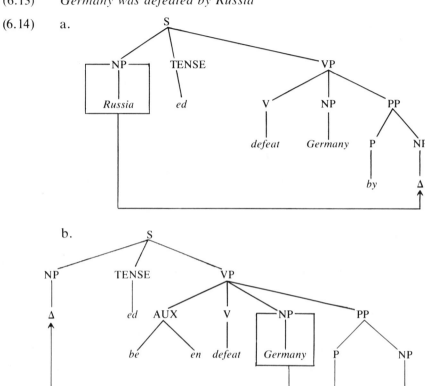

First, the deep structure subject, *Russia*, is postposed to fill the empty NP node following *by*. Then *Germany* fills the empty node left as a result of the postposing of the subject.

The constraining effect of this approach to movement can be appreciated from a consideration of the following ungrammatical sentences:

(6.15)   a. **Germany Russia was defeated by*
           b. **Germany was Russia defeated by*
           c. **Germany was by Russia defeated*
           d. **Germany was defeated Russia by*

Under traditional treatments, the ungrammaticality of (6.15a–d) follows simply from the statement of the Passive rule. Note that this rule could be modified trivially to generate any one of them. But the Structure Preserving Constraint PREDICTS their ungrammaticality from a general fact about English structure—none of these sentences correspond to structures generated by independently motivated base rules.

There are two formally characterizable classes of transformations which are not structure preserving in Emonds's theory:

A. Root transformations—transformations which attach elements to a "root sentence" (essentially, the highest clause in the P-marker). Topicalization is an example.

B. Local transformations—transformations which refer to a single non-phrase node and one adjacent constituent. Particle Movement is an example.

Hooper and Thompson (1973) have argued that root transformations are best defined semantically (they apply only in asserted clauses) rather than structurally as in Emonds (1976). They point out that a number of apparent counterexamples to the structural definition—cases where root transformations do indeed apply in embedded clauses—are thus explained. While the Hooper–Thompson proposal has gained much support, it has not diminished the significance of the Structure Preserving Constraint nor of the tripartite division of movement rules.

Historically speaking, the Structure Preserving Constraint has had a somewhat paradoxical character. On the one hand, it is one of the most widely accepted proposals in syntax. But on the other, it is seldom actually referred to or utilized in deciding between competing analyses of some syntactic phenomenon. For example, while there are innumerable passages in the literature that read "we must reject the X analysis of Y because it violates such-and-such Ross–Constraint," we almost never find "we must reject the X analysis of Y because it violates the Structure Preserving Constraint."

There are several reasons, I think, for the noncentral role of the Structure Preserving Constraint in linguistic argumentation. First, while the constraint excludes innumerable POSSIBLE analyses, it barely restricts the class of PLAUSIBLE ones. In general, competing analyses of the same phenomena all turn out to be structure preserving. By way of example, Emonds himself vastly revised his analysis of Extraposition between 1970 and 1976. Yet both alternatives are consistent with the constraint. Even a large percentage of the rules proposed by generative semanticists have been structure preserving. Second, the claim that a rule is structure preserving is tantamount to the claim that its output could be base-generated without any great complication ensuing. For reasons which will be discussed in Chapter 8, the tendency in the late 1970s has been to favor, for many constructions, base-generation rather than transformational derivation—a tendency which has diminished the direct applicability of the constraint. And finally, some of the most problematic areas of English syntax—the analysis of Extraposition and *Wh*-Fronting, for example—have also been the most problematic for the Structure Preserving Constraint. Emonds's treatments of both have been widely criticized. In 1970, his proposal for including the former involved the dubious device of "doubly filled nodes," and his treatment of the latter required recourse to obligatorily empty deep structure nodes, which seemed equally dubious. In 1976 his treatment of the latter involved a significant weakening of the constraint itself, and that of the former necessitated an otherwise unmotivated local transformation. The perceived problems in both his earlier and later solutions (see Higgins 1973; Hooper 1973; Freidin 1978a; Grimshaw 1979) have prevented the Structure Preserving Constraint from playing an important role in choosing the "correct" analysis of these phenomena.

6.2.3. Constraints on Rules of Anaphora

Recall from Section 5.2 that interpretivists suggested base generation and derived interpretation of pronouns as a means of avoiding the many problems of the strict transformational approach. However throughout the early 1970s, McCawley's alternative of considering pronouns bound variables unreplaced by lowered noun phrases continued to receive support (see Fauconnier 1973; Partee 1975a). The most thoroughgoing critique of this latter position is Wasow (1975), where it is argued that several cyclic transformations must be sensitive to the difference between full noun phrases and pronouns—i.e., pronouns must be base generated. Since then, there have been few supporters of noninterpretive theories of pronominalization.[2]

However the more extreme attempt to limit the power of transformational rules by handling ALL anaphoric processes interpretively (Jackendoff 1972; Wasow 1972; Shopen 1972; Fiengo 1974) has not met with widespread acceptance. The strongest arguments against this position appear in Ross (1969c), Grinder and Postal (1971a), Hankamer (1973), and Morgan (1973b), and typically involve rules sensitive to identity of sense rather than identity of reference. A few arguments for the existence of such deletion rules are briefly paraphrased below:

Consider sentence (6.16):

(6.16)   *We can't prove that there are such rules, but there are*

This suggests that Verb Phrase Deletion applies syntactically in the second conjunct to delete *such rules*. Otherwise, how could we account for the presence of the word *there* (which has an extremely limited distribution) and plural number agreement in that clause?

[PARAPHRASING ROSS 1969c]

Consider (6.17):

(6.17)   *I've never cooked a skunk, but Paul has, and it tasted terrible*

The *it* in the third clause cannot refer to *a skunk* in the first because of the

---

[2] A notable exception being Jacobson (1977), where Wasow's conclusions are rebutted. Jacobson argues that some pronouns derive transformationally from full NP's and some from bound variables.

ungrammaticality of (6.18):

(6.18)   * *I've never cooked a skunk, and it tasted terrible*

It must therefore refer to an NP in the second clause. This strongly suggests the presence of an underlying verb phrase in the second clause containing the NP *a skunk*, which was subsequently deleted under identity to the verb phrase in the first clause.

[PARAPHRASING GRINDER and POSTAL 1971a]

Consider the following questions and their answers:

(6.19)   a.   *Is John healthy?*
            b.   *No, sick*
            c.   *No, ill*

(6.20)   a.   *Is he a healthy boy?*
            b.   *No, sick*
            c.   **No, ill*

We can explain the deviance of (6.20c) on the basis of the deviance of **he is an ill boy* IF we assume that it is derived by an Ellipsis transformation. Otherwise, its ungrammaticality would have to be treated in a totally ad hoc fashion.

[PARAPHRASING POPE 1971]

Some interpretivists (e.g., Wasow 1972) have attempted to circumvent these arguments by hypothesizing that elliptical constructions in deep structure are fully structured syntactically, but terminate in empty nodes rather than in lexical items. All transformational rules apply to these structures. At surface structure, interpretive rules which are essentially inverses of deletion transformations apply, supplying empty nodes with the readings of their antecedent nodes and filtering out those derivations where readings cannot be supplied. However, many regard this alternative as (at best) a notational variant of the deletion approach, with the added disadvantage of necessitating a huge set of excrescent empty nodes.

The most thorough treatment of anaphoric processes to date is Hankamer and Sag (1976). They argue that anaphoric processes divide fundamentally into two classes: DEEP ANAPHORA, which allows pragmatic control and in which the anaphoric relation is determined at deep structure, and SURFACE ANAPHORA, which does not allow pragmatic control and in which the anaphoric relation is determined at a superficial level of syntactic structure. A typical deep anaphoric element is the definite pronoun. Note that *his* in (6.21) can be identified from the nonlinguistic (i.e., pragmatic) context:

(6.21)   *His face is turning red*

Verb Phrase Deletion is a typical surface anaphoric process. The missing VP in (6.22) must appear in the immediately preceding linguistic context in order for (6.22) to be used appropriately:

(6.22)   *It's not clear you'll be able to*

Hankamer and Sag point out that while the following correlations usually hold, deep anaphora cannot be identified exclusively with identity of reference anaphora nor with anaphora which leaves a nonnull element behind, nor can surface anaphora be identified exclusively with identity of sense anaphora nor with anaphora in which there is no pro-form. Note that (6.23) clearly admits pragmatic control of its understood "object" even though the identity is one of sense, not reference. On the other hand, the process involved in (6.24) is clearly surface anaphora. *So*, unlike definite pronouns, requires a linguistic antecedent:

(6.23)   *I don't approve*

(6.24)   *I don't believe so*

The Hankamer–Sag claims have been debated extensively in *Linguistic Inquiry*. For a critique of the deep–surface dichotomy, see Williams (1977a) and Schachter (1977); for a defense, see Sag (1979).

6.3. "BLIND APPLICATION" AND ITS IMPLICATIONS

In the earliest formulations of grammatical transformations, these rules were defined as applying "blindly" to factored strings, with no regard to grammatical relations or meaning, and without Boolean conditions on structural factors:

> We can formulate such a notion of "grammatical transformation" in the following way. Suppose that Q is a P-marker of the terminal string t and that t can be subdivided into successive segments $t_1, \ldots, t_n$ in such a way that each t_i is traceable, in Q, to a node labeled A_i. We say, in such a case, that
>
> t is analyzable as $(t_1, \ldots, t_n; A_1, \ldots, A_n)$ with respect to Q.
>
> In the simplest case, a transformation T will be specified in part by a sequence of symbols $(A_1, \ldots, A_n)$ that defines its domain by the following rule:
>
> a string t with P-marker Q is in the domain of T if t is analyzable as $(t_1, \ldots, t_n; A_1, \ldots, A_n)$ with respect to Q.
>
> In this case, we will call $(t_1, \ldots, t_n)$ a *proper analysis* of t with respect to Q, T, and we will call $(A_1 \ldots, A_n)$ the structure index of T [Chomsky 1961b: 19].

Chomsky in *Aspects* (1965) reiterated that "each transformation is fully defined by a structure index, which is a Boolean condition on Analyzability, and a sequence of elementary transformations [pp. 142–143]."

Yet very few actually formulated transformations met this extremely restrictive condition. In particular, rules were often stated in terms of Boolean conditions on factors, as in one popular formulation of Extraposition which required part of the structural analysis to be simultaneously "NP" and "*it* S." Rules were written with clause mate conditions, identity conditions, and special ad hoc conditions which even seemed to defy formalization.[3]

Chomsky, in a 1969 presentation (see Chomsky 1972a:118) and in "Conditions on Transformations" (written a year later, and published in 1973) reasserted the principle of blind application and explored its consequences further. They turned out to be cataclysmic. Carried to its logical conclusion, this principle was to lead to a vastly revised view of the organization of the syntactic component and ultimately to a model in which surface structure (or a level very close to it) is the sole input to the rules of semantic interpretation. And this furthermore resulted in the first major schism in the interpretivist camp. The early progress of this model is outlined in Sections 6.3.1 and 6.3.2; later developments in Section 8.2.

6.3.1. Chomsky-Conditions

The heart of Chomsky's argument is that not only is the principle of blind application desirable in itself, but it leads to a set of extremely restrictive (and therefore desirable) conditions on the application of transformational rules. His first step in the long chain of argumentation was to point out that, given the principle, we would expect (without further assumptions) (6.25a) to be transformed by the rule of Passive into ungrammatical (6.25b). If rules apply blindly, then Passive could not "know" that the NP *the dog* was the subject of *is hungry* rather than the object of *believe*:

(6.25)   a.   *I believe the dog is hungry*
           b.   **The dog is believed is hungry (by me)*

Chomsky proposed to explain (6.25b) by the following constraint:

A. **Tensed-S Condition.** *No rule can involve* X, Y *in the structure* $X \ldots [_\alpha \ldots Y \ldots] \ldots$, *where α is a tensed S.*

There were still problems, however. Chomsky was assuming a rule of *Each* Movement, which transforms (6.26a) into (6.26b):

(6.26)   a.   *The candidates each hated the other(s)*
           b.   *The candidates hated each other*

This rule is correctly blocked by the Tensed-S Condition:

(6.27)   a.   *The candidates each expected that the other would win*
           b.   **The candidates expected that each other would win*

---

[3] Chomsky (1976:310) catalogues in detail the manner in which the principle of blind application had been violated in the literature, and Postal (1976b:151–152) lists a number of papers violating this principle.

But by what principle would this rule successfully transform (6.28a) into (6.28b), but fail to apply to map (6.29a) into (6.29b)? Note that in both cases the embedded S is untensed:

(6.28)   a.   *The candidates each expected [$_s$PRO to defeat the other]*
         b.   *The candidates expected to defeat each other.*

(6.29)   a.   *The men each expected [$_s$the soldier to shoot the other]*
         b.   **The men expected the soldier to shoot each other*

The crucial difference, Chomsky claimed, lies in the nature of the embedded subject.[4] In (6.28a) it is a null pronoun, controlled by the higher subject. In (6.29a) it is fully specified. This suggested the following constraint:

   B.   **Specified Subject Condition.** *No rule can involve X, Y in the structure . . . X . . . [$_\alpha$ . . . Z . . . −WYV . . .] . . . , where Z is the specified (i.e., nonpronominal) subject of WYV and α is a cyclic node (NP or S).*

Note that this constraint would have applied to "subjects" of noun phrases, supporting Chomsky's hypothesis (see Sections 4.3 and 6.4) that rules and grammatical relations generalize to apply within noun phrases as well as sentences:

(6.30)   a.   *The men saw the pictures of each other*
         b.   **The men saw John's pictures of each other*

But there appeared to be a very obvious counterexample to both the Tensed-S Condition and the Specified Subject Condition. Under previous treatments of *Wh*-Fronting, this rule moved a *wh*-phrase over a variable to the left, transforming, for example, (6.31a) into (6.31b):

(6.31)   a.   *You told me that Bill saw who*
         b.   *Who did you tell me that Bill saw?*

Who appears to have been moved out of a tensed S and over a specified subject. The explanation of this led to Chomsky's most radical revision of all of then current analyses. First, he adopted the idea from Bresnan (1970b, 1972a) and Emonds (1970) that the rule of *Wh*-Fronting is allowed to move a *wh*-phrase only into complementizer position:

(6.32)   a.   COMP *you saw who→*
         b.   *who you saw → who did you see*

Then he further assumed that the rule would be cyclic and would apply to ANY COMP node (as opposed to Bresnan and others who assumed that a

---

[4] In order for his constraints to be stated with maximum generality, it was necessary for Chomsky to consider "PRO" in (6.28a) and *the soldier* in (6.29a) to be the subjects of *defeat* in derived as well as deep structure. In other words, the existence of a rule of Raising-to-Object (making "PRO" and *the soldier* objects of *expect*) is incompatible with his framework.

wh-phrase would move only to a COMP node marked "+WH"). Finally, he added a condition that an element can "escape" FROM a COMP only if it is moved INTO a COMP, it being irrelevant if the COMP from which that element originates is part of a tensed S or a sentence with a specified subject. Hence (6.31b) can be derived. The COMP–COMP condition has been known informally as the "Escape Clause":

C. **Escape Clause.** *No rule can involve X, Y in the structure* ... *X* ... [$_\alpha$ ... *Z* ... − *WYV* ...] ... , *where Y is in COMP and X is not in COMP and α is a cyclic node.*

Notice that the system of conditions now disallows a single step fronting of *who* from (6.31a) to (6.31b)—*who* has to be moved into COMP position on the lowest cycle so that it can escape from the embedded clause. The derivation of (6.31b), then, would proceed as follows:

(6.33)   a. COMP *you told me* [$_S$COMP *Bill saw who*]→
            b. COMP *you told me* [$_S$*who Bill saw*]→
            c. *who you told me Bill saw* →
            d. *who did you tell me Bill saw*

Chomsky went on to argue that COMP-to-COMP movement allows an EXTREMELY strong condition to be placed on the application of transformational rules—the Principle of Subjacency:

D. **Principle of Subjacency.** *Transformational rules are constrained to apply only within the domain of one cyclic node or the domain of two successive (i.e., adjacent) cyclic nodes (The cyclic nodes, that is, nodes marking domains within which the transformations of the cycle must apply, include for Chomsky at least S and NP.)*

Unbounded movements and unbounded deletions in this framework are thus completely excluded.

These principles combined to handle most of the phenomena for which Ross proposed his set of constraints.[5] For example, consider (6.6), repeated for convenience:

[6.6]   * *Who do you believe the claim that Bill saw?*

Its deep structure in the Chomsky (1973) framework would be approximately (6.34):

(6.34)   COMP *you believe* [$_{NP}$*the claim* [$_S$COMP *Bill saw who*]

---

[5] Chomsky also resurrected the A-over-A Principle, giving it a somewhat different interpretation from that in the (1964a) paper. He proposed several other conditions as well, which space limitations prevent me from discussing.

In the first cycle, *who* is moved into COMP position. But there is no way for it to escape from the lower clause since the next higher cyclic node, NP, does not have a COMP. Hence, extraction is blocked and the ungrammaticality of the sentence follows as a consequence. Most of Ross's Complex NP Constraint violations can be treated in a similar fashion.

Likewise, these principles were claimed to explain why two *wh*-phrases from the same clause cannot both be fronted. Note:

(6.35)   *What does he wonder where John put?*

Since *wh*-phrases move only into COMP, the ungrammaticality of (6.35) follows from the impossibility of both *what* and *where* simultaneously occupying COMP on the lowest cycle.

6.3.2. The Trace Theory of Movement Rules

Chomsky (again, 1973) immediately observed a serious problem with the conditions as formulated. They were incapable of blocking the following sentence:

(6.36)   *John seems to the men to like each other*

The movement of *each* violates neither the Tensed-S Condition nor the Specified Subject Condition. Chomsky proposed to deal with the problem by assuming that every time movement of a noun phrase takes place, a TRACE (*t*) is left behind at the site from which the NP was moved, and is indexed to the moved NP. This trace acts as a specified subject. The derivation of (6.36) thus proceeds as follows:

(6.37)   a. *it seems to each of the men* [COMP *John to like the other*] →

b. *John seems to each of the men t to like the other* →

c. **John seems to the men to like each other* = (6.36)

The ungrammaticality of (6.36) is predicted by the movement of *each* over a specified subject.

Now, on the face of it, this was a totally ad hoc solution, and Chomsky knew it. If the only motivation for traces was to save the constraints and the principle of blind application which engendered them, then the entire principle would be cast in jeopardy. However, the trace theory of movement rules did not arise in a vacuum—numerous proposals had been made in the years preceding the "Conditions" paper and concurrently with it which embodied the idea of leaving behind a marker of some sort at a movement or "deletion" site. For example, Postal (1970b) and Ross (1969c) had suggested that certain "deletion" rules in reality leave behind a "doom marker" for reference by later rules. This idea was developed in different ways in Emonds (1970), with its claim that movement rules leave behind an empty node, and later in Perlmutter (1972), where it is proposed that such rules leave behind a "shadow pronoun." The Baker and Brame (1972) and Selkirk (1972) indexing proposals (see Section 5.6.2) also had many features of trace theory.

Chomsky and his early 1970s students set to work to find independent evidence for traces. An interesting argument is found in Wasow (1972) and Chomsky (1975b). They proposed first that any trace left in the position occupied in deep structure by a moved *wh*-phrase be considered a variable bound by the *wh*-phrase acting as a logical quantifier.[6] Given that assumption, Wasow and Chomsky argued that it is transparently easy to convert surface structures with *wh*-phrases and traces to their logical forms. A relatively trivial interpretive rule maps (6.38a) directly onto (6.38b):

(6.38)   a. *The police know who the FBI discovered that Bill shot t* →
          b. *The police know for which person x, the FBI discovered that Bill shot x*

This suggested a solution to the "crossover" problem (see Postal 1971). Postal observed that in (6.39a) *who* and *him* can be interpreted as co-referential, while this is not possible in (6.39b):

(6.39)   a. *Who said Mary kissed him?*
          b. *Who did he say Mary kissed?*

Postal offered an explanation based on the observation that in the derivation of (6.39b), but not (6.39a), co-referential NP's "cross" each other. Wasow argued that trace theory explains this phenomenon without any additional assumptions. Under trace theory, the surface structures of (6.39a–b) are (6.40a–b), respectively:

(6.40)   a. *who [t said Mary kissed him]*
          b. *who [he said Mary kissed t]*

By the principle mentioned above, these would be mapped into (6.41a–b), respectively:

(6.41)   a. *for which person x, x said that Mary kissed him?*
          b. *for which person x, he said that Mary kissed x?*

But now, in Wasow's view, independently motivated principles governing the distribution of anaphoric pronouns block the co-referential reading in (6.39b)—this sentence would be excluded by the same rule which excludes *he said Mary kissed someone,* where *he* and *someone* are co-referential.

Syntactic motivation for traces has been adduced most vigorously by

---

[6] While neither Wasow nor Chomsky mentioned the fact, as Bach (1977b) points out, the idea of considering question words like *who* and *what* as being logically equivalent to quantifiers is relatively old. This conception is found in the writings of Jespersen (1965:302–305), Carnap (1937:296), Reichenbach (1947:340), and, more recently, Bach (1968) and Baker (1970b).

Fiengo (1974, 1977) and Lightfoot (1976). Fiengo observed that if traces are, in effect, pronouns, an asymmetry in the types of movement rules can be explained. He pointed out that while movement transformations move NP's to the left within a clause or to the left to the next higher clause, they do not (generally!—see the following) move NP's downward to the right or to the right within a clause. That is, after movement we may have the trace-antecedent relations (6.42a–b), but not (6.42c–d):

(6.42)

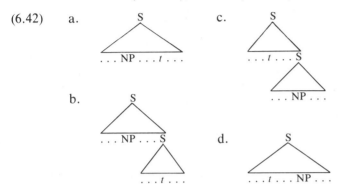

This fact as well was argued to fall out from independent principles on the interpretation of anaphora. In (6.42a) and (6.42b), the trace follows the moved NP—a pronoun can always follow its antecedent. But in (6.42c) and (6.42d), the trace both precedes and commands its antecedent, resulting in ungrammaticality. The asymmetry could thus be explained.

What made this explanation seem particularly interesting is the fact that there ARE rules that move NP's to the right, leaving behind a potentially dangerous trace. But these are rules which in many cases can be argued to "obliterate" the trace by replacing it with some dummy element, so that at surface structure there is no trace-antecedent configuration that would lead to the sentence being ruled ungrammatical. For example, consider the rule of *There*-Insertion, which in the view of trace theorists postposes a subject NP, leaving behind a trace:

(6.43)   a. *three books are on the table* →
         b. *t are three books on the table*

If nothing else happened, the derivation would be blocked by virtue of *t* both preceding and commanding *three books*. But Fiengo (1974) and Dresher and Hornstein (1979) have argued that since the trace is replaced by the noun phrase *there*, the traceless surface structure does not yield a pronominalization violation.

Trace theory has developed considerably beyond what I have outlined in this section. And this theory, and every hypothesis which contributed to it, have been subjected to extensive criticism. Both developments will be dealt with in Chapter 8.

6.4. CONSTRAINTS ON BASE RULES

Recall that the most skeptically received aspects of Chomsky's "Remarks on Nominalization" were his proposals for allowing transformational rules and co-occurrence restrictions to generalize across major categories. Not only did Chomsky not succeed in capturing the desired parallels formally, but the requirement of features on major categories that the X-bar convention entailed resulted in a real weakening of linguistic theory.

Not surprisingly, quite a bit of work has gone into refining the X-bar convention with the goal of simplifying the base rules while enabling the proper cross-categorial generalizations to be expressed. And there certainly seems to be no lack of such generalizations. The assumptions of the lexicalist hypothesis, of course, demanded that every abstract syntactic argument that two categories are really one be reinterpreted as a generalization to be captured by means of the X-bar convention. Interpretivists themselves pointed out a number of other cross-categorial generalizations. For example:

> Both Gapping (6.44a–b) and Verb Phrase Deletion (6.45a–b) have analogs in which nouns (or nouns and their specifiers and/or complements) are deleted:
>
> (6.44) a. *Max ate the apple and Sally ____ the hamburgers*
>   b. *I bought three quarts of wine and two ____ of Clorox*
>
> (6.45) a. *Bill ate the peaches and Harry did ____ too*
>   b. *I like John's yellow shirt, but not Max's ____*
>
> [PARAPHRASING JACKENDOFF 1971c]
>
> *Wh*-Fronting (6.46a–d), Comparative Deletion (6.47a–d), and Heavy-NP-Shift (6.48a–b) generalize to apply across major categories:
>
> (6.46) a. [$_{NP}$*what book*] *did you read* ____
>   b. [$_{Adj P}$*how long*] *is it* ____
>   c. [$_{Adv P}$*how quickly*] *did you read it* ____
>   d. [$_{QP}$*how much*] *did it cost* ____
>
> (6.47) a. *it costs more than it weighs* [$_{QP}$ ____]
>   b. *it looks more costly than it is* [$_{Adj P}$ ____]
>   c. *she drives more dynamically than he drives* [$_{Adv P}$ ____]
>   d. *she had more friends than he had* [$_{NP}$ ____]
>
> (6.48) a. *he considers stupid* [$_{NP}$*many of my best friends*]
>   b. *he talked about their stupidity* [$_{PP}$*to many of my best friends*]
>
> [PARAPHRASING BRESNAN 1976a]

But it seems fair to say that even after a dozen years, researchers have been far more successful in demonstrating that there are generalizations to be captured than they have been in actually capturing them. Advocates of the X-bar convention have not even come close to agreeing on the most basic aspects of the theoretical apparatus needed. The answers to the most fundamental questions have not achieved a consensus. Among them are the following:

A. **How many "levels" are to be hypothesized for each category?** That is, if all phrase-structure rules are of the form $X^n \rightarrow X^{n-1}$ (see Section 4.3), what is the maximum value of n? As Jackendoff (1977) has pointed out, there have been many answers to this question:

> In Chomsky's original formulation, n equals 2 for nouns and 3 for verbs (assuming the verb is the head of the sentence). Vergnaud (1974) and Siegel (1974) have n equal to 4, at least for nouns; Dougherty (1968) has n equal to 3 for nouns and 6 for verbs; Jackendoff (1971c; 1974a) has n equal to 2 for all categories [p. 35].

In Jackendoff (1977) a uniform three-level analysis is proposed for all categories.

B. **How are the categories themselves subcategorized with respect to features?** In Bresnan (1976) and Chomsky and Lasnik (1977), verbs, nouns, adjectives, and prepositions are subcategorized as follows:

(6.49)

$$\text{a. } V = \begin{bmatrix} +V \\ -N \end{bmatrix}$$

$$\text{b. } N = \begin{bmatrix} -V \\ +N \end{bmatrix}$$

$$\text{c. } A = \begin{bmatrix} +V \\ +N \end{bmatrix}$$

$$\text{d. } P = \begin{bmatrix} -V \\ -N \end{bmatrix}$$

But Jackendoff (1977) proposes a different (and quite incompatible) feature assignment:

(6.50)

$$\text{a. } V = \begin{bmatrix} +\text{Subj} \\ +\text{Obj} \end{bmatrix}$$

$$\text{b. } N = \begin{bmatrix} +\text{Subj} \\ -\text{Obj} \end{bmatrix}$$

$$\text{c. } A = \begin{bmatrix} -\text{Subj} \\ -\text{Obj} \end{bmatrix}$$

$$\text{d. } P = \begin{bmatrix} -\text{Subj} \\ +\text{Obj} \end{bmatrix}$$

C. **How are grammatical relations generalized to apply with noun phrases as well as sentences?** Jackendoff (1977) proposed deep structures (6.52a-b) for (6.51a-b), respectively, capturing the parallels in grammatical relations and thereby avoiding the grave defects of Chomsky's analysis in "Remarks on Nominalization'' (see Section 4.3):

(6.51)   a. *John has proved the theorem*
           b. *John's proof of the theorem*

(6.52)   a.

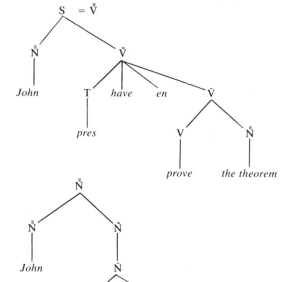

           b.

But Hornstein (1977) has challenged the idea that the node S participates in the X-bar convention AT ALL, a view which necessitates a very different approach to the grammatical relation problem.

   D. **How can the theory be constrained?** The notation allows for a vast number of cross-categorial generalizations which never seem to occur. By the same token, it allows for various categories having "levels" that play no role in any grammatical process. For example, Jackendoff (1977) proposes the categories M (modal), M̄, M̿, and M̄̄, but no rules apply to any of them except M̿ in his grammar.

   E. **What principle determines which rules will generalize across categories and which will not?** (See Section 4.3 for discussion of this problem.) Emonds (1976) suggests that no rule which moves a constituent leftward applies within both NP and S.[7] Akmajian (1975) proposes that neither root transformations nor structure preserving transformations governed by verbs

---

   [7] In Emonds's view, the rule of Passive does NOT generalize to apply within both NP and S.

apply within NP. For Jackendoff (1977), the internal structural DIFFERENCES of NP's and S's combined with the statements of the rules themselves determine their domain of applicability.

F. **How are structurally "mixed" languages to be handled?** Jackendoff (1977) points out that German, which has a verb final V but a noun initial N, poses a serious problem for the X-bar convention. The same can be said for any structurally "mixed" language (see Greenberg 1963 for a summary of data on many such languages).

6.5. SURFACE STRUCTURE CONSTRAINTS

One addition to syntactic theory which has its roots in the 1960s and continued to be developed in the 1970s is the SURFACE STRUCTURE CONSTRAINT (or OUTPUT CONDITION or SURFACE FILTER). A constraint of this type applies at surface structure to filter out (i.e., rule ungrammatical) certain derivations that survive the transformational rules.

Despite their name, surface structure constraints cannot be thought of as "constraining" the grammar, since they add a new mechanism of great expressive power to the already existing mechanisms. Typically, they have been proposed to capture generalizations unstatable transformationally. In the classic case, Perlmutter (1971) argued at length that the order of preverbal clitics in Spanish cannot be stated by any imaginable combination of transformational rules, but the following positive output condition (6.53) expresses the correct generalization quite elegantly (the Roman numerals refer to grammatical person):

(6.53)   *se*   II   I   III

Perlmutter recognized the resultant weakening to linguistic theory of an unconstrained set of surface filters, and therefore sought to characterize universally the phenomena to which such constraints were applicable:

(6.54)   *The word is universally subject to surface structure con-*
           straints on morpheme order, expressed in positive output
           constraint notation.

However, Emonds (1975) has argued that clitic order in French can and should be expressed via base rules and transformations alone. The issue is still under debate.

Below are two more examples of surface structure constraints which have been proposed as a result of the apparent impossibility of a transformational formulation:

Note that the subject cannot be extraposed to the end of the sentence in (6.55), nor the direct object postposed by Heavy-NP-Shift in (6.56):

(6.55)   a.   *That his fingernails were on my throat proves that he was unfond
               of me*
          b.   **It proves that he was unfond of me that his fingernails were on
               my throat*

(6.56)   a.   *We found the fact that she has blood on her hands indicative of
               the fact that she killed him*
          b.   **We found indicative of the fact that she killed him the fact that
               she had blood on her hands*

Facts like these suggest the following output condition:
The Same Side Filter: *No surface structure can have both complements
of a bisentential verb on the same side of that verb.*
                                            [PARAPHRASING ROSS 1973d]

In most cases, two consecutive words ending in *-ing* result in grammaticality violations:

(6.57)   a.   **It is continuing raining*
          b.   **I'm stopping watching it*
          c.   **He's going drinking beer*

But in certain cases there is no violation:

(6.58)   a.   *Waldo keeps molesting sleeping gorillas*
          b.   *His avoiding contacting Harriet is understandable*
          c.   *His having getting into college to consider is a drag*

As a result of the many interactions of rules which serve to create *-ing* . . .
-ing sequences, there is no way to state the relevant constraint transformationally without loss of generality. However, it can be stated elegantly
at the level of surface structure:
Double *-ing* Constraint: *Surface Sequences of V -ing are prohibited
unless a NP boundary intervenes.*
     [PARAPHRASING EMONDS 1973—a reinterpretation of Ross 1972b]

The principle of blind application has led Chomsky to propose a rich
set of surface filters. Here the motivation is not so much the impossibility
of a transformational formulation per se, but the impossibility of one consistent with the principle. In Chomsky (1973) two such filters are proposed,
and are paraphrased below:

The structure $[_{NP}NP\ V_T \ . \ . \ . \ ]$ is excluded, where V_T is an element containing tense (T). This accounts for the fact that in (6.59b), but not in (6.59a),
the deletion of the relative pronoun results in ungrammaticality:

(6.59)   a.   *the woman who Mary saw* → *the woman Mary saw*
          b.   *the woman who saw Mary* → * *the woman saw Mary*

The structure +WH NP *to* is excluded. This accounts for (6.60):

(6.60)   * *I don't know who Bill to ask*

In Chomsky's later work, surface filters have played an even more important role. See Section 8.2 for further discussion.

6.6. RULE INTERACTION AND GRAMMATICAL ORGANIZATION

In this section I will discuss some other important questions which consumed the attention of grammarians in the early and mid 1970s: the question of rule ordering (Section 6.6.1), the cyclic principle (Section 6.6.2), the interaction of syntax and semantics (Section 6.6.3), and the interaction of syntax and phonology (Section 6.6.4).

6.6.1 Rule Ordering

It was clear from the earliest work in transformational generative syntax that transformational rules apply to each other's outputs. Hence, in any derivation it is possible to specify the ORDER of application of rules in that derivation. The question naturally arose, then, whether it was necessary for the grammar itself to specify that order. In this regard, Chomsky (1965) wrote:

> In connection with ordering of rules, it is necessary to distinguish EXTRINSIC ORDER, imposed by the explicit ordering of rules, from INTRINSIC ORDER, which is simply a consequence of how rules are formulated. Thus if the rule R_1 introduces the symbol A and R_2 analyzes A, there is an intrinsic order relating R_1 and R_2, but not necessarily any extrinsic order. Similarly, if a certain transformation T_1 applies to a certain structure that is formed only by application of T_2, there is an intrinsic order T_1, T_2 . . . . [*sic*] Generative grammars have ordinarily required both [intrinsic and extrinsic ordering] [p. 223].

A classic argument for extrinsic ordering involves the Reflexive (6.61) and Imperative (6.62) transformations:

$$(6.61) \quad X \ - \ NP_i \ - \ X \ - \quad NP_i \quad \ - \ X$$

$$1 \quad\quad 2 \quad\quad 3 \quad\quad\quad 4 \quad\quad\quad 5$$

$$\Rightarrow 1 \quad\quad 2 \quad\quad 3 \quad \begin{bmatrix} +PRO \\ +REFLEXIVE \end{bmatrix} \quad 5$$

Condition: 2 and 4 are clause mates

$$(6.62) \quad You\text{---}will\text{---}X$$

$$1 \quad 2 \quad 3$$

$$\Rightarrow \phi \quad \phi \quad 3$$

Unless the rules are ordered (1)–Reflexive, (2)–Imperative, the argument goes, nothing will block Imperative from deleting the subject in (6.63), rendering Reflexive inapplicable and resulting in ungrammatical (6.64):

(6.63)   *you will shave you*

(6.64)   **shave you*

Extrinsic ordering had for many years been looked on as a necessary evil, "evil" because it VASTLY increases the number of possible grammars for any given language. This point is argued persuasively in Pullum (1979a):

> The number of distinct well orderings that can be imposed on a set of *n* elements is *n*! . . . Burt (1971) provides a partial grammar for English which has 27 transformational rules. The [no extrinsic ordering] hypothesis defines one grammar as the only one containing only those rules that is well-formed . . . . But the linear [i.e., extrinsic] ordering hypothesis defines 27! (i.e., 27 × 26 × 25 × · · · × 1) grammars as well-formed for the same set of rules. This number is approximately ten thousand quadrillion. . . . It makes an absurdly weak claim about language acquisition: that even if Burt's rules were correct, [infants] would still face the task of isolating the correct grammar for English from among a set of possible grammars of cardinality 200,000 million times greater than the number of seconds in the estimated age of the universe [pp. 28–29].

Providing arguments against those circulating in favor of extrinsic ordering and formulating universal principles to explain order of application became the best-known occupation of the Department of Linguistics at Indiana University. Koutsoudas (1972, 1973) discussed at length two common fallacies in conventional arguments for extrinsic order. The first is based on the a priori (and incorrect) assumption that if it can be shown that SOME rules must be extrinsically ordered, then ALL must be. He showed that many ordering arguments collapse given the possibility of a random ordering of the rules in question. He also pointed out what Pullum (1979a) has since called "The Fallacy of Neglecting Cyclicity." For example, in the derivation of (6.65) it is clear that Passive applied before Relative Clause Formation. But this does not have to be put in the form of an extrinsic ordering statement since Passive applies on an earlier cyclic domain (see (6.66)):

(6.65)   *The man who was arrested by the police went mad.*

(6.66)

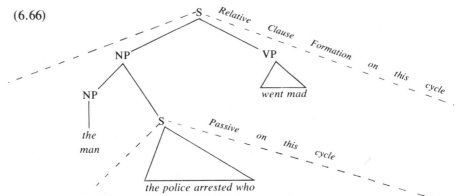

To argue that the grammar must specify this ordering explicitly is to commit "The Fallacy of Neglecting Cyclicity."

Two important universal principles of rule application proposed at Indiana are (A) the Obligatory–Optional Principle and (B) the Proper Inclusion Principle:

A. Obligatory–Optional Principle (Ringen 1972). If a phrase-marker meets the structural description of both an optional and an obligatory rule, the obligatory rule must apply to that phrase-marker. This explains why Reflexive precedes Imperative.

B. Proper Inclusion Principle (Sanders 1974). Rule A applies before Rule B if the structural description of A properly includes that of B. Since the structural description of Extraposition [under formulation (6.67)] properly includes that of It-Deletion (6.68), the former rule applies before the latter:

(6.67)
$$X \ [_{NP}it \ [_S\begin{Bmatrix} that \\ for \end{Bmatrix} X \ ]] \ X$$

(6.68)
$$X \ [_{NP}it \ [_S \ X \ ]] \ X$$

There have been several attempts to work out a universal algorithm for rule applicability. Those of Eckman (1974) and Pullum (1979a) are based essentially on these two principles. And Williams (1974) has attempted to predict order of application in terms of domain of application, hypothesizing that rules with smaller domains apply before rules with larger domains.

Those few transformational rules remaining in the grammars of trace theorists are now assumed to be optional and intrinsically ordered (see Fiengo 1977). I will return to this in Section 8.2.1.

6.6.2. The Cycle

As we have seen in Section 3.5.2, Chomsky proposed in *Aspects* that rules apply cyclically, preserving their linear order, first to the most deeply embedded sentence, then to the next most deeply embedded one, and so on. But while he was able to argue that cyclic application of rules is possible (it presumably allows the generation of all and only the sentences of any language) and desirable (cyclic grammars are more restrictive—again presumably—than noncyclic ones), he never demonstrated that cyclic application is NECESSARY. G. Lakoff's (1968c) argument to that effect, then, was very important in the development of syntactic theory.[8] It involves the rules

---

[8] Lakoff's preface to the original manuscript version of (1968c) explaining why it would never be published serves as further documentation of the generative semantic dynamic described in Chapter 5:

This is the first draft of what was intended to be a revision and extension of my dissertation. The project was abandoned in January 1967, when it became clear that deeper things than I had imagined were going on in syntax.

Lakoff's original argument is easily accessible in published form in Grinder and Elgin (1973).

of Passive (P) and Raising-to-Object (R), and takes the following form: Assume that these rules are linearly ordered, but do not apply cyclically. Sentence S can be derived only by two applications of (P), one before (R) and one after (R). That this is a safe conclusion is evidenced by the fact that the first application of (P) creates the structure to which (R) applies; likewise (P)'s second application is dependent upon a structure created by (R). Hence, we must posit the following rule ordering:

(6.69)   a. (P)
          b. (R)
          c. (P)

But S can occur embedded in another sentence, allowing repeated applications of (R) and (P). Since there is no limit to the amount of embedding possible, (R) and (P) can continue to apply in sequential fashion indefinitely:

(6.70)   a. (P)
          b. (R)
          c. (P)
          d. (R)
          e. (P)
          ⋮   ⋮

Given the principle of linear ordering with no further assumptions about the organization of rules, we would need to specify an infinite number of rules for English—a clearly undesirable conclusion. However, if we assume that rules, by universal convention, apply cyclically, we need to state (P) and (R) in the grammar only once. The principle of the cycle will account for the infinite number of possible applications.

It was not long before Lakoff realized that this (and other) arguments for the cycle could be gotten around if it was hypothesized that each rule applied on its OWN cycle. That is, if each rule applied cycling up the tree to the topmost S before the next rule applied on the most deeply embedded S. He and J. R. Ross campaigned vigorously for this view (the "Individual Cycle" or "Linear Grammar") in 1966–1967, but soon dropped it. Nevertheness, it remained a popular idea, and was defended in Kimball (1972b) and Grinder (1972), the latter claiming that the individual cyclic hypothesis results in a more highly constrained grammar.[9] Today this view seems to have few, if any, adherents.

Another popular type of argument for the cycle involves showing that rule A must precede rule B in the derivation of one sentence, but follow it in another. The only way to avoid this paradox (the argument goes) is to hypothesize the cyclic principle. For example, Akmajian and Heny (1975) point out that Equi must precede Raising-to-Subject in the derivation of

---

[9] A claim rebutted in Freidin (1976), who argues that cyclic application is more restrictive.

(6.71a) but follow it in the derivation of (6.71b):

(6.71)   a. *John appears to want to know physics*
          b. *John wants to appear to know physics*

They argue that only the principle of cyclic application can avoid an ordering paradox involving the two rules.

Pullum (1979a), the most exhaustive defense of the cyclic principle, points out that most arguments for the cycle (such as the two which I have just presented) crucially depend on the discredited notion of language-particular extrinsic ordering. If rules apply freely (i.e., are intrinsically ordered), then many arguments for the cycle collapse. However, he does argue that one argument along the lines of Lakoff's, which involves the rules of Raising-to-Object and Reflexive, cannot be subverted by a noncyclic but unordered grammar. Given deep structure (6.73), only the cyclic principle can block Raising (and then Reflexive) from applying in S_2 before Reflexive has a chance to apply in S_1, resulting in ungrammatical (6.72):

(6.72)   **Melvin believes himself to have proved Melvin innocent.*

(6.73)

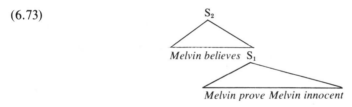

Pullum also points to a number of constraints which can be stated only on cycle-final structures, thereby providing strong indirect support for the principle.

For another defense of the cyclic principle which does not depend on extrinsic ordering, see Jacobson and Neubauer (1976).

One might think that since so many of the direct arguments for the cycle involve rules whose existence most interpretivists consider quite dubious (Raising-to-Object, Equi, Reflexive, etc.), this principle would not have strong interpretivist support. Just the opposite is the case, however. All of the Chomsky-Conditions, and in particular the principle of Subjacency, presuppose cyclic application. Attempts at reformulating the conditions without reference to the cycle have only recently begun (see Freidin 1978b). Recall also that in order for rules to generalize in the fashion demanded by the lexicalist hypothesis (Section 4.3, 6.4), NP as well as S must be a cyclic category.

The cyclic principle has repeatedly been supplemented with various other organizing principles. One possibility suggested is that certain rules apply PRECYCLICALLY, that is, over an entire phrase-marker before the first application of a cyclic rule on the lowest cycle. The first such proposal (G. Lakoff 1968c) has no current support due to the universal abandonment of the assumptions which underlie the argument, and does not bear repeating. Other proposals for precyclic rules have been made, however. Aissen (1974) argues that the verb raising rule forming multimorphemic causative constructions in languages such as Turkish is universally precyclic. And Newmeyer (1976a) claims that many of the rules peculiar to generative semantics, in particular lexical incorporation rules such as Nominalization and Predicate Raising, apply precyclically. The consequence of this, he argues, is that the empirical claims of early generative semantics and interpretive semantics with respect to overall grammatical organization turn out to be much less distinct than is generally believed. However, it seems fair to say that only a small minority of syntacticians are convinced of the existence of ANY precyclic rules.

POSTCYCLIC (or LAST-CYCLIC) rules appear to be on much stronger ground. Originally (G. Lakoff 1968c), the former term referred to rules that follow all cyclic rules; the latter to rules that apply only on the last cycle, but still might precede a cyclic rule on that cycle. No convincing examples bearing out the latter possibility were ever found, however, and the two terms are now used interchangeably. (Though, for some reason, interpretivists favor the term "last-cyclic" and noninterpretivists the term "postcyclic.")

The class of last-cyclic transformations is generally identified with the class of Emonds's root transformations (see Section 6.2.2). This is hardly surprising, since by definition a root transformation applies (essentially) in the topmost S (i.e., on the last cycle). It is logically possible, however, that a rule could be constrained so as to apply only on the last cycle yet affect a domain that is NOT the root S. Such transformations have in fact been proposed (for discussion, see Noll 1974; Pullum 1979a), but typically have either been rules whose existence is controversial or whose last-cyclic motivation involves interaction with controversial rules. In general, it has proved very difficult to argue for last-cyclicity, since a slight alteration in the formulation of a rule often affects its domain of application.

6.6.3. Syntax and Semantics

Before the mid 1970s, it was mainly generative semanticists who addressed the problem of grammar and meaning. The neglect of semantics by interpretivists was partly a result of the all-absorbing work taking place constraining the syntactic rules, which seemed to be yielding such promising results. But partly it resulted as well from a lingering feeling that semantics was, for the time being at least, simply "undoable"—too nebulous and unsystematizable to admit formalization with the descriptive tools then available. Surely, the negative example of both the Katz–Fodor work and the efforts of generative semanticists did much to reinforce this feeling among interpretivists. While assertions like "sentence (43) is filtered out by the interpretive rules . . . [Dougherty 1969:499]'' fill the pages of the interpretivist literature, such rules were rarely even characterized, much less formalized.

Nevertheless, there were several important semantic studies by interpretivists in this period. All agreed on two fundamental points, which distinguished them from generative semanticists: (1) semantic representations are not single formal objects; rather, different types of rules "fill in" different aspects of the meaning; and (2) some interpretive rules apply at levels more shallow than deep structure. Ray Jackendoff's *Semantic Interpretation in Generative Grammar* (1972), the most extensive account of semantic interpretation, was typical in this respect.[10] In Jackendoff's view, there are four distinct parts to a semantic representation:

1. **Functional structure:** The main propositional content of the sentence, essentially the semantic relationship between a verb and its noun phrase co-constituents within its clause.
2. **Modal structure:** The specification of the scope of logical elements such as negation and quantifiers, and the referential properties of noun phrases.
3. **The table of co-reference:** The specification of which noun phrases in a sentence are understood as co-referential.
4. **Focus and presupposition:** The designation of what information in the sentence is understood as new and what is understood as old.

In all pretrace-theory models, the rules determining functional structure applied to deep structures (see S. Anderson 1971a and Jackendoff 1974b for two examples). Modal structure, in Jackendoff's view, was normally dependent on surface structure (capturing the intuitions discussed in earlier chapters that surface order is relevant to the interpretation of quantifier scope), though he also proposed a few modal operators whose scope properties suggested deep structure interpretation. Jackendoff's rules of co-reference assignment applied cyclically, a position later criticized by Wasow (1972) and Lasnik (1976), who opted for surface structure interpretation. Both Jackendoff and Chomsky (1971) proposed surface structure interpretation of focus and presupposition. However, Postal pointed out (1972:164) that this stress-dependent interpretive rule could not really operate on surface structure, given the then uncontroversial assumption that this level contains no stress markings. Nor could it apply to the phonetic representation, since this level contains no constituent boundaries. This problem was never really resolved.

---

[10] This book incorporates and expands on several of his earlier papers (1968a,b; 1969; 1971a,b). For critiques of Jackendoff's work from interpretivist viewpoints, see Gee 1974, Freidin 1975a, Lasnik 1976, and Hust and Brame 1976, and for a general critique of his theory of anaphora, see McCawley 1976c.

In the mid 1970s, semantics began to be taken more and more seriously by interpretivists. Partly this resulted from the realization that as more and more rules were struck from the transformational roster, doing formal grammar was going to mean going beyond syntax as it had been traditionally conceived, like it or not. Partly it resulted from the fact that trace theory suggested (at least to many interpretivists) a solution to some traditional semantic problems. And partly it resulted from the fact that as the achievements of model theoretic semantics (which were made largely outside the "linguistic" tradition) became known to linguists, the needed formal devices became available to express the desired generalizations about meaning. Hence, in the late 1970s, semantic studies flourished as never before. I will return to this in Chapter 8.

6.6.4. Syntax and Phonology

Generativists, in probing the interaction of syntax and phonology, have attempted to answer three distinct, though interrelated, questions:

1. What is the nature of the interface between the syntactic component and the phonological component of the grammar?
2. To what extent (if any) may syntactic rules have access to phonological information?
3. To what extent (if any) may phonological rules have access to syntactic information?

I will not discuss the third question at all in this book, since it belongs more properly to a study of developments in generative phonology. For interesting remarks on the problems involved here, see Zwicky (1970).

The earliest answer to the first question was that the boundary between the two components is sharp: "In short, the input to the phonological rules is identical to the output of the syntactic rules [Postal 1968: xii]." However, Chomsky and Halle were soon forced to recognize that things were not so simple:

> Thus we have two concepts of surface structure: input to the phonological component and output of the syntactic component. It is an empirical question whether these two concepts coincide. In fact, they do coincide to a very significant degree, but there are also certain discrepancies [Chomsky and Halle 1968: 9].

To handle these discrepancies, which involved the noncorrespondence of phonological phrases to the labeled bracketings provided by the syntactic component, they proposed "readjustment rules" to apply between the syntax and the phonology.

A drastic reanalysis of the syntax–phonology interface came with Joan Bresnan's (1971a) paper "Sentence Stress and Syntactic Transformations." Bresnan argued that stress assignment rules have to precede the rules of

Question Formation and Relative Clause Formation, and therefore must be ordered within the syntactic cycle (while she did not emphasize it, this position entails that ALL phonological rules be in the syntactic cycle, since stress assignment rules and the rules of segmental phonology are interspersed). She claimed, furthermore, that this provided independent support for the lexicalist hypothesis, since in order to work it demanded that stems and their derivational affixes be present in the deep structure. A lively debate ensued in *Language*, with G. Lakoff (1972f) and Berman and Szamosi (1972) attacking this view, followed by a defense by Bresnan (1972b). Lakoff (who defended a global account of the same facts) was certainly right in pointing out (1972f:301) that Bresnan's position entailed a real weakening of linguistic theory, since it allowed for the possibility that cyclic syntactic rules might refer to the stress levels of items in embedded clauses. Bresnan could only cite a highly controversial cliticization rule from her own unpublished work (1971b) that this was necessary.

While no elaborative work at all was done in Bresnan's framework, most interpretivists seem to have assumed its correctness. With the more recent developments in this model, however, it is unclear how her position could be maintained in anything like its original form. For example, Chomsky and Lasnik (1977) suggest that "there is little reason to suppose that lexical items are inserted in base structure . . . [p. 432]," a view totally incompatible with Bresnan's syntactic stress assignment. And it would seem that Bresnan's most recent radical interpretivist views that no cyclic transformations exist at all (see Section 8.3.2) are likewise in conflict with her 1971 position.

From time to time, syntactic rules have been proposed that have access to phonological information. Many rules, for example, have been formulated with "heaviness restrictions" governing their applicability (see Section 7.3). Also, a subset of syntactic rules, namely rules of word-formation (especially cliticization) have been repeatedly given access to syllable structure and other phonological information. Zwicky (1969) and Pullum and Zwicky (forthcoming) have argued at length that the strong position that syntax is phonology-free can be maintained. In their view, heaviness restrictions can be attributed to pragmatic factors, and word-formation rules can be removed from the syntax and reanalyzed as lexical or morphological.

6.7. SYNTAX IN THE 1970s: SOME SOCIOLOGICAL ASPECTS

6.7.1. Publications

Before 1970, there was no journal devoted exclusively to papers in the transformationalist framework. That year saw the founding of *Linguistic Inquiry* by Jay Keyser, then at Brandeis, later chairman of the linguistics department at the University of Massachusetts, and now MIT's chairman. Under Keyser's editorship, *Linguistic Inquiry* has become the unofficial organ of transformational generative grammar—in the last few years, the number of citations to papers published in *Linguistic Inquiry* in works on syntax and phonology exceeds the number of those published in all other journals put together. Not surprisingly, the subscription rate (2500) and the rejection rate (90%) have both been consistently high. Papers in the late generative semantic tradition aside, all varieties of transformationalist work have had some representation in the pages of *Linguistic Inquiry*. However, with the exception of Susumu Kuno and Paul Postal, noninterpretivists have not found it easy to get their submissions accepted, and there has been much (underground) grumbling that papers critical of Chomsky's work are judged excessively severely.

In 1975, Michael Brame of the University of Washington founded the journal *Linguistic Analysis*, which soon attained a high subscription (1500) and rejection (35%) rate as well. Every syntax paper in this journal has been within the interpretivist framework.

The North Eastern Linguistic Society (NELS) is the closest thing to an interpretivist's CLS. However, its meetings and published conference proceedings (which have appeared since 1974) have not played nearly the crucial role in the development of interpretivism that those of the CLS did in the development of generative semantics. This is a function of the availability of *Linguistic Inquiry* and *Linguistic Analysis* to partisans of the former model, and NELS's problem of promoting and distributing its publication—a problem which arises largely from its practice of holding its conference at a different college each year.

6.7.2. Three Groups of Syntacticians

Most of the specific proposals discussed in this chapter are mutually compatible. One can believe in the structure preserving constraint, the X-bar Convention, Ross-Constraints (or some variant of them), the nonexistence of extrinsic ordering, and the cyclic principle without contradiction. (Of course Ross-Constraints are incompatible with Chomsky-Conditions and trace theory.) Yet only in rare cases did we (or do we) find any particular linguist adopting the full range of possible compatible positions. There has consistently been a CLUSTERING of positions and different—and to a large extent sociologically identifiable—groupings of linguists who have adopted different clusters. While boundaries are fuzzy and loyalties can and have changed, the existence of three groupings seems unquestionable.

The first group is made up of many of Chomsky's early 1960s students and their students, and the bulk of syntacticians who have had little or no direct contact with the MIT Linguistics Department. Most of its members have either been at one time or another conscious generative semanticists or would consider themselves to have been influenced by that model. Their analyses reflect a favoring of transformational over lexical or interpretive solutions to problems when possible. Those in this group have generally been skeptical about the Structure Preserving Constraint and hostile to the X-bar Convention. Developing Ross-Constraints, motivating the cycle, and demotivating extrinsic ordering have been special concerns of these individuals.

The second group is composed primarily of Chomsky's late 1960s students and their students. Its members have concentrated on defending and extending the lexicalist hypothesis and have devoted much energy to elaborating the Structure Preserving Constraint and the X-bar Convention, and a certain amount to work on morphology. Their reaction to Chomsky-Conditions and trace theory has ranged from skepticism to open opposition. For the most part, questions of rule ordering and the cycle have not occupied much of their attention.

The third group contains Chomsky's early and mid 1970s students and others in close contact with the MIT Linguistics Department in this period. Its members have generally been absorbed with further motivating and developing Chomsky-Conditions and trace theory.

The pivotal factor in all of this, of course, is Chomsky. What greater testament can there be to his impact than the fact that his students adopt his then-current views and continue to develop them even after his direct influence on them ceases—and even after he himself has gone on to some new position, often contradicting the one he taught them. Chomsky in the early 1960s was an "abstract syntactician"—and many of his students from that period still are! Chomsky in the late 1960s proposed the lexicalist alternative to abstract syntax—and those who were then his students are still developing this model. And we can predict that Chomsky's 1970s students will be refining trace theory long after Chomsky has developed his ideas along other lines.

Chapter 7

On the Boundary of Formal Grammar

7.1. INTRODUCTION

The unifying theme of this chapter is the attempt to deal with linguistic phenomena, whether pragmatic (Section 7.2), perceptual (Section 7.3), or "functional" (Section 7.4), which have traditionally either defied or resisted a strict grammatical treatment. We will see that in each case, the history of the attempt has been quite similar. Initially, the phenomena were dismissed from being worthy of investigation by linguists at all, often with the unstated implication that they are unamenable to ANY type of systematic study. Then, the exact opposite position was taken by many, as formal grammar itself was broadened to incorporate them. More recently, a synthesis of these two counterposed positions has become quite popular, as a number of linguists have readopted the position that the domain of formal grammar is limited and its properties constrained, yet argue that the formal properties of the independent systems governing the behavior of these phenomena are amenable to systematic study, as is their interaction with the theory of grammar.

7.2. PRAGMATICS

In the first decade of transformational research, nobody had much faith in the possibility of constructing a theory of how language is used in communication. This was not simply a matter of the belief of the PREMATURITY of attempting such a theory, given the current state of knowledge—it was a matter of PRINCIPLED impossibility. Katz and Fodor (1963) stated the prevailing view succinctly: "But a complete theory of this kind is not possible in principle; for to satisfy the above necessary condition it would be required that the theory represent ALL the knowledge speakers have about the world [p. 178]." The fact that such knowledge is not normally available to investigators tended to put a damper on studies of the pragmatic aspects of language.

But in the late 1960s, quite a few linguists were won away from this hard position against the study of pragmatic phenomena. The most important factor in this change was the work of a number of philosophers in the ordinary language tradition, especially J. L. Austin (1962), John Searle (1969), and H. P. Grice (1975). These philosophers were able to demonstrate that beyond a shadow of a doubt, aspects of language use are systematic and amenable to study, without necessitating access to "all the knowledge speakers have about the world." They showed that strategies for successful communication are not only to a certain extent rule governed, but interact with what might be considered strictly grammatical phenomena in subtle and interesting ways.

At the same time, the methodology which had come to characterize generative semantics (see especially Section 5.5.1) resulted in a climate highly receptive to the incorporation of these insights directly into grammatical theory. Since, to generative semanticists in this period, one's intuitions about, say, the correct use of honorifics (R. Lakoff 1972) carried the same theoretical weight as those about the surface order of auxiliary morphemes, there was no alternative to developing a full grammatical treatment of pragmatic phenomena. In fact, it does not seem unfair to say that the early 1970s saw many generative semanticists gradually transformed into ordinary language philosophers, as informal descriptions of language use replaced the construction of a grammatical theory as their immediate priority.

7.2.1. Grammatical Approaches

Ross (1970) and Sadock (1969, 1974) argued that the type of speech act which a sentence represents should be encoded directly in its semantic representation (i.e., underlying syntactic structure). By and large, their arguments were no different in form from those typical of abstract syntax (see Section 4.1). For example, Ross argued that all declarative sentences are dominated in the most remote level of syntactic structure by an S which has subject *I*, indirect object *you*, and a main verb which has the features [+V, + performative, + communication, + linguistic, + declarative]. The following supporting argument was typical of the many adduced by Ross:

Consider the sentences of (7.1):

(7.1)　　a.　*I told Albert that physicists like* $\left\{\begin{array}{l} myself \\ himself \\ *yourself \\ *themselves \end{array}\right\}$
　　　　　　are hard to find.

　　　　　b.　*Physicists like* $\left\{\begin{array}{l} myself \\ yourself \\ *himself \\ *themselves \end{array}\right\}$ *are hard to find.*

(7.1a) illustrates that reflexives in the *like . . . -self* construction must agree in person, number, and gender with a noun phrase in a dominating sentence. This suggests that a simple uniclausal declarative like (7.1b) is derived from a deep structure headed by a "performative" sentence containing the noun phrases *I* and *you*.

[PARAPHRASING ROSS 1970]

Sadock (1970, 1972, 1974) extended the performative analysis to indirect speech acts as well. He pointed out that while the words *please* and vocative *someone* typically occur in imperative utterances, parenthetical *tell me* never occurs with true imperatives:

(7.2)　　a.　*Give me a drink, please*
　　　　　b.　*Give me a drink, someone*
　　　　　c.　**Tell me, give me a drink*

He then noted that sentences with the superficial form of questions in which an imperative sense is conveyed manifest the same distributional properties as the true imperatives just mentioned:

(7.3)　　a.　*Would you give me a drink, please*
　　　　　b.　*Would you give me a drink, someone*
　　　　　c.　**Tell me, would you give me a drink*

This suggested to Sadock a deep structure for (7.4a) roughly like (7.4b), which contains a conjunction of imperative and interrogative performative verbs:

(7.4)   a. *Would you give me a drink.*
         b.

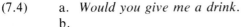

While George Lakoff accepted the performative hypothesis for direct speech acts, he chose to treat indirect speech acts quite differently—but still within the domain of formal grammar. He first noted an observation of Searle's (1975) that one can convey a request by either asserting a speaker-based sincerity condition relevant to that request or questioning a hearer-based condition. Hence (7.5b) and (7.5c) can both be used to convey (7.5a):

(7.5)   a. *Pass the salt*
         b. *I'd like the salt*
         c. *Can you pass the salt?*

He and his collaborator David Gordon chose to formalize this (Gordon and Lakoff 1971; G. Lakoff 1975b) by treating conveyed meanings as logical entailments. Just as the entailment relation between (7.6a) and (7.6b) was to be stated by meaning postulate (7.7), the generalizations just stated were to be captured by conversational postulates (7.8a–b):

(7.6)   a. *It is certain that Harry will lose*
         b. *It is possible that Harry will lose*

(7.7)   CERTAIN (S_1) → POSSIBLE (S_1)

(7.8)   a. SAY (a, b, WANT (a, Q)) → REQUEST (a, b, Q)
         b. ASK (a, b, CAN (b, Q)) → REQUEST (a, b, Q)

For Lakoff, the main difference between (7.8) and (7.7) was that conversational postulates were considered to be entailments with respect to a particular context and speaker-intention. In Lakoff's opinion, the outstanding benefit of such an approach was its property of integrating the treatment of one of the least understood aspects of language into a familiar framework: "What we have done is to largely, if not entirely, eliminate pragmatics, reducing it to garden variety semantics [Lakoff 1972b:655]."

Gordon and Lakoff also gave an example of a transformational rule that itself seems to need to make transderivational reference to a set of contexts and conversational postulates. They noted the following sentences:

(7.9)   a. *Why do you paint your house purple?*
          b. *Why paint your house purple?*

(7.9a) can be construed as a normal question or as a suggestion that the addressee should NOT be painting the house purple. The latter reading was explained by linking the logical structure of sentences of the form of (7.9a) by a conversational postulate to a conveyed meaning something like 'unless you have a good reason for painting your house purple, you shouldn't paint your house purple' in a "class of contexts" in which the judgmental reading is appropriate. Since (7.9b), however, ALWAYS conveys the judgmental meaning. Gordon and Lakoff stated the transformational rule of *You +* Tense Deletion (informally) as follows:

WHY YOU TENSE $x \rightarrow$ WHY x
ONLY IF C $\Vdash$ ('*Unless you have some good reason for doing x, you should not do x.*')
In (43), C $\Vdash$ indicates that the application of the rules is relative only to those contexts and conversational postulates such that they together with the logical structure of the sentence entail what is on the right-hand side of C $\Vdash$ [Gordon and Lakoff 1971:73].

A debate was carried on in the early 1970s between Sadock (1975) and Green (1975) on the one side and George Lakoff on the other about whether indirect illocutionary force should be encoded directly into the logical structure (à la Sadock) or should be handled semantically (à la Lakoff). Sadock pointed out that transderivational rules undermine the entire performative analysis—given such devices there could be no principled objection to a transderivational rule of "performative addition," which would refer to performativeless semantic representations. Green (1975) stated the case in even stronger terms: "In fact, the possibility of having global syntactic rules that refer to conversational entailments of deep structures removes the basis for all arguments in favor of generative semantics and makes 'generative semantics' an interpretive theory [p. 131]."

However, the debate was dropped as more and more problems were discovered with ANY type of grammatical solution to these phenomena (see Section 7.2.2).

In this period, many other seeming interactions of syntactic rules and pragmatic phenomena were discovered. A few are paraphrased below:

Sentences like (7.10a–b) can be interpreted in three ways: as *yes–no* questions, as requests for information, or as rhetorical exclamations:

(7.10)   a. *Have you seen John lately?*
          b. *Do you have any idea how much that vase was worth?*

But if a rule that deletes the subject and the auxiliary applies, they may be interpreted only as requests for information:

(7.11)   a. *Seen John lately?*
          b. *Any idea how much that vase was worth?*

[PARAPHRASING SCHMERLING 1973]

In comparative constructions, the second occurrence of a verb may optionally be replaced by the pro-verb *do*, or be deleted:

(7.12)   a. *John is taller than Bill (is)*
          b. *John runs faster than Bill (runs, does)*
          c. *John walks like his father (walks, does)*

Comparatives and similes have a sense in which they are used as "conventionalized hyperbole":

(7.13)   a. *Mary is bigger than a house*
          b. *John runs as fast as a deer*
          c. *Hans leaps like a gazelle*

But in order to convey this figurative sense, the deletion rule MUST take place. (7.14a–c) are not understood as hyperbolic:

(7.14)   a. *Mary is bigger than a house is*
          b. *John runs as fast as a deer runs*
          c. *Hans leaps like a gazelle does*

[PARAPHRASING MORGAN 1975]

The derivation of imperative sentences normally involves deletion of the underlying *you* subject. If the subject is NOT deleted, the sentence can be interpreted only as a conveyed warning:

(7.15)   *Don't you eat too much*

[PARAPHRASING SADOCK 1977]

7.2.2. Current Thinking

Virtually nobody today accepts a strictly grammatical explanation of all pragmatic phenomena, whether syntactic or semantic. The mid and late 1970s saw an accelerating number of papers and books which convincingly cast into doubt the possibility of one homogeneous syntax–semantics–pragmatics and its consequent abandonment of the competence–performance distinction.

The syntactic arguments for the performative hypothesis were challenged very early and in many papers (see S. Anderson 1971b; Banfield

1973b; Fraser 1974; Heal 1977; Gildin 1978; Gazdar 1979).[1] They all added up to the conclusion that there was simply no syntactic motivation for positing an abstract performative verb of declaring, requesting, commanding, etc. in the deep structure. For example, Fraser pointed out that arguments like the one of Ross's recently cited based on the distribution of reflexives are invalidated by the possibility of a reflexive occurring in the performative clause itself:

(7.16) a. *You are hereby authorized by John and myself to buy that ship*
   b. *You are hereby advised by Mary and myself that we are married*
   c. *The court rejects any such remarks directed at the other jurors and myself*

In Lakoff's view, there is a relationship of semantic entailment between a speech act and its felicity conditions—in fact, a NECESSARY one for Lakoff's analysis in terms of conversational postulates to go through. Gazdar (1979) demonstrated that no such relationship exists. If Lakoff were right, he argued, (7.17a) should entail (7.17b):

(7.17) a. *Sue requested of Tom that he meet Harry*
   b. *Sue attempted to get Tom to meet Harry*

But if such an entailment exists, Gazdar argued, (7.18a) should make Sue sound irrational, and (7.18b) should be contradictory:

(7.18) a. *Sue requested of Tom that he meet Harry, because it was the only way she knew of preventing him from doing so*
   b. *Sue requested of Tom that he meet Harry, but she was only attempting to shock him*

That (7.18a–b) do not behave as predicted demonstrates that the relationship between a speech act and its felicity conditions cannot be one of entailment. This supports a pragmatic over a semantic treatment of such phenomena.

Since all arguments against a syntactic treatment of direct speech acts carry over to refute such a treatment of indirect speech acts as well, the special syntactic problems of the Sadock analysis just described were pointed out more often verbally than in writing. As far as semantic treatments of indirect speech acts are concerned, Morgan (1977) discussed at length the problems of treating them (and conversational implicature in general) in terms of semantic entailment. He pointed that while, indeed,

---

[1] There have also been objections to grammatical approaches to performatives from a philosophical standpoint. See, for example, Searle (1976) and Pelletier (1977).

(7.19a) is often used to convey (7.19b):

(7.19)   a. *Can you open the door?*
           b. *Open the door*

the relationship cannot be one of entailment:

> one cannot always be sure of success, either from the speaker's standpoint or from the
> hearer's, since at least some contexts are ambiguous, in any useful sense of context; i.e.,
> the hearer is equally justified in concluding either that a certain implicature was intended,
> or that it was not intended. I do not mean by this any sort of performance error on the
> hearer's part that might ensue from failure to observe some aspect of context, or failure
> to apply some principle of reasoning—a special kind of dullness—but rather cases where
> the idealized, perfectly rational human being cannot deduce whether a certain implicature
> was intended, but is equally justified in concluding either that it was or that it was
> not . . . . THE VERY PROPERTY OF IMPLICATURE THAT MAKES IT SO USEFUL AS A CON-
> VERSATIONAL PLOY IS THAT IT IS NOT ENTAILED, BUT MERELY SUGGESTED OR HINTED
> AT [pp. 279-280, emphasis added].

Kempson (1975) has carried that attack a step farther, arguing that ANY attempt to include speaker-relative concepts (such as intentions or assumptions) in a grammatical statement will result in the semantics automatically losing its predictive power. Focusing on Robin Lakoff's (1971) analysis of conjunction, which is based on the grammatical notion "presupposed common topic," she demonstrated that any mechanism with sufficient power to predict the required sentence-presupposition pairs would need to have quite unconstrainable power. From this, she concluded that notions such as "speaker assumptions" and the like cannot be part of a formal semantic theory.

It is now generally agreed upon that, despite the claims of an early influential article by Keenan (1971), no logical relation of presupposition has a role in a semantic theory.[2] Keenan contrasted two types of presuppositions: logical (i.e., semantic) and pragmatic. A sentence A was said to logically presuppose a sentence B if when A is true, B is true; when not A is true, B is true; and when B is false, A has no truth value. Keenan cited factive predicates (7.20a-b), definite names (7.21a-b), and cleft sentences (7.22a-b) as examples illustrating logical presupposition:

(7.20)   a. (A) *John regrets that he left Seattle*
           b. (B) *John left Seattle*

(7.21)   a. (A) *The mayor of Birmingham wears a hat*
           b. (B) *There exists a mayor of Birmingham*

(7.22)   a. (A) *It was John who caught the thief*
           b. (B) *Someone caught the thief*

A pragmatic presupposition was defined on the relation between the utterance of a sentence and the context in which it is uttered—the utterance

---

[2] But see Katz and Langendoen (1976) for a defense of the contrary position.

of a sentence. was said to presuppose pragmatically that its context is appropriate. In this view, the utterance of (7.23a) (by a Spanish speaker) pragmatically presupposes that the speaker is female; (7.23b) male:

(7.23)   a. *Estoy cansada*
         b. *Estoy cansado*

Many linguists in recent years (see Kuroda 1974, Wilson 1975; Kempson 1975; Boër and Lycan 1976; Karttunen and Peters 1977; Gazdar 1979) have challenged the existence of logical presupposition. They argue that the "presuppositions" in simple affirmative clauses are really entailments, while in negative clauses, the so-called "presuppositions" are really conversational implicatures (i.e., pragmatic phenomena). A typical argument involves the citation of sentences like the following:

(7.24)   a. **John regrets that he left Seattle—but he didn't really leave*
         b. *John doesn't regret that he left Seattle—how could he? He never really left*

(7.25)   a. **The mayor of Birmingham wears a hat—but in fact there really is no such person*
         b. *The mayor of Birmingham doesn't wear a hat—in fact there really is no such person*

(7.26)   a. **It was John who caught the thief—actually, nobody did*
         b. *It wasn't John who caught the thief—actually, nobody did*

The (a) sentences of examples (7.24)-(7.26) are all contradictory, as we would expect from the entailment of *John left Seattle* by *John regrets that he left Seattle*, etc. But the corresponding negative (b) sentences allow cancellation—a test for implicature (see Grice 1975). Therefore the conclusion is reached that the relationship between *John doesn't regret that he left Seattle* and *John left Seattle* must be one of implicature rather than presupposition. Many other tests were proposed in these publications, all of which lead to the same conclusion.

Deirdre Wilson (1975) constructed an argument to explain WHY the implicature cited in the preceding paragraph holds, based on the strategy outlined in Grice (1975), by which conversationalists optimize brevity and attempt to avoid obscurity in communicating. More recently, she and Daniel Sperber (Wilson and Sperber 1979) have developed an alternative to presuppositional theories based on the notion "ordered entailment."

There have been many studies of the various logical and pragmatic properties of predicates in the last decade (see, for example, Kiparsky and Kiparsky 1970; Fillmore 1969b, 1971a; and Karttunen 1970, 1971, 1973). Probably the most noteworthy is Laurence Horn's *On The Semantic Properties of Logical Operators in English* (1972). Horn investigated in particular scalar predicates of various sorts, and hypothesized that they are lower bounded by assertion and upper bounded by implicature. He noted the following contrasts:

(7.27)   a.   *John is five years old, if not six*
          b.   **John is five years old, if not four*

(7.28)   a.   *Mary was seriously, if not critically, wounded*
          b.   **Mary was critically, if not seriously, wounded*

(7.29)   a.   *John can go—in fact, he will*
          b.   **John will go—in fact, he can*

These facts fall out automatically, he claimed, if the lower bound of a scalar predicate is asserted, and hence unsuspendable, while the upper bound is simply conversationally implicated, and hence suspendable. The importance of this observation was that it led to a number of interesting explanations of seemingly unrelated phenomena. To cite only one example, Horn observed that there are lexicalizations of (i.e., lexical items corresponding to) the (a) expressions of Examples (7.30)–(7.32), but not of the (b) expressions:

(7.30)   a.   *~some*   =   *no/none*
          b.   *some~*

(7.31)   a.   *~much*   =   *little*
          b.   *much~*

(7.32)   a.   *~frequently*   =   *rarely*
          b.   *frequently~*

He showed that his principle of scalar predicates being upper bounded by implicature can explain this fact, that is, expressions that can be conversationally implicated by others resist lexicalization. Since, for example, (7.33a) implicates (7.33b), no lexicalization of *some not* is possible:

(7.33)   a.   *Some have greatness thrust upon them*
          b.   *Not all have greatness thrust upon them (=Some do not)*

Since, however, no expression implicates *not some*, it has a lexicalization— *no* (or *none*)—as predicted.

There are many other examples of phenomena which a few years ago were treated syntactically or semantically and are now assigned to pragmatics. For example, the correct treatment of the scope of logical elements such as quantifiers and negatives was once at the center of the debate between generative and interpretive semantics—partisans of the former opting for a syntactic treatment, partisans of the latter a semantic one. Yet more and more linguists are coming to the conclusion that scope relations do not enter into the determination of truth conditions at all; that is, the interpretation of "logical" scope is a pragmatically determined phenomenon. Fauconnier (1975) writes: " 'Logical' properties of sentences, such as quantification and scope, are not necessarily represented in a logical form;

rather several factors, some of them pragmatic, may be at work to produce logical effects and scope differences [p. 374]."

Along the same lines, Morgan (1978) has argued that the fact that some linguistic phenomenon might be conventionalized is not in itself evidence that it demands a grammatical treatment. To take a clear-cut case, (7.34a–b) are conventionalized ways of answering the telephone, while (7.34c–d), their logical equivalents, are not:

(7.34) a. *This is Edith Thornton*
        b. *Edith Thornton speaking*
        c. *Here is Edith Thornton*
        d. *Edith Thornton is speaking*

Nobody but a 1970-model generative semanticist would argue that this is a GRAMMATICAL fact—clearly it reflects a conventionalized rule of usage. Yet once the possibility of such rules was admitted, the door was opened to a pragmatic treatment of many other conventionalized phenomena.

It is very interesting (and a bit ironic) that intensive investigation of pragmatic phenomena is leading to a model of grammar very much in the spirit of "classical" Chomskyan theory, recognizing a system of formal grammar with properties fundamentally independent of pragmatics and other performance phenomena. In fact, the most detailed and formalized study of pragmatic phenomena to date, Gerald Gazdar's *Pragmatics: Implicature, Presupposition, and Logical Form* (1979), specifically postulates syntactic, semantic, and pragmatic rules, each quite distinct in their form and function. For the first time in well over a decade, a real rapproachment is underway between the two camps which had split in the late 1960s over the abstractness of underlying syntactic representation.

7.3. PERCEPTUAL EXPLANATIONS

Very early in the history of transformational research, investigators realized that there were phenomena which did not lend themselves to a neat grammatical treatment, yet could not be explained by recourse to any "sociological" factors (nonlinguistic context, principles of conversation and cooperation, etc.). For example, Miller and Chomsky (1963) noted the extreme unacceptability of multiply self-embedded constructions such as (7.35):

(7.35) *The cheese that the rat that the cat chased ate was rotten*

There was no obvious GRAMMATICAL explanation of this unacceptability. For one thing, it was clear that the structure underlying (7.35) is well-formed, given the acceptability of (7.36):

(7.36) *The cheese was rotten that the rat which was chased by the cat ate*

That meant that if (7.35) was to be excluded grammatically, it would have to be blocked at some derived level of structure. But where and how? It seemed that to filter it grammatically would require some sort of ad hoc "recursion counter" to be built into the grammar. Yet such a device would vastly increase the power of the grammar, and was unneeded elsewhere. Miller and Chomsky suggested that (7.35) IS in fact generated by the grammar (i.e., is a grammatical sentence) and that its unacceptability can be explained by a PERFORMANCE principle, that is, essentially, the limit of the amount of information storable in immediate memory.

Given the implausibility of a grammatical explanation of (7.35) and the clearly independently motivated performance principle, the Miller–Chomsky explanation was generally accepted. In fact, for a number of years discussions of "theories of performance" were normally restricted to proposals involving perceptually based strategies for language processing.

Nevertheless, until very recently syntacticians have tended to opt for a full grammatical treatment of phenomena which seem (at least intuitively) to be a reflection of perceptual abilities. A fairly clear example involves attempts to build "heaviness" conditions on rules into the statement of the rules themselves. For example, Ross (1968) noted the apparent inapplicability of Particle Movement if the direct object is "complex" [cf. (7.37a–b); (7.38a–b)] and that of Heavy-NP-Shift if the direct object is not "complex" [cf. (7.39a–b)–(7.40a–b)]:

(7.37)   a. *A sudden gust of wind knocked down the old man*
          b. *A sudden gust of wind knocked the old man down*

(7.38)   a. *A sudden gust of wind knocked down the old man who I saw get out of the car a few minutes ago*
          b. **A sudden gust of wind knocked the old man who I saw get out of the car a few minutes ago down*

(7.39)   a. *I consider John a fool*
          b. **I consider a fool John*

(7.40)   a. *I consider all the people who I met at the party fools*
          b. *I consider fools all the people who I met at the party*

Ross attempted to block (7.38b) and (7.39b) grammatically, by postulating complex conditions on the rules of Particle Movement and Heavy-NP-Shift. Langendoen (1970), however, opted for a performance explanation of the same facts. He argued that these sentences are fully grammatical, their unacceptability following from their not providing easy access to their deep structures. But since the notion of "accessibility" is far fuzzier than that of "human memory limitation," the Langendoen explanation was not nearly as widely accepted as Miller and Chomsky's. Nevertheless, it seems fair to say that most linguists today would favor some sort of performance explanation for such phenomena.

Even proposed grammatical universals have been reanalyzed in recent years as following from some independent perceptual principle and hence outside of the realm of formal grammar. For example, Ross (1973e) proposed what he called the "Penthouse Principle," the principle that the reordering rules that apply in subordinate clauses are a subset of those that apply in main clauses, and those that apply in final subordinate clauses are a subset of those that apply in initial subordinate clauses. But Bever (1975) argued that Ross's observations are an automatic consequence of the following nonlinguistic principle:[3]

> Since the subordinate clause must be maintained unrecoded in short-term memory for a longer time, we might expect more restrictions on word order in subordinate clauses than in main clauses: the special processing load imposed by subordinate clauses constrains word order to be closer to the canonical order than would be the case in main clauses [p. 597].

He concluded:

> Consider the implications of the discovery that the penthouse principle is not a property of universal grammar but rather due to the perceptual mechanisms associated with clause segmentation and recoding. [Ross's formulation] . . . captures the observed facts, but provides an explanation for them only by terminological fiat, or by the claim that the penthouse principle is innate. In contrast to this, the perceptual explanation follows from an independently motivated theory of perceptual functioning, and thereby explains the facts without recourse to new hypothetical universals [p. 598].

The investigation of possible perceptual explanations for linguistic phenomena has been carried out most extensively by Thomas Bever, Terence Langendoen, and their associates (see especially Bever 1970, 1975; Bever and Langendoen 1971; Langendoen 1970, 1976; Langendoen, Kalish-Landon, and Dore 1974). Bever (1970), the most comprehensive study of perception and acceptability, proposes many such explanations, of which the following is perhaps representative:

The Double Function Hypothesis
In a sequence of constituents x, y, z, if x has an internal relation R_i to y and y has the same internal relation to z, and x, y, and z are superficially identical, then the stimulus is relatively complex, due to y's double function in the perceptual strategy S_i

$$S_i : x\ y \to x\ R_i\ y \qquad\qquad [\text{p. 337}]$$

For example, he noted that (7.41a) is harder to process than (7.41b), and (7.42a) harder than (7.42b):

(7.41)   a. *They were tired <u>of the discussion</u> <u>of the consideration</u> <u>of the</u>*
                       x y z
                <u>production</u> of toys
        b. *They were tired <u>of the discussion</u> <u>of the evolution</u> <u>of the pro-</u>*
                       x y z
                <u>duction</u> of toys

(7.42)   a. *<u>John claimed</u> <u>Mary believed</u> <u>Bill left</u>*
                  x y z
        b. *<u>John claimed</u> <u>Mary believed</u> <u>Bill to have left</u>*
                  x y z

---

[3] The Penthouse Principle is, of course, a reinterpretation of Emonds's work (see Section 6.2.2). Ross's formulation has been attacked on empirical grounds in Andersson and Dahl (1974).

In Bever's view, (7.41a) creates more processing difficulties than (7.41b) because in the former the x,y relation and the y,z relation are both nominalization–direct object. In the latter, however, x and y are related as nominalization–direct object, and y and z as nominalization–subject. (7.42b) is easier to process than (7.42a) because in (7.42b) z is superficially distinct from x,y, while in (7.42a) x,y and z are superficially identical.

Kuno (1974) is an interesting attempt to explain many of the universal tendencies first noted in Greenberg (1963) on the basis of the perceptual difficulties engendered by center-embedded structures. For example, Greenberg noted that *SOV* (subject–object–verb) languages invariably have prenominal relative clauses, while *VSO* (verb–subject–object) languages invariably have postnominal relatives. Kuno showed that these correlations are a consequence of the avoidance of center-embedded structures—the opposite correlations would increase the amount of center-embedding in the language. This point is illustrated in (7.43)–(7.46), where the (a) sentences contain intransitive verbs, the (b) sentences transitive verbs with a relative clause on the subject, and the (c) sentences transitive verbs with a relative clause on the object:

(7.43)   *SOV* with Prenominal Relative Clauses.
          a. *[Mary loved] boy died*
          b. *[Mary loved] boy Jane hated*
          c. *Jane [Mary loved] boy hated*   (center-embedding)

(7.44)   *SOV* with Postnominal Relative Clauses.
          a. *Boy [Mary loved] died*   (center-embedding)
          b. *Boy [Mary loved] Jane hated*   (center-embedding)
          c. *Jane boy [Mary loved] hated*   (center-embedding)

(7.45)   *VSO* with Prenominal Relative Clauses.
          a. *Died [loved Mary] boy*   (center-embedding)
          b. *Hated [loved Mary] boy Jane*   (center-embedding)
          c. *Hated Jane [loved Mary] boy*   (center-embedding)

(7.46)   *VSO* with Postnominal Relative Clauses.
          a. *Died boy [loved Mary]*
          b. *Hated boy [loved Mary] Jane*   (center-embedding)
          c. *Hated Jane boy [loved Mary]*

Kuno also constructed analogous arguments to explain the typical positions of complementizers and prepositions in *VSO*, *SVO*, and *SOV* languages.

The principle of blind application of transformational rules (Section 6.3) has speeded up the search for perceptually based explanations of acceptability judgments, since such explanations generally allow complex conditions to be removed from the statement of transformational rules. To handle such phenomena, Chomsky has proposed a rich set of surface filters (see Section 6.5 and 8.2.1) rather than advocate strictly perceptual (i.e., performance) explanations, remarking on "the possibility that surface filters might be regarded as a point of contact between a performance theory and a competence theory, as might some of the conditions on transformations [Chomsky 1973:284]." Except in the most obvious cases, there has been little agreement on the question of whether a transformational, surface filter, or strictly perceptual explanation is appropriate.

7.4. FUNCTIONAL EXPLANATIONS

Numerous studies have been published attempting to explain linguistic phenomena by reference to discourse-oriented concepts, such as "new information," "old information," "speaker's viewpoint," "theme," and "empathy." Approaches in which such concepts play an important role have been termed "functional sentence perspective," "functional syntax," or simply "functionalism."

The history of the treatment of such phenomena within generative grammar parallels that of pragmatics and perceptually related phenomena. In the early 1970s, many linguists advocated treating these concepts to the fullest extent possible in the syntactic derivation of the sentence itself. But more and more, the tendency has been to follow the example of an early treatment of narrative style by Banfield (1973b), and consider discourse concepts as phenomena which are outside the domain of formal grammar, but which interact in various ways with a tightly constrained syntax.

The first work within transformational generative grammar to attempt to introduce discourse factors directly in the syntax was Cantrall (1974). Cantrall attacked the problem of "picture noun reflexives" (see Postal 1971; Jackendoff 1972) such as (7.47):

(7.47) *John said that there was a picture of himself in the post office*

They pose a problem for the traditional analysis of reflexives since the occurrences of *John* and *himself* are in different clauses. Cantrall attempted to explain them by a syntactic treatment of the notion of "point of view." He argued that the deep structure of (7.47) is approximately (7.48), in which "point of view" is encoded directly into the syntactic structure:

(7.48) *John said that there was what he perceived as a picture of himself in the post office*

In that way, he argued, the clause mate condition on Reflexivization might be maintained.

Langacker (1975) is a summary of a program for a complete synthesis of generative semantics and functional syntax. He argued that each of the many levels of embeddings in the semantic representation of a simple sentence can be characterized by its functional properties.

By far, the most influential functionalist within the general framework of transformational generative grammar is Susumu Kuno (see especially 1972a, 1972b, 1975a, 1975b, 1976a, 1976b, 1978). Kuno's approach to discourse-based phenomena has gradually moved from a syntactic one to one in which the generalizations are to be stated outside of formal grammar. For example, in an early paper (1972b) he noted the far greater acceptability of (7.49a–b) than (7.50a–b):

(7.49) a. *?That John$_i$ was sick was denied by him$_i$*
        b. *?That John$_i$ had an appointment at two was denied by him$_i$*

(7.50) a. **That John$_i$ will be elected is expected by him$_i$*
        b. **That John$_i$ was the best boxer in the world was claimed by him$_i$*

Kuno hypothesized that the difference lies in the deep structure differences between (7.49) and (7.50). In (7.49), the deep structure has some marking in it that indicates that the complement clause represents an abstract fact or someone else's discourse or feeling. In (7.50), the deep structure has some marking in it that the complement clause represents the direct discourse (or direct feeling) of the referent of the matrix subject.

However, Kuno (1978) advocates removing such notions from the syntax entirely, "making the theory of syntax less powerful, and hence, more desirable [p. 280]." In that way, "a discourse-based approach to syntactic analysis can make a significant contribution in constructing a theory of generative syntax [p. 282]." For example, consider his response to the claims of Hankamer (1973). In an attempt to explain the unexpected non-ambiguity of certain sentences derived by the rule of Gapping, Hankamer proposed the following condition on that rule:

(7.51)   **The No-Ambiguity Condition:** *Any application of Gapping which would yield an output structure identical to a structure by Gapping from another source, but with the "gap" at the left extremity, is disallowed.*

This explains why (7.52) has only interpretation (7.53a); interpretation (7.53b) is impossible BECAUSE OF THE EXISTENCE of (7.53a):

(7.52)   *Mary hit John with a stick and Sue with a club*

(7.53)   a. *Mary hit John with a stick and [Mary hit] Sue with a club*
            b. *Mary hit John with a stick and Sue [hit John] with a club*

Kuno, however, advocates an alternative, functional, approach to this problem. He suggested (1976a) that the facts of Examples (7.52)–(7.53) have nothing to do with the rule of Gapping itself, but fall out from the following four nonsyntactic constraints:

(7.54)   **Minimal Distance Principle:** *The more recently a constituent has been processed, the easier it is to recall. As a consequence,* *the two constituents left behind by Gapping can most readily be coupled with the constituents in the first conjunct that were processed last.*

(7.55)   **Functional Sentence Perspective (FSP) Principle on Constituents Left Behind after Gapping:** *Material left behind after Gapping must represent new information. When the first conjunct is pronounced without emphatic stress, the two constituents that appear in final position are ordinarily interpreted as representing new information. Hence, the constituents left behind after Gapping are most readily coupled with these.*

(7.56)   **FSP Principle on Constituents Deleted by Gapping:** *Material deleted by Gapping must be discourse anaphoric. It is not sufficient that a copy of the deleted string be present in the first conjunct; what is deleted must represent subject matter which has been talked about in the preceding discourse, or which the preceding discourse (or nonlinguistic context) has led one to expect.*

(7.57)   **Subject–Predicate Interpretation Tendency:** *When both an NP and a VP are left behind by Gapping, they tend to take on a subject-predicate interpretation; namely, it is readily assumed that the NP is (or is co-referential with) the underlying subject of the VP.*

By and large, Kuno's functional explanations have dealt with anaphoric processes in the grammar—processes such as Pronominalization, Reflexivization, Verb Phrase Deletion, and Gapping. For example, he proposed a constraint on Backward Pronominalization (1972a) to the effect that it can take place only when the referent of the pronoun is determinable from the preceding context. This explains why (7.58b) is an acceptable response to (7.58a), while (7.59b) and (7.60b) are bizarre responses to (7.59a) and (7.60a), respectively:

(7.58)   a. Speaker A: *Who is visiting John$_i$?*
            b. Speaker B: *His$_i$ brother is visiting John$_i$.*

(7.59)   a. Speaker A: *Who is visiting who?*
            b. Speaker B: *His$_i$ brother is visiting John$_i$.*

(7.60)   a. Speaker A: *Who are John$_i$'s brother and Bill$_j$'s brother visiting?*
            b. Speaker B: *His$_i$ brother is visiting John$_i$, but I don't know about Bill$_j$'s brother.*

It is interesting to note that the distinction between sentence grammar and discourse grammar is now well accepted (see Hankamer 1971; Hankamer and Sag 1976; Williams 1977b; Sag 1977). However, Kuno's general approach has met with quite a bit of opposition from syntacticians. The problem is the fuzziness of the basic concepts involved and the belief on the part of many linguists that such concepts can be manipulated at will to explain anything. Bever (1975) was probably echoing the majority sentiment when he wrote:

> I have taken care to argue that each specific linguistic phenomenon is interpreted as due to independently motivated aspects of speech perception. I have attempted to avoid vague reference to properties such as "mental effort," "informativeness," "importance," "focus," "empathy," and so on. I do not mean that these terms are empty in principle: however, they are empty at the moment, and consequently can have no clear explanatory force [pp. 601–602].

Chapter 8

Recent Developments in
Syntax and Semantics

8.1. WORK IN PROGRESS

It is not easy to treat the present as history. Lacking the advantage of at least a few years hindsight, I run the risk in this chapter of distorting the importance of some current development by assigning it (by virtue of too great or too little coverage) a significance which history will show it does not deserve. Nevertheless, I will do my best in the following pages to survey what are generally recognized to be the major contemporary currents in syntax and semantics.

8.2. DEVELOPMENTS IN TRACE THEORY

Chomsky has continued to develop the trace theory of movement rules beyond the model described in Section 6.3. His current views of grammatical organization, which Section 8.2.1 outlines, are as different from early 1970s interpretivism as that was from the *Aspects* model. Every step Chomsky has taken, however, has been resisted by a significant number of linguists, this resistance being composed of as many interpretivists as (former) generative semanticists. The character of the resistance is the subject matter of Section 8.2.2.

8.2.1. Chomsky's Recent Work

In several important recent papers (Chomsky 1976, 1977b, 1978; Chomsky and Lasnik 1977), Chomsky has developed a model whose major syntactic consequences follow from a strengthening of the principle of blind application of transformational rules and whose semantic consequences follow from a theory of enriched "surface structure" which allows all interpretation to take place at that level.

He suggested (1976) that a condition of MINIMAL FACTORIZATION could be imposed on the structural descriptions of transformational rules, a condition which disallows an SD from containing two successive categorial terms unless one or the other is satisfied by a factor changed by the rule. This condition, as one of its many consequences, rules out the following SD for Passive, since only NP is directly affected by the rule:

(8.1)   X, NP, Aux, V, NP, *by*, Δ, X

Chomsky argued that this condition vastly restricts the expressive power of transformations. So much so, that it leaves (8.2a), or equivalently (8.2b), as the only possible statement of the Passive rule:

(8.2)   a. X NP X NP X
         b. Move NP

The effect of strengthening blind application by minimal factorization was the resultant collapsing of a number of rules which were previously considered distinct into (8.2). For example, it followed as a consequence that Passive and Raising-to-Subject (which had always been assumed to relate (8.3a) and (8.3b)) had to be the same rule:

(8.3)   a. *It is likely for John to be nominated*
         b. *John is likely (for) to be nominated*

It is clear that rule (8.2), by virtue of its lack of specificity, results in massive overgeneration. For example, "Move NP" allows the generation of all of the sentences of (8.4) (trace theory is assumed):

(8.4)   a. **John is believed [t is incompetent]*
         b. *John is believed [t to be incompetent]*
         c. **John('s) was read [t book]*
         d. *John seems [t to like Bill]*
         e. **John seems [Bill to like t]*
         f. **Yesterday was lectured t*
         g. *Yesterday's lecture*

If (8.4a,c,e,f) had to be excluded by ad hoc statements, then the correctness of the (further strengthened) principle of blind application would be doubtful. But, Chomsky claimed, all are excluded by independently motivated constraints: (8.4a) by the Tensed-S Condition (Section 6.3.1), (8.4c) by the A-over-A Principle (Section 6.2.1), (8.4e) by the Specified Subject Condition (Section 6.3.1), and (8.4f) (more vaguely) by a "principle of semantic interpretation of surface structures [Chomsky 1976:317]."

Chomsky suggested that a number of other processes previously considered to be distinct could be collapsed into the following rule, which along with (8.2) make up the two rules of "core grammar":

(8.5) Move *Wh*-Phrase

Rule (8.5) differs from (8.2) in that the moved element becomes dominated by COMP rather than NP (see Section 6.3.1). Chomsky (1977b) proposed that not just relative clause and question formation, but that ALL of the following rules (and several others) be reanalyzed as the rule of "Move *Wh*-Phrase" [the (a) sentences of Examples (8.6)–(8.9) schematize the traditional derivation, the (b) sentence, Chomsky's, in which supplementary rules to guarantee deletion of *wh*-phrases in COMP must additionally be assumed]:

A. COMPARATIVE DELETION

(8.6) a. *John is taller than Mary is* [*tall*]
                                    ↓
                                    ∅

       b. *John is taller than* [COMP] *Mary is what*

B. TOPICALIZATION

(8.7) a. *I like beans* → *beans I like*
       b. [TOP *beans*] [COMP] *I like what*

C. CLEFT SENTENCE FORMATION

(8.8) a. *What I like are beans* → *it is beans that I like*
       b. *it is* [TOP *beans*] [COMP *that*] *I like what*

D. TOUGH MOVEMENT

(8.9) a. *it is easy to please John* → *John is easy to please*
       b. *John is easy* [COMP *for*] *PRO to please who*

The fact that all of these rules obey constraints on extraction would follow as an automatic consequence of their reanalysis as *Wh*-Movement.

As for the Tensed-S Condition (renamed the "Propositional Island Condition") and the Specified Subject Condition; Chomsky suggested that they be reinterpreted as conditions on well-formed surface structures rather than as conditions on transformations. While recognizing that the empirical consequences of this move are "not easy to sort out [Chomsky 1976:320]," he later (1977b) stated that this reinterpretation allows conditions on rules of construal (see the following) and conditions on movement to be collapsed in an interesting way. (8.10a–c) are thereby all filtered at the same level and for the same reason:

(8.10)   a.   *Bill seems [John to like t]
           b.   *Bill expected [Mary to like himself]
           c.   *Bill expected [Mary to find his way home]

By the late 1970s, Chomsky and his co-workers had developed the following overall picture of grammatical organization:

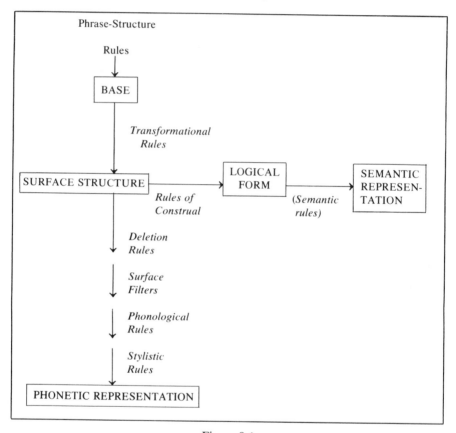

Figure 8.1

Note that in this model all interpretation takes place at surface structure, though this level differs in two important ways from earlier conceptions. First, it is "enriched" by virtue of its containing traces left by application of the movement rules (8.2) and (8.5). Second, it is considerably more "abstract" than in earlier conceptions, since deletions, filters, and stylistic rules apply AFTER the transformations have defined that level.

The rules of construal include Reciprocal Interpretation, which assigns the appropriate sense to sentences of the form NP . . . each other, and the rule of Disjoint Reference, which assigns disjoint reference to NP, pronoun pairs such as *the men* and *them* in (8.11) under specific conditions:

(8.11)   *the men like them*

Logical form is claimed to have a syntax close to that of standard forms of predicate calculus (though Chomsky in fact provides no explicit syntax for this level) and incorporates "whatever features of sentence structure (1) enter directly into semantic interpretation of sentences and (2) are strictly determined by properties of (sentence-) grammar [Chomsky 1976:305–306]." This entails that whatever rules are involved in the interpretation of pragmatically controlled anaphora (see Section 6.2.3) are not rules of construal, but are part of the unnamed system of rules applying between logical form and semantic representation. Semantic representations involve beliefs, expectations, etc., and "in addition to properties of logical form determined by grammatical rule, should suffice to determine role in inference, conditions of appropriate use, etc. . . . [Chomsky 1976:306]."

Chomsky and Lasnik (1977) further motivates and develops the theory of "surface filters" (see Sections 6.5 and 7.3). (8.12) is an example of one which is claimed to be universal ($\pm$ WH means a *wh-* or *that* complementizer):

(8.12)   *[$_{\bar{S}}$ $\pm$ WH [$_{NP}$ Δ] . . .], unless $\bar{S}$ or its trace is in the context [$_{NP}$NP _____ . . .]

(8.12) accounts for the fact that embedded sentences in English headed by *that* or *whether* complementizers have to have subjects. The "unless . . ." clause is necessary to allow the generation of relatives like (8.13):

(8.13)   *a book t arrived* [$_{\bar{S}}$ *that* [$_{NP}$ *e*] *may interest you*] *(t* the trace of $\bar{S}$)

Perlmutter (1971) had proposed an earlier version of this filter, which stated simply that all nonimperative sentences in English, French, and other languages have to have subjects. However, he recognized that this filter could not be universal since languages (such as Spanish) with a rule of Subject Deletion could not obey it. However, Chomsky and Lasnik claim their filter (8.12) CAN be universal—Subject Deletion will delete "empty" subjects of the form [$_{NP}$ Δ], thus voiding the filter. (Note that for this solution to work, filters must follow deletion rules—see Figure 8.1.)

Chomsky and Lasnik proposed quite a few other filters, all specific to English. All involved, directly or indirectly, the complementizer system, leading them to speculate that filters might necessarily be restricted in this way. Furthermore, they claim, their adoption leads to a grammatical model more constrained in its descriptive power:

> [Filters] will have to bear the burden of accounting for constraints which, in the earlier and far richer theory, were expressed in statements of ordering and obligatoriness, as well as all contextual dependencies that cannot be formulated in the narrower framework

of core grammar. Our hypothesis, then, is that the consequences of ordering, obligato-
riness, and contextual dependency can be captured in terms of surface filters, something
that surely need not be the case in principle; and further, that these properties can be
expressed in a natural way at this level [Chomsky and Lasnik 1977:433].

They suggested that the origin of surface filters lies in the facilitation
of perceptual strategies, by "sharply reduc[ing] the range of possible out-
comes from well-formed base-generated structures, while still permitting at
least one outcome in each case [Chomsky and Lasnik 1977:470]."

The central theme of Chomsky's paper 'On Binding' (1978) is the
reformulation of the Tensed-S Condition (now called the "Nominative Island Condition") and the Specified Subject Condition (now the "Opacity
Condition") as conditions on logical form, which is now explicitly claimed
to be a level at which representations are in the form of phrase-markers.
Recently, he and his co-thinkers (see especially van Riemsdijk 1978b and
Koster 1978c) have been developing the notion of 'markedness' in syntax.
The thrust of their work is the attempt to explain what might otherwise be
taken as counterexamples to Chomsky-conditions and trace theory by pos-
tulating that they involve 'marked' constructions.

8.2.2. The Resistance to Chomsky's Model

Not one step of Chomsky's reasoning has been without scathing attack.
Naturally, nobody objected in principle with the desirability of constraining
transformational power to the fullest extent possible. Such an endeavor was
the principal occupation of syntacticians throughout the 1970s (see Chapter
6). But many linguists (eg., Bresnan 1976b; Bach 1977b; Newmeyer 1978)
pointed out that reduction of the power of the transformational rules, if
accompanied by an INCREASE in the power of other rule-types does not lead
to a more overall constrained grammar. As Bresnan (1976b) put it:

Nevertheless, a reduction in the class of possible TRANSFORMATIONS is not equivalent to
a reduction in the class of permissible RULES; so for the above argument from restrictiveness to apply, it must be shown that the proposed restrictions on transformations are
not offset by extensions of permissible rules elsewhere in the grammar. Otherwise, we
have, not a "more restrictive" theory of grammar, but simply a different theory of
grammar, for which there is no a priori preference [p. 356].

Many have argued that unconstrainedness HAS simply been shifted to devices such as surface filters, lexical rules, and the two types of semantic
rules, resulting in only the illusion that the grammar as a whole has been
further constrained.

Paul Postal devoted an entire 450 page volume, *On Raising* (1974), to
arguing that the rule of Raising-to-Object, a major victim of the principle of
blind application (see Chapter 6, footnote 4) does in fact exist, and that the
principle is thereby (indirectly) falsified. While a summary of his arguments
is, of course, impossible, the following is perhaps typical:

Note that the rule of Heavy-NP-Shift applies to objects, but not to subjects:

(8.14)   a.   *I showed all of the coffee ground and lettuce cookies to Jack*

          b.   *I showed to Jack all of the coffee ground and lettuce cookies*

(8.15)   a.   *I think all of the men who recovered from mononucleosis are happy*

          b.   **I think are happy all of the men who recovered from mononucleosis*

Now we have a test to determine whether in sentences like (8.16), the lower clause subject has been raised to the position of higher clause object:

(8.16)   *John believed [$_{NP}$Bill] to have left*

If so, that NP should be movable by Heavy-NP-Shift. In fact, it is:

(8.17)   a.   *I believe [$_{NP}$all of the gang members who were caught] to have been innocent*

          b.   *I believe to have been innocent [$_{NP}$all of the gang members who were caught]*

Therefore, a rule which transforms (8.18a) into (8.18b) must exist:

(8.18)   a.   *John believed [$_S$Bill (to have) left]*

          b.   *John believed Bill [$_S$to have left]*

The conditions which follow as a consequence of the principle have been attacked in literally dozens of publications. Subjacency, which prohibits unbounded movements and deletions, has been the most severely criticized. Since this principle goes hand-in-hand with a reanalysis of all seeming unbounded movements and deletions as instances of *Wh*-Movement applying on successive cycles, it has proved particularly vulnerable. Bresnan (1976b) has argued that the principle of subjacency leads to completely artificial treatments of the many (mainly verb-final) languages with no complementizers, since almost all have what seem to be unbounded movements and/or deletions, and of languages such as Basque (see De Rijk 1972) which have neither relative pronouns nor any signs of a question movement rule. Treating rules such as Topicalization as *Wh*-Movement leads to analogous problems, according to Bach and Horn (1976). In almost all languages, Topicalization moves an element to the left—even in Japanese, which has its COMP on the right.[1]

---

[1] The existence of languages like Sharanahua (see Frantz 1973), which apparently has obligatory *Wh*-Movement to the left, but clause-final complementizers, and Polish (see Wachowicz 1974), which apparently allows several interrogative movements in the same clause, also pose problems for Chomsky. But they are equally problematic for anybody who views *Wh*-Movement as complementizer replacement, a view first put forward in Bresnan (1970b).

Support for the existence of unbounded deletion rules can be found in Bresnan (1975, 1976b, 1977), Grimshaw (1974), and Maling (1977). Bresnan defends the claim that sentences like (8.19) result from the rule of Comparative Deletion, a rule which deletes the identical NP over a variable, rather than from a local deletion after COMP-to-COMP movement by rule (8.5), as Chomsky suggests:

(8.19)   *He uttered more homilies than I'd ever listened to ____ in one sitting*

Her argument can be broken into steps (A)–(D):

(A) The obeying of constraints on extraction is not a diagnostic for movement. Note (8.20b) and (8.21b) where movement clearly did not take place:

(8.20)   a.   *Who saw pictures of whom?*
          b.   **Who heard claims about pictures of whom?*

(8.21)   a.   *Who has evidence about which crimes?*
          b.   **Who has information about evidence of which crimes?*

Therefore the fact that Comparative Deletion obeys such constraints is not evidence that a movement rule applied (i.e., it is not evidence for Chomsky).

(B) The rule of Subdeletion, illustrated in (8.22), can be shown to be a special case of Comparative Deletion:

(8.22)   *They have many more enemies than we have ____friends*

(C) But Subdeletion cannot possibly be a movement rule, since it violates the Left Branch Condition (see Section 6.2.1), a condition on movement:

(8.23)   *Maggie is as fine a doctor as her sister is ____ a lawyer*

(D) Therefore, Comparative Deletion cannot be a movement rule—it must be an unbounded deletion.

Grimshaw and Maling have presented evidence for an unbounded rule of relativization by deletion in Middle English and Old Icelandic, respectively. Grimshaw argued that if in Middle English relativization took place by means of movement only, there would be no non-ad hoc way to account for the fact that with *that*-relatives any preposition associated with the relativized NP must be left in place, while with *which*-relatives such a preposition must be fronted:

(8.24)   a.   *this bok of which I make mencioun*
          b.   **this bok which I make mencioun of*

(8.25)   a.   **this bok of that I make mencioun*
          b.   *this bok that I make mencioun of*

These facts, she claimed, have a natural explanation if in *that*-relatives, the "target" NP is simply deleted over a variable under identity to the head noun. Otherwise, an ad hoc filter would be required to block (8.25a).

The other conditions proposed in Chomsky (1973) have been attacked in various publications, particularly Postal (1976b), Bach and Horn (1976), Bach (1977b), and Brame (1977). Brame, for example, has argued that while the Specified Subject Condition will exclude (8.26), it will have no effect on (8.27):

(8.26)   *Who did you see John's pictures of?*

(8.27)   *Which artist did Bill see those paintings by?*

He concluded that since (intuitively) the sentences are deviant for the same reason, the Specified Subject Condition should be replaced by a prohibition against extraction over constructions bearing heads.

Finally, the trace theory of movement rules has been subject to heavy criticism (see especially Postal and Pullum 1978; Pullum and Postal 1979; and Pullum 1979b). Pullum (1979b) argues that at present the theory is entirely empty, since no successful algorithm exists for determining that a particular trace is the trace of a particular noun phrase. Simply assuming that a moved phrase leaves its own index behind at every move will not work, since such leads to the derivation of (8.28d) from (8.28a) by the steps outlined:

(8.28)   a. $[_{COMP}[_{NP1}\Delta]]$ $[_S[_{NP2}\Delta]$ *hit* $[_{NP3}who]]$
             b. $[_{COMP}[_{NP1}\Delta]]$ $[_S[_{NP3}who]$ *hit* $[_{NP3}$ $t]]$
             c. $[_{COMP}[_{NP3}$ *who*$]]$ $[_S[_{NP3}$ $t]$ *hit* $[_{NP3}$ $t]]$
             d. *who hit?*

After considering a couple (unsuccessful) attempts to patch up the indexing procedure, Pullum (1979b) asks:

> What, then, is the indexing procedure that defines the trace/mover relations in trace theory? How can indexing be controlled during derivations so that at shallow structure the generalizations that Chomsky and Fiengo seek can be stated? Until a clear and explicit answer is given to these questions, it cannot truly be said that trace theory provides an explanation for anything—not even the very simple example (1b) [= *was seen by John*—F.N.] [p. 361].

As far as the semantic effect of traces is concerned, the inexplicitness of Chomsky's discussion has made direct criticism difficult. However, several linguists (e.g., Bresnan 1976; Bach 1977b) have observed that the traces left in COMP as a result of iterative *Wh*-Movement have no semantic function whatever, and might well complicate the retrieval of the underlying grammatical relations needed for interpretation from the "enriched" trace-containing surface structures. And Postal and Pullum (1978) point to syntactic difficulties they give rise to. But of course, such unneeded traces are an inevitable consequence of the principle of subjacency, which demands COMP-to-COMP movement.

8.3. TOWARD NONTRANSFORMATIONAL GRAMMAR

8.3.1. The Autonomy Thesis[2]

As we have seen, Chomsky's position on the interaction of syntax and semantics until the mid 1970s was rather ill-defined. Initially (see Section 2.2.5), while opposing semantic motivation for syntactic structures, he assumed that the independently motivated rules would lead to the grammar's explaining ambiguity directly. Later, after his adoption of the Katz–Postal hypothesis, he had no choice but to admit semantic motivation, since it was a condition on deep structures that they contain all information necessary for semantic interpretation (see Chapter 3). Even after the Katz–Postal hypothesis was rejected, in many early 1970s interpretivist papers we find semantic constructs entering syntactic descriptions. For example, in the syntactic analyses in Dougherty (1970b), the most extensive formal grammar fragment by an interpretivist, the semantic features "totality," "individual," "disjunctive," and "negative" play a crucial role. Even Chomsky, in "Conditions on Transformations" (1973), concludes that in order for Passive to apply correctly, the third term in its factorization must be either a morphological or a semantic unit.

But by 1975, Chomsky had taken an extremely strong position on the relation of syntax to semantics, formulating and justifying what he called the "absolute autonomy thesis":[3]

> the absolute autonomy thesis implies that the formal conditions on "possible grammars" and a formal property of "optimality" are so narrow and restrictive that a formal grammar can in principle be selected (and its structures generated) on the basis of a preliminary analysis of data in terms of formal primitives excluding the core notions of semantics, and that the systematic connections between formal grammar and semantics are determined on the basis of this independently selected system and the analysis of data in terms of the full range of semantic primitives [Chomsky 1975c:92].

The "core notions of semantics" include such notions as "synonymous," "significant," "denotes," and "refers to concrete objects."

The absolute autonomy thesis is generally understood to embody the

---

[2] Much of the material in this section was first published in Newmeyer (1978).

[3] Oddly, Chomsky (1975c) wrote that "the absolute thesis of autonomy . . . was in fact tentatively put forth as a working hypothesis in the earliest work on transformational generative grammar [p. 93]." Given his remarks which I cited in Section 2.2.5, Chomsky could not possibly have held this position at that time. Actually his 1975 paper argues that the absolute thesis is a bit too strong and has to be "parameterized" to handle certain facts about lexical semantics.

following two claims:

A. **The Semantic Motivation Prohibition:** *Semantic evidence may not be used to motivate the existence of a transformational rule.*

B. **The Semantic Construct Prohibition:** *Semantic constructs may not appear in the formulation of a transformational rule.*

Chomsky's followers have adopted both prohibitions explicitly. For example, Akmajian (1977) is a clearly argued defense of the Semantic Motivation Prohibition. Jackendoff (1972), and Hale, Jeanne, and Platero (1977) state the Semantic Construct Prohibition explicitly. The latter points out, for example, that the autonomy thesis forbids semantic constructs such as "specific" or "generic" from appearing in the statement of a transformational rule. Along the same lines, Liberman (1974) remarks that Klima's (1964) analysis of negation violates the autonomy thesis because his rules refer to the notion "affective," which Liberman takes to be semantic.

The absolute autonomy thesis and the principle of blind application, while logically independent, of course complement each other directly. As they gradually took shape in the early 1970s, they resulted in numerous postulated transformations being eliminated. For example, the many pre-lexical transformations proposed by generative semanticists, such as Quantifier Lowering, Predicate Raising, and Nominalization, clearly run afoul of both principles, and cannot therefore be transformations. Since nobody questioned that the RELATIONSHIPS captured by these putative transformations were real, it became necessary to develop other devices in the grammar to incorporate these generalizations. So, for example, a rich set of surface structure rules of semantic interpretation (see Section 6.6.3) was postulated to handle scope of logical operators, and render transformations like Quantifier Lowering unnecessary. Likewise a highly developed set of rules applying in the lexicon (see Jackendoff 1975, Aronoff 1976, Hust 1978) was postulated to do the work of the generative semanticists' word-forming transformations like Predicate Raising and Nominalization.

Part of the appeal of the interpretive model (the "Extended Standard Theory") in the early 1970s was that those REMAINING transformations seemed to obey an extremely interesting set of constraints. That is, it seemed to be just those remaining rules which could be characterized as structure preserving, root, or local (see [6.2.2]), which could be conflated under the X-bar convention, and which behaved in a unitary fashion in other respects. And furthermore, the deep structure level which served as input to those rules seemed at exactly the correct degree of "abstractness" to capture a host of syntactic generalizations.

But the "classic" interpretivist model of this period proved to have a built-in instability, which has led in recent years to a splintering of the once monolithic interpretivist camp, as well as to a de facto renunciation of the absolute autonomy thesis by some of its staunchest erstwhile defenders. We have already seen the opposition (largely by interpretivists) to Chomsky's recent work. Many of his critics have wondered what content the concept of ''autonomy of syntax'' could possibly have in a theory in which the syntactic rules so massively overgenerate that virtually any imaginable string of phrases (conforming to the X-bar Convention) is considered ''syntactically well-formed.''[4]

However, the interpretivists who are not followers of Chomsky have carried the negation of the autonomy thesis much farther than Chomsky has—some to the point where transformations have been totally eliminated, and it is not clear that any interesting syntactic component remains to be ''autonomous.'' In the remainder of this section I will outline their argumentation.

There have been traditionally, two (nonsemantic) steps involved in motivating the transformational status of a grammatical process. The first is to show that the phenomena involved could be captured only in a cumbersome fashion by base rules alone but have a natural elegant treatment utilizing the more descriptively powerful transformational rules. The classic *Syntactic Structures* arguments for the various auxiliary transformations and Passive are arguments of this type, and have been cited as models for motivating transformations in many works. The second is to defend the fully productive nature of the process. This seems to be in keeping with the *Aspects* hypothesis that exceptionality and irregularity be localized in the lexicon.

But ironically, the twin criteria of simplification and productivity have led a number of linguists to strike all (or virtually all) rules from the transformational roster. The first criterion has been effectively nullified by the Structure Preserving Constraint. Freidin (1974) was the first to point out that if transformational rules are structure preserving, then that fact undermines the most persuasive criterion for their existence, which is overall simplification of the grammar. Clearly, positing such processes as transformational could not lead to a simplification of the base rules because, figuratively speaking, the base rules ''apply'' throughout the transformational derivation. That is, if passives are base generated, then of course the rule of Passive would appear to be ''structure preserving.''

Consider now the productivity argument. Chomsky in *Aspects* argued that *destroy* and *destruction* ARE related transformationally (since the relationship is productive), while the nonproductive *horror–horrid* relationship is lexical. By Chomsky (1970), however, his criteria for productivity had become more stringent. In that paper, the NONproductivity of the *destroy–*

---

[4] Along the same lines, Bach (1977b) in his comments on Chomsky (1977b) writes:

However, the net effect of an explicit set of rules [by Chomsky] treating completely a reasonably rich fragment of English will, I suspect, lead to the following question: why should we have any transformations at all? And what conceivable role would deep structure play in such a theory [Bach 1977b: 140]?

destruction relationship pointed to its lexicality as opposed to the productive active–passive relationship.

However, in the 1970s many interpretivists have taken the productivity requirement so stringently that they have found ALL (or virtually all) rules to be nonproductive and therefore nontransformational. For example, one of Freidin's (1975b) arguments against the rule of Passive is its lack of productivity, as illustrated by the following pairs of sentences:

(8.29)   a.   *Max resembles Harry*
         b.   **Harry is resembled by Max*

(8.30)   a.   *The kimono fits Dorothy*
         b.   **Dorothy is fit by the kimono*

(8.31)   a.   *That picnic basket weighs a ton*
         b.   **A ton is weighed by that picnic basket*

Along the same lines, Oehrle (1976) claims that the following contrasts demonstrate that Dative Movement must be lexical rather than transformational:

(8.32)   a.   *I'll get a ticket for you ~ I'll get you a ticket*
         b.   *I'll obtain a ticket for you ~ *I'll obtain you a ticket*

(8.33)   a.   *you should give back the package to the owner ~ you should give the owner back the package*
         b.   *you should return the package to the owner ~ *you should return the owner the package*

Brame (1976) constructed different sorts of arguments to illustrate the nonproductivity (and therefore nonexistence) of Equi-NP-Deletion. For example, he claimed that this rule, which has been posited to transform (8.34a) to (8.34b), requires that the verb *try* take an S complement in deep structure:

(8.34)   a.   *A few students tried [$_S$for a few students to be in class on time]*
         b.   *A few students tried [$_{VP}$to be in class on time]*

But if so, what is to prevent *There*-Insertion from applying in the embedded sentence to derive ungrammatical (8.35)?:

(8.35)   **A few students tried for there to be a few students in class on time.*

Brame suggested that if Equi were eliminated and (8.34b) be the DEEP structure, this problem does not arise. But note that if Equi does not exist, then the many rules which have been postulated to feed it, such as Passive, Raising, *There*-Insertion, and *Tough*-Movement must also not exist as transformations.

While the "long distance" transformations such as *Wh*-Movement and Topicalization had always been thought to be immune to charges of non-productivity, Brame (1978a) has argued that even they are guilty on this count. For example, he has offered as evidence against the rule of *Wh*-Movement the fact that it leads to the postulation of an unnatural source for (8.36a), as the ungrammaticality of (8.36b–c) indicates:

(8.36)   a.   *What the hell did you see?*
          b.   **You saw something the hell*
          c.   **You saw what the hell?*   (echo question)

Brame (1976) contains the first hint within "transformational" generative grammar that ALL transformations might be eliminable in favor of base-generated surface structures and an expanded role for the interpretive rules. This conception has been (slowly) gaining adherents over the last few years.[5] I will discuss some specific proposals in the following section.

8.3.2. Nontransformational Models

Bresnan (1978) develops in greater depth the arguments for treating rules such as Passive, *There*-Insertion, and Raising lexically, and proposes a formalism for computing functional and semantic relations directly from structures which would have been considered transformationally derived in earlier models. However, the main interest of this paper is in its appeal to the notions of "psychological reality" and "suitability for incorporation into an adequate model of speech production and perception" as justification for its analyses. Taking note of both the multitudinous published analyses for any given phenomenon and the findings of psycholinguists (reported in detail in Fodor, Bever, and Garrett (1974)) that there is no evidence to support the idea that grammatical transformations are psychologically real, Bresnan (1978) suggests that

> the proper conclusion to draw about the familiar model of transformational grammar presented in Chomsky's *Aspects of the Theory of Syntax* (1965) may simply be that it is psychologically unrealistic. Linguistic research by Chomsky and many others on the characterization problem has shown the *Aspects* model to be inadequate in significant ways as a theory of language, and the model had undergone important changes. I will argue that these new developments in transformational linguistics, together with independent developments in computational linguists and the psychology of language, make it feasible to begin to construct realistic grammars [pp. 2–3].

Pointing to the results of computational linguists (e.g., Woods 1973) and psychologists (e.g., Brown 1973, and Wanner and Maratsos 1978), Bresnan concludes that "function-dependent" rules (Passive, etc.) must be reinterpreted as essentially lexical operations, while "structure-dependent" rules (*Wh*-Movement, etc.) are transformational.

---

[5] But see Wasow (1977) for an attempt to set up firm criteria for characterizing the differences between transformational rules and lexical rules.

For Brame (1978a, 1978b, 1979), NO transformations exist. In his model, rules of composition build surface structures from the bottom up. The work of transformations is accomplished by lexical operations analogous to those of Bresnan's and by a procedure called "Operator Binding," which is essentially an interpretive analogue of unbounded movement and deletion rules. Brame argues that his approach leads to a unified explanation of the deviance of (8.37) and (8.38), which is impossible in a transformational model:

(8.37)   *What did John put the car in the garage?*

(8.38)   *the car which John put the bike in the garage*

He further argues that the various postulated constraints on movement transformations, which he had termed "artifacts" (1977:383), in fact follow as an automatic consequence of surface subcategorization and Operator Binding.

8.4. RELATIONAL GRAMMAR

In the early 1970s, syntacticians from all quarters began to develop an increased interest in "grammatical relations" such as subject, direct object, and indirect object. Recall that Chomsky's most important constraint, the Specified Subject Condition, demands a characterization of the notion "subject"—universally, in fact, if the condition has any claim to universality. And on the basis of extensive empirical research, Edward Keenan and Bernard Comrie discovered numerous processes in numerous languages which seem to "pay attention to" grammatical relations. They postulated for example (see Keenan and Comrie 1977) that grammatical relations universally form the hierarchy in (8.39) in regard to relative clause formation. All languages relativize from subject position; if a language relativizes from a position lower on the hierarchy, it will also relativize from higher positions:

(8.39)   Subject > Direct Object > Indirect Object > Major Oblique Case
           NP > Genitive NP > Object of Comparison

This "Accessibility Hierarchy" has been argued to govern other grammatical processes as well, for example, determining the grammatical relation assumed by embedded subjects after clause-merging causative transformations apply (Comrie 1976) and selecting the particular NP which is affected by a wide variety of rules which change grammatical relations (Johnson 1974; Trithart 1975).

While working together at IBM in the summer of 1972, David Perlmutter and Paul Postal began to investigate the possibility of a theory in which these relations themselves are taken to be the primitives, with linear order derivative. This developed into a nascent theory called "relational grammar," which soon gained the reputation of being an important alternative to all varieties of "standard" transformational grammar.[6]

Relational grammar quickly won a sizeable number of adherents, and this was not due merely to the prestige of its formulators. The greatest attraction of the theory was that it seemed to be able to capture universal generalizations about language which defied expression in linear-order-based models. Most importantly, it made possible a universal rule inventory not statable in nonrelational terms. Take the rule of Passive, for example, as linear-order-based transformational grammar would handle it from language to language. In some languages (eg., English) this rule (more or less) interchanges the object and the subject. In others (eg., Chinese) it moves the object to the left of the verb. In others (eg., Japanese) it moves the object to the left of the subject. And in others (eg., Cebuano) it moves nothing at all. Clearly, stated in terms of linear order changes, Passive admits no universal statement. But Perlmutter and Postal (1977) argue that if grammatical relations are basic, Passive can be stated UNIVERSALLY as (8.40), all language-independent surface orderings following from principles needed independently for the language in question:

(8.40)   Direct Object → Subject

In addition, Postal and Perlmutter were able to formulate a significant number of universal laws in relational terms governing grammatical operations which also appeared inexpressible in linear terms. The following three (from around 1974) were among the most important, though well over a dozen others were proposed:[7]

A. **The Relational Succession Law.** *When a rule turns an NP bearing a particular grammatical relation in a lower clause into a relation-bearer in a higher clause, that NP assumes the grammatical relation of the NP which originally dominated it. (For example, the rule of Raising-to-Subject in English moves an NP out of a clause which is in subject position; the rule of Raising-to-Object moves an NP out of a clause which is in object posi-*

---

[6] John Kimball in the late 1960s had pointed out that the class of cyclic rules and the class of rules affecting grammatical relations is roughly coextensive (see Kimball 1972b). The first proposal known to me for stating these rules IN TERMS OF grammatical relations was put forward in class lectures at the University of Illinois by Jerry Morgan in the fall of 1971. While Morgan did not follow up this idea immediately, his lectures inspired David Johnson's 1974 Illinois dissertation *Toward a Theory of Relationally-Based Grammar* (Johnson 1976). Johnson later joined Postal at IBM. The first actually published hint of the developing theory is in Postal (1974), in which in various footnotes and sections of the text relational solutions are briefly sketched.

[7] At the expense of slight misrepresentaion, I have simplified the statement of these laws, and recast them in more familiar terminology.

tion. This law PREDICTS *that derived higher subjects cannot be raised from object clauses, nor higher objects from subject clauses.)*

B. **The Relational Annihilation Law.** *When a NP, NP$_i$, assumes the grammatical relation borne by another NP, NP$_j$, then NP$_j$ ceases to bear any grammatical relation whatever. (Hence the displaced subjects from Passive,* **There-Insertion,** *etc. cannot partake in any rules sensitive to grammatical relations.)*

C. **The Reranking Law.** *A rule that alters an NP with respect to its grammatical relation status can only increase its rank on hierarchy (8.39). (Hence there are rules which turn direct objects into subjects, but none which turn subjects into direct objects.)*

Another reason for the immediate popularity of relational grammar was its ability to capture directly the descriptions of the great traditional grammarians in a way that standard transformational grammar could not. By and large, such linguists as Jespersen, Poutsma, Curme, *et al.* talked about syntactic rules as changes of grammatical relations, not linear order—hence relational grammarians felt that they had more right to claim such persons as their direct predecessors than did the mainstream transformational grammarians.[8]

Finally, relational grammar has appealed to the many who have been attracted by the easily tested universal claims that it makes. This model, by virtue of its numerous "laws" that make fairly direct claims about linguistic structure, has encouraged an intensive empirical investigation of grammatical structure in numerous languages.

The crowning moment of relational grammar was the 1974 LSA Summer Institute in Amherst. There Postal and Perlmutter jointly taught the fundamentals of relational grammar to hundreds—the best attended Institute class since Chomsky's at UCLA in 1966.

The Postal–Perlmutter lecture series was complemented by the publication of Sandra Chung's paper "An Object-Creating Rule in Bahasa Indonesia" (1976), widely agreed to be the most compelling defense of relational grammar in print. Chung argues that if rules are sensitive to linear order, then there is no non-ad hoc way to block NP's in Indonesian which underlyingly (prior to Dative Movement) were direct objects from undergoing a number of transformations. However, the Relational Annihilation Law PREDICTS that these NP's will be immune to any subsequent relation-affecting transformations.

However, relational grammar has unquestionably been losing momen-

---

[8] Although Fiengo and Lasnik (1976) pointed out that Jespersen considered *John* in BOTH sentences (i) and (ii) to be the indirect object:

(i)   *Mary gave the book to John*
(ii)   *Mary gave John the book*

tum over the last few years. There seem to be several reasons for this. The first has to be Postal and Perlmutter's long delay in publishing a concise outline of the theory. Nothing couched in a relational framework appeared in a printed journal or book until Postal (1977), and even in the photo-litho format of the "parajournals" put out by the linguistic societies, nothing appeared until Aissen and Perlmutter (1976). Neither of these articles gives an account of the theory as a whole. While Johnson (1976) partially filled the gap, the transmission by word-of-mouth (and word-of-ditto machine) of relational principles in the mid 1970s seriously impeded the acceptance and general credibility of the theory.[9]

Second, many linguists, already exasperated with the style of the generative semanticists (see Section 5.7.3), groaned to see many of the same traits reappear in relational grammar. These traits, which manifested themselves in the bewilderingly opaque and ever-changing technical vocabulary of the theory, were another impediment to its widespread adoption by the linguistic public.

Third, relational grammar has run counter to the renewed interest in semantics in the late 1970s. While its partisans have claimed (see Perlmutter and Postal 1977; Perlmutter 1978) that initial grammatical relations are semantically determined, almost no work has been produced to demonstrated that this is in fact the case, nor have any intensive investigations of the relationship between semantic case and syntactic grammatical relation been undertaken. In fact, Newmeyer (1976b) has argued that only rather low-level syntactic processes give any real support to the model, suggesting an intimate connection between relational grammar and autonomous syntax. If this is correct, then the situation is not without irony, given the generative semantics-oriented background of many leading relational grammarians.

Finally and most importantly, relational grammar is on the retreat because a large percentage of the universal laws proposed within the framework have been falsified or weakened. Significantly, this has been accomplished by linguists highly sympathetic to—or even working within—the model. For example, the Accessibility Hierarchy has been attacked by Cole (1976a, 1976b); the Reranking Law by A. Harris (1976a, 1976b), "Stratal Uniqueness" and the Relational Annihilation Law by Dalgish and Sheintuch (1976) and Gary and Keenan (1977), and so on.

In the late 1970s, an important battle concerned the status of the "Motivated Chomage Law" (see Perlmutter and Postal 1977). This law states that the only way a noun phrase can become a chomeur (i.e., an "ex-

---

[9] The cause of this seems to be the favoring of a different research strategy by each of the two linguists. Perlmutter's priorities were to begin by carrying out intensive cross-language studies of relational phenomena; Postal's by developing and refining the formalism in which relational generalizations might be expressed, and proposing candidate laws on the basis of the known facts of English and the other well-known languages. These different priorities impeded collaboration at the level necessary to publish a synopsis of the theory.

grammatical relation") is for it to be displaced from its original grammatical relation status by another noun phrase. That is, rules like the following are excluded:

(8.41)   Subject → Chomeur

Comrie (1977) argued that such rules, "spontaneous demotions" as he calls them, do exist, and are involved in the derivation of impersonal passive constructions in many languages. Comrie's arguments have been rebutted in Perlmutter (1978), but the matter is far from settled.

For the last few years, some relational grammarians have put forward a "nonderivational" model, in which all grammatically relevant aspects of a sentence are depicted in one graph-theoretic object, a "relational network." It is not clear at this point to what extent this model (now formalized in an elaborated and modified version as "arc pair grammar"), older relational models, and standard transformational grammar are descriptively equivalent. The future of relational grammar will perhaps be clearer after the publication of Johnson and Postal's mammoth *Arc-Pair Grammar* (1979), in which the theory is minutely outlined and formalized, and the two volumes edited by Perlmutter under the title *Studies in Relational Grammar*.

8.5. MONTAGUE GRAMMAR

Logicians for many years scoffed at the treatment of semantics within transformational generative grammar. In their view, the abstract semantic "representations" of both the generativists and the interpretivists were not interpretations at all. Rather, they simply belonged to the syntax of another metalanguage into which the syntactic constructs of the theory are translated. David Lewis (1972) scornfully called this metalanguage "Markerese", and commented:

> But we can know the Markerese translation of an English sentence without knowing the first thing about the meaning of the English sentence: namely, the conditions under which it would be true. Semantics with no treatment of truth conditions is no semantics [p. 169].

Logicians were also appalled at the lack of rigor in transformationalist descriptions. Richard Montague's (1970a) view was probably typical:

> One could also object to existing syntactical efforts by Chomsky and his associates on grounds of adequacy, mathematical precision, and elegance; but such criticism should perhaps await more definitive and intelligible expositions than are yet available [p. 373].

But the barriers between logicians and linguists began to break down in the late 1960s as a number of theoretical linguists also began to seek an adequate model theoretic semantics for natural language. By the early 1970s, most agreed that the general approach of Montague seemed the most promising. Montague's work, as reinterpreted and redirected by his UCLA colleague Barbara Partee after his senseless murder in 1971, has attracted a small but growing number of linguists, and has become one of the principal alternative models of syntactic–semantic description.

Montague broke with the two leading Anglo-American philosophical schools—the logical positivists and the ordinary language philosophers. The former, dismayed at the apparent chaotic nature of natural language, sought to "do it one better" by constructing artificial logical languages. The latter, believing artificial languages shed no light on real problems of linguistic philosophy, did study natural language, but highly informally. Montague (1970b), on the other hand, believed that natural languages THEMSELVES can be constructed as formal languages: "I reject the contention that an important theoretical difference exists between formal and natural languages [p. 189]." In this view, the same formal devices suffice to describe the properties of both types of languages.

Now it needs to be stressed that Montague was no empirical scientist. That is, he was not constructing a competence model with empirical constraints on its formulation. In fact, he had no real interest in syntax at all: "I fail to see any great interest in syntax except as a preliminary to semantics [Montague 1970a: 373]." Nevertheless, his model, in the hands of Partee and others, lent itself easily to a REINTERPRETATION as a competence model, and this is its significance for linguistics.

It may prove useful to outline briefly the basics of the theory. A Montague grammar consists of three components:

A. **The Lexicon.** This consists of a list of the lexical items in the language, each provided with a syntactic category and a translation into intensional logic.

B. **A Set of Syntactic Rules.** These build a sentence from the "bottom up," in the manner of categorial grammar (see Ajdukiewicz 1935 and Bar-Hillel 1953). Each has the form given in (8.42), where α, β, γ are strings of terminal symbols and A, B, and C are syntactic categories:

(8.42)   If $\alpha \in A$ and $\beta \in B$, then $\gamma \in C$, where $\gamma = F_i(\alpha, \beta)$

For Montague, F_i was NORMALLY simple concatenation. However, he also proposed some transformation-like rules to handle quantification. All rules can apply in mixed and variable orders. That is, there is no level resembling "deep structure."

C. **A Set of Semantic Rules.** For each syntactic rule, there is precisely one translation rule, giving the translation of the resulting phrase into intensional logic as a specified function of the translations of its parts. The second stage of interpretation is the model-theoretic semantics for the intensional logic.

What linguists have found most interesting about Montague grammar is its claim that for each syntactic rule there exists a semantic rule. Note that this idea is not novel—each of the generalized transformations of the 1963–1965 theory had an accompanying "P2" projection rule (see Section 3.3.2). In fact, under one interpretation of the Katz–Fodor (1963) "P1" projection rules, each phrase-structure rule corresponds to a different P1 rule, resulting in a model even more strikingly like Montague Grammar.[10]

Partee (1973) maintains that the hypothesis of syntactic rule–semantic rule association is very strong, allowing for the principled selection of only one out of a number of competing analyses of the same phenomenon. For example, (8.43a) and (8.43b) have long been put forward as alternative analyses for relative clauses (using *the boy who lives in the park* as an illustration):

(8.43)   a.

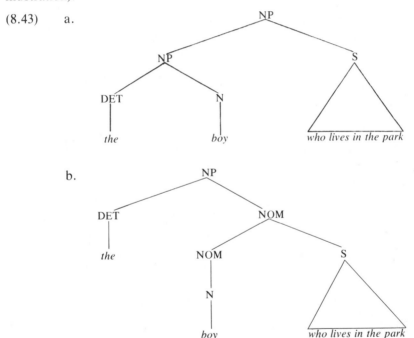

     b.

She argues that if each syntactic rule must have semantic consequences, then (8.43b), not (8.43a), must be the structure. Only in (8.43b) are

> the two class-denoting phrases [*boy* and *who lives in the park*] . . . first combined to form a complex class-denoting phrase, which can be interpreted as denoting the intersection of the two classes, namely the class of entities which both live in the park and are boys; combining *the* with the results leads to the correct assertion that it is that class that has one and only one member [Partee 1973:512].

[10] Bach (1976) discusses certain formal similarities between Montague grammar and pre-*Aspects* transformational grammar.

Others have felt, however, that the claim of semantic rule–syntactic rule pairing might not be so strong after all, since in principle there is nothing to prevent a "stubborn" (i.e., semantically nonunified) syntactic rule from being split into two or more parts, each part being assigned its own corresponding semantic rule. And in the very case of relative clauses, Bach and Cooper (1978) have shown how a Montague semantics for the NP-S structure COULD be provided.

There are many ways in which Partee and others have brought Montague grammar closer to mainstream transformational grammar.[11] Most importantly, Partee (1975:258) has proposed that rules be stated in terms of labeled bracketed structures, rather than simply in terms of strings as in Montague's original conception. Furthermore, she has added operations virtually identical to transformations to the stock of syntactic rules. While they are interspersed with the concatenatory rules, their formal properties are nevertheless much like the standard transformations familiar to linguists.

There is no question that interest in Montague grammar is continuing to grow. Besides Partee, many linguists with a history of research in transformational grammar are now publishing Montague analyses; Dowty (1976, 1978), Karttunen (1977), Karttunen and Peters (1975), and Schmerling (1978) is a small sample of papers in the Montague framework which illustrates this point.

So far, there has been no knock-down debate between proponents of Montague grammar and those of transformational grammar. Aside from a few negative comments (made, essentially, in passing) in Chomsky (1975c) and (1976), few transformationalists have even mentioned Montague grammar. This seems odd, given the potential of this theory to grow still further and the (apparently?) incompatible assumptions of the two approaches. No doubt this stems at least partially from the extreme DIFFICULTY of Montague grammar—linguists with little or no training in formal logic find its semantic descriptions impossible to comprehend. And many have taken Cooper and Parsons's (1976) proof that for one fragment of English, Montague grammar and transformational grammar (of both the generative and interpretive semantic types) are equivalent as a proof that there are NO empirical differences between the two theories, so there is no need to master the difficult formalism of Montague grammar.

But whatever the ultimate fate of Partee-modified Montague grammar as a model of linguistic competence, it seems clear that model theoretic semantics is here to stay. As Janet Fodor (1977) has put it, "The indications are that we are drawing to the end of the period in which semantic representations form an abstract uninterpreted system which can be connected with reality only by identifying its primitive terms with some universal innate mental entities [p. 61]."

---

[11] There is an interesting discussion in McCawley (1977b) of the evolutionary parallels between Montague grammar and transformational grammar.

8.6. SOME CONCLUDING REMARKS

At the time of this writing, a rather perplexing situation exists within the universe of linguistic theory. On the one hand, the FUNDAMENTAL goals and assumptions of the theory of transformational generative grammar—those which were first articulated by Chomsky in the 1950s—have more adherents (who represent a greater percentage of the linguistic community) than ever before. The internal challenge from generative semantics has been repelled, while the true rival theories with distinct assumptions and methodologies like tagmemics, stratificational grammar, and form–content grammar, have attracted little general interest. There are still, of course, a huge number of linguists who would describe themselves as "atheoretical."[12] But the vast majority who take theory seriously acknowledge (explicitly or implicitly) their adoption of Chomsky's view of language.

On the other hand, the fragmentation WITHIN the Chomskyan paradigm is more severe than at any time in the past, and this shows signs of worsening.[13] That is, there continues to be less and less agreement on the concrete realization of a model within the general framework. Confounding the entire problem is the fact that few, if any, of these models have been formalized with sufficient care to allow the ascertaining of their empirical differences. Many harbor the suspicion that even two such superficially different models as relational grammar and Montague grammar (for example) might upon close examination turn out to be descriptively equivalent. But nobody is really sure.

The most "visible" model—the one most worked in, discussed, and attacked—is Chomsky's. But even so, a rather small percentage of practicing transformationalists claim allegiance to it. Interestingly, the majority of Chomsky's closest adherents these days are Europeans. Even the bulk of analyses published IN ENGLISH supporting Chomsky's current views are by Europeans: Koster (1978a,b,c), Pollock (1978), Rizzi (1978), van Riemsdijk (1978a,b), Taraldsen (1978), and den Besten (1978) are a few examples. Chomsky's European supporters have organized a society called 'Generative Linguists of the Old World' (GLOW). The 'GLOW Manifesto' does not merely endorse generative grammar IN GENERAL, but specifically points to

---

[12] An essentially atheoretical approach to syntax has emerged at several linguistics departments in California, where the sentiment that "we must be prepared to devote much more time to empirical investigation" (Li 1977:xix) is regarded as COUNTERPOSED to theory construction, rather than COMPLEMENTARY to it. Many of the papers in the three volumes of conference proceedings edited by Charles Li (Li 1975, 1976, 1977) illustrate this regression to descriptivism. For an extremely persuasive critique of the papers in Li (1977), see Lightfoot (1979).

[13] Symptomatic of this fact is the "Conference on Current Approaches to Syntax," held in Milwaukee in April 1979. At this conference, which has been jokingly referred to as the "Syntax Sweepstakes," no fewer than 14 different syntactic models were presented and defended.

'Conditions on Transformations' as "epoch-making" and states that "a significant number of members of GLOW have found their common ground in the research program that grew out of Conditions." (Koster, van Riemsdijk, and Vergnaud 1978:5) In recent years, the GLOW conferences, held annually at a different European university, have taken on the atmosphere of the Chicago Linguistic Society meetings of the early 1970's, boosting trace theory and the enthusiasm of its supporters in the way that the CLS meetings advanced generative semantics.

The opposition to Chomsky has been too divided internally to benefit from its superior numbers. Many of their critiques have been so defensive in approach (eg. Postal's *On Raising*) that, whatever the strength of their argumentation, they have left the reader with the feeling that, flawed though it may be, no viable alternative exists to Chomsky's approach. Bresnan may be right that the problem represented by the proliferation of models will be solvable only by evaluating now how each model might be realized in a performance theory. But she will have a difficult time convincing theoretical linguists of this, most of whom have been extremely skeptical about the applicability of the results in artificial intelligence and other computation-oriented fields to linguistic theory. For as Dresher and Hornstein (1976) have argued at great length, they have had every reason to be skeptical.

It is difficult to predict which of the competing models discussed in Chapters 6 and 8 will ultimately win out, or whether the victor will represent a synthesis of more than one of them. But in an important sense, it hardly matters. For the differences among them are almost trivial compared to the foundation which they hold in common—the recognition that a linguistic theory is a formal model of a speaker's abstract linguistic competence. It is this scientific idealization more than any specific proposal about transformational rules, deep structures, or semantic representations that has enabled linguistics to break from the grip of taxonomy and anecdotality. On the basis of this idealization, more has been learned about the nature of language in the last 25 years than in the previous 2500.

References

Abercrombie, David. 1965 (1956). "Pseudo-Procedures in Linguistics. *"Studies in Phonetics and Linguistics,* edited by David Abercrombie, pp. 114–119. London: Oxford University Press.

Aissen, Judith. 1973. "Shifty Objects in Spanish." *Papers from the Ninth Regional Meeting of the Chicago Linguistic Society,* pp. 11–22.

Aissen, Judith. 1974. "Verb Raising." *Linguistic Inquiry* 5: 325–366.

Aissen, Judith, and Hankamer, Jorge. 1972. "Shifty Subjects: A Conspiracy in Syntax?" *Linguistic Inquiry* 3: 501–504.

Aissen, Judith, and Perlmutter, David. 1976. "Clause Reduction in Spanish." *Papers from the Second Annual Meeting of the Berkeley Linguistics Society,* pp. 1–30.

Ajdukiewicz, Kasimierz. 1935. "Die Syntaktische Konnexitat." *Studia Philosophica* 1: 1–27.

Akmajian, Adrian. 1975. "More Evidence for an NP Cycle." *Linguistic Inquiry* 6: 115–129.

———. 1977. "The Complement Structure of Perception Verbs in an Autonomous Syntax Framework." In *Formal Syntax,* edited by Peter Culicover *et al.* (1977), pp. 427–460. New York: Academic Press.

Akmajian, Adrian, and Heny, Frank. 1975. *An Introduction to the Principles of Transformational Syntax.* Cambridge, Massachusetts: MIT Press.

Allen, Harold B., ed. 1958. *Readings in Applied English Linguistics.* New York: Appleton-Century-Crofts.

Anderson, John. 1971. *The Grammar of Case: Towards a Localist Theory.* London: Cambridge University Press.

———. 1977. *On Case Grammar.* London: Croom Helm.

Anderson, Stephen. 1971a. "On the Role of Deep Structure in Semantic Interpretation." *Foundations of Language* 7: 387-396.

———. 1971b. "On the Linguistic Status of the Performative/Constative Distinction." Indiana University Linguistics Club Publication.

———. 1976 (1967). "Concerning the Notion 'Base Component of a Transformational Grammar.'" In *Syntax and Seminars,* vol. 7, edited by James McCawley (1976a), pp. 113-128. New York: Academic Press.

251

Anderson, Stephen, and Chung, Sandra. 1977. "On Grammatical Relations and Clause Structure in Verb-Initial Languages." In *Syntax and Semantics,* vol. 8, edited by Peter Cole and Jerrold Sadock pp. 1-26. New York: Academic Press.

Anderson, Stephen, and Kiparsky, Paul, eds. 1973. *A Festschrift for Morris Halle.* New York: Holt, Rinehart and Winston.

Andersson, Anders-Börje, and Dahl, Östen. 1974. "Against the Penthouse Principle." *Linguistic Inquiry* 5: 451-453.

Andrews, Avery. 1971. "Case Agreement of Predicate Modifiers in Ancient Greek." *Linguistic Inquiry* 2: 127-152.

Aronoff, Marc. 1976. *Word Formation in Generative Grammar.* Cambridge, Massachusetts: MIT Press.

Austin, J. L. 1962. *How to Do Things with Words.* Oxford: Oxford University Press.

Bach, Emmon. 1962. "The Order of Elements in a Transformational Grammar of German." *Language* 38: 263-269.

———. 1964a. *An Introduction to Transformational Grammars.* New York: Holt, Rinehart and Winston.

———. 1964b. "Subcategories in Transformational Grammars." In *Proceedings of the Ninth International Congress of Linguists,* edited by H. Lunt, pp. 672-677. The Hague: Mouton.

———. 1968. "Nouns and Noun Phrases." In *Universals in Linguistic Theory,* edited by Emmon Bach and Robert Harms (1968), pp. 91-124. New York: Holt, Rinehart and Winston.

———. 1970. "Problominalization." *Linguistic Inquiry* 1: 121-122.

———. 1974. *Syntactic Theory.* New York: Holt, Rinehart and Winston.

———. 1976. "An Extension of Classical Transformational Grammar." In *Problems in Linguistic Metatheory.* East Lansing, Michigan: Michigan State University.

———. 1977a (1974). "'The Position of Embedding Transformations in a Grammar' Revisited." In *Linguistic Structures Processing,* edited by A. Zampolli. New York: North-Holland.

———. 1977b. "Comments on the Paper by Chomsky." In *Formal Syntax,* edited by Peter Culicover, *et al.* (1977), pp. 133-156. New York: Academic Press.

Bach, Emmon, and Cooper, Robin. 1978. "The NP-S Analysis of Relative Clauses and Compositional Semantics." *Linguistics and Philosophy* 2: 145-150.

Bach, Emmon, and Harms, Robert, eds. 1968. *Universals in Linguistic Theory.* New York: Holt, Rinehart and Winston.

Bach, Emmon, and Horn, George. 1976. "Remarks on 'Conditions on Transformations'." *Linguistic Inquiry* 7: 265-279.

Bailey, Charles-James, and Shuy, Roger, eds. 1973. *New Ways of Analyzing Variation in English.* Washington: Georgetown University Press.

Baker, C. L. 1973 (1966). "Definiteness and Indefiniteness in English." Indiana University Linguistics Club Publication.

———. 1970a. "Double Negatives." *Linguistic Inquiry* 1: 169-186.

———. 1970b. "Notes on the Descriptions of English Questions: The Role of an Abstract Question Morpheme." *Foundations of Language* 6: 179-219.

———. 1975. "The Role of Part of Speech Distinctions in Generative Grammar." *Theoretical Linguistics* 2: 113-131.

———. 1977. "Comments on the Paper by Culicover and Wexler." In *Formal Syntax,* edited by Culicover, *et al.* (1977), pp. 61-70. New York: Academic Press.

———. 1978. *Introduction to Generative-Transformational Syntax.* Englewood Cliffs: Prentice-Hall.

Baker, C. L., and Brame, Michael. 1972. "Global Rules: A Rejoinder." *Language* 48: 51-77.

Banfield, Ann. 1973a. *Stylistic Transformations in "Paradise Lost."* Ph.D. dissertation, University of Wisconsin.

———. 1973b. "Narrative Style and the Grammar of Direct and Indirect Speech." *Foundations of Language* 10: 1-40.

Bar-Hillel, Yehoshua. 1953. "A Quasi-Arithmetical Notation for Syntactic Description." *Language* 29: 47-58.

Bar-Hillel, Yehoshua, Gaifman, C., and Shamir, E. 1960. "On Categorial and Phrase Structure Grammars." *Bulletin of the Research Council of Israel* 9F: 1-16.

Becker, A. L., and Arms, D. G. 1969. "Prepositions as Predicates." *Papers from the Fifth Regional Meeting of the Chicago Linguistic Society,* pp. 1-11.

Bedell, George. 1974. "The Arguments about Deep Structure." *Language* 50: 423-445.

Berman, Arlene. 1974. "On the *VSO* Hypothesis." *Linguistic Inquiry* 5: 1-37.

Berman, Arlene, and Szamosi, Michael. 1972. "Observations on Sentential Stress." *Language* 48: 304-325.

Bever, Thomas. 1970. "The Cognitive Basis for Linguistic Structures." In *Cognition and the Development of Language,* edited by R. Hayes, pp. 277-360. New York: Wiley.

———. 1975. "Functional Explanations Require Independently Motivated Functional Theories." In *Papers from the Parasession on Functionalism,* edited by R. Grossman, *et al.* (1975), pp. 580-609.

Bever, Thomas, Katz, Jerrold, and Langendoen, D. Terence, eds. 1976. *An Integrated Theory of Linguistic Ability.* New York: Crowell.

Bever, Thomas, and Langendoen, D. Terence. 1971. "A Dynamic Model of the Evolution of Language." *Linguistic Inquiry* 2: 433-463. Reprinted in *An Integrated Theory of Linguistic Ability,* edited by Thomas Bever, *et al.* (1976), pp. 115-148. New York: Crowell.

Bierwisch, Manfred, and Heidolph, Karl, eds. 1970. *Progress in Linguistics.* The Hague: Mouton.

Binnick, Robert. 1971. "'Bring' and 'Come.'" *Linguistic Inquiry* 2: 260-265.

Bloch, Bernard. 1941. "Phonemic Overlapping." *American Speech* 16: 278-284. Reprinted in *Readings in Linguistics,* edited by Martin Joos (1958), pp. 93-96. Washington: American Council of Learned Societies.

———. 1946. "Studies in Colloquial Japanese II: Syntax." *Language* 22: 200-248. Reprinted in *Readings in Linguistics,* edited by Martin Joos (1958), pp. 154-185. Washington: American Council of Learned Societies.

———. 1947. "English Verb Inflection." *Language* 23: 399-418. Reprinted in *Readings in Linguistics,* edited by Martin Joos (1958), pp. 243-254. Washington: American Council of Learned Societies.

———. 1948. "A Set of Postulates for Phonemic Analysis." *Language* 24: 3-46.

———. 1950. "Studies in Colloquial Japanese IV: Phonemics." *Language* 26: 86-125.

Bloomfield, Leonard. 1933. *Language.* New York: Holt, Rinehart and Winston.

———. 1939a. *Linguistic Aspects of Science. International Encyclopedia of Unified Science,* vol. 1, no. 4. Chicago: University of Chicago Press.

———. 1939b. "Menomini Morphophonemics." *Travaux du Cercle Linguistique de Prague* 8: 105-115.

Boër, Steven, and Lycan, William. 1976. *The Myth of Semantic Presupposition.* Indiana University Linguistics Club Publication.

Bolinger, Dwight. 1965. "The Atomization of Meaning." *Language* 41: 555-573.

Borkin, Ann, *et al.* 1972. "Where the Rules Fail: A Student's Guide. An Unauthorized Appendix to M. K. Burt's *From Deep to Surface Structure.*" Indiana University Linguistics Club Publication.

Botha, Rudolph. 1976. "'The Theory Comparison Method' vs. 'The Theory Exposition Method.'" Indiana University Linguistics Club Publication.

Bowers, John. 1970. "A Note on 'Remind.'" *Linguistic Inquiry* 1: 559-560.

Brame, Michael. 1976. *Conjectures and Refutations in Syntax and Semantics.* New York: North-Holland.

———. 1977. "Alternatives to the Tensed S and Specified Subject Conditions." *Linguistics and Philosophy* 1: 381-411.

———. 1978a. *Base Generated Syntax.* Seattle: Noit Amrofer Press.

————. 1978b. "Binding and Discourse without Transformations." *Linguistic Analysis* 4: 321–360.

Brame, Michael. 1979. "Realistic Grammar." Paper presented at the Conference on Current Approaches to Syntax, Milwaukee, Wisconsin.

Brekle, H. E. 1969. Review of N. Chomsky, *Cartesian Linguistics*. *Linguistics* 49: 74–91.

Bresnan, Joan. 1970a. "An Argument against Pronominalization." *Linguistic Inquiry* 1: 122–123.

————. 1970b. "On Complementizers: Towards a Syntactic Theory of Complement Types." *Foundations of Language* 6: 297–321.

————. 1971a. "Sentence Stress and Syntactic Transformations." *Language* 47: 257–281.

————. 1971b. "Contraction and the Transformational Cycle in English." Unpublished manuscript.

————. 1972a. *Theory of Complementation in English Syntax*. Ph.D. dissertation, MIT.

————. 1972b. "Stress and Syntax: A Reply." *Language* 48: 326–342.

————. 1975. "Comparative Deletion and Constraints on Transformations." *Linguistic Analysis* 1: 25–74.

————. 1976a. "On the Form and Functioning of Transformations." *Linguistic Inquiry* 7: 3–40.

————. 1976b. "Evidence for a Theory of Unbounded Transformations." *Linguistic Analysis* 2: 353–394.

————. 1977. "Variables in the Theory of Transformations." In *Formal Syntax*, edited by Peter Culicover, *et al.* (1977), pp. 157–196. New York: Academic Press.

————. 1978. "A Realistic Transformational Grammar." In *Linguistic Theory and Psychological Reality*, edited by Morris Halle, *et al.* (1978), pp. 1–59. Cambridge, Massachusetts: MIT Press.

Brown, Roger. 1973. *A First Language: The Early Stages*. Cambridge, Massachusetts: Harvard University Press.

Burt, Marina. 1971. *From Deep to Surface Structure*. New York: Harper and Row.

Cantrall, William. 1970. "If You Hiss or Anything, I'll Do It Back." *Papers from the Sixth Regional Meeting of the Chicago Linguistic Society*, pp. 168–177.

————. 1974 (1969). *Viewpoint, Reflexives, and the Nature of Noun Phrases*. The Hague: Mouton.

Carden, Guy. 1968. "English Quantifiers." In *The Computation Laboratory of Harvard University, Mathematical Linguistics and Automatic Translation, Report No. NSF-20 to the National Science Foundation*, pp. IX-1–IX-45.

————. 1976. "Syntactic and Semantic Data: Replication Results." *Language in Society* 5: 99–104.

Cardona, George. 1976. *Pāṇini: A Survey of Research*. The Hague: Mouton.

Carnap, Rudolf. 1937 (1934). *The Logical Syntax of Language*. London: Routledge and Kegan Paul.

Carroll, John B. 1953. *The Study of Language*. Cambridge, Massachusetts: Harvard University Press.

Cattell, Ray. 1976. "Constraints on Movement Rules." *Language* 52: 18–50.

Chafe, Wallace. 1970. *Meaning and the Structure of Language*. Chicago: University of Chicago Press.

Chao, Yuen-Ren. 1934. "The Non-Uniqueness of Phonemic Solutions of Phonetic Systems." *Bulletin of the Institute of History and Philology, Academia Sinica*, vol. IV, part 4, pp. 363–397. Reprinted in *Readings in Linguistics*, edited by Martin Joos (1958), pp. 38–54. Washington: American Council of Learned Societies.

Chapin, Paul. 1967. *The Syntax of Word-Derivation in English*. Bedford, Massachusetts: MITRE Corporation Information System Language Studies No. 16.

Chomsky, Noam. 1951. *Morphophonemics of Modern Hebrew*. M.A. thesis, University of Pennsylvania.

————. 1953. "Systems of Syntactic Analysis." *Journal of Symbolic Logic* 18: 242–256.

————. 1955. *The Logical Structure of Linguistic Theory.* Mimeographed. Cambridge, Massachusetts: MIT.

————. 1956. "Three Models for the Description of Language." *IRE Transactions on Information Theory,* pp. II–2, 113–124.

————. 1957. *Syntactic Structures.* The Hague: Mouton.

————. 1959a. "On Certain Formal Properties of Grammars." *Information and Control* 2: 2.

————. 1959b. Review of B. F. Skinner, *Verbal Behavior. Language* 35: 26–57. Reprinted in *The Structure of Language: Readings in the Philosophy of Language,* edited by Jerry A. Fodor and Jerrold Katz (1964). pp. 547–578. Englewood Cliffs, New Jersey: Prentice-Hall; and in *Readings in the Psychology of Language,* edited by Leon Jakobovits and Murray Miron (1967), pp. 142–171. Englewood Cliffs, New Jersey: Prentice-Hall.

————. 1961a. "Some Methodological Remarks on Generative Grammar." *Word* 17: 219–239.

————. 1961b. "On the Notion 'Rule of Grammar.'" In *Structure of Language and Its Mathematical Aspects.* Proceedings of Symposia in Applied Mathematics, vol. XII, edited by Roman Jackobson (1961), pp. 6–24. Providence, Rhode Island: American Mathematical Society. Reprinted in *The Structure of Language: Readings in the Philosophy of Language,* edited by Jerry A. Fodor and Jerrold Katz (1964), pp. 119–136. Englewood Cliffs, New Jersey, Prentice-Hall.

————. 1962 (1958). "A Transformational Approach to Syntax." In *Proceedings of the Third Texas Conference on Problems of Linguistic Analysis in English,* edited by Archibald Hill (1962), pp. 124–158. Austin, Texas: University of Texas Press. Reprinted in *The Structure of Language: Readings in the Philosophy of Language,* edited by Jerry A. Fodor and Jerrold Katz (1964), pp. 211–245. Englewood Cliffs, New Jersey: Prentice -Hall.

————. 1964a. "The Logical Basis of Linguistic Theory." In *Proceedings of the Ninth International Congress of Linguists,* edited by H. Lunt, pp. 914–978. The Hague: Mouton. (A revised version was published as Chomsky 1964b.)

————. 1964b. *Current Issues in Linguistic Theory.* The Hague: Mouton. (A slightly different version appears in *The Structure of Language: Readings in the Philosophy of Language,* edited by Jerry A. Fodor and Jerrold Katz (1964), pp. 50–118. Englewood Cliffs, New Jersey: Prentice-Hall.)

————. 1965. *Aspects of the Theory of Syntax.* Cambridge, Massachusetts: MIT Press.

————. 1966a. *Topics in the Theory of Generative Grammar.* The Hague: Mouton.

————. 1966b. *Cartesian Linguistics.* New York: Harper and Row.

————. 1967. "The Formal Nature of Language." In *Biological Foundations of Language,* edited by Eric Lenneberg, pp. 397–442. New York: Wiley.

————. 1968. *Language and Mind.* (First ed..) New York: Harcourt.

————. 1970 (1967). "Remarks on Nominalization." In *Readings in English Transformational Grammar,* edited by Roderick Jacobs and Peter Rosenbaum (1970), pp. 184–221. Waltham, Massachusetts: Ginn and Co. Reprinted in *Studies on Semantics in Generative Grammar,* by Noam Chomsky (1972b), pp. 11–61. The Hague: Mouton.

————. 1971 (1969). "Deep Structure, Surface Structure, and Semantic Interpretation." In *Semantics: An Interdisciplinary Reader,* edited by Danny Steinberg and Leon Jakobovits (1971), pp. 183–216. Cambridge, England: Cambridge University Press. Reprinted in *Studies on Semantics in Generative Grammar,* by Noam Chomsky (1972b), pp. 62–119. The Hague: Mouton.

————. 1972a (1969). "Some Empirical Issues in the Theory of Transformational Grammar." In S. Peters (1972), pp. 63–130. Reprinted in *Studies on Semantics in Generative Grammar,* by Noam Chomsky (1972b), pp. 120–202. The Hague: Mouton.

————. 1972b. *Studies on Semantics in Generative Grammar.* The Hague: Mouton.

————. 1973. "Conditions on Transformations." In S. Anderson and P. Kiparsky (1973), pp. 232–286. Reprinted in *Essays on Form and Interpretation,* by Noam Chomsky (1977a), pp. 81–162. Amsterdam: North-Holland.

————. 1975a (1955). *The Logical Structure of Linguistic Theory* (with a new Introduction). New York: Plenum.

————. 1975b. *Reflections on Language.* New York: Pantheon.

————. 1975c. "Questions of Form and Interpretation." *Linguistic Analysis* 1: 75–109. Reprinted in *Essays on Form and Interpretation,* by Noam Chomsky (1977a), pp. 25–62. New York: North-Holland.

————. 1976. "Conditions on Rules of Grammar." *Linguistic Analysis* 2: 303–351. Reprinted in *Essays on Form and Interpretation,* by Noam Chomsky (1977a), pp. 163–210. New York: North-Holland.

————. 1977a. *Essays on Form and Interpretation.* New York: North-Holland.

————. 1977b. "On *Wh*-Movement." In *Formal Syntax,* edited by Peter Culicover, *et al.* (1977), pp. 71–132. New York: Academic Press.

————. 1978. "On Binding." Unpublished manuscript.

————. 1979. *Language and Responsibility.* New York: Pantheon.

Chomsky, Noam, and Halle, Morris. 1960. "The Morphophonemics of English." *MIT Research Laboratory of Electronics Quarterly Progress Report,* p. 58.

————. 1965. "Some Controversial Questions in Phonological Theory." *Journal of Linguistics* 1: 97–138.

————. 1968. *The Sound Pattern of English.* New York: Harper and Row.

Chomsky, Noam, Halle, Morris, and Lukoff, Fred. 1966. "On Accent and Juncture in English." In Morris Halle *et al.* (compilers), *For Roman Jakobson,* pp. 65–80. The Hague: Mouton.

Chomsky, Noam, and Lasnik, Howard. 1977. "Filters and Control." *Linguistic Inquiry* 8: 425–504.

Chomsky, Noam, and Miller, George. 1963. "Introduction to the Formal Analysis of Natural Languages." In *Handbook of Mathematical Psychology,* edited by P. Luce, R. Bush, and E. Galanter, vol. II, pp. 269–322. New York: Wiley.

Chung, Sandra. 1976. "An Object-Creating Rule in Bahasa Indonesia." *Linguistic Inquiry* 7: 41–88.

Cohen, David, ed. 1972. *Limiting the Domain of Linguistics.* Milwaukee: University of Wisconsin at Milwaukee Linguistics Group.

Cole, Peter. 1976a. "An Apparent Asymmetry in the Formation of Relative Clauses in Modern Hebrew." In *Studies in Modern Hebrew-Syntax and Semantics,* edited by P. Cole, pp. 231–247. Amsterdam: North-Holland.

————. 1976b. "The Interface of Theory and Description." *Language* 53: 563–583.

————., ed. 1978. *Syntax and Semantics,* vol. 9. New York: Academic Press.

Cole, Peter, and Morgan, Jerry, eds. 1975. *Syntax and Semantics,* vol. 3. New York: Academic Press.

Cole, Peter, and Sadock, Jerrold, eds. 1977. *Syntax and Semantics,* vol. 8. New York: Academic Press.

Comrie, Bernard. 1976. "The Syntax of Causative Constructions: Cross-Language Similarities and Divergences." In *Syntax and Semantics,* vol. 6, edited by Masayoshi Shibatani (1976), pp. 261–312. New York: Academic Press.

————. 1977. "In Defense of Spontaneous Demotion: The Impersonal Passive." In *Syntax and Semantics,* vol. 8, edited by Peter Cole and Jerrold Sadock (1977), pp. 47–58. New York: Academic Press.

Contreras, Heles. 1973. "Grammaticality vs. Acceptability: The Spanish 'se' Case." *Linguistic Inquiry* 4: 83–88.

Cooper, Robin, and Parsons, Terence. 1976. "Montague Grammar, Generative Semantics, and Interpretive Semantics." In *Montague Grammar,* edited by Barbara Partee (1976), pp. 311–362. New York: Academic Press.

Corcoran, John. 1972. "Harris on the Structures of Language." In *Transformationelle Analyse,* edited by S. Plötz pp. 275–291. Frankfurt: Athenäum Verlag.

Corum, Claudia, Smith-Stark, T. Cedric, and Weiser, Ann, eds. 1973. *You Take the High Node and I'll Take the Low Node.* Chicago: Chicago Linguistic Society.

Culicover, Peter. 1976. *Syntax.* New York: Academic Press.

————. 1977. "An Invalid Evaluation Metric." *Linguistic Analysis* 3: 65-100.

Culicover, Peter, Wasow, Thomas, and Akamaijan, Adrian, eds. 1977. *Formal Syntax.* New York: Academic Press.

Culicover, Peter, and Wexler, Kenneth. 1977. *"Some Syntactic Implications of a Theory of Language Learnability."* In *Formal Syntax,* edited by Peter Culicover, *et al.* (1977), pp. 7-60. New York: Academic Press.

Dalgish, Gerard, and Sheintuch, Gloria. 1976. "On the Justification for Language-Specific Sub-Grammatical Relations." *Studies in the Linguistic Sciences* 6: 2.

Darden, Bill. 1974. "Introduction." In *Papers from the Parasession on Natural Phonology,* edited by A. Bruck, R. Fox, and M. LeGaly. Chicago: Chicago Linguistic Society.

Davidson, Donald, and Harmon, Gilbert, eds. 1972. *Semantics of Natural Language.* Dordrecht: D. Reidel.

Davis, Philip W. 1973. *Modern Theories of Language.* Englewood Cliffs, New Jersey: Prentice-Hall.

Dean, Janet. See Fodor, Janet Dean.

Den Besten, Hans. 1978. "On the Presence and Absence of *Wh*-Elements in Dutch Comparatives." *Linguistic Inquiry* 9: 641-672.

De Rijk, Rudolf. 1972. *Studies in Basque Syntax: Relative Clauses.* Ph.D. dissertation, MIT.

Dixon, R. M. W. 1963a. *Linguistic Science and Logic.* The Hague: Mouton.

————. 1963b. "A Trend in Semantics." *Linguistics* 1: 30-57.

————. 1964. "A Trend in Semantics—A Rejoinder." *Linguistics* 3: 19-22.

————. 1970. "Olgolo Syllable Structure and What They Are Doing about It." *Linguistic Inquiry* 1: 273-276.

————. 1972. *The Dyirbal Language of North Queensland.* Cambridge: Cambridge University Press.

————. 1977. "Some Phonological Rules in Yidin." *Linguistic Inquiry* 8: 1-34.

Dougherty, Ray. 1968. *A Transformational Grammar of Conjoined Coordinate Structures.* Ph.D. dissertation, MIT.

————. 1969. "An Interpretive Theory of Pronominal Reference." *Foundations of Language* 5: 488-519.

————. 1970a. "Recent Studies on Language Universals." *Foundations of Language* 6: 505-561.

————. 1970b. "A Grammar of Conjoined Coordinate Structures." *Language* 46: 850-898; 47: 298-339.

————. 1974. "Generative Semantic Methods: A Bloomfieldian Counterrevolution." *International Journal of Dravidian Linguistics* 3: 255-286.

Dowty, David. 1972. *Studies in the Logic of Verb Aspect and Time Reference in English.* Austin, Texas: Department of Linguistics, University of Texas.

————. 1976. "Montague Grammar and the Lexical Decomposition of Causative Verbs." In *Montague Grammar,* edited by Barbara Partee (1976), pp. 201-246. New York: Academic Press.

————. 1978. "Governed Transformations as Lexical Rules in a Montague Grammar." *Linguistic Inquiry* 9: 393-426.

Dresher, B. Elan, and Hornstein, Norbert. 1976. "On Some Supposed Contributions of Artificial Intelligence to the Scientific Study of Language." *Cognition* 4: 321-398.

————. 1979. "Trace Theory and NP Movement Rules" *Linguistic Inquiry* 10: 65-82.

Earned Degrees Conferred. Published yearly by the Department of Health, Education, and Welfare, U.S. National Center for Educational Statistics.

Eckman, Fred. 1974. "Optional Rules and Inclusion Relations." Indiana University Linguistics Club Publication.

Emonds, Joseph. 1970. *Root and Structure-Preserving Transformations.* Indiana University Linguistics Club Publication.

———. 1973. "Alternatives to Global Constraints." *Glossa* 7: 39–62.

———. 1975. "A Transformational Analysis of French Clitics without Positive Output Constraints." *Linguistic Analysis* 1: 3–24.

———. 1976. *A Transformational Approach to English Syntax.* New York: Academic Press.

Emonds-Banfield, Peter. In press. "English Syntactic Competence." Berkeley, California: Thousand Oaks Elementary School.

Fauconnier, Giles. 1973. "Cyclic Attraction into Networks of Coreference." *Language* 49: 1–18.

———. 1975. "Pragmatic Scales and Logical Structure." *Linguistic Inquiry* 6: 357–375.

Fiengo, Robert. 1974. *Semantic Conditions on Surface Structure.* Ph.D. dissertation, MIT.

———. 1977. "On Trace Theory." *Linguistic Inquiry* 8: 35–61.

Fiengo, Robert, and Lasnik, Howard. 1976. "Some Issues in the Theory of Transformations." *Linguistic Inquiry* 7: 182–192.

Fillmore, Charles. 1962. "Indirect Object Constructions and the Ordering of Transformations." *Project on Syntactic Analysis, Report No. 1.* (1965) pp. 1–49. The Hague: Mouton.

———. 1963. "The Position of Embedding Transformations in a Grammar." *Word* 19: 208–231.

———. 1966. "A Proposal Concerning English Prepositions." *Monograph Series on Languages and Linguistics* 19: 19–34.

———. 1968. "The Case for Case." In *Universals in Linguistic Theory,* edited by Emmon Bach and Robert Harms (1968), pp. 1–90. New York: Holt, Rinehart and Winston.

———. 1969a. "Toward a Modern Theory of Case." In *Modern Studies in English*, edited by David Riebel and Sanford Schane (1969), pp. 361–375. Englewood Cliffs, New Jersey: Prentice-Hall.

———. 1969b. "Verbs of Judging: An Exercise in Semantic Description." *Papers in Linguistics* 1: 91–117. Reprinted in *Studies in Linguistic Semantics,* edited by Charles Fillmore and D. Terence Langendoen (1971), pp. 273–290. New York: Holt, Rinehart and Winston.

———. 1971a. "Types of Lexical Information." In *Semantics: An Interdisciplinary Reader,* edited by Danny Steinberg and Leon Jakobovits (1971), pp. 370–392. Cambridge, England: Cambridge University Press.

———. 1971b. "Some Problems for Case Grammar." *Monograph Series on Languages and Linguistics* 24: 35–56.

———, ed. 1971c. *Ohio State University Working Papers in Linguistics,* No. 10.

———. 1972 (1969). "On Generativity." In *Goals of Linguistic Theory,* edited by Stanley Peters, pp. 1–20. Englewood Cliffs, New Jersey: Prentice-Hall.

———. 1977. "The Case for Case Reopened." In *Syntax and Semantics,* vol. 8, edited by Peter Cole and Jerrold Sadock (1977), pp. 59–82. New York: Academic Press.

Fillmore, Charles, and Langendoen, D. Terence, eds. 1971. *Studies in Linguistic Semantics.* New York: Holt, Rinehart and Winston.

Fodor, Janet Dean. 1968. "Nonspecific Noun Phrases in English." In *The Computation Laboratory of Harvard University, Mathematical Linguistics and Automatic Translation, Report No. NSF-20 to the National Science Foundation,* pp. VII-1–VII-43.

———. 1977. *Semantics: Theories of Meaning in Generative Grammar.* New York: Crowell.

Fodor, Jerry A. 1961. "Projection and Paraphrase in Semantics." *Analysis* 21: 73–77.

———. 1970. "Three Reasons for not Deriving 'Kill' from 'Cause to Die.'" *Linguistic Inquiry* 1: 429–438.

Fodor, Jerry A., and Bever, Thomas. 1965. "The Psychological Reality of Linguistic Segments." *Journal of Verbal Learning and Verbal Behavior* 4: 414–420. Reprinted in *Readings in the Psychology of Language,* edited by Leon Jakobovits and Murray Miron (1967), pp. 325–332. Englewood Cliffs, New Jersey: Prentice-Hall.

Fodor, Jerry A., Bever, Thomas, and Garrett, M. F. 1974. *The Psychology of Language.* New York: McGraw-Hill.

Fodor, Jerry A., and Katz, Jerrold, eds. 1964. *The Structure of Language: Readings in the Philosophy of Language.* Englewood Cliffs: Prentice-Hall.

Fox, Robin. 1970. "The Cultural Animal." *Encounter* 35: 31–42.

Frantz, Donald. 1973. "On Question Word Movement." *Linguistic Inquiry* 4: 531–534.

———. 1974. "Generative Semantics: An Introduction, with Bibliography." Indiana University Linguistics Club Publication.

Fraser, Bruce. 1970. "Some Remarks on the Action Nominalization in English." In *Readings in English Transformational Grammar,* edited by Roderick Jacobs and Peter Rosenbaum (1970), pp. 83–98. Waltham, Massachusetts: Ginn and Co.

———. 1974 (1969). "An Examination of the Performative Analysis." *Papers in Linguistics* 7: 1–40.

Freidin, Robert. 1974 (1972). "Transformations and Interpretive Semantics." In *Towards Tomorrow's Linguistics,* edited by Roger Shuy and C. J. Bailey, pp. 12–22. Washington: Georgetown University Press.

———. 1975a. Review of R. Jackendoff, *Semantic Interpretation in Generative Grammar. Language* 51: 189–204.

———. 1975b. "The Analysis of Passives." *Language* 51: 384–405.

———. 1976. "The Syntactic Cycle: Proposals and Alternatives." Indiana University Linguistics Club Publication.

———. 1978a. Review of J. Emonds, *A Transformational Approach to English Syntax. Language* 54: 407–415.

———. 1978b. "Cyclicity and the Theory of Grammar." *Linguistic Inquiry* 9: 519–550.

Fries, Charles C. 1963. "The Bloomfield 'School.'" In *Trends in European and American Linguistics 1930–1960,* edited by C. Mohrmann, A. Sommerfelt, and J. Whatmough. Utrecht: Spectrum.

Fujimura, Osamu, ed. 1973. *Three Dimensions of Linguistic Theory.* Tokyo: TEC Corporation.

Gary, Judith, and Keenan, Edward. 1977. "On Collapsing Grammatical Relations in Universal Grammar." In *Syntax and Semantics,* vol. 8, edited by Peter Cole and Jerrold Sadock (1977), pp. 83–120. New York: Academic Press.

Gazdar, Gerald. 1979 (1977). *Pragmatics: Implicature, Presupposition and Logical Form.* New York: Academic Press.

Gazdar, Gerald, and Klein, Ewan. 1978. Review of E. Keenan, ed., *Formal Semantics of Natural Language. Language* 54: 661–667.

Gee, James. 1974. "Jackendoff's Thematic Hierarchy Condition and the Passive Construction." *Linguistic Inquiry* 5: 304–308.

Gildin, Bonny. 1978. "Concerning Radios in Performative Clauses." *Pragmatics Microfiche* 3: 4.

Gleason, Henry. 1955 (Second ed. 1961). *An Introduction to Descriptive Linguistics.* New York: Holt, Rinehart and Winston.

Gordon, David, and Lakoff, George. 1971. "Conversational Postulates." *Papers from the Seventh Regional Meeting of the Chicago Linguistic Society, pp. 63–84.* Reprinted in *Syntax and Semantics,* vol. 3, edited by Peter Cole and Jerry Morgan (1975), pp. 83–106. New York: Academic Press.

Green, Georgia. 1972. "Some Observations on the Syntax and Semantics of Instrumental Verbs." *Papers from the Eighth Regional Meeting of the Chicago Linguistic Society,* pp. 83–97.

———. 1974 (1971). *Semantics and Syntactic Regularity.* Bloomington, Indiana: Indiana University Press.

———. 1975. "How to Get People to Do Things with Words: The Whimperative Question." In *Syntax and Semantics,* vol. 3, edited by Peter Cole and Jerry Morgan (1975), pp. 107–142. New York: Academic Press.

Greenberg, Joseph, ed. 1963. *Universals of Language*. Cambridge, Massachusetts: MIT Press.
———. 1973. "Linguistics as a Pilot Science." In *Themes in Linguistics: The 1970's*, edited by E. Hamp, pp. 45–60. The Hague: Mouton.
Grice, H. P. 1975 (1967). "Logic and Conversation." In *Syntax and Semantics*, vol. 3, edited by Peter Cole and Jerry Morgan (1975), pp. 41–58. New York: Academic Press.
Grimshaw, Jane. 1974. "Evidence for Relativization by Deletion in Chaucerian Middle English." *Papers from the Fifth Annual Meeting of the North Eastern Linguistic Society*, pp. 216–224.
———. 1979. "The Structure-Preserving Constraint: A Review of *A Transformational Approach to English Syntax* by J. E. Emonds." *Linguistic Analysis* 5: 313–343.
Grinder, John. 1972. "On the Cycle in Syntax." In *Syntax and Semantics*, vol. 1, edited by John Kimball (1972a), pp. 81–111. New York: Academic Press.
Grinder, John, and Elgin, Suzette. 1973. *Guide to Transformational Grammar*. New York: Holt, Rinehart and Winston.
Grinder, John, and Postal, Paul. 1971a. "Missing Antecedents." *Linguistic Inquiry* 2: 269–312.
———. 1971b. "A Global Constraint on Deletion." *Linguistic Inquiry* 2: 110–112.
Grossman, Robin, San, L. J., and Vance, Timothy, eds. 1975. *Papers from the Parasession on Functionalism*. Chicago: Chicago Linguistic Society.
Grosu, Alexander. 1972. "The Strategic Nature of Island Constraints." *Ohio State University Working Papers in Linguistics* 13: 1–225.
Gruber, Jeffrey. 1976 (1965–1967). *Lexical Structures in Syntax and Semantics*. New York: North-Holland.
Hagège, Claude. 1976. *La Grammaire Générative: Réflexions Critiques*. Paris: Presses Universitaires de France.
Hale, Kenneth, La Verne, Jeanne, and Platero, Paul. 1977. "Three Cases of Overgeneration." In *Formal Syntax*, edited by Peter Culicover, *et al.* (1977), pp. 379–416. New York: Academic Press.
Hall, Robert. 1951. "American Linguistics, 1925–1950." *Archivum Linguisticum* 3: 101–125.
———. 1966. *Pidgin and Creole Languages*. Ithaca, New York: Cornell University Press.
———. 1975. *Stormy Petrel in Linguistics*. Ithaca, New York: Spoken Language Services, Inc.
———. 1977. Review of C. Hagège, *La Grammaire Générative: Réflexions Critiques*. *Forum Linguisticum* 2: 75–79.
Halle, Morris. 1959. *The Sound Pattern of Russian*. The Hague: Mouton.
———. 1962. "Phonology in Generative Grammar." *Word* 18: 54–72. Reprinted in *The Structure of Language*, edited by Jerry A. Fodor and Jerrold Katz (1964), pp. 334–352. Englewood Cliffs, New Jersey: Prentice-Hall.
Halle, Morris, Bresnan, Joan, and Miller, George, eds. 1978. *Linguistic Theory and Psychological Reality*. Cambridge, Massachusetts: MIT Press.
Halliday, Michael. 1961. "Categories of the Theory of Grammar." *Word* 17: 241–292.
Hankamer, Jorge. 1971. *Constraints on Deletion in Syntax*. Ph.D. dissertation, Yale University.
———. 1972. "Analogical Rules in Syntax." *Papers from the Eighth Regional Meeting of the Chicago Linguistic Society*, pp. 111–123.
———. 1973. "Unacceptable Ambiguity." *Linguistic Inquiry* 4: 17–68.
Hankamer, Jorge, and Sag, Ivan. 1976. "Deep and Surface Anaphora." *Linguistic Inquiry* 7: 391–428.
Harris, Alice. 1976a. *Grammatical Relations in Modern Georgian*. Ph.D. dissertation, Harvard University.
———. 1976b. "Inversion as a Rule in Universal Grammar." Paper presented at 1976 LSA Meeting.
Harris, Zellig. 1946. "From Morpheme to Utterance." *Language* 22: 161–183. Reprinted in

Readings in Linguistics, edited by Martin Joos (1958), pp. 142-153. Washington: American Council of Learned Societies.

———. 1951. *Methods in Structural Linguistics.* Chicago: University of Chicago Press.

———. 1954. "Transfer Grammar." *International Journal of American Linguistics* 20: 259-270.

———. 1955. "From Phoneme to Morpheme." *Language* 31: 190-222.

———. 1957. "Co-Occurrence and Transformation in Linguistic Structure." *Language* 33: 283-340.

———. 1965. "Transformational Theory." *Language* 41: 363-401.

Haugen, Einar. 1951. "Directions in Modern Linguistics." *Language* 27: 211-222.

Heal, Jane. 1977. "Ross and Lakoff on Declarative Sentences." *Studies in Language* 1: 337-362.

Hempel, Carl. 1950. "Problems and Changes in the Empiricist Criterion of Meaning." *Revue Internationale de Philosophie* 11: 41-63.

———. 1951. "The Concept of Cognitive Significance: A Reconsideration." *Proceedings of the American Academy of Arts and Sciences* 80: 61-77.

———. 1965. "Empiricist Criteria of Cognitive Significance: Problems and Changes." In *Aspects of Scientific Explanation,* edited by Carl Hempel, pp. 101-122. New York: Free Press.

Higgins, F. Roger. 1973. "On J. Emonds' Analysis of Extraposition." In *Syntax and Semantics,* vol. 2, edited by John Kimball (1973), pp. 149-196. New York: Seminar Press.

Hill, Archibald. 1958. *Introduction to Linguistic Structures.* New York: Harcourt, Brace and World.

———. 1961. "Grammaticality." *Word* 17: 1-10.

———, ed. 1962 (1958). *Proceedings of the Third Texas Conference on Problems of Linguistic Analysis in English.* Austin, Texas: University of Texas Press.

Hockett, Charles. 1942. "A System of Descriptive Phonology." *Language* 18: 3-21. Reprinted in *Readings in Linguistics,* edited by Martin Joos (1958), pp. 97-108. Washington: American Council of Learned Societies.

———. 1948a. "Biophysics, Linguistics, and the Unity of Science." *American Scientist* 36: 558-572.

———. 1948b. "A Note on Structure." *International Journal of American Linguistics* 14: 269-271.

———. 1951. Review of A. Martinet, *Phonology as Functional Phonetics. Language* 27: 333-341.

———. 1953. Review of C. Shannon and W. Weaver, *The Mathematical Theory of Communication. Language* 29: 69-93.

———. 1954. "Two Models of Grammatical Description." *Word* 10: 210-231. Reprinted in *Readings in Linguistics,* edited by Martin Joos (1958), pp. 386-399. Washington: American Council of Learned Societies.

———. 1955. *A Manual of Phonology.* Baltimore: Waverly Press.

———. 1958. *A Course in Modern Linguistics.* New York: Macmillan.

———. 1965. "Sound Change." *Language* 41: 185-204.

———. 1966. *Language, Mathematics, and Linguistics.* The Hague: Mouton.

———. 1968. *The State of the Art.* The Hague: Mouton.

Hooper, Joan. 1973. "A Critical Look at the Structure Preserving Constraint." *UCLA Papers in Syntax* 4: 34-72.

Hooper, Joan, and Thompson, Sandra. 1973. "On the Applicability of Root Transformations." *Linguistic Inquiry* 4: 465-497.

Horn, George. 1977 (1974). *The Noun Phrase Constraint.* Indiana University Linguistics Club Publication.

Horn, Laurence. 1969. "A Presuppositional Analysis of Only and Even." *Papers from the Fifth Regional Meeting of the Chicago Linguistic Society,* pp. 98-107.

——. 1970. "Ain't It Hard (Anymore)?" *Papers from the Sixth Regional Meeting of the Chicago Linguistic Society,* pp. 318-327.

——. 1972. *On the Semantic Properties of Logical Operators in English.* Indiana University Linguistics Club Publication.

Hornstein, Norbert. 1977. "S and X-Bar Convention." *Linguistic Analysis* 3: 137-176.

Householder, Fred. 1952. Review of Z. Harris, *Methods in Structural Linguistics. International Journal of American Linguistics* 18: 260-268.

——. 1957. "Rough Justice in Linguistics." *Monograph Series on Languages and Linguistics* 7: 153-160.

——. 1965. "On Some Recent Claims in Phonological Theory." *Journal of Linguistics* 1: 13-34.

——. 1973. "On Arguments from Asterisks." *Foundations of Language* 10: 365-376.

Hudson, Richard. 1976. *Arguments for a Non-Transformational Grammar.* Chicago: University of Chicago Press.

Hull, Clark. 1943. *Principles of Behavior.* New York: Appleton-Century-Crofts.

Hume, David. 1961. *An Inquiry Concerning Human Understanding.* In *Enquiries Concerning the Human Understanding and Concerning the Principles of Morals by David Hume,* edited by L. A. Selby-Bigge. London: Oxford University Press. (Reprint of 1777 edition.)

Hust, Joel. 1978. "Lexical Redundancy Rules and the Unpassive Construction." *Linguistic Analysis* 4: 61-89.

Hust, Joel, and Brame, Michael. 1976. "Jackendoff on Interpretive Semantics." *Linguistic Analysis* 2: 243-278.

Hymes, Dell. 1971. *On Communicative Competence.* Philadelphia: University of Pennsylvania Press.

Hymes, Dell, and Fought, John. 1975. "American Structuralism." In *Historiography of Linguistics,* edited by T. Sebeok. *Current Trends in Linguistics,* vol. 13, pp. 903-1178. The Hague: Mouton.

Jackendoff, Ray. 1968a. "Quantifiers in English." *Foundations of Language* 4: 422-442.

——. 1968b. "An Interpretive Theory of Pronouns and Reflexives." Indiana University Linguistics Club Publication.

——. 1969. "An Interpretive Theory of Negation." *Foundations of Language* 5: 218-241.

——. 1971a. "On Some Questionable Arguments about Quantifiers and Negation." *Language* 47: 282-297.

——. 1971b. "Modal Structure in Semantic Representation." *Linguistic Inquiry* 2: 479-538.

——. 1971c. "Gapping and Related Rules,"*Linguistic Inquiry* 2: 21-36.

——. 1972 (1966-1969). *Semantic Interpretation in Generative Grammar.* Cambridge, Massachusetts: MIT Press.

——. 1974a. "Introduction to the X-Bar Convention." Indiana University Linguistics Club Publication.

——. 1974b. "A Deep Structure Projection Rule." *Linguistic Inquiry* 5: 481-505.

——. 1975. "Morphological and Semantic Regularities in the Lexicon." *Language* 51: 639-671.

——. 1977. *X-Bar Syntax: A Study of Phrase Structure.* Cambridge, Massachusetts: MIT Press.

Jacobs, Roderick, and Rosenbaum, Peter, eds. 1970. *Readings in English Transformational Grammar.* Waltham, Massachusetts: Ginn and Co.

Jacobson, Pauline. 1977. *The Syntax of Crossing Coreference Sentences.* Ph.D. dissertation, University of California-Berkeley.

Jacobson, Pauline, and Neubauer, Paul. 1976. "Rule Cyclicity: Evidence from the Intervention Constraint." *Linguistic Inquiry* 7: 429-462.

Jakobovits, Leon, and Miron, Murray, eds. 1967. *Readings in the Psychology of Language.* Englewood Cliffs, New Jersey: Prentice-Hall.

Jakobson, Roman. 1941. *Kindersprache, Aphasie und allgemeine Lautgesetze.* Uppsala Universitets Aarsskrift. (Translated as *Child Language, Aphasia and Phonological Universals.* 1968. The Hague: Mouton.

————. 1948. "Russian Conjugation." *Word* 4: 155–167.

————, ed. 1961. *Structure of Language and Its Mathematical Aspects* (= *Proceedings of Symposia in Applied Mathematics,* volume XII). Providence, Rhode Island: American Mathematical Society.

Jakobson, Roman, Fant, Gunnar, and Halle, Morris. 1952. *Preliminaries to Speech Analysis.* Cambridge, Massachusetts: MIT Press.

Jakobson, Roman, and Halle, Morris. 1956. *Fundamentals of Language.* The Hague: Mouton.

Jespersen, Otto. 1965 (1924). *The Philosophy of Grammar.* New York: Norton.

Johnson, David. 1974. "Prepaper on Relational Constraints on Grammars." Unpublished manuscript.

————. 1976 (1974). *Toward a Theory of Relationally-Based Grammar.* Indiana University Linguistics Club Publication.

Johnson, David, and Postal, Paul. 1979. *Arc-Pair Grammar.* Princeton: Princeton University Press.

Joos, Martin, ed. (1958). *Readings in Linguistics.* Washington: American Council of Learned Societies.

————. 1961. "Linguistic Prospects in the United States." In *Trends in European and American Linguistics, 1930–1960,* edited by C. Mohrmann, *et al.* Utrecht: Spectrum.

————. 1964. *The English Verb.* Madison: University of Wisconsin Press.

Kac, Michael. 1972. "Action and Result: Two Aspects of Predication in English." In *Syntax and Semantics,* vol. 1, edited by John Kimball (1972), pp. 117–124. New York: Seminar Press.

————. 1978. *Corepresentation of Grammatical Structure.* Minneapolis: University of Minnesota Press.

Karttunen, Lauri. 1970. "On the Semantics of Complement Sentences." *Papers from the Sixth Regional Meeting of the Chicago Linguistic Society,* pp. 328–339.

————. 1971. "Implicative Verbs." *Language* 47: 340–358.

————. 1973. "Presuppositions of Compound Sentences." *Linguistic Inquiry* 4: 169–193.

————. 1977. "Syntax and Semantics of Questions." *Linguistics and Philosophy* 1: 3–44.

Karttunen, Lauri, and Peters, Stanley. 1975. "Conventional Implicature and Montague Grammar." *Papers from the First Annual Meeting of the Berkeley Linguistics Society,* pp. 266–278.

————. 1977. "Requiem for Presupposition." *Papers from the Third Annual Meeting of the Berkeley Linguistics Society,* pp. 360–371.

Katz, Jerrold. 1962. "A Reply to 'Projection and Paraphrase in Semantics.'" *Analysis* 22: 36–41.

————. 1967. "Recent Issues in Semantic Theory." *Foundations of Language* 3: 124–194.

————. 1972. *Semantic Theory.* New York: Harper and Row.

Katz, Jerrold, and Bever, Thomas. 1976. "The Fall and Rise of Empiricism." In *An Integrated Theory of Linguistic Ability,* edited by Thomas Bever, *et al* (1976), pp. 11–64. New York: Crowell.

Katz, Jerrold, and Fodor, Jerry. 1963. "The Structure of a Semantic Theory." *Language* 39: 170–210. Reprinted in *The Structure of Language,* edited by Jerry A. Fodor and Jerrold Katz (1964), pp. 479–518. Englewood Cliffs, New Jersey: Prentice-Hall.

Katz, Jerrold, and Langendoen, D. Terence. 1976. "Pragmatics and Presupposition." *Language* 52: 1–17.

Katz, Jerrold, and Postal, Paul. 1964. *An Integrated Theory of Linguistic Descriptions.* Cambridge, Massachusetts: MIT Press.

Keenan, Edward. 1971. "Two Kinds of Presupposition in Natural Language." In *Studies in Linguistic Semantics,* edited by Charles Fillmore and D. Terence Langendoen (1971), pp. 45–54. New York: Holt, Rinehart and Winston.

Keenan, Edward, ed. 1975. *Formal Semantics of Natural Language.* London: Cambridge University Press.

Keenan, Edward, and Comrie, Bernard. 1977 (1972). "Noun Phrase Accessibility and Universal Grammar." *Linguistic Inquiry* 8: 63–99.

Kempson, Ruth. 1975. *Presupposition and the Delimitation of Semantics.* Cambridge: Cambridge University Press.

Keyser, S. Jay, ed. 1978. *Recent Transformational Studies in European Languages.* Cambridge, Massachusetts: MIT Press.

Kimball, John, ed. 1972a. *Syntax and Semantics,* vol. 1. New York: Seminar Press.

———. 1972b. "Cyclic and Linear Grammars." In *Syntax and Semantics,* vol. 1, edited by John Kimball (1972a), pp. 63–80. New York: Seminar Press.

———. ed. 1973. *Syntax and Semantics,* vol. 2. New York: Seminar Press.

King, Harold. 1970. "On Blocking the Rules for Contraction in English." *Linguistic Inquiry* 1: 134–136.

Kiparsky, Paul, and Kiparsky, Carol. 1970 (1967). "Fact." In *Progress in Linguistics,* edited by Manfred Bierwisch and Karl Heidolph (1970), pp. 143–173. The Hague: Mouton. Reprinted in *Semantics,* edited by Danny Steinberg and Leon Jakobovits (1971), pp. 345–369. Cambridge, England: Cambridge University Press.

Klima, Edward. 1964. "Negation in English." In *The Structure of Language,* edited by Jerry A. Fodor and Jerrold Katz (1964), pp. 246–323. Englewood Cliffs, New Jersey: Prentice-Hall.

Knowles, John. 1974. "On Acceptable Agrammaticality." *Linguistic Inquiry* 5: 622–628.

Koster, Jan. 1978a. "Why Subject Sentences Don't Exist." In *Recent Transformational Studies in European Languages,* edited by S. Jay Keyser (1978), pp. 53–64. Cambridge, Massachusetts: MIT Press.

———. 1978b. *Locality Principles in Syntax.* Dordrecht: Forsi Publications.

———. 1978c. "Conditions, Empty Nodes, and Markedness." *Linguistic Inquiry* 9: 551–594.

Koster, Jan, van Riemsdijk, Henk, and Vergnaud, Jean Roger. 1978. "GLOW Manifesto." *GLOW Newsletter* 1: 2–5.

Koutsoudas, Andreas. 1972. "The Strict Order Fallacy." *Language* 48: 88–96.

———. 1973. "Unordered Rule Hypotheses." Indiana University Linguistics Club Publication.

Koutsoudas, Andreas, Sanders, Gerald, and Noll, Craig. 1974 (1971). "On the Application of Phonological Rules." *Language* 50: 1–28.

Kroeber, A. L. 1952. "Culture." In *Papers of the Peabody Museum in American Archaeology and Ethnology,* edited by A. L. Kroeber and C. H. Kluckholn, p. 47.

Kuno, Susumu. 1972a. "Functional Sentence Perspective: A Case Study from Japanese and English." *Linguistic Inquiry* 3: 269–320.

———. 1972b. "Pronominalization, Reflexivization, and Direct Discourse." *Linguistic Inquiry* 3: 161–195.

———. 1973. "Constraints on Internal Clauses and Sentential Subjects." *Linguistic Inquiry* 4: 363–386.

———. 1974. "The Position of Relative Clauses and Conjunctions." *Linguistic Inquiry* 5: 117–136.

———. 1975a. "Three Perspectives in the Functional Approach to Syntax." In *Papers from the Parasession on Functionalism,* edited by Robin Grossman, *et al.* (1975), pp. 276–336. Chicago: Chicago Linguistic Society.

—————. 1975b. "Conditions for Verb Phrase Deletion." *Foundations of Language* 13: 161–175.

—————. 1976a. "Gapping: A Functional Analysis." *Linguistic Inquiry* 7: 330–318.

—————. 1976b. "Subject, Theme , and Speaker's Empathy: A Reexamination of Relativization Phenomena." In *Subject and Topic,* edited by C. Li, pp. 417–444. New York: Academic Press.

—————. 1978. "Generative Discourse Analysis in America." In *Current Trends in Textlinguistics,* edited by W. Dressler, pp. 275–294. New York: Walter de Gruyter.

Kuroda, S.-Y. 1969 (1965). "Attachment Transformations." In *Modern Studies in English,* edited by David Riebel and Sanford Schane (1969), pp. 331–351. Engelwood Cliffs, New Jersey: Prentice-Hall.

—————. 1972. "Anton Marty and the Transformational Theory of Grammar." *Foundations of Language* 9: 1–37.

—————. 1974. "Geach and Katz on Presupposition." *Foundations of Language* 12: 177–200.

La Barre, Weston. 1958. "What Linguists Tell Anthropologists." *Monograph Series on Languages and Linguistics* 9: 73–78.

Lakoff, George. 1968a. "Instrumental Adverbs and the Concept of Deep Structure." *Foundations of Language* 4: 4–29.

—————. 1968b. "Some Verbs of Change and Causation." In *The Computation Laboratory of Harvard University, Mathematical Linguistics and Automatic Translation, Report No. NSF-20 to the National Science Foundation,* pp. III-1–III-27.

—————. 1968c (1966). "Deep and Surface Grammar." Indiana University Linguistics Club Publication.

—————. 1969a. "Empiricism without Facts." *Foundations of Language* 5: 118–127.

—————. 1969b. "On Derivational Constraints." *Papers from the Fifth Regional Meeting of the Chicago Linguistic Society,* pp. 117–139.

—————. 1970a (1965). *Irregularity in Syntax.* New York: Holt, Rinehart and Winston.

—————. 1970b. "Pronominalization, Negation, and the Analysis of Adverbs." In *Readings in English Transformational Grammar,* edited by Roderick Jacobs and Peter Rosenbaum (1970), pp. 145–165. Waltham, Massachusetts: Ginn and Co.

—————. 1970c. "Global Rules." *Language* 46: 627–639.

—————. 1971a (1969). "On Generative Semantics." In *Semantics,* edited by Danny Steinberg and Leon Jakobovits (1971), pp. 232–296. Cambridge, England: Cambridge University Press.

—————. 1971b. "The Role of Deduction in Grammar." In *Studies in Linguistic Semantics,* edited by Charles Fillmore and D. Terence Langendoen (1971), pp. 63–72. New York: Holt, Rinehart and Winston.

—————. 1971c. "Presupposition and Relative Well-Formedness." In *Semantics,* edited by Danny Steinberg and Leon Jakobovits (1971), pp. 329–340. Cambridge, England: Cambridge University Press.

—————. 1972a. "Forward." To "Where the Rules Fail," by Ann Borkin, *et al.* (1972), pp. i–v. Indiana University Linguistics Club Publication.

—————. 1972b. "Linguistics and Natural Logic." In *Semantics of Natural Language,* edited by Donald Davidson and Gilbert Harmon (1972), pp. 545–665. Dordrecht: D. Reidel.

—————. 1972c. "The Arbitrary Basis of Transformational Grammar." *Language* 48: 76–87.

—————. 1972d. Quotation from *The New York Times,* 10 September 1972.

—————. 1972e. "Hedges: A Study in Meaning Criteria and the Logic of Fuzzy Concepts." *Papers from the Eighth Regional Meeting of the Chicago Linguistic Society,* pp. 183–228.

—————. 1972f. "The Global Nature of the Nuclear Stress Rule." *Language* 48: 285–303.

—————. 1973. "Fuzzy Grammar and the Performance/Competence Terminology Game." *Papers from the Ninth Regional Meeting of the Chicago Linguistic Society,* pp. 271–291.

—————. 1974a (1972). "Interview." In *Discussing Langauge,* by Herman Parret (1974), pp. 151–178. The Hague: Mouton.

————. 1974b. "Notes Toward a Theory of Global Transderivational Well-Formedness Grammar." Unpublished manuscript.

————. 1975a. "Dual-Hierarchy Grammar." Unpublished manuscript.

————. 1975b (1973). "Pragmatics in Natural Logic." In *Formal Semantics of Natural Language,* edited by Edward Keenan (1975), pp. 253-286. London: Cambridge University Press. Reprinted in *Proceedings of the Texas Conference,* edited by Andy Rogers, *et al.,* pp. 107-134. Arlington: Center for Applied Linguistics.

————. 1976a (1963). "Toward Generative Semantics." In *Syntax and Semantics,* vol. 7, edited by James McCawley (1976), pp. 43-62. New York: Academic Press.

————. 1976b (1968). "Pronouns and Reference." In *Syntax and Semantics,* vol. 7, edited by James McCawley (1976), pp. 275-335. New York: Academic Press.

————. 1977. "Linguistic Gestalts." *Papers from the Thirteenth Regional Meeting of the Chicago Linguistic Society,* pp. 236-287.

Lakoff, George, and Peters, Stanley. 1969. "Phrasal Conjunction and Symmetric Predicates." In *Modern Studies in English,* edited by David Reibel and Sanford Schane (1969), pp. 113-142. Englewood Cliffs, New Jersey: Prentice-Hall.

Lakoff, George, and Ross, John R. 1976 (1967). "Is Deep Structure Necessary?" In *Syntax and Semantics,* vol. 7, edited by James McCawley (1976a), pp. 159-164. New York: Academic Press.

Lakoff, George, and Thompson, Henry. 1975. "Introducing Cognitive Grammar." *Papers from the First Annual Meeting of the Berkeley Linguistics Society,* pp. 295-313.

Lakoff, Robin. 1968. *Abstract Syntax and Latin Complementation.* Cambridge, Massachusetts: MIT Press.

————. 1971. "If's, And's, and But's about Conjunction." In *Studies in Linguistic Semantics,* edited by Charles Fillmore and D. Terence Langendoen (1971), pp. 115-150. New York: Holt, Rinehart and Winston.

————. 1972. "Language in Context." *Language* 48: 907-927.

————. 1974. "Pluralism in Linguistics." In *Berkeley Studies in Syntax and Semantics,* vol. 1, pp. XIV-1-XIV-36. Berkeley: Department of Linguistics, University of California.

Lamb, Sidney. 1963. "On Redefining the Phoneme." Paper presented to Linguistic Society of America.

Lane, Michael. 1970. *Introduction to Structuralism.* New York: Basic Books.

Langacker, Ronald. 1969 (1966). "On Pronominalization and the Chain of Command." In *Modern Studies in English,* edited by David Reibel and Sanford Schane (1969), pp. 160-186. Englewood Cliffs, New Jersey: Prentice-Hall.

————. 1975. "Functional Stratigraphy." In *Papers from the Parasession on Functionalism,* edited by Robin Grossman, *et al.* (1975), pp. 351-397. Chicago: Chicago Linguistic Society.

————. 1978. "The Form and Meaning of the English Auxiliary." *Language* 54: 853-882.

Langendoen, D. Terence. 1970. "The Accessibility of Deep Structure." In *Readings in English Transformational Grammar,* edited by Roderick Jacobs and Peter Rosenbaum (1970), pp. 99-106. Waltham, Massachusetts: Ginn and Co.

————. 1976. "A Case of Apparent Ungrammaticality." In *An Integrated Theory,* edited by Thomas Bever, *et al.* (1976), pp. 183-194. New York: Crowell.

Langendoen, D. Terence, Kalish-Landon, Nancy, and Dore, John. 1974. "Dative Questions: A Study in the Relation of Acceptability to Grammaticality of an English Sentence Type." *Cognition* 2: 451-478. Reprinted in *An Integrated Theory,* edited by Thomas Bever, *et al.* (1976), pp. 195-223. New York: Crowell.

Lashley, Karl. 1951. "The Problem of Serial Order in Behavior." In *Cerebral Mechanisms in Behavior,* edited by L. A. Jeffress, pp. 112-136. New York: John Wiley and Sons. Reprinted in *Psycholinguistics: A Book of Readings,* edited by Sol Saporta (1961), pp. 180-197. New York: Holt, Rinehart and Winston.

Lasnik, Howard. 1976. "Remarks on Coreference." *Linguistic Analysis* 2: 1-22.

Lawler, John. 1973. "Tracking the Generic Toad." *Papers from the Ninth Regional Meeting of the Chicago Linguistic Society*, pp. 320-331.

_____. 1977. "*A* Agrees with *B* in Achinese: A Problem for Relational Grammar." In *Syntax and Semantics*, vol. 8, edited by Peter Cole and Jerrold Sadock (1977), pp. 219-248. New York: Academic Press.

Lees, Robert B. 1953. "The Basis of Glottochronology." *Language* 29: 113-127.

_____. 1957. Review of Noam Chomsky, *Syntactic Structures*. *Language* 33: 375-408.

_____. 1960. *The Grammar of English Nominalizations*. The Hague: Mouton.

_____. 1961. "Grammatical Analysis of the English Comparative Construction." *Word* 17: 171-185. Reprinted in *Modern Studies in English*, edited by David Reibel and Sanford Schane (1969), pp. 303-315. Englewood Cliffs, New Jersey: Prentice-Hall.

_____. 1963. "Analysis of the 'Cleft Sentence in English.'" *Zeitschrift für Phonetik* 16: 311-388.

_____. 1964. "On Passives and Imperatives in English." *Gengo Kenkyu* 46: 28-41.

Lees, Robert B., and Klima, Edward. 1963. "Rules for English Pronominalization." *Language* 39: 17-28. Reprinted in *Modern Studies in English*, edited by David Reibel and Sanford Schane (1969), pp. 145-159. Englewood Cliffs, New Jersey: Prentice-Hall.

Lehmann, Winfred. 1978. "The Great Underlying Ground-Plans." In *Syntactic Typology*, edited by W. Lehmann, pp. 3-56. Austin: University of Texas Press.

Lenneberg, Eric. 1964 (1959). "The Capacity for Language Acquisition." In *The Structure of Language*, edited by Jerry A. Fodor and Jerrold Katz (1964), pp. 579-603. Englewood Cliffs, New Jersey: Prentice-Hall.

Le Page, R. B. 1964. *The National Language Question*. London: Oxford University Press.

Levelt, W. J. M. 1974. *Applications in Linguistic Theory. Formal Grammars in Linguistics and Psycholinguistics*, vol. II. The Hague: Mouton.

Levi, Judith. 1978 (1974). *The Syntax and Semantics of Complex Nominals*. New York: Academic Press.

Lévi-Strauss, Claude. 1953. "Remarks." In *An Appraisal of Anthropology Today*, edited by Sol Tax, *et al.*, pp. 349-352. Chicago: University of Chicago Press.

Levy, Mary, Carroll, John B, and Roberts, A. Hood. 1976. *Present and Future Needs for Specialists in Linguistics and the Uncommonly Taught Languages*. Arlington: Center for Applied Linguistics and Linguistic Society of America.

Lewis, David. 1972. "General Semantics." In *Semantics of Natural Language*, edited by Donald Davidson and Gilbert Harmon (1972), pp. 169-218. Dordrecht: D. Reidel. Reprinted in *Montague Grammar*, edited by Barbara Partee (1976), pp. 1-50. New York: Academic Press.

Li, Charles (Ed.). 1975. *Word Order and Word Order Change*. Austin: University of Texas Press.

_____. 1976 (Ed.) *Subject and Topic*. New York: Academic Press.

_____. 1977 (Ed.) *Mechanisms of Syntactic Change*. Austin: University of Texas Press.

Liberman, Mark. 1974. "On Conditioning the Rule of Subject-Aux Inversion." *Papers from the Fifth Annual Meeting of the North Eastern Linguistic Society*, pp. 77-91.

Lieberman, Philip. 1965. "On the Acoustic Basis of the Perception of Intonation by Linguists." *Word* 21: 40-54.

Lightfoot, David. 1976. "Trace Theory and Twice-Moved NP's." *Linguistic Inquiry* 7: 559-582.

_____. 1979. Review of C. Li, *Mechanisms of Syntactic Change*. *Language* 55: 381-395.

Locke, William N. 1955. "Machine Translation to Date." *Monograph Series on Languages and Linguistics* 6: 101-113.

Lyons, John. 1968. *Introduction to Theoretical Linguistics*. Cambridge, England: Cambridge University Press.

Maclay, Howard. 1973. "Linguistics and Psycholinguistics." In *Issues in Linguistics: Papers in Honor of Henry and Renee Kahane,* edited by B. Kachru, *et al.,* pp. 569-587. Urbana: University of Illinois Press.

Maclay, Howard, and Sleator, Mary. 1960. "Responses to Language: Judgments of Grammaticalness." *International Journal of American Linguistics* 30: 275-282.

Maling, Joan. 1977. "Old Icelandic Relative Clauses: An Unbounded Deletion Rule." *Papers from the Seventh Annual Meeting of the North Eastern Linguistic Society,* pp. 175-188.

Matthews, G. H. 1961. "Analysis by Synthesis of Sentences of Natural Language." *First International Conference on Machine Translation.* Teddington, England.

McCawley, James. 1968a. "The Role of Semantics in Grammar." In *Universals in Linguistic Theory,* edited by Emmon Bach and Robert Harms (1968), pp. 125-170. New York: Holt, Rinehart and Winston. Reprinted in *Grammar and Meaning,* by James McCawley (1976b), pp. 59-98. New York: Academic Press.

———. 1968b. "Concerning the Base Component of a Transformational Grammar." *Foundations of Language* 4: 243-269. Reprinted in *Grammar and Meaning,* by James McCawley (1976b), pp. 35-58. New York: Academic Press.

———. 1968c. "Lexical Insertion in a Transformational Grammar without Deep Structure." *Papers from the Fourth Regional Meeting of the Chicago Linguistic Society,* pp. 71-80. Reprinted in *Grammar and Meaning,* by James McCawley (1976b), pp. 155-166. New York: Academic Press.

———. 1970a. "Semantic Representation." In *Cognition: A Multiple View,* edited by P. Garvin, pp. 227-247. New York: Spartan Books. Reprinted in *Grammar and Meaning,* by McCawley (1976b), pp. 240-256. New York: Academic Press.

———. 1970b. "Where Do Noun Phrases Come From?" In *Readings in English Transformational Grammar,* edited by Roderick Jacobs and Peter Rosenbaum (1970), pp. 166-183. Waltham, Massachusetts: Ginn and Co. Reprinted in *Grammar and Meaning,* by James McCawley (1976b), pp. 133-154. New York: Academic Press.

———. 1970c. "English as a *VSO* Language." *Language* 46: 286-299. Reprinted in *Grammar and Meaning,* by James McCawley (1976b), pp. 211-228. New York: Academic Press.

———. 1971. "Interpretive Semantics Meets Frankenstein." *Foundations of Language* 7: 285-296. Reprinted in *Grammar and Meaning,* by James McCawley (1976b), pp. 333-342. New York: Academic Press.

———. 1972. "On Interpreting the Theme of This Conference." In *Limiting the Domain of Linguistics,* edited by David Cohen (1972), n.p. Milwaukee: University of Wisconsin Linguistics Group.

———. 1974 (1972). "Interview." In *Discussing Language,* by Herman Parret (1974), pp. 249-278. The Hague: Mouton.

———. 1975. Review of N. Chomsky, *Studies on Semantics in Generative Grammar. Studies in English Linguistics* 3: 209-311.

———, ed. 1976a. *Syntax and Semantics,* vol. 7. New York: Academic Press.

———. 1976b. *Grammar and Meaning.* New York: Academic Press.

———. 1976c. "Notes on Jackendoff's Theory of Anaphora." *Linguistic Inquiry* 7: 319-341.

———. 1977a. "The Nonexistence of Syntactic Categories." In *Second Annual Linguistic Metatheory Conference Proceedings,* pp. 212-222. East Lansing, Michigan: Department of Linguistics, Michigan State University.

———. 1977b. "Evolutionary Parallels between Montague Grammar and Transformational Grammar." *Papers from the Seventh Annual Meeting of the North Eastern Linguistic Society,* pp. 219-232.

Mehta, Ved. 1971. *John Is Easy to Please.* New York: Farrar, Strauss and Giroux.

Mellema, Paul. 1974. "A Brief against Case Grammar." *Foundations of Language* 11: 39-76.

Miller, George. 1962. "Some Psychological Studies of Grammar." *American Psychologist* 17: 748-762. Reprinted in *Readings in the Psychology of Language,* edited by Leon Jakobovits and Murray Miron (1967), pp. 201-218. Englewood Cliffs, New Jersey: Prentice-Hall.

Miller, George, and Chomsky, Noam. 1963. "Finitary Models of Language Users." In *Handbook of Mathematical Psychology*, vol. II, edited by P. Luce, R. Bush, and E. Galanter, pp. 419–492. New York: Wiley.

Miller, George, and Isard, Stephen. 1963. "Some Perceptual Consequences of Linguistic Rules." *Journal of Verbal Learning and Verbal Behavior* 2: 217–228. Reprinted in *Readings in the Psychology of Language*, edited by Leon Jakobovits and Murray Miron (1967), pp. 219–231. Englewood Cliffs, New Jersey: Prentice-Hall.

Montague, Richard. 1970a. "Universal Grammar." *Theoria* 36: 373–398. Reprinted in *Formal Philosophy*, edited by Richmond Thomason (1974), pp. 222–246. New Haven: Yale University Press.

———. 1970b. "English as a Formal Language." In *Linguaggi nella Società e nella Tecnica*, edited by B. Visentini *et al.*, pp. 189–224. Milan: Edizioni di Comunità. Reprinted in *Formal Philosophy*, edited by Richmond Thomason (1974), pp. 188–221. New Haven: Yale University Press.

Morgan, Charles Grady, and Pelletier, Francis Jeffry. 1977. "Some Notes Concerning Fuzzy Logics." *Linguistics and Philosophy* 1: 79–98.

Morgan, Jerry. 1969a. "On Arguing about Semantics." *Papers in Linguistics* 1: 49–70.

———. 1969b. "On the Treatment of Presupposition in Transformational Grammar." *Papers from the Fifth Regional Meeting of the Chicago Linguistic Society*, pp. 167–177.

———. 1973a. "How Can You Be in Two Places at Once, When You're Not Anywhere at All?" *Papers from the Ninth Regional Meeting of the Chicago Linguistic Society*, pp. 410–427.

———. 1973b. "Sentence Fragments and the Notion 'Sentence.'" In *Issues in Linguistics: Papers in Honor of Henry and Renee Kahane*, edited by B. Kachru, *et al.*, pp. 719–751. Urbana: University of Illinois Press.

———. 1975. "Some Interactions of Syntax and Pragmatics." In *Syntax and Semantics*, vol. 3, edited by Peter Cole and Jerry Morgan (1975), pp. 289–304. New York: Academic Press.

———. 1977. "Conversational Postulates Revisited." *Language* 53: 277–284.

———. 1978. "Two Types of Convention in Indirect Speech Acts." In *Syntax and Semantics*, vol. 9, edited by Peter Cole (1978), pp. 261–280. New York: Academic Press.

Newman, Paul. 1978. Review of C. Hagège, *La Grammaire Générative*. *Language* 54: 925–929.

Newman, Stanley. 1941. "Behavior Patterns in Linguistic Structure: A Case Study." In *Language, Culture, and Personality*, edited by L. Spier, A. Hallowell, and S. Newman, pp. 94–108. Menasha, Wisconsin: Sapir Memorial Publication Fund.

Newmeyer, Frederick. 1970. "On the Alleged Boundary between Syntax and Semantics." *Foundations of Language* 6: 178–186.

———. 1971. "The Source of Derived Nominals in English." *Language* 47: 786–796.

———. 1975 (1969). *English Aspectual Verbs*. The Hague: Mouton.

———. 1976a. "The Precyclic Nature of Predicate Raising." In *Syntax and Semantics*, vol. 6, edited by Mayayoshi Shibatani (1976), pp. 131–164. New York: Academic Press.

———. 1976b. "Relational Grammar and Autonomous Syntax." *Papers from the Twelfth Regional Meeting of the Chicago Linguistic Society*, pp. 506–515.

———. 1977. Review of F. Rossi-Landi, *Linguistics and Economics*. *Language* 53: 254–256.

———. 1978. "The Self-Defeating Autonomy Thesis." *Papers from the Fourteenth Regional Meeting of the Chicago Linguistic Society*, pp. 316–325.

———. In Preparation. "Remarks on American Structuralism and the 'Chomskyan Revolution.'"

Newmeyer, Frederick, and Emonds, Joseph. 1971. "The Linguist in American Society." *Papers from the Seventh Regional Meeting of the Chicago Linguistic Society*, pp. 285–306.

Noll, Craig. 1974. "Predicting Postcyclicity for English Transformations." Paper presented to LSA Meeting, Amherst, Massachusetts.

Oehrle, Richard. 1976. *The Grammatical Status of the English Dative Alternation.* Ph.D. dissertation, MIT.

———. 1977. Review of G. Green, *Semantics and Syntactic Regularity. Language* 53: 198–208.

Olmsted, David. 1955. Review of C. Osgood and T. Sebeok, *Psycholinguistics. Language* 31: 46–59.

Osgood, Charles, and Miron, Murray. 1963. *Approaches to the Study of Aphasia.* Urbana: University of Illinois Press.

Osgood, Charles, and Sebeok, Thomas. 1954. *Psycholinguistics.* Indiana University Publications in Anthropology and Linguistics, Memoir 10 of the *International Journal of American Linguistics.* Bloomington: Indiana University Press.

Osgood, Charles, Suci, George, and Tannenbaum, Percy. 1957. *The Measurement of Meaning.* Urbana: University of Illinois Press.

Otero, Carlos. 1972. "Acceptable Ungrammatical Sentences in Spanish." *Linguistic Inquiry* 3: 233–242.

———. 1973. "Agrammaticality in Performance." *Linguistic Inquiry* 4: 551–562.

———. 1976. "On Acceptable Agrammaticality: A Rejoinder." *Linguistic Inquiry* 7: 342–362.

Parret, Herman. 1974. *Discussing Language.* The Hague: Mouton.

Partee, Barbara. 1970 (1968). "Negation, Conjunction, and Quantifiers: Syntax vs. Semantics." *Foundations of Language* 6: 153–165.

———. 1971. "On the Requirement That Transformations Preserve Meaning." In *Studies in Linguistic Semantics,* edited by Charles Fillmore and D. Terence Langendoen (1971), pp. 1–22. New York: Holt, Rinehart and Winston.

———. 1973. "Some Transformational Extensions of Montague Grammar." *Journal of Philosophical Logic* 2: 509–534. Reprinted in *Montague Grammar,* edited by Barbara Partee (1976), pp. 51–76. New York: Academic Press.

———. 1975a. "Deletion and Variable Binding." In *Formal Semantics of Natural Language,* edited by Edward Keenan (1975), pp. 16–34. London: Cambridge University Press.

———. 1975b. "Montague Grammar and Transformational Grammar." *Linguistic Inquiry* 6: 203–300.

———, ed. 1976. *Montague Grammar.* New York: Academic Press.

Pelletier, Francis Jeffry. 1977. "How/Why Does Linguistics Matter to Philosophy?" *Southern Journal of Philosophy* 15: 393–426.

Peranteau, Paul. 1973. "The Chicago Linguistic Society: A Report." Unpublished manuscript.

Peranteau, Paul, Levi, Judith, and Phares, Gloria, eds. 1972. *The Chicago Which Hunt.* Chicago: Chicago Linguistic Society.

Percival, W. Keith. 1971. Review of P. Salus, *Linguistics. Language* 47: 181–185.

———. 1977. Review of E. F. K. Koerner, *Ferdinand de Saussure. Language* 53: 383–405.

Perlmutter, David. 1971 (1968). *Deep and Surface Structure Constraints in Syntax.* New York: Holt, Rinehart and Winston.

———. 1972. "Evidence for Shadow Pronouns in French Relativization." In *The Chicago Which Hunt,* edited by Paul Peranteau, *et al.* (1972), pp. 73–105.

———. 1978. "Impersonal Passives and the Unaccusative Hypothesis." *Papers from the Fourth Annual Meeting of the Berkeley Linguistics Society,* pp. 157–189.

Perlmutter, David, and Postal, Paul. 1977. "Toward a Universal Characterization of Passive." *Papers from the Third Annual Meeting of the Berkeley Linguistics Society,* pp. 394–417.

Peters, Stanley, ed. 1972. *Goals of Linguistic Theory.* Englewood Cliffs, New Jersey: Prentice-Hall.

Peters, Stanley, and Ritchie, Robert. 1969. "A Note on the Universal Base Hypothesis." *Journal of Linguistics* 5: 150–152.

———. 1971. "On Restricting the Base Component of Transformational Grammars." *Information and Control* 18: 483–501.

———. 1973. "On the Generative Power of Transformational Grammars." *Informatio...*

Sciences 6: 49–83.

Pike, Kenneth. 1947a. "On the Phonemic Status of English Diphthongs." *Language* 23: 151–159.

———. 1947b. "Grammatical Prerequisites to Phonemic Analysis." *Word* 3: 155–172.

———. 1952. "More on Grammatical Prerequisites." *Word* 8: 106–121.

———. 1954. *Language in Relation to a Unified Theory of the Structure of Human Behavior.* Glendale, California: Summer Institute of Linguistics.

———. 1958. "Discussion." *Proceedings of the Eighth International Congress of Linguists.* Oslo: Oslo University Press.

Pollock, Jean-Yves. 1978. "Trace Theory and French Syntax." In *Recent Transformational Studies in European Languages,* edited by S. Jay Keyser (1978), pp. 65–112. Cambridge, Massachusetts: MIT Press.

Pool, I. de Sola. 1959. *Trends in Content Analysis.* Urbana: University of Illinois Press.

Pope, Emily. 1971. "Answers to Yes-No Questions." *Linguistic Inquiry* 2, 69-82.

Post, Emil. 1936. "Finite Combinatory Processes: Formulation I." *Journal of Symbolic Logic* 1: 103–105.

———. 1944. "Recursively Enumerable Sets of Positive Integers and Their Decision Procedures." *Bulletin of the American Mathematical Society* 50: 284–316.

Postal, Paul. 1962. *Some Syntactic Rules in Mohawk.* Ph.D. dissertation, Yale University.

———. 1964a. "Limitations of Phrase Structure Grammars." In *The Structure of Language,* edited by Jerry A. Fodor and Jerrold Katz (1964), pp. 137–151. Englewood Cliffs, New Jersey: Prentice-Hall.

———. 1964b. *Constituent Structure: A Study of Contemporary Models of Syntactic Description.* The Hague: Mouton.

———. 1964c. "Underlying and Superficial Linguistic Structure." *Harvard Educational Review* 34: 246–266.

———. 1966. Review of R. M. W. Dixon, *Linguistic Science and Logic. Language* 42: 84–92.

———. 1968. *Aspects of Phonological Theory.* New York: Harper and Row.

———. 1969. "Anaphoric Islands." *Papers from the Fifth Regional Meeting of the Chicago Linguistic Society,* pp. 205–239.

———. 1970a. "On the Surface Verb 'Remind.'" *Linguistic Inquiry* 1: 37–120. Reprinted in *Studies in Linguistic Semantics,* edited by Charles Fillmore and D. Terence Langendoen (1971), pp. 181–272. New York: Holt, Rinehart and Winston.

———. 1970b. "On Coreferential Complement Subject Deletion." *Linguistic Inquiry* 1: 439–500.

———. 1971 (1967). *Cross-Over Phenomena.* New York: Holt, Rinehart and Winston.

———. 1972 (1969). "The Best Theory." In *Goals of Linguistic Theory,* edited by Stanley Peters, pp. 131–170. Englewood Cliffs, New Jersey: Prentice-Hall.

———. 1974. *On Raising.* Cambridge, Massachusetts: MIT Press.

———. 1976a. (1967). "Linguistic Anarchy Notes." In *Syntax and Semantics,* vol. 7, edited by James McCawley (1976a), pp. 201–226. New York: Academic Press.

———. 1976b. "Avoiding Reference to Subject." *Linguistic Inquiry* 7: 151–181.

———. 1977. "Antipassive in French." *Lingvisticae Investigationes* 1: 333–374.

Postal, Paul, and Pullum, Geoffrey. 1978. "Traces and the Description of English Complementizer Contraction." *Linguistic Inquiry* 9: 1–30.

Pullum, Geoffrey. 1978. Review of J. Wirth, ed., *Assessing Linguistic Arguments. Language* 54: 399–401.

———. 1979a (1976). *Rule Interaction and the Organization of a Grammar.* New York: Garland.

———. 1979b. "The Nonexistence of the Trace-Binding Algorithm." *Linguistic Inquiry* 10: 356–362.

Pullum, Geoffrey, and Postal, Paul. 1979. "On an Inadequate Defense of 'Trace Theory.'" *Linguistic Inquiry* 10: 689–706.

Pullum, Geoffrey, and Zwicky, Arnold. Forthcoming. *The Syntax-Phonology Interface*. New York: Academic Press.

Quicoli, A. C. 1972. *Aspects of Portuguese Complementation*. Ph.D. dissertation, State University of New York at Buffalo.

Quine, Willard. 1953. "The Problem of Meaning in Linguistics." In *From a Logical Point of View*, pp. 47–64. New York: Harper and Row.

———. 1970. *Philosophy of Logic*. Englewood Cliffs, New Jersey: Prentice-Hall.

Reibel, David, and Schane, Sanford, eds. 1969. *Modern Studies in English*. Englewood Cliffs, New Jersey: Prentice-Hall.

Reich, Peter. 1969. "The Finiteness of Natural Language." *Language* 45: 831–843.

Reichenbach, Hans. 1947. *Elements of Symbolic Logic*. New York: Macmillan.

Reichling, Anton. 1961. "Principles and Methods of Syntax: Cryptanalytical Formalism." *Lingua* 10: 1–17.

Ringen, Catharine. 1972. "On Arguments for Rule Ordering." *Foundations of Language* 8: 266–273.

Rizzi, Luigi. 1978. "A Restructuring Rule in Italian Syntax." In *Recent Transformational Studies in European Languages*, edited by S. Jay Keyser (1978), pp. 113–158. Cambridge, Massachusetts: MIT Press.

Robinson, Jane. 1970. "Dependency Structures and Transformational Rules." *Language* 46: 259–285.

Rodman, Robert. 1975. "The Nondiscrete Nature of Islands." Indiana University Linguistics Club Publication.

Rogers, Andy. 1974. "A Transderivational Constraint on Richard?" *Papers from the Tenth Regional Meeting of the Chicago Linguistic Society*, pp. 551–558.

Rogers, Andy, Wall, Bob, and Murphy, John P., eds. 1977 (1973). *Proceedings of the Texas Conference on Performatives, Presuppositions, and Implicatures*. Arlington: Center for Applied Linguistics.

Ronat, Mitsou. 1972 (1970). *A Propos du Verbe 'Remind' selon P. M. Postal, La Sémantique Générative: Une Réminiscence du Structuralisme?* Padova: Liviana Editrice.

Rosenbaum, Peter. 1967 (1965). *The Grammar of English Predicate Complement Constructions*. Cambridge, Massachusetts: MIT Press.

Rosenbloom, Paul. 1950. *The Elements of Mathematical Logic*. New York: Dover.

Ross, John R. 1967. "On the Cyclic Nature of English Pronominalization." In *To Honor Roman Jakobson*, 1669–1682. The Hague: Mouton. Reprinted in *Modern Studies in English*, edited by David Reibel and Sanford Schane (1969), pp. 187–200. Englewood Cliffs, New Jersey: Prentice-Hall.

———. 1968 (1967). *Constraints on Variables in Syntax*. Indiana University Linguistics Club Publication.

———. 1969a. "Adjectives as Noun Phrases." In *Modern Studies in English*, edited by David Reibel and Sanford Schane (1969), pp. 352–360. Englewood Cliffs, New Jersey: Prentice-Hall.

———. 1969b. "Auxiliaries as Main Verbs." In *Studies in Philosophical Linguistics 1*, edited by W. Todd, pp. 77–102. Evanston, Illinois: Great Expectations Press.

———. 1969c. "Guess Who?" *Papers from the Fifth Regional Meeting of the Chicago Linguistic Society*, pp. 252–286.

———. 1970 (1967). "On Declarative Sentences." In *Readings in English Transformational Grammar*, edited by Roderick Jacobs and Peter Rosenbaum (1970), pp. 222–272. Waltham, Massachusetts: Ginn and Co.

———. 1972a. "Act." In *Semantics of Natural Language*, edited by Donald Davidson and Gilbert Harmon (1972), pp. 70–126. Dordrecht: D. Reidel.

──────. 1972b. "Doubl-ing." *Linguistic Inquiry* 3: 61-86. Reprinted in *Syntax and Semantics*, vol. 1, edited by John Kimball (1972), pp. 157-186. New York: Seminar Press.

──────. 1973a. "Nouniness." In *Three Dimensions of Linguistic Theory*, edited by Osamu Fujimura (1973), pp. 137-258. Tokyo: TEC Corporation.

──────. 1973b. "Slifting." In *The Formal Analysis of Natural Language*, edited by M. Gross, *et al.*, pp. 133-172. The Hague: Mouton.

──────. 1973c. "A Fake NP Squish." In *New Ways of Analyzing*, edited by Charles-James Bailey and Roger Shuy (1973), pp. 96-140. Washington: Georgetown University Press.

──────. 1973d. "The Same Side Filter." *Papers from the Ninth Regional Meeting of the Chicago Linguistic Society*, pp. 549-567.

──────. 1973e. "The Penthouse Principle and the Order of Constituents." In *You Take the High Node*, edited by Claudia Corum, *et al.* (1973), pp. 397-422. Chicago: Chicago Linguistic Society.

──────. 1974. "Three Batons for Cognitive Psychology." In *Cognition and the Symbolic Processes*, edited by D. Palermo and W. Weimar, pp. 63-124. Washington: V. H. Winston and Sons.

──────. 1975. "Clausematiness." In *Formal Semantics of Natural Language*, edited by Edward Keenan (1975), pp. 422-475. London: Cambridge University Press.

Sadock, Jerrold. 1969. "Hypersentences." *Papers in Linguistics* 1: 283-370.

──────. 1970. "Whimperatives." In *Studies Presented to Robert B. Lees by His Students*, edited by J. Sadock and A. Vanek, pp. 223-238. Edmonton: Linguistic Research Inc.

──────. 1972. "Speech Act Idioms." *Papers from the Eighth Regional Meeting of the Chicago Linguistic Society*, pp. 329-339.

──────. 1974. *Toward a Linguistic Theory of Speech Acts*. New York: Academic Press.

──────. 1975. "The Soft Interpretive Underbelly of Generative Semantics." In *Syntax and Semantics*, vol. 3, edited by Peter Cole and Jerry Morgan (1975), pp. 383-396. New York: Academic Press.

──────. 1977. "Aspects of Linguistic Pragmatics." In *Proceedings of the Texas Conference*, edited by Andy Rogers, *et al.* (1977), pp. 67-78. Arlington: Center for Applied Linguistics.

Sag, Ivan. 1977. *Deletion and Logical Form*. Indiana University Linguistics Club Publication.

──────. 1979. "The Nonunity of Anaphora." *Linguistic Inquiry* 10: 152-164.

Sampson, Geoffrey. 1976. Review of D. Cohen, ed., *Explaining Linguistic Phenomena*. *Journal of Linguistics* 12: 177-181.

Sanders, Gerald. 1974 (1970). "Precedence Relations in Language." *Foundations of Language* 11: 361-400.

Sapir, Edward. 1921. *Language* New York: Harcourt, Brace, and World.

de Saussure, Ferdinand. 1959. *Course in General Linguistics*. New York: McGraw-Hill. (Translation of *Cours de Linguistique Générale*. 1916. Paris: Payot.)

Schachter, Paul. 1962. Review of Robert B. Lees, *The Grammar of English Nominalizations*. *International Journal of American Linguistics* 28: 134-145.

──────. 1973. "On Syntactic Categories." In *UCLA Papers in Syntax* 4: 138-192.

──────. 1977. "Does She or Doesn't She?" *Linguistic Inquiry* 8: 763-767.

──────. 1978. Review of R. Hudson, *Arguments for a Non-Transformational Grammar*. *Language* 54: 348-376.

Schlick, Moritz. 1936. "Meaning and Verification." *Philosophical Review* 45: 339-369. Reprinted in *Theory of Meaning*, edited by A. and K. Lehrer (1970). Englewood Cliffs, New Jersey: Prentice-Hall.

Schmerling, Susan. 1973. "Subjectless Sentences and the Notion of Surface Structure." *Papers from the Ninth Regional Meeting of the Chicago Linguistic Society*, pp. 577-586.

──────. 1978. "A Categorial Analysis of Dyirbal Ergativity." Paper presented at Winter LSA Meeting.

Searle, John. 1969. *Speech Acts*. Cambridge, England: Cambridge University Press.

————. 1972. "Chomsky's Revolution in Linguistics." *The New York Review*, 29 June 1972, pp. 16–24.

————. 1975. "Indirect Speech Acts." In *Syntax and Semantics*, vol. 3, edited by Peter Cole and Jerry Morgan (1975), pp. 59–82. New York: Academic Press.

————. 1976. Review of J. Sadock, *Toward a Linguistic Theory of Speech Acts*. *Language* 52: 966–971.

Sebeok, Thomas, ed. 1960. *Style in Language*. Cambridge, Massachusetts: MIT Press.

Seegmiller, Milton. 1974. *Lexical Insertion in a Transformational Grammar*. Doctoral Dissertation, New York University.

Selkirk, Elizabeth. 1972. *The Phrase Phonology of English and French*. Ph.D. dissertation, MIT.

Seuren, Pieter. 1972. "Autonomous versus Semantic Syntax." *Foundations of Language* 8: 237–265.

Shannon, Claude E., and Weaver, Warren. 1949. *The Mathematical Theory of Communication*. Urbana: University of Illinois Press.

Shibatani, Masayoshi, ed. 1976. *Syntax and Semantics*, vol. 6. New York: Academic Press.

Shir, Nomi Erteschik. 1977 (1973). *On the Nature of Island Constraints*. Indiana University Linguistics Club Publication.

Shopen, Timothy. 1972. *A Generative Theory of Ellipsis*. Indiana University Linguistics Club Publication.

Siegel, Dorothy. 1974. *Topics in English Morphology*. Ph.D. dissertation, MIT.

Skinner, B. F. 1957. *Verbal Behavior*. New York: Appleton-Century-Crofts.

Sklar, Robert. 1968. "Chomsky's Revolution in Linguistics." *The Nation*, 9 September 1968, pp. 213–217.

Sledd, James. 1955. Reviews of G. Trager and H. L. Smith, *An Outline of English Structure* and C. C. Fries, *The Structure of English*. *Language* 31: 312–345.

Smith, Carlota. 1964. "Determiners and Relative Clauses in a Generative Grammar of English." *Language* 40: 37–52. Reprinted in *Modern Studies in English*, edited by David Reibel and Sanford Schane (1969), pp. 247–263. Englewood Cliffs, New Jersey: Prentice-Hall.

Smith, Neil, and Wilson, Deirdre. 1979. *Modern Linguistics: The Results of Chomsky's Revolution*. Bloomington, Indiana: Indiana University Press.

Sommerstein, Alan. 1977. *Modern Phonology*. London: Edward Arnold.

Stalker, Douglas. 1973. "Some Problems with Lakoff's Natural Logic." *Foundations of Language* 10: 527–544.

Starosta, Stanley. 1971. "Lexical Derivation in Case Grammar." *University of Hawaii Working Papers in Linguistics* 3: 83–101.

————. 1973. "The Faces of Case." *Language Sciences* 25: 1–14.

Steinberg, Danny, and Jakobovits, Leon, eds. 1971. *Semantics: An Interdisciplinary Reader*. Cambridge, England: Cambridge University Press.

Stockwell, Robert. 1960. "The Place of Intonation in a Generative Grammar of English." *Language* 36: 360–367.

Stockwell, Robert, and Schachter, Paul. 1962. "Rules for a Segment of English Syntax." Mimeographed. Los Angeles: University of California.

Stockwell, Robert, Schachter, Paul, and Partee, Barbara. 1973 (1969). *The Major Syntactic Structures of English*. New York: Holt, Rinehart and Winston.

Swadesh, Morris. 1947. "On the Analysis of English Syllabics." *Language* 23: 137–150.

Taraldsen, Knut. 1978. "The Scope of *Wh* Movement in Norwegian." *Linguistic Inquiry* 9: 623–640.

Thomason, Richmond, ed. 1974. *Formal Philosophy: Selected Papers of Richard Montague*. New Haven: Yale University Press.

Thorne, James. 1965. Review of P. Postal, *Constituent Structure*. *Journal of Linguistics* 1: 73–76.

Trager, George L. 1950. Review of Tadeusz Milewski, *Zarys Jezykoznawstwa Ogolnego.* *Studies in Linguistics* 8: 99–100.

Trager, George L., and Bloch, Bernard. 1941. "The Syllabic Phonemes of English." *Language* 17: 223–246.

Trager, George L., and Smith, Henry Lee. 1951. *An Outline of English Structure.* Studies in Linguistics: Occasional Papers, no. 3. Norman, Oklahoma: Battenberg Press.

Trithart, Lee. 1975. "Relational Grammar and Chicewa Subjectivization Rules." *Papers from the Eleventh Regional Meeting of the Chicago Linguistic Society,* pp. 615–624.

Trubetskoi, N. S. 1939. *Grundzüge der Phonologie. Travaux du Cercle Linguistique de Prague* 7 (Translated by Christiane A. M. Baltaxe as *Principles of Phonology.* 1969. Los Angeles: University of California Press.)

Twaddell, W. Freeman. 1935. "On Defining the Phoneme." *Language Monograph* No. 16. Reprinted in *Readings in Linguistics,* edited by Martin Joos (1958), pp. 55–80. Washington: American Council of Learned Societies.

Uhlenbeck, E. M. 1963. "An Appraisal of Transformational Theory." *Lingua* 12: 1–18.

Vergnaud, J.-R. 1974. *French Relative Clauses.* Ph.D. dissertation, MIT.

Van Riemsdijk, Henk. 1978a. "On the Diagnosis of *Wh* Movement." In *Recent Transformational Studies in European Languages,* edited by S. Jay Keyser (1978), pp. 189–206. Cambridge, Massachusetts: MIT Press.

———. 1978b. *A Case Study in Syntactic Markedness.* Lisse: Peter de Ridder Press.

Voegelin, C. F. 1958. Review of Noam Chomsky, *Syntactic Structures. International Journal of American Linguistics* 24: 229–231.

Wachowicz, Krystyna. 1974. "Against the Universality of a Single *Wh*-Question Movement." *Foundations of Language* 11: 155–169.

Wang, William S.-Y. 1964. "Some Syntactic Rules for Mandarin." In *Proceedings of the Ninth International Congress of Linguists,* edited by H. Lunt, pp. 191–202. The Hague: Mouton.

Wanner, Eric, and Maratsos, Michael. 1978. "An ATN Approach to Comprehension." In *Linguistic Theory and Psychological Reality,* edited by Morris Halle, *et al.* (1978), pp. 119–161. Cambridge, Massachusetts: MIT Press.

Wasow, Thomas. 1972. *Anaphoric Relations in English.* Ph.D. dissertation, MIT.

———. 1975. "Anaphoric Pronouns and Bound Variables." *Language* 51: 368–373.

———. 1976. "McCawley on Generative Semantics." *Linguistic Analysis* 2: 279–301.

———. 1977. "Transformations and the Lexicon." In *Formal Syntax,* edited by Peter Culicover, *et al.* (1977), pp. 327–360. New York: Academic Press.

Weinreich, Uriel. 1966. "Explorations in Semantic Theory." In *Current Trends in Linguistics,* vol. 3, edited by T. Sebeok, pp. 395–478. The Hague: Mouton.

Wells, Rulon. 1945. "The Pitch Phonemes of English." *Language* 21: 27–39.

———. 1947. "Immediate Constituents." *Language* 23: 81–117. Reprinted in *Readings in Linguistics,* edited by Martin Joos. (1958), pp. 186–207. Washington: American Council of Learned Societies.

Whitehall, Harold. 1951. *Structural Essentials of English.* New York: Harcourt, Brace and Co.

Williams, Edwin. 1974. *Rule Ordering in Syntax.* Ph.D. dissertation, MIT.

———. 1977a. "On Deep and Surface Anaphora." *Linguistic Inquiry* 8: 692–696.

———. 1977b. "Discourse and Logical Form." *Linguistic Inquiry* 8: 101–139.

Wilson, Deirdre. 1975. *Presupposition and Non-Truth Conditional Semantics.* London: Academic Press.

Wilson, Deirdre, and Sperber, Daniel. 1979. "Ordered Entailments: An Alternative to Presuppositional Theories." In *Presuppositions. Syntax and Semantics,* vol. 11, edited by C. K. Oh and D. Dinneen, pp. 299–323. New York: Academic Press.

Winter, Werner. 1965. "Transforms without Kernels?" *Language* 41: 484–489.

Woods, William. 1973. "An Experimental Parsing System for Transition Network Grammars."

In *Natural Language Processing,* edited by R. Rustin. Englewood Cliffs, New Jersey: Prentice-Hall.

Yngve, Victor. 1960. "A Model and an Hypothesis for Language Structure." *Proceedings of the American Philosophical Society* 104: 444–466.

———. 1961. "The Depth Hypothesis." In *Structure of Language and Its Mathematical Aspects,* edited by Roman Jakobson (1961), pp. 130–138. Providence, Rhode Island: American Mathematical Society.

Zadeh, Lofti. 1965. "Fuzzy Sets." *Information and Control* 8: 338–353.

———. 1971. "Quantitative Fuzzy Semantics." *Information Sciences* 3: 159–176.

Zwicky, Arnold. 1968. "Naturalness Arguments in Syntax." *Papers from the Fourth Regional Meeting of the Chicago Linguistic Society,* pp. 94–102.

———. 1969. "Phonological Constraints in Syntactic Description." *Papers in Linguistics* 1: 411–463.

———. 1970. "Auxiliary Reduction in English." *Linguistic Inquiry* 1: 323–336.

———. 1972. "Remarks on Directionality." *Journal of Linguistics* 8: 103–109.

Name Index

General Index

Index of Rules and Constraints